Physical Education for Lifelong Fitness

The Physical Best Teacher's Guide

**American Alliance
for Health, Physical Education,
Recreation and Dance**

Human Kinetics

Library of Congress Cataloging-in-Publication Data

Physical Best (Program)
    Physical education for lifelong fitness : the Physical Best
teacher's guide / American Alliance for Health, Physical Education,
Recreation, and Dance.
        p.   cm.
    Includes bibliographical references (p.) and index.
    ISBN 0-88011-983-7
    1. Physical education and training--Study and teaching--United
States.   2. Physical fitness--Study and teaching--United States.
I. American Alliance for Health, Physical Education, Recreation, and
Dance.   II. Title.   III. Title: Physical Best teacher's guide.
GV365.P4992   1999
613.7--dc21   99-22701
                                                            CIP

ISBN 0-88011-983-7

Acquisition Editor: Scott Wikgren; **Writer:** Bonnie Pettifor, MA Ed; **Developmental Editors:** C.E. Petit, JD, and Lynn M. Hooper-Davenport; **Assistant Editors:** Amanda Ewing, Melissa Feld, Amy Flaig, Susan Hagan, Phil Natividad, and Stephan Seyfert; **Permissions Managers:** Katie Aquino, Cesar Barradas, and Terri Hamer; **Proofreader:** Erin Cler; **Graphic Designer:** Nancy Rasmus; **Graphic Artists:** Kathleen Boudreau-Fuoss, Nancy Rasmus, and Tara Welsch; **Photo Editor:** Clark Brooks; **Cover Designer:** Jack W. Davis; **Photographer (cover):** Tom Roberts; **Photographer (interior):** Tom Roberts, except where otherwise noted; **Illustrators:**Tom Roberts (Mac); Roberto Sabas (line art); Michael D. Richardson (Figure 8.2); Tim Shedelbower (Figure 5.1); Tim Offenstein (Figure 9.1); Susan Carson (Figure 18.1); **Printer:** United Graphics

Printed in the United States of America   10 9 8 7 6 5

Human Kinetics
Web site: www.HumanKinetics.com

United States: Human Kinetics
P.O. Box 5076
Champaign, IL 61825-5076
800-747-4457
e-mail: humank@hkusa.com

Canada: Human Kinetics
475 Devonshire Road, Unit 100
Windsor, ON N8Y 2L5
800-465-7301 (in Canada only)
e-mail: orders@hkcanada.com

Europe: Human Kinetics
107 Bradford Road
Stanningley
Leeds LS28 6AT, United Kingdom
+44 (0)113 255 5665
e-mail: hk@hkeurope.com

Australia: Human Kinetics
57A Price Avenue
Lower Mitcham, South Australia 5062
08 8277 1555
e-mail: liahka@senet.com.au

New Zealand: Human Kinetics
P.O. Box 105-231, Auckland Central
09-523-3462
e-mail: hkp@ihug.co.nz

Contents

Preface

As a physical educator, you have an awesome opportunity to have a powerful and positive impact on hundreds of young people each year. By teaching them the skills and knowledge, and giving them the appreciation and confidence they need to live physically active lives, you are preparing them to avoid many major diseases and live healthier, less stressful, and more productive lives than those who live sedentary lives.

And what greater preparation can a teacher give students than readiness for a healthy life? In 300 BC Herophiles (considered the "father of anatomy") stated: "When health is absent, wisdom cannot reveal itself, art cannot become manifest, strength cannot be exerted, wealth is useless, and reason is powerless." For all the technological advances that have taken place since 300 BC, this one constant remains—without one's health, all else is useless.

The role physical education plays in preparing students for lifelong health is clear—there is a direct link between participation in regular physical activity and good health. It is physical education in the schools that affords the best opportunity to reach the majority of the population. However, we also know that for a physical education program to successfully prepare students for healthy lives, it must be far more than the "roll-out-the-ball" programs we see stereotyped on television, and, sadly, still see in a few schools today.

This book was written to provide a comprehensive guide to successfully incorporating health-related fitness and lifetime physical activity into physical education programs. It provides a conceptual framework, based on recent research, and a wealth of examples from experienced physical educators. It provides specific advice on integrating all aspects of a quality physical education program. For example, it will show how to teach fitness concepts through enjoyable physical activities and how to use fitness testing as an educational and motivational tool.

For veteran teachers, this book outlines strategies for placing a greater emphasis on health-related fitness while still maintaining all the excellent aspects of an existing program. For new teachers, this book details all components of creating an excellent fitness education program, illustrating these details with specific examples from master teachers.

In part I, we provide an overview of health-related fitness, including an in-depth look at physical activity and motivation. We also examine how health-related fitness education can be integrated into a physical education program. Part I concludes with strategies for effective management of health-related physical fitness education programs.

A review of health-related physical fitness concepts is provided in part II. Specifically, we address basic training principles, aerobic fitness, muscular strength and endurance, flexibility, and body composition and nutrition as they relate to the teaching of kindergarten through 12th-grade students. Because our knowledge of fitness has been rapidly evolving and some disagreement still exists even among exercise physiologists as to appropriate exercise protocols, we provide discussions of controversial topics with recommendations for addressing these issues in your program.

In part III, we outline strategies for developing a health-related fitness education curriculum that will serve your needs whatever your unique situation. We also examine effective teaching strategies that allow for the inclusion of all students, whether in the gymnasium, on the field, or in the classroom.

Assessment is an important component of effective teaching, and in part IV, we provide a detailed look at assessing health-related fitness, including using fitness testing appropriately, assessing knowledge of fitness concepts, assessing participation in physical activity, and assessing evidence of growth in the affective domain.

Part V provides an easy-to-follow review of the entire book and is designed to help you prepare for the Physical Best Health-Fitness Specialist Certification Exam.

This book concludes with ready-to-use worksheets and masters, recommended reading, contact information for national organizations, detailed information on the American Fitness Alliance, and in-depth information on nutrition.

Physical Best

While this book can stand alone as a blueprint for incorporating health-related fitness into physical education, it was developed specifically to be part of the Physical Best program.

Physical Best is the educational component of a comprehensive health-related physical fitness education program. It complements and supports—but not necessarily replaces—existing physical education curricula, helping teachers assist students in meeting the National Association for Sport and Physical Education (NASPE) National Physical Education Standards related to health-related fitness. It will also help teachers assist students in meeting the national standards in health, dance, and adapted physical education that relate to health-related fitness.

In addition to this book, Physical Best resources include:

- *Physical Best Activity Guide—Elementary Level*

- *Physical Best Activity Guide—Secondary Level*
- *Physical Best Instructor Video* (for use by Physical Best Health-Fitness instructors)
- *Physical Best Instructor Guide* (for use by Physical Best Health-Fitness instructors)
- Physical Best Health-Fitness Specialist Certification Workshop and Exam
- Physical Best Health-Fitness Instructor Certification Workshop and Exam

Physical Best also endorses the use of *FITNESSGRAM* (developed by the Cooper Institute for Aerobics Research) as the physical fitness test battery of choice.

For more information on the Physical Best Health-Fitness Specialist Certification or on becoming a Physical Best Health-Fitness Instructor, call the American Alliance for Health, Physical Education, Recreation and Dance (AAHPERD) at 1-800-213-7193, ext. 426.

Additional products are available through the American Fitness Alliance to complement Physical Best. These include the Brockport Physical Fitness Test for Youths with Disabilities; FitSmart, a national fitness knowledge test for high school students; and *Physical Best and Individuals with Disabilities: A Handbook for Inclusion in Fitness Programs*. A lifelong physical activity and personal fitness text for high school students is also being developed.

All Physical Best materials, resources, and workshops will do the following:

- Emphasize enjoyable participation in physical activities that are relevant to students
- Offer a diverse range of noncompetitive and competitive activities appropriate for different ages and abilities, allowing all students to successfully participate
- Emphasize the personal nature of participation in lifelong physical activity
- Provide appropriate and authentic assessment as part of the learning process, designed so students take on increasing responsibility for their own learning

- Follow proven educational progressions that lead to students taking increasing responsibility for their own health-related fitness
- Assist students in meeting the NASPE National Standards for Physical Education for health-related fitness as well as the health-related fitness components of the national standards for dance, health, and adapted physical education

Based on these concepts, scholars and practitioners at AAHPERD developed Physical Best to be educational, individualized, and integrated into a comprehensive, on-going health-related fitness program.

Skill Development

It is important to note that in our emphasis on health-related fitness and lifetime physical activity, we do not mean to imply that other aspects of a quality physical education program, such as skill development and the teaching of sport strategies, are not important. Learning skills and strategies helps prepare students to be active for a lifetime. However, detailed information on these components of physical education is available in many other books and space does not allow us to repeat it here and still give adequate attention to health-related fitness. Indeed, each of the chapters in this book could be entire books in themselves; therefore, we encourage you to pursue more information (see appendix C, the reference list, and the recommended reading list at the back of this book.

How This Book Was Developed

Good teaching is both an art and a science. We developed this book by combining extensive research on the science of physical activity for children and young adults with the vast knowledge and experience of master physical education teachers from across the country. Once this information was compiled, it was given to a professional writer to provide continuity and an enjoyable, easy-to-read text. Then the AAHPERD Physical Best Steering Committee and a number of other physical educators provided detailed reviews at multiple stages, which were used to craft this final product—an invaluable summary of accurate information and countless years of teaching experience. Please see page ix for a listing of physical educators who were involved as reviewers and consultants.

Your Physical Best

As a physical educator, you have a very important job, one that can literally shape the future health of the nation. It is our hope that you will find this book both informational and inspirational in being the best physical educator you can be.

Scott Wikgren
Director
Health, Physical Education,
Recreation and Dance Division
Human Kinetics

Acknowledgments

The information used to write this book came from the contributions of many physical educators who generously shared their ideas and experiences and from those researchers who have dedicated their lives to learning more about how to improve the health and well-being of children and young adults. We have made every effort to acknowledge the contributions of these individuals throughout the book via attribution and reference.

In addition, the AAHPERD Physical Best Steering committee and Physical Best Experts served to review the drafts and provide specific feedback that was used to revise and improve this book. Robin Brookfield, Physical Best Program Administrator for AAHPERD, and her predecessors, Anne Cahill and Linda Thompson-Fuller, played significant roles in coordinating this process.

The following individuals contributed greatly to the development of this book in their roles as members of the AAHPERD Physical Best Steering Committee and/or as an AAHPERD Physical Best Expert.

Ellen Abbadessa
Arizona

Laura Borsdorf
Pennsylvania

Larry Cain
Wisconsin

Jeff Carpenter
Washington

Ron Feingold
New York

Marian Franck
Pennsylvania

Jennie Gilbert Hartman
California

Dawn Graff-Haight
Oregon

Aleita Hass-Holcombe
Oregon

Linda Hatchett
Alabama

Vicki Highstreet
Nebraska

John Kading
Wisconsin

Carolyn Masterson, Chair 1998–1999
New Jersey

Nancy Raso-Eklund
Wyoming

Jennifer Reeves, Chair 1999-2000
Arizona

Nannette Wolford
Missouri

The following individuals served as contributors and/or reviewers in the development of this book.

W. Larry Bruce
Cuba

Barbara Cusimano
Oregon

Richard Hohn
South Carolina

Deborah Loper
Nebraska

Marilu Meredith
Texas

Lawrence Rohner
New Mexico

Suzann Schiemer
Pennsylvania

Kathleen Thorton
Maryland

Stephen J. Virgilio
New York

Greg Welk
Texas

We also want to acknowledge the many wonderful authors and researchers who we have referenced throughout this book. Their contributions to the profession provided the foundation for the development of Physical Best.

Sponsorship

AAHPERD would also like to thank the late Dr. Paul Saltman of the University of California at San Diego for his guidance on nutritional issues, and Mars, Incorporated, and Gopher Sport for their financial and developmental support of the Physical Best Program.

Endorsement

The Physical Best program is endorsed by the National Association of Governor's Councils on Physical Fitness and Sport.

Part I

Foundations of Health-Related Fitness and Physical Activity

Chapter 1

Introduction to Physical Best

Physical Best is the educational component of a comprehensive health-related fitness education program. It provides for one of the two critical foundation content components of physical education. It also helps teachers assist students in meeting the National Association of Sport and Physical Education (NASPE) National Standards for Physical Education pertaining to health-related fitness. The ultimate goal of Physical Best is to help young people develop the skills, knowledge, attitudes, and behaviors that lead to physically active, healthy lifestyles.

Why Physical Best?

The scientific and empirical evidence is indisputable—lifelong participation in physical activity has a significant positive impact on people's health and well-being. In turn, improved health and well-being have significant positive consequences for both individuals and society as a whole. The best opportunity to prepare the majority of children and adolescents to live physically active, healthy lives is through physical education in the schools. However, some physical education programs have done an unsatisfactory job by ignoring

Physical Activity and Health

Physical educators have always considered that one of the aims of physical education is the understanding of principles of physical fitness and physical activity for health. Similarly, most western societies, and probably others, have shown an unprecedented interest in health during the past few years. The time would appear right, therefore, for a significant impact on children's physical activity and health from physical education. Schools have at least three obvious advantages in the targeting of physical activity:

- Schools contain people at ages where change is most likely to occur.
- Schoolwide strategies should enable virtually all members of an age cohort to be targeted.
- A delivery structure is already in place, mainly through physical education, but also available through other curriculum areas and school practices (Vanden Auweele 1999).

the teaching of concepts of health-related factors of fitness and the relation of physical activities to establishing healthier levels of fitness. These factors inspired the creation of Physical Best.

A Brief History

In 1987, the American Alliance for Health, Physical Education, Recreation and Dance (AAHPERD) recognized the need to create a program that would assist physical educators in helping youths understand the importance of a lifetime of activity and that would focus on educating *all* students, regardless of their abilities, from a health-related viewpoint. Health-minded organizations, such as the American Academy of Pediatrics, the American Medical Association, the Centers for Disease Control and Prevention, the President's Council on Physical Fitness and Sports, the U.S. Department of Health and Human Services, and the allied health community, emphasize the importance of lifelong physical activity to good health. This is true for all people, including those with physical and mental challenges, the sedentary population, and even elite athletes, who need to understand the health aspects of lifelong physical activity so they do not become sedentary after completing their athletic careers.

Based on these concepts, scholars and practitioners at AAHPERD developed Physical Best. First and foremost, Physical Best is educa-

tional and individualized. The Physical Best activities (available in the *Physical Best Activity Guide—Elementary Level* and *Physical Best Activity Guide—Secondary Level*) are designed to teach health-related fitness concepts through enjoyable physical activities that are developmentally appropriate and individualized so that all students' needs and interests may be met.

Why Physical Best Is Different

There are many excellent physical educators who have been using the Physical Best approach for years—indeed, these experts helped create the Physical Best resources and program. Unfortunately, however, many more physical education programs in the United States have been doing more harm than good, because they have turned children off to physical activity as a lifestyle choice. Because of this, physical education in the nation's schools has been getting shortchanged at a time when an increasing number of American adults view exercise as important to their health. Pate and Hohn (1994) explain:

In our view, tax-paying adults are convinced, on the one hand, that children need exercise, that they should develop reasonable levels of fitness, and that they should master fundamental motor skills. Yet, on the other hand, these same taxpayers appear skeptical that school physical education is contributing much to these goals. We suspect that this skepticism is fueled by the largely negative recollections that many adults have of their own experience in physical education. We fear that many adults associate physical education with embarrassment, pain, boredom, triviality, and irrelevance.

In some districts, the physical education programs have not significantly changed from when the teachers and administrators were children. Fitness education has been associated with fitness tests, comparing one against another, touting the "no pain, no gain" philosophy, and using fitness activities for punishment and embarrassment. Many programs have not made a change from preparing for war—when fitness status was critical and our military strength and programs were focused on physical "training" rather than the "education" necessary to maintain personal health in a new and high-tech age.

It should come as no surprise, then, that the availability of physical education and the rate of physical activity among young people are declining:

- Daily participation in physical education fell from 42 percent of high school students in 1991 to a mere 25 percent in 1995 (CDC 1995).
- Almost half of young people ages 12 to 21 and over a third of high school students do not participate in vigorous physical activity on a regular basis (CDC 1995).
- At the very best, physical education classes account for less than 1.75 hours of physical activity per week (International Life Sciences Institute [ILSI] 1997a).
- Too often disinterested (and unqualified) classroom teachers teach physical education (NASPE 1993; Siedentop 1990).
- In many states, requirements for physical education are gradually being reduced (NASPE 1993).

Thus, not surprisingly, children carry more body fat than ever and are more likely to display one or more risk factors for developing heart disease in the future. Many studies show children's activity levels decline sharply in high school (figure 1.1). Those young athletes who are in better shape are typically found on elite and select club teams that require significant financial and time commitments from parents. The key issue, however, is, How well are all children and adolescents prepared to be active and to stay fit for life? Unfortunately, fitness is temporary and being fit as a child does not guarantee fitness as an adult unless one remains active. Naturally, the health benefits related to activity and fitness are good only as long as activity and fitness are maintained. Learning how to remain fit is the essential educational component of physical education.

The American Academy of Pediatrics (AAPC) Statement on Physical Fitness and the Schools

Because financial support for fitness programs in the schools is unlikely to increase in the foreseeable future, and television is unlikely to become less attractive, we must anticipate the probability that our children's degree of physical fitness will decline. Pediatricians must acquaint themselves with this problem and appeal to their local school boards to maintain, if not increase, the schools' physical education program of physical fitness. School programs should emphasize the so-called lifetime "athletic" activities such as cycling, swimming, and tennis. Schools should decrease time spent teaching the skills used in team sports such as football, basketball, and baseball. Physical fitness activities at school should promote a lifelong habit of aerobic exercise. During anticipatory guidance sessions, pediatricians should encourage parents to see that all family members are involved in fitness-enhancing physical activities, so that these activities become an integral part of the family's lifestyle (AAPCSMSH 1987).

Reprinted, by permission, from R. Pate & R. Hohn, 1994, *Health and Fitness Through Physical Education*. (Champaign, IL: Human Kinetics), 4.

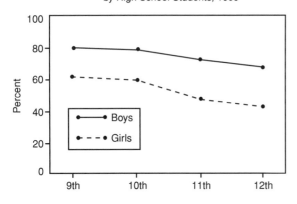

Regular Participation in Vigorous Physical Activity*
by High School Students, 1995

*On three or more of the seven days preceding the survey, at least 20 minutes of participation in activities that made the students breathe hard and sweat.

Figure 1.1 Physical activity levels decline in high school, and high school girls tend to be less active than high school boys.

Reprinted by permission from Human Kinetics, 1998, *Active Youth*. (Champaign, IL: Human Kinetics), 3.

Lifetime Activity Must Be Taught

According to the U.S. Department of Health and Human Services (USDHHS 1999), young people must be taught the skills, knowledge, attitudes, and behaviors that lead to regular participation in physical activity. As physical educators, we know the value of physical education; we've seen it with our own eyes.

Back in 1991, over 100,000 specialists were teaching physical education—evidence that society has been making a considerable investment in physical education. But today many in our society question whether this investment is yielding a reasonable return (Pate and Hohn 1994). Pass the information in this chapter on to those who doubt the necessity of our profession.

Different reports, particularly in the popular media, often fail to distinguish among the terms *fitness*, *physical activity*, and *exercise*. The USDHHS (1996) offers technical definitions of these terms:

- *Physical activity* is strictly defined as any bodily movement produced by skeletal muscles that results in an expenditure of energy. It includes a broad range of occupational, leisure time, and routine daily activities—from manual labor to gardening, walking, or household chores. These activities can require light, moderate, or vigorous effort and can lead to improved health if they are practiced regularly.

- *Exercise* is physical activity that is planned, structured, and repetitive bodily movement done to improve or maintain one or more of the components of [health-related] physical fitness.

What About Parents?

Using data collected by Louis Harris and Associates in September and October 1996, the International Life Sciences Institute (1997a) surveyed parents and children on their physical activity patterns. According to this survey, fewer than 25 percent of children (4th–12th grade) participated in vigorous physical activity every day of the week (figure 1.2). Furthermore, 23 percent of children do not have any physical education classes through their schools, and only about one in three have physical education class every school day (figure 1.3). "Daily physical activity for children needs to become a priority for parents equal to that of buckling seat belts," says Dr. James O. Hill, chairman of the Centers for Disease Control and Prevention's Physical Activity and Nutrition (PAN) Advisory Committee and professor of pediatrics and medicine at the University of Colorado Health Sciences Center. "Adopting a 'no more excuses' attitude when a child pleads lack of time is an important beginning. Furthermore, parents need to demand that schools put the fourth R back into their curriculum: Recreation. . . ." The report goes on to recommend that "Daily physical education classes should be reinstated at all grade levels, and the content of these classes should be revamped so that children receive maximum benefit and enjoyment." Furthermore, genuine interest exists among parents and children in volunteering to "help bring physical activity opportunities to families and communities . . . [including] helping turn community schools into recreational centers during nonschool hours. . . ."

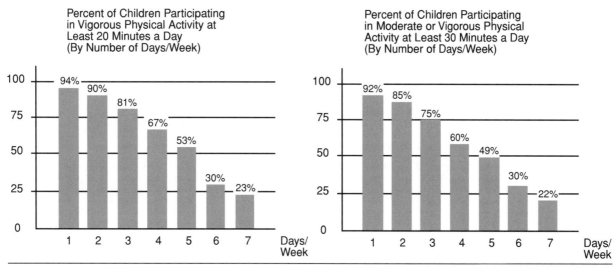

Figure 1.2 Fewer than 25 percent of children in grades 4–12 participate in physical activity every day of the week.

Source: *Improving Children's Health Through Physical Activity: A New Opportunity, Executive Summary.* Adapted, with permission. © 1997 International Life Sciences Institute, Washington, DC, USA.

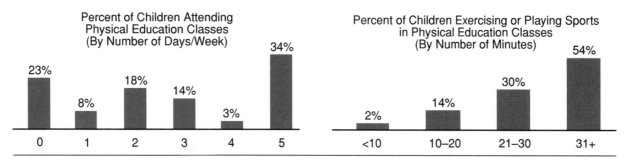

Figure 1.3 Only one in three children have physical education classes every school day, and only 54 percent of students spend more than 30 minutes exercising or playing sports during each physical education class.

Source: *Improving Children's Health Through Physical Activity: A New Opportunity, Executive Summary.* Adapted, with permission. © 1997 International Life Sciences Institute, Washington, DC, USA.

• *[Health-related] physical fitness* is a measure of a person's ability to perform physical activities that require endurance, strength, or flexibility. It is achieved through a combination of regular exercise and inherent ability (performance-related fitness: agility, balance, coordination, speed, power, and reaction time). The components of [health-related] physical fitness are aerobic capacity [cardiorespiratory endurance], muscular strength, muscular endurance, flexibility, and body composition as they relate specifically to health enhancement.

Each of the health-related fitness concepts is specific to physical health—cardiovascular (heart), muscular strength and endurance and flexibility (back), and body composition (obesity).

Michael Pratt summarizes these terms very succinctly: "In a nutshell, *physical activity* is something you *do. Physical fitness* is something you *acquire*—a characteristic or an attribute one can achieve by being physically active. *Exercise* is structured and tends to have *fitness* as its goal" (USDHHS 1999).

Definitions aside, since research shows participants, in general, may view the word *exercise* in a negative light (CDC 1995), it is best to use the term *physical activity* and emphasize enjoyable activity, not regimen.

Society does value lifelong physical activity as a very important health behavior. Indeed, in the last several years, youth sport programs, fitness-oriented recreational programs for youth, and other fitness activities for kids

The Surgeon General Supports Physical Education

The Surgeon General of the United States supports physical education as a path to choosing physical activity as a healthful lifestyle choice. In a report released July 11, 1996, the Surgeon General advocated the following (USDHHS 1996):

- Inactive people can improve their health and well-being by becoming moderately and regularly active.
- Physical activity does not have to be vigorous to achieve health benefits.
- Those who are already physically active will benefit more by becoming more active (figure 1.4).

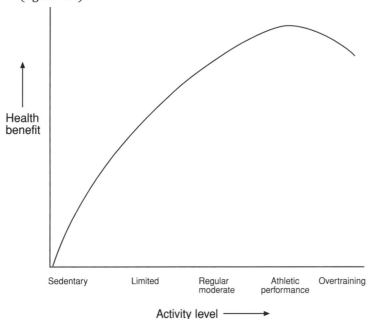

Figure 1.4 Individuals gain significant health benefits when they move to a physically active lifestyle from an inactive lifestyle. Health benefits continue to increase, though less dramatically, with increased activity. When an individual reaches the point of overtraining, however, some health benefits may be lost.

The next step in this progression is the Healthy People 2010 initiative, a successor to the Surgeon General's Healthy People 1990 and Healthy People 2000 programs. Of the 13 objectives of Healthy People 2000, failure to progress in ensuring daily school physical education and in the quality of physical education are of direct concern for physical educators. Specifically, objective 11 emphasizes that "the quantity, and in particular the quality, of school physical education programs have a significant positive effect on the health-related fitness of children and youth by increasing their participation in moderate to vigorous activities" (NASPE 1999).

The American Heart Association Position Statement on the Benefits of Exercise

Children should be introduced to the principles of regular physical exercise and recreational activities at an early age. Schools at all levels should develop and encourage positive attitudes toward physical exercise, providing opportunities to learn physical skills and to perform physical activities, especially those that can be enjoyed for many years. The school curriculum should not overemphasize sports and activities that selectively eliminate children who are less skilled. Schools should teach the benefits of exercise and the development and maintenance of exercise conditioning throughout life.

Some studies demonstrate that such organized school programs are not only feasible but can also be successful. In addition these programs can be used to promote proper nutrition and cigarette smoking prevention and cessation (Pate and Hohn 1994).

have multiplied prolifically (Pate and Hohn 1994). People in our society do seem to understand what the CDC keeps telling us: Physically active people tend to be healthier and better able to enjoy life to its fullest, whereas physically inactive people are more likely to suffer from a variety of ailments. Also in our favor as physical educators is that health care professionals are advocating physical education programs that focus on promoting lifetime physical activities (Pate and Hohn 1994; see sidebars). Furthermore, in general, the public believes education is vital to preparing "happy, healthy, and productive" adults (Pate and Hohn 1994, p. 4). We believe that promoting healthful and active lifestyles through physical education—which includes a solid foundation of health-related fitness education—is the best way to help students be happy, healthy, and productive.

Physical Best Certification

The Physical Best program seeks to improve physical education by providing accurate, up-to-date information and training for today's physical educators to create a conceptual, integrated format for health-related fitness education within their programs. AAHPERD offers a certification program that allows physical education teachers to become Physical Best Health-Fitness Specialists. This certification is similar in concept to the health-related fitness certifications available through other organizations, but Physical Best has been created specifically for the purpose of updating physical educators on the most effective strategies for helping their students gain the knowledge, skills, appreciation, and confidence needed to lead physically active, healthy lives. It focuses on application: how to teach fitness and nutrition concepts through age- and developmentally appropriate games and activities.

To earn certification through AAHPERD as a Physical Best Health-Fitness Specialist you will need to do the following:

- Attend the one-day Physical Best Health-Fitness Specialists Workshop.
- Read this book (*Physical Education for Lifelong Fitness: The Physical Best Teacher's Guide*) and either the *Physical Best Activity Guide—Elementary Level* or the *Physical Best Activity Guide—Secondary Level.*
- Using the required resources mentioned above, complete a take-home examination and submit it to AAHPERD. Successful and timely completion and submission to AAHPERD will result in certification.

For more information or to learn about becoming a Physical Best Health-Fitness Instructor (to train other treachers) or Specialist, call Physical Best at 1-800-213-7193, ext. 426.

Benefits of Lifelong Participation

Because inactivity and poor diet are second only to tobacco use as the leading causes of preventable death in the United States (figure 1.5), students need to know the risks of a sedentary lifestyle. However, it's also crucial—and more meaningful—to your students to know about the many benefits of getting enough physical activity today and remaining active for life—especially the benefits they'll see today. Regular physical activity can (adapted from USDHHS 1996)

- build muscular strength and endurance as well as stronger bones and joints, enhancing both sport and nonsport physical performance;
- improve aerobic endurance;
- enhance flexibility;
- burn kilocalories while preserving lean muscle mass, leading to improved weight control;
- reduce stress; and
- increase feelings of well-being.

In short, physical activity can help *everyone* look better, feel better, and be healthier—not just athletes.

Beyond the many positive benefits associated with adequate physical activity, students need to know what diseases can be prevented by being active for life. According to the U.S. Department of Health and Human Services (1996), regular physical activity can prevent health problems such as the following:

- Premature death in general

How Physical Best Is Different

Physical Best is different from what is commonly referred to as "traditional" physical education, because Physical Best is:

- **educational**—students learn why activity is important and how it benefits them today and for a lifetime. Traditional physical education tells students *what* to do, but not *why*.
- **health oriented**—it emphasizes health-related fitness in addition to the skill-related focus of traditional programs.
- **individualized**—students are not treated as clones of each other, but rather are helped at their own levels so they can become the best they are capable of becoming. Traditional physical education provides the same instruction for all students at the same time.
- **fair**—students are assessed based on personal improvement, not judged against each other or a standardized norm. Physical Best uses physical fitness test results to help students understand the components of health-related fitness and to set individualized goals for improvement. Traditional physical education uses fitness test scores to determine grades and awards.
- **enjoyable**—it advocates the use of physical activity that students enjoy and promotes individual choices whenever possible. Traditional physical education uses the same drills and games regardless of student interest, offering no student choices.
- **realistic**—students explore many ways to be physically active and improve health-related fitness so that there may be greater transfer to real-life settings. Traditional physical education offers a narrow curriculum, often repeating the same activities year after year without proper mastery of the sequence to achieve a basic level of performance competence.

Physical Best is a flexible program, whereas many traditional physical education programs have been rigid. Physical Best teachers say, "I teach children and young adults the hows and whys of a physically active, healthy lifestyle." In the past, some physical educators have said, "I teach football, basketball, volleyball, and softball." We believe that each of our emphases increases students' chances of reaching our ultimate goal—producing individuals who seek health-related fitness as a way of life.

- Death caused by heart disease
- Diabetes
- High blood pressure
- Colon cancer
- High cholesterol levels

Not only does physical activity provide tremendous individual health benefits, a physically active population also benefits society as a whole. It is important that we help community members understand this so physical education doesn't get the "short end of the stick" when it comes to financial decisions. Garner support from others who understand this concept, such as physicians, and let your community know that physical activity can help save society money and prevent drug abuse, violence, and depression. In fact, if we think of a school as a child's "worksite," a health-related physical fitness education program that teaches children about a wide range of healthy habits is similar to a business instituting a worksite health promotion program. Figure 1.6 lists the economic benefits to industry of promoting health where people spend most of their waking hours. To these data we add that less illness means individuals and families incur lower medical costs, need to take less time off work for doctor's visits and sick days, and so on. All these benefits lead to improved productivity and increased quality of life. Children in school deserve the same assistance to be healthy as adults in the workplace, and it's a good time to reach them in order to prevent the development of bad habits.

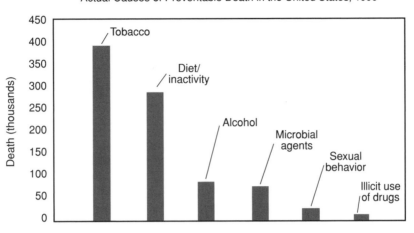

Actual Causes of Preventable Death in the United States, 1990

Figure 1.5 Inactivity and poor diet are second only to tobacco use as the leading cause of preventable death in the United States. Reprinted, by permission, from Human Kinetics, 1998, *Active Youth*. (Champaign, IL: Human Kinetics), v.

Focus on the Positive

Let's say all your students can rattle off several benefits of physical activity and several diseases it can prevent. Now they're all healthy, right? Wrong! Merely memorizing benefits and disease prevention statistics will not inoculate your students against poor health arising from physical inactivity. While this knowledge is important for them to know for the long term, it does not motivate children to become or stay physically active. The answer to this dilemma is three-fold: (1) focus on the positive benefits of physical activity rather than the disease prevention aspects, (2) offer an enjoyable and emotionally and physically safe health-related fitness program in which students may apply the knowledge in ways relevant to their individual lives, and (3) teach them the basic physical skills they need to possess in order to be confident and reasonably successful in a wide range of physical activities and movement forms.

In *Active Youth* (Human Kinetics 1998, pp. 5–7), the Centers for Disease Control and Prevention outline the following 10 recommendations for ensuring quality physical activity programs (see appendix A for further guidelines on implementing the CDC recommendations). (The following list is reprinted, by permission, from Human Kinetics, 1998, *Active Youth*. (Champaign, IL: Human Kinetics), 5-7):

1. Policy: Establish policies that promote enjoyable, lifelong physical activity among young people.

2. Environment: Provide physical and social environments that encourage and enable safe and enjoyable physical activity.

3. Physical education: Implement physical education curricula and instruction that emphasize enjoyable participation in physical activity and that help students develop the knowledge, attitudes, motor skills, behavioral skills, and confidence needed to adopt and maintain physically active lifestyles.

4. Health education: Implement health education curricula and instruction that help students develop the knowledge, attitudes, behavioral skills, and confidence

Developmentally Appropriate Health-Related Fitness

The Council on Physical Education for Children (COPEC) and the Middle and Secondary School Physical Education Council (MASSPEC), committees of the National Association for Sport and Physical Education (NASPE), have published documents outlining developmentally appropriate practices on major physical education issues, including health-related fitness teaching approaches. See tables 1.1, 1.2, and 1.3.

Table 1.1   Elementary Physical Education Practices

	Appropriate practices	Inappropriate practices
Concepts of fitness	• Children participate in activities that are designed to help them understand and value the important concepts of physical fitness and the contribution they make to a healthy lifestyle.	• Children are required to participate in fitness activities, but are not helped to understand the reasons why.
Physical fitness tests	• Ongoing fitness assessment is used as part of the ongoing process of helping children understand, enjoy, improve and/or maintain their physical health and well-being. • Test results are shared privately with children and their parents as a tool for developing their physical fitness knowledge, understanding, and competence. • As part of an ongoing program of physical education, children are physically prepared so they can safely complete each component of a physical test battery.	• Physical fitness tests are given once or twice a year solely for the purpose of qualifying children for awards or because they are required by a school district or state department. • Children are required to complete a physical fitness test battery without understanding why they are performing the tests or the implications of their individual results as they apply to their future health and well-being. • Children are required to take physical fitness tests without adequate conditioning (e.g., students are made to run a mile after "practicing" it only one day the week before).
Fitness as punishment	• Fitness activities are used to help children increase personal physical fitness levels in a supportive, motivating, and progressive manner, thereby promoting positive lifetime fitness attitudes.	• Physical fitness activities are used by teachers as punishment for children's misbehavior.
Active participation	• All children are involved in activities that allow them to remain continuously active. • Classes are designed to meet a child's need for active participation in all learning experiences.	• Activity time is limited because children are waiting in lines for a turn in relay races, to be chosen for a team, or because of limited equipment or playing games such as Duck, Duck, Goose. • Children are organized into large groups where getting a turn is based on individual competitiveness or aggressive behavior. • Children are eliminated with no chance to reenter the activity, or they must sit for long periods of time.
Number of children on a team	• Children participate in team games (e.g., 2–3 per team) that allow for numerous practice opportunities while also allowing time to learn about the various aspects of the game being taught.	• Children participate in full-sided games (e.g., the class of 30 is split into two teams of 15 and these two teams play each other), thereby leading to few practice opportunities.
Competition	• Activities emphasize self-improvement, participation, and cooperation instead of winning and losing. • Teachers are aware of the nature of competition and do not require higher levels of competition from children before they are ready. For example, children are allowed to choose between a game in which a score is kept and one that is just for practice.	• Children are required to participate in activities that label children as "winners" and "losers." • Children are required to participate in activities that compare one child's or team's performance against others (e.g., a race in which the winning child or team is clearly identified).

Reprinted from *Developmentally Appropriate Physical Education Practices for Children* (1992) with permission from the National Association for Sport and Physical Education (NASPE), 1900 Association Drive, Reston, VA 20191-1599.

Table 1.2 Middle School Physical Education Practices

	Appropriate practices	Inappropriate practices
Physical fitness activities	• Students participate in activities that are designed to help them understand and value physical fitness and its contribution toward a healthy lifestyle. • Physical fitness development is an ongoing process and is incorporated into the daily lesson. • Each component of physical fitness receives equal emphasis.	• Students are required to participate in fitness activities without understanding the relevance to their lives. • Programmatically, fitness is taught as a separate unit, is over- or under-emphasized, and scores on normative tests are used as the basis for grading.
Knowledge	• Emphasis is placed on acquiring the knowledge necessary to develop critical thinking and problem-solving skills within the context of physical activity. [This knowledge includes]…fitness assessment and the role of physical activity…within their lives.	• Sport skill acquisition and participation are the only objectives emphasized or valued. The program does not contribute to the student's knowledge of how to use physical activity in their lives.
Individualization of instruction	• Instruction is individualized by giving the students choices, providing additional necessary practice time, or modifying the task difficulty depending on the student's achievement of prerequisite objective.	• All students are doing the same thing at the same time regardless of their skill level, success at prerequisite objective, or developmental level.
Warming up	• Warm-up is activity-specific, conforms to guidelines for safe exercises, and accomodates different fitness levels.	• A single warm-up routine is used regardless of the activity, ignores individual fitness levels, and is potentially unsafe.
Physical fitness testing	• Scores on fitness tests are used to help students set personal goals and to determine individual progress.	• Students are assessed under the pressure of having to perform alone in front of the entire class or when not ready.
Student choices	• Students are given choices in matters such as (a) equipment, (b) modification of rules, numbers of players, size of playing spaces, as well as (c) selection of activities to accomodate skill levels and interest, such as choosing among competitive games, cooperative games, or solitary skill practice.	• Teacher always determines and controls the activity, game rules, equipment, and type of participation.

Reprinted from *Appropriate Practices for Middle School Physical Education* (1995) with permission from the National Association for Sport and Physical Education (NASPE), 1900 Association Drive, Reston, VA 20191-1599.

Table 1.3   High School Physical Education Practices

	Appropriate practices	Inappropriate practices
Physical fitness activities	• Students participate in activities that are designed to help them understand and develop the components of health-related fitness and value physical activity and its contributions to a healthy lifestyle. • Development of all components of health-related physical fitness is an ongoing process and is incorporated into daily lessons.	• Students are required to participate in specific physical activities but with no education context (e.g., running laps). • Fitness testing may be emphasized but scores on normative tests are used as the basis for grading. • Fitness testing is not presented as a self-assessment and goal-setting activity. • Fitness activities are used as punishments for inappropriate behaviors.
Variety	• A wide range of physical activity forms are provided that fully utilize school and community resources and address student needs and interest. . . .	• Curriculum offerings are limited to only a few movement forms based on physical activity interests of a few students and/or faculty. School and community resources are not fully used.
Warming up	• Warm-up is activity-specific, consists only of safe, appropriately selected and executed exercises, and accommodates different fitness levels. • Students learn about the purpose, benefit, and correct uses of warm-up activities.	• A single warm-up routine is used regardless of the lesson, ignores individual fitness levels, and/or is potentially unsafe. • Mass exercise sessions are conducted without instructional focus.
Physical fitness testing	• Scores on fitness tests are used for prescription and for individual goal setting. • Students perform periodic self-assessments and record progress toward personal goals.	• Fitness tests are done in isolation or used only for assigning grades.

Reprinted from *Appropriate Practices for High School Physical Education* (1996) with permission from the National Association for Sport and Physical Education (NASPE), 1900 Association Drive, Reston, VA 20191-1599.

WORKSITE HEALTH PROMOTION PROGRAMS

Upon mounting evidence that worksite health promotion cuts costs and produces a healthier workforce, more employers are giving WHP programs greater attention. Much of this newfound respect is probably due to the impressive savings reported by 12 companies in *Fortune* magazine. Here are some highlights:

Aetna: Five state-of-the-art centers kept exercisers' health care costs $282 lower than nonexercisers.

L.L. Bean: Due to a healthy workforce, annual health insurance premiums were one half the national average.

Dow Corporation: On-the-job injury strains dropped 90 percent.

Johnson & Johnson: Health screening saved $13 million a year in absenteeism and health care costs.

Quaker Oats: Because of an integrated health management approach, health insurance premiums were nearly a third less than the national average.

Steelcase: Personal health counselors motivated high-risk employees to reduce major risk factors, generating an estimated $20 million over 10 years.

Union Pacific: Reduced hypertension and smoking saves more than $3 million a year.

Figure 1.6 The benefits of worksite health promotion lead to improved productivity and increased quality of life. Children in school deserve the same assistance that adults in the workplace receive.

Reprinted, by permission, from D. Chenoweth, 1998, *Health Promotion* (Champaign, IL: Human Kinetics), 12.

needed to adopt and maintain physically active lifestyles.

5. Extracurricular activities: Provide extracurricular physical activity programs that meet the needs and interests of all students.

6. Parental involvement: Include parents and guardians in physical activity instruction and in extracurricular and community physical activity programs, and encourage them to support their children's participation in enjoyable physical activities.

Cognitive Performance Benefits of Physical Activity

Cognitive performance, whether in or out of the classroom, greatly benefits from physical activity. For example, most championship caliber chess players spend the last several weeks before important matches or tournaments preparing physically for top performance. Garry Kasparov, the reigning world champion, runs several miles a day starting at least one month before the tournament. Other world-class players swim, walk, bike, or engage in other physical activity in addition to the intense study required for these tournaments (Chelminski 1998).

7. Personnel training: Provide training for education, coaching, recreation, health care, and other school and community personnel that imparts the knowledge and skills needed to effectively promote enjoyable, lifelong physical activity among young people.

8. Health services: Assess physical activity patterns among young people, counsel them about physical activity, refer them to appropriate programs, and advocate for physical activity instruction and programs for them.

9. Community programs: Provide a range of developmentally appropriate community sports and recreation programs that are attractive to all young people.

10. Evaluation: Regularly evaluate school and community physical activity instruction, programs, and facilities.

More specifically, here are several suggestions for ways to create an enjoyable and beneficial health-related physical fitness education program (adapted from USDHHS 1999):

• Place greater emphasis on physical activities that can be enjoyed over a lifetime. Consider offering electives such as aerobic

Mental Health Benefits of Physical Activity

Several studies have revealed that regular physical activity can prevent or reduce symptoms of depression in the short term, regardless of a person's age, gender, race, or socioeconomic status, and whether or not he or she is medicated with antidepressant drugs. Jackson et al. (1999) comment that "Being sedentary increases the risk for depression, but high levels of physical activity may not be any more protective than moderate amounts of physical activity." Finally, most people rated themselves as less depressed after exercise—whether or not they worked hard enough to increase aerobic endurance. According to the American College of Sports Medicine (ACSM), three to five days a week, 20 to 60 minutes each session, at 40 to 85 percent of aerobic capacity is safe and appropriate for people with depression (ACSM 1998).

One study in Sweden (Engstrom 1991) found a clear relationship between regular activity at 15 years of age and high psychological readiness at age 30. The study also found a strong relationship between that psychological readiness at age 30 and continued involvement in physical activity, for both men and women.

dance classes, step aerobics, stretching or weight training classes, racewalking, golf, tennis, cross-country skiing, or swimming.

- Help each student master motor skills and develop a perception of physical competence that supports a wide range of developmentally appropriate physical activity options. For example, teach how to walk, run, or play individual sports; *how* to stretch or warm up and *why* so that students can learn to tailor warm-ups to the activity; or how to design a program of muscle strengthening activities.

- Explore options so that all children can participate and all can feel like winners—not only those who are more athletically gifted. Create incentives or some form of recognition for reasons other than physical achievement, such as most improved, best attitude, full participation, or best team worker. Provide an environment free of ridicule or embarrassment. . . . (*Note*: Handling of awards is a serious issue in physical education and fitness. See the sidebar discussing this in chapter 2.)

- Place greater emphasis throughout the health or physical education curriculum on the physical, social, and mental benefits of physical activity and on the development of personal skills needed to adopt, maintain, and support physically active lifestyles—skills such as self-assessment, goal setting, self-monitoring and self-regulation, decision making, identifying and overcoming barriers, self-reinforcement, communication, and advocacy skills.

Pate and Hohn (1994) offer the following themes on which you should build a sound physical education program:

1. Make promoting lifelong physical activity and fitness the primary goal of physical education.

2. Balance the physical education curriculum so it will function effectively in all three educational domains—psychomotor, cognitive, and affective (social). In fact, knowledge and attitudes are the keys to physical education that promote lifelong physical activity and fitness.

Definitions of Domains

A child should be educated across the three main domains of learning, being, and doing:

- Psychomotor—physical abilities and neuromuscular skills (Rink 1998)
- Cognitive—intellectual aspects
- Affective—values, attitudes, interests, and social skills

3. Ensure that students leave their physical education experience with a heightened sense of "physical activity competence." Those who feel competent in physical activities and see themselves in control of their activity seem likely to engage in exercise as a way of life.

Opinion Statement on Physical Fitness in Children and Youth by the American College of Sports Medicine

It is the opinion of the ACSM that physical fitness programs for children and youth should be developed with the primary goal of encouraging the adoption of appropriate lifelong exercise behavior in order to develop and maintain sufficient physical fitness for adequate functional capacity and health enhancement.

Recommendations for Action

1. School physical education programs are an important part of the overall educational process and should give increased emphasis to the development and maintenance of lifelong exercise habits and provide instruction about how to attain and maintain appropriate physical fitness. The amount of exercise required for optimal functional capacity and health at various ages has not been precisely defined. Until more definitive evidence is available, current recommendations are that children and youth obtain 20-30 minutes of vigorous exercise each day. Physical education classes typically devote instructional time to physical fitness activities, but class time is generally insufficient to develop and maintain optimal physical fitness. Therefore, school programs also must focus on education and behavior change to engagement in appropriate activities outside of class. Recreational and fun aspects of exercise should be emphasized.

2. Home influences are important, and parents should be encouraged to show concern for physical fitness as an important factor that affects their child's health and well-being. Parents should work with local school officials and teachers to promote physical fitness. Parents should strive to be appropriate physical fitness role models.

3. Community opportunities for exercise and physical fitness activities must be expanded. There are many opportunities for children interested in such sports as baseball, basketball, football, swimming, soccer, and gymnastics. Other activities, especially those that are individual in nature and likely to be performed throughout life, need to be more widely available and packaged and promoted in an attractive manner.

4. The health care professions need to become more actively involved in promoting physical fitness for children and youth. More continuing education programs on childhood and youth physical activity and physical fitness should be offered to health professionals. Medical and public health authorities should view the physical fitness of children and youth as being within their sphere of responsibility in addition to traditional undertakings such as immunization and scoliosis screening. Physicians can have a major impact in promoting and supporting physical fitness programs for children and youth.

5. Physical fitness testing is a highly visible and important part of physical fitness programs. School, community, state, and national organizations must adopt a logical, consistent, and scientifically sound approach to physical fitness testing. The focus of physical fitness testing should be health-related rather than athletic-related. Characteristics such as speed, muscular power, and agility are important for athletic success and are primarily genetically determined. These traits should not be assessed in physical fitness testing, although physical education teachers and coaches may wish to measure them for other purposes. Aerobic power, body composition, joint flexibility, and strength and endurance of the skeletal muscles are partly influenced by heredity but can be changed significantly by appropriate exercise patterns.

6. Educational programs designed to increase knowledge and appreciation of the role and value of exercise of physical fitness and health are virtually nonexistent in schools, although such programs are common at colleges and universities. Professional efforts need to be taken to develop, pretest, and publish educational materials suitable for use in schools. Training programs need to be developed and initiated to provide school teachers with the knowledge and skills to help their students achieve cognitive, affective, and behavioral skills objectives associated with exercise, health and fitness. Teachers also need assistance in ways to integrate other aspects of health promotion (good nutrition and not smoking, for

(continued)

example) into instruction about exercise and physical fitness. The educational components of testing, teaching physical fitness activities, and recognition through awards should be complementary and need to be coordinated for a comprehensive program.

7. The ACSM recommends that physical fitness test scores be interpreted in relation to acceptable standards, rather than by normative comparison. It is illogical to declare that American children and youth are physically unfit as a group and then use group norms to interpret a student's fitness test scores. A standards approach establishes a desirable physical fitness score for each fitness component. Current research is inadequate to establish with scientific precision acceptable standards for all fitness components, but preliminary standards should be developed based on the best available evidence and professional opinion. Additional research to refine, modify, and validate standards is a crucial need.

8. Awards systems that require excellent or exemplary performance on physical fitness tests are inadequate. Awards attainable only by students with superior athletic ability may discourage the majority of children and youth because they cannot qualify. A graduated awards system that rewards exercise behavior and achievement in relation to achievable physical fitness standards should be developed and implemented.

Reprinted, by permission, from the American College of Sports Medicine, 1998, "Physical Fitness in Children and Youth," *MMSE* 20(4):422423.

4. Provide reasonable amounts of physical activity in physical education.

5. Ensure that physical fitness testing procedures used are designed to help students attain long-term activity and fitness objectives. (To which we add, teach students to self-test so they can measure their own health-related physical fitness, as well as measure their progress and improvement.)

6. Work to meet the needs of all students, especially those who have special needs and/or are low fit.

7. Ensure that professional preparation programs prepare future physical education teachers to develop balanced curricula and to deliver instruction that is effective in all three educational domains.

We'll look more closely at ways to create and implement a fun and beneficial health-related physical fitness program in parts III and IV. We'll also more fully define "fun" as what students find enjoyable, challenging, personally satisfying, and success-oriented— all of which vary depending on students' ages and interests.

Summary

Physical Best complements and supports existing physical education programs by teaching and applying health-related physical fitness concepts to promote lifelong physical activity. Physical Best excels at providing this component of a well-rounded physical education curriculum by

- basing its philosophy and materials on current research and expert, field-tested input,

- teaching the benefits of lifelong physical activity,

- offering national certification (the Physical Best Health-Fitness Specialist program),

- focusing on the positive (such as student strengths, enjoyable activities), and

- individualizing curricula so that all students may benefit and succeed.

Physical Best believes that this approach enhances the likelihood that students will pursue healthy, physically active lifestyles after they leave your program and into adulthood.

Chapter 2

Physical Activity Behavior and Motivation

School activity and fitness education and testing programs should place less emphasis on the development of current levels of fitness. . . . Instead, health professionals and educators should work to develop activity and fitness programs that increase the likelihood that the participating children will maintain appropriate levels of activity and fitness throughout life.

—Steven N. Blair (1995, p. 151)

As adults, we all have our reasons for being physically active or inactive, and, of course, children do too. In this chapter, we look at several factors affecting physical activity levels. Some motivating factors are common to both children and adults, but others are not. We also offer strategies for helping students learn to set goals and show how this is an important tool for motivating children and adolescents to be active.

Why Children Choose to Be Active

Children seem to be the most active age group in our society; even so, physical activity declines in early adolescence (USDHHS 1999). Why are some children more physically active than others? Why do some children stay more physically active than their peers during adolescence? The answers to these questions provide valuable information as to how to structure developmentally appropriate physical education programs that promote physical activity as a way of life.

Personal Factors Influencing Physical Activity Behavior

The possible personal factors (both biological and psychological) affecting physical activity in children reveal interesting data we can use to improve our approaches to help individual students.

Biological Factors

As shown in table 2.1, gender, age, and obesity have been studied as possible biological influences on physical activity behavior. Studies

Table 2.1 Biological Factors and Children's Physical Activity

Variable	Relation to physical activity
Gender	Boys are more active.
Age	Activity declines with age.
Obesity	Unclear, conflicting findings. Obese children prefer low-intensity activities.

Reprinted, by permission, from J. Sallis, 1994, "Determinants of Physical Activity Behavior in Children." In *Health and Fitness Through Physical Education*, edited by R. Pate and R. Hohn (Champaign, IL: Human Kinetics), 31.

investigating gender and age factors have shown fairly clear-cut trends: boys are generally slightly more active than girls (Fuchs et al. 1988; Kraft 1989; Tell and Vellar 1988; Verschuur and Kemper 1985), and a substantial decline in physical activity levels occurs between the

ages of 6 and 18, with the most drastic change occurring between the ages of 11 and 13 (USDHHS 1999; Sallis et al. 1993). The International Life Sciences Institute (ILSI 1997a) has also confirmed these trends. Once individuals enter the workforce, rates of physical activity drop off farther: "Whereas 70 percent of 12-year-old children report that they engage in vigorous physical activity, by age 21 these rates drop off to 40 percent for men and 30 percent for women" (Jackson et al. 1999). Genetics plays a role as well. In answer to the question, Are physical activity habits inherited? Jackson et al. (1999) write ". . . Only about 20 percent of the variation in a person's physical activity is explainable by genetic inheritance. . . ."

Discerning obesity's influence on physical activity levels, however, is harder to do. Sallis (1994) asks the question, Does lack of physical activity produce obesity, or are obese children particularly inactive because it is so hard for them to move around? He goes on to assert that both factors are probably true. What is known is that obese children prefer low-intensity activities and obese children with obese parents view endurance activities more negatively than do lean children with lean parents (Epstein et al. 1989).

You Can Lead a Horse to Water . . .

. . . but you can't make him drink. In terms of physical education, you can teach a student about health-related physical fitness but you can't make him or her physically active. With proper attention to motivation, however, you won't have to *make* your students be active because they'll *want* to be—and this is far more valuable, especially in the long term.

Psychological Factors

A myriad of possible psychological factors may affect physical activity behaviors. The results of the research have sometimes been conclusive and sometimes inconclusive. Table 2.2 summarizes some of this body of work.

First, as alluded to in chapter 1, knowing that it's healthy to be physically active does not always influence physical activity levels. Knowing *how* to be physically active is also

Table 2.2 Psychological Factors and Children's Physical Activity

Variable	Relation to physical activity
Knowledge of health effects	Not related
Knowledge of how to exercise	Related
Barriers to physical activity	Related
Cues to be active	Related
Perceived susceptibility to obesity	Not related
Intention to be active	Related
Attitudes about activity	Weakly related?
Subjective norms (perceptions of others' beliefs)	Weakly related?
Self-efficacy about activity	Related
Personality	Probably not related

Reprinted, by permission, from J. Sallis, 1994, "Determinants of Physical Activity Behavior in Children." In *Health and Fitness Through Physical Education*, edited by R. Pate and R. Hohn (Champaign, IL: Human Kinetics), 34.

very important (Sallis 1994; Desmond et al. 1990). Moreover, feeling confident in one's own effectiveness or ability (self-efficacy) in physical activity is vital to adolescents' continuing to be active into adulthood. Another strong psychological factor is a person's perception of not having enough time for physical activity (Jackson et al. 1999).

Environmental Factors Influencing Physical Activity Behavior

Naturally, the world a child lives in influences his or her physical activity level and choices. Social and physical factors must be taken into consideration.

Youth and Physical Activity Statistics

Although youth are a more active segment of the U.S. population when compared to adults, the important thing to note about youth activity patterns is the drastic change that takes place in the 11 to 13 age range. As grade in school increases, a number of factors create personal and environmental barriers to physical activity and make it less likely for adolescents to continue an active lifestyle into adulthood (USDHHS 1999):

- Physical activity levels among both girls and boys tend to decline steadily during adolescence (USDHHS 1996).

- Many American high school students do not engage in regular physical activities that maintain or improve their cardiorespiratory fitness, strength, and flexibility. Results of the 1997 national school-based Youth Risk Behavior Surveillance (YRBS) system revealed that 63.8 percent of high school students reported being vigorously active for at least 20 minutes on three or more of the past seven days. Only about half reported participating in stretching or strengthening exercises on three or more of the past seven days (Kann et al. 1998).

- According to the 1997 YRBS, high school girls are less likely to be vigorously active than are high school boys (53.5 percent and 72.3 percent, respectively), African-American girls are less active than caucasian girls (53.9 percent and 66.8 percent, respectively), and students in grades 11 and 12 are less active than students in grade 9 (60 percent, 57.5 percent, and 72.7 percent, respectively) (Kann et al. 1998).

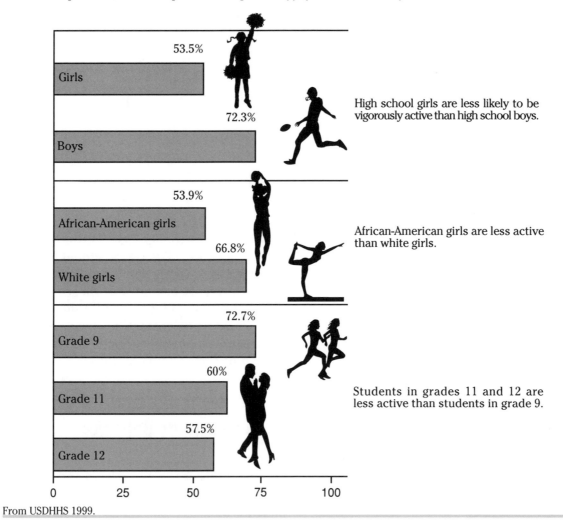

High school girls are less likely to be vigorously active than high school boys.

African-American girls are less active than white girls.

Students in grades 11 and 12 are less active than students in grade 9.

From USDHHS 1999.

Social Factors

Parents and siblings greatly influence a child's choices in life, but an adolescent is more likely to seek peer approval and support. "Families can also transmit a home culture that promotes or hinders physical activity" (Jackson et al. 1999). Parents must serve as role models, as the ILSI survey revealed that very physically active parents have very physically active children. Two-thirds of parents who reported they felt their children were not active enough blamed lack of interest and competition from TV, video games, and computers (ILSI 1997a). Other adults, including teachers, coaches, and physicians, also influence a child's choices. All these influences affect physical activity behavior. Table 2.3 summarizes the research in this area.

The various people in a child's life can influence physical activity behavior in many ways:

- Peers—Naturally, if a child's friends are out biking or in-line skating, the child is more likely to be doing the same. By the same token, if television or video games are their thing, they're more likely to be the child's too. The older the child, the more likely it is that peers will significantly influence physical activity behavior.

Table 2.3 Social Factors and Children's Physical Activity

Variable	Relation to physical activity
Peer modeling and support	Probably related
Parent modeling and support	Related, but probably weaker in adolescence
Teacher modeling and support	Unknown

Reprinted, by permission, from J. Sallis, 1994, "Determinants of Physical Activity Behavior in Children." In *Health and Fitness Through Physical Education*, edited by R. Pate and R. Hohn (Champaign, IL: Human Kinetics), 35.

- Parents and siblings—As with peers, if a child's family is out hiking or playing basketball regularly, the child is more likely to feel competent in these areas through experience and therefore is more likely to be physically active. Conversely, if the child's family is into sedentary activities and avoiding physical activity, the child is less likely to be motivated to be physically active. Parents also influence a child's physical activity level by being able or unable to finance community-based physical activities. As any parent knows, chauffeuring for these activities alone can be a tremendous time and energy commitment.

- Teachers—Most of us can think of at least one teacher who greatly influenced at least one life choice we have made in one area or another. In relation to physical activity behavior, Sallis (1994) writes, "... It is likely that physical educators who are active and enthusiastic about teaching will be more successful in stimulating their students' enjoyment of physical activity." Coaches are likely to have the same degree of influence.

- Physicians—Although knowledge of the need for physical activity is definitely not a motivator, apparently even adolescents have great respect for the authority of their physicians and will follow doctor-given advice regarding physical activity (Sallis 1994). Doctors have even written prescriptions for physical activity, which seems to be a powerful motivator for most kids. In addition, physicians, like physical educators, should be physically active and fit themselves, serving as role models in the community.

Physical Factors

Many different physical factors may promote or discourage physical activity. This is an especially important area to consider as most physical activity must take place outside of physical education class and school itself. Table 2.4 summarizes the research into the influences in this area.

The European Perspective

Physical educators in Europe have developed guidelines very similar to those developed in the United States (Vanden Auweele 1999, pp. 23–24):

- A primary aim of physical education should be to encourage long-term changes in physical activity. Where short-term interventions aim to increase activity, they should ultimately have the objective of effecting permanent change.

- Attitudes about physical activity and social norms influence intentions to be physically active. Attitudes include both beliefs about the outcomes of physical activity and the value or importance attached to such beliefs. Social norms are associated with the beliefs of important others, such as family members, and the degree to which one wishes to comply with those beliefs.

- Intrinsic motivation is associated with highly perceived competence and feelings of autonomy about self-determination. External events affect intrinsic motivation through their perceived effects on personal control and personal competence.

- Positive feelings derived from physical education activities are likely to be the single best determinant of intentions, at least in the short term. Therefore, physical education lessons should aim to be purposeful yet enjoyable.

Table 2.4 Physical Environment Factors and Children's Physical Activity

Variable	Relation to physical activity
Day of week	Probably more active on weekend
Season	Most active in summer, least active in winter
Setting	More active outdoors
Organized programs	Related
Television and video games	Probably related

Reprinted, by permission, from J. Sallis, 1994, "Determinants of Physical Activity Behavior in Children." In *Health and Fitness Through Physical Education*, edited by R. Pate and R. Hohn (Champaign, IL: Human Kinetics), 36.

In addition, the neighborhood a child lives in can greatly influence physical activity behavior. For example, in many urban environments, parents are reluctant or unwilling to allow their children to play outdoors, prefer-

ring they engage in sedentary indoor activities, such as watching television, where they are safer. In a rural area, facilities to use and friends to play with are often several miles away. In contrast, the child living in a suburban neighborhood is likely to have greater freedom as well as more attractive and conveniently located physical activity facilities, such as parks, gymnasiums, and swimming pools.

Motivating Students to Be Active for Life

How can we as teachers prevent our students' levels of physical activity from decreasing as the students get older?

Why Physical Activity Decreases With Age

Young children naturally want to move. What happens, then, to this natural inclination to be physically active as children grow into early adolescence? The reason teens give for low activity levels are much like those adults give: lack of time [or so they perceive] and interest (Sallis 1994). Teens also say, "I don't

Physical Best Summer Shape-Up Challenge

Each summer Nancy Raso-Eklund runs a Summer Shape-Up Challenge for her students in Green River, Wyoming. Examples from one summer's program are shared on pages 25–27. This program encourages students to take the initiative to participate in summer activities like street basketball tournaments such as Gus Macker.

Dear Students and Parents,

Welcome to the Physical Best Summer Shape-Up Challenge.

This program is designed as an incentive to keep your bodies in good physical condition during the summer. I hope you all accept the challenge to stay fit. Set your goals high! Be responsible for a healthy, active lifestyle.

This is how it works:

Accept at least 3 of the 6 challenges. You can do more if you'd like. Each time you participate, jot the information down on the fitness log the best that you can. Return your Physical Best Summer Shape-Up Challenge contract and log sheet when school starts and you will receive your certificate.

Let's work together to establish a lifetime of fitness and health. Good luck, have fun, and be your physical best!

Healthfully yours,
Nancy Raso-Eklund
P.E. Specialist

Physical Best Summer Shape-Up Challenge

A quality physical fitness education program prepares students to take self-responsibility for engaging in healthful physical activities. It also encourages students to choose activities they enjoy. The Summer Shape-Up Challenge provides students the opportunity to take responsibility and make choices regarding their physical activity levels.

Activity Log
for Summer Shape-Up Challenge

Name _____

Date	Activity	Time/Distance	Challenge
6/1	Walk	30 min.	1
6/1	Bike ride	2 miles	3
6/3	Bike ride	3 miles	3
6/4	Jump rope	30 min.	2
6/5	Bike ride	3 miles	3
6/6	Basketball practice	1 hour	6
6/7	Bike ride	3 miles	3
6/8	Basketball game	3 hours	6
6/9	Bike ride	3 miles	3
6/12	Bike ride	3 miles	3
6/13	Walking	1 hour	2
6/15	Hoop jump	30 min.	4
6/16	Bike ride	3 miles	3

Physical Best
Summer Shape-Up Challenge

In order to earn the Physical Best Summer Shape-Up Challenge certificate, I will complete at least 3 of the 6 Summer Shape-Up Challenges.

_____
Student Signature

_____
Parent Signature

Summer Shape-Up Challenges

1. The Vacation Run!

Select a relative or friend you'd like to visit who lives in a nearby town. Determine the distance to their house. Draw a map to plot the course of your trip. As you run or walk this summer, log and chart your mileage until you've reached your destination.

2. Parents Like to Play, Too!

To complete this challenge, you must participate with one or both parents or guardians at least 1 day per week for 10 weeks. Your activity session should be at least 20 minutes long.

3. Wheels in Motion

Using your bike, scooter, roller skates/blades or skateboard challenge yourself to log 20 miles between June 5 and August 24. Record the date and distance.

4. Try Something New

The challenge is for you to participate in an activity you have not tried before. Find a friend or family member to help teach you necessary skills to complete this challenge. Participate at least 5 more times and log the dates and time spent.

5. The Green River Float Trip

The challenge is to log two miles of the Green River by swimming laps in the pool. Each time you go swimming, do some lap swimming. 1 lap = 2 lengths; 30 laps or 60 lengths = 1 mile.

6. Keep the Log Rolling

Keep a log of your favorite activities. Challenge yourself to three activities a week at 20 minutes in duration. Record date and time spent. Suggested activities: ballet, basketball, baseball/T-ball, bowling, golf, gymnastics, hiking, jog, hula hoop, jump rope, karate, playing catch, soccer, tennis, dance class, waterskiing, wrestling.

Involvement with peers in community events can be a powerful motivator for getting young people to be active.

care for all the competition" and "It's [physical activity is] not fun anymore." Virgilio (1997) offers the following explanation:

> As children reach about 10 years of age, they discover various interests and hobbies that may pull them away from physical activity. Moreover, they resist being labeled a "child," and so they may stop playing active childhood games. Too often, parents and teachers convey the message that physical activity must have a purpose, such as joining a team to compete or taking karate lessons to become a black belt. Children who are not very athletic may become inactive if they feel incompetent and unsupported. We must stop treating 10-year-olds as miniature adult athletes and start letting them develop as children who need to move freely and express their physical selves (p. 3).

Teens may also have suffered through years of boring or developmentally inappropriate physical education programs, and once given the choice, avoid physical activity as much as possible. Moreover, teens may lack the knowledge they need to be physically active in safe and interesting ways. In other words, they may not know how to set up a personal physical activity program that meets their individual needs, set goals, monitor their own progress, or reward themselves appropriately and effectively. In addition, teens may not have learned the basic physical skills that lead to physical activity success and confidence.

Students need to understand that although mastering physical skills obviously helps them achieve more success in activities and therefore be more confident, people do not need to be highly skilled to enjoy the benefits of physical activity. For example, the person finishing last in a 5K run is still gaining health benefits and enjoyment from participating. Likewise, players on the company basketball team might not be able to even touch the rim, but they still benefit from and enjoy the activity. Not everyone can or needs to perform at an elite level; when it comes to a person's health and well-being, it is better to have played and lost than not to have played at all. In addition, because self-confidence is so important to participation in physical activity, *perceived* competence may be even more important than actual competence. Moreover, *all* students can learn and improve. So encourage *all* students, regardless of their levels of natural ability, to participate in physical activities. This can be done through individualizing instruction (see

Overcoming Barriers to Physical Activity for Children With Disabilities

"Easier said than done" could be the motto for many families who try to provide expanded opportunities to participate in physical activity to their children with disabilities. Although the Individuals with Disabilities Act (see chapter 15) mandates accessibility to public buildings and accessible transportation for all, it still takes a lot of resolve for families to facilitate getting these children into the arena of physical activity. Some examples:

- James, a teenager with cerebral palsy, wanted to prepare for a swim meet, requiring him to travel alone by bus to the pool. His mother felt comfortable with this as James is able to communicate clearly, but the bus driver refused to help James position his heavy wheelchair to use the lift. His mother had to fight to get the bus company to change its "policy," forcing the bus driver to give James the assistance he needed.

- Sara's father wanted her to play soccer, but the city league was not receptive to including a child with a disability. Sara's father organized his own special team, which thrived for many years because of this parent's dedication.

Contributed by Aleita Hass-Holcombe, Corvallis (Oregon) School District.

chapter 12). Also keep in mind that students tend to gravitate toward partners of their own skill levels. In an appropriate setting in which they can succeed, students learn that enjoyment and reward lie in the participation itself.

Therefore, the question to ask when assessing the value of a physical education program is, "Does the particular program contribute to increased physical activity when a child reaches adulthood?" (Pate 1995). Pate goes on to assert that "The three primary self-management skills are self-monitoring of behavior, self-evaluation through goal setting, and self-reinforcement. . . . This type of training is especially critical for high school students who will soon leave structured physical education programs" (p. 131). In general, then, physical education programs must emphasize teaching students to apply what they're learning to real-life community settings and activities available to adults, while helping students develop the basic skills they need for their activities of choice. Note that focusing on preparing students for the rest of their lives is more likely to meet the overall school mission, as learning self-responsibility is an invaluable life skill.

Motivation

We can describe motivation as being either extrinsic or intrinsic. *Extrinsic motivation* involves factors outside the individual, unre-

lated to the task being performed (Ormrod 1995). Examples include stickers and treats at the elementary level and T-shirts at the middle and high school levels. Although extrinsic rewards motivate children to achieve activity goals to some extent, they also have many drawbacks when used to manipulate children into participating. Children view the extrinsic rewards as the reason to participate in activities they might have chosen to do on their own anyway (Raffini 1993). Extrinsic rewards offered to entice children to be physically active encourage children to focus on the reward instead of on participating in the activity itself, and they may stop working once they have received the reward. Therefore, extrinsic rewards alone are unlikely to promote lifetime physical activity patterns. When children choose to participate on their own, however, and experience feelings of competence, then unexpected extrinsic rewards may help reinforce those feelings. This in turn enhances their intrinsic motivation to participate in physical activity. Another way teachers have handled this issue is to reward physical activity behavior extrinsically (as with stickers, ribbons, gift certificates) long enough to help children see the intrinsic rewards. This may be appropriate with younger children if they are "weaned" into appreciating the intrinsic value of physical activity. Make sure to award the *process*, being active, rather than the *product*, such as a fast time in the

Why Are Competitive Physical Education Programs Still So Common?

Physical education courses are still more likely to feature competitive team sports instead of activities that people could enjoy lifelong (Pate et al. 1995). One possible reason is that many physical educators were excellent athletes and enjoyed competitive sports, and it's simply hard for them to imagine that not all children and young adults feel the same way they do. For example, a teacher (and former college baseball player) may ask students, Who wants to play baseball? and the top athletes raise their hands. The rest of the students go along with this "vote" because they are intimidated (e.g., an elementary student might think, "If I don't go along with the big kids, I'll get beat up at recess"; a high school student may worry about peer ridicule in the locker room). Meanwhile, the teacher incorrectly assumes he or she is running a happy and productive class while long lines of students wait for turns at bat and stand around in right field bored to death. Although many sports can be used to enhance health-related fitness, simply having the students choose an activity to keep them busy without using the opportunity to teach both psychomotor skills and health-related fitness concepts is not physical *education*; it is physical *neglect,* as the students who need the activity the most are likely to get the least. Nor will anyone learn *why* physical activity is important or *how* to apply it to real life. In short, students need to be taught the connections between sports and lifelong health-related fitness for sports to be valuable as lifelong physical activities. Remember, competitive sports are not bad, it is poor teaching methods and the lack of connections to adult life that turns students off.

mile run (see also chapter 17). Keep in mind, however, that it is really choice plus physical skill that equals a physically active person, regardless of extrinsic rewards.

Choice + Skill = A Person Motivated to Be Physically Active

Intrinsic motivation is an individual's internal desire to perform a particular task (Ormrod 1995). A primary example is participating in an activity simply because one enjoys it. Unlike extrinsic rewards, intrinsic motivators encourage long-term behavior changes fairly effectively. In contrast to children working in learning environments that emphasize extrinsic motivation, those encouraged to develop intrinsic motivation tend to view physical activity as a process, and this continual process can lead to feelings of personal satisfaction and competence.

The major intrinsic motivator for children is, of course, "fun." Indeed, fun is the primary intrinsic reason students give for participating in physical activity. And enjoyable, intrinsically motivating activities have four characteristics: challenge, curiosity, control [chances for self-responsibility], and creativity (Raffini 1993). (See sidebar titled "What Is Fun?") The activities you use should embody these characteristics. Another intrinsic motivator is the

natural urge to learn. If the child learns from the class activity, he or she is more likely to be motivated to continue being physically active. Finally, don't forget skill teaching: It's not enjoyable to participate in an activity for which the student lacks the basic skills.

No matter your approach, however, students must perceive your program in the right light to reach the goal of physical activity for life. Whitehead (1994) offers a flowchart outlining the ways in which students may perceive a physical education program and the possible outcomes, depending on their perceptions, in figure 2.1.

Of course, we want students to have positive perceptions of physical activity as a worthwhile endeavor in itself. The following summarizes the ways in which we can help increase students' intrinsic motivation to be active for life. (The following list is reprinted from J.R. Whitehead, 1994, "Enhancing Fitness and Activity Motivation in Children." In *Health and Fitness Through Physical Education*, edited by R. Pate and R. Hohn (Champaign, IL: Human Kinetics, 85.):

1. Help all children *feel competent* at physical activity, exercise, and fitness. To do this, try to structure teaching sequences and learning evaluations relative to individual task mastery. Remember that

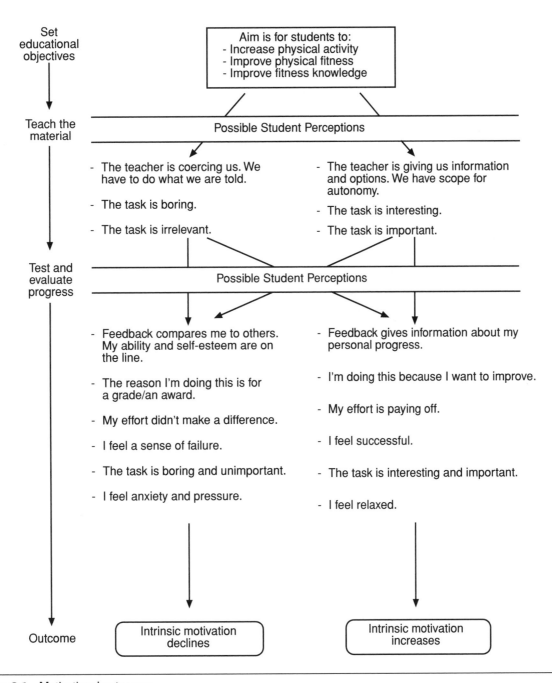

Figure 2.1 Motivational outcomes.

Adapted, by permission, from J. Whitehead, 1994, "Enhancing Fitness and Activity Motivation in Children." In *Health and Fitness Through Physical Education*, edited by R. Pate and R. Hohn (Champaign, IL: Human Kinetics), 86.

peer comparisons of ability may be highly counterproductive, particularly to those children who need our help the most—the most unfit.

2. Promote *perceptions of self-determination through choice* in fitness activity and programming. Remember that, like most adults, children feel coerced when told what activities they must do.

3. Be *informational* rather than controlling when giving necessary directions or feedback; take care to explain the good reasons for and meanings of instructions and rules.

4. Kids are intrinsically interested in what they think is *important* to them personally. Foster children's interest in activity by making them aware of its benefits. This

Having fun is the primary intrinsic reason students give for choosing to be physically active on their own.

can range from helping elementary kids equate sports with fun to teaching the social, appearance, and health bene-fits of exercise to high school students.

5. Enhance the intrinsic pleasures of physical activity by heightening *interest, fun,* and *excitement* in exercise-learning and fitness-promoting situations. Don't unnecessarily turn healthful exercise into com-

petition, drudgery, or punishment. It should feel like play, not work!

Enhancing the intrinsic pleasures of physical activity is the strength of Physical Best.

Guidelines for Physical Education Programs That Motivate

We cannot stress enough that too often in attempting to get children fit, we turn them off to physical activity. Boring laps, the "no pain, no gain" philosophy, and comparisons to others have too often been deterrents to physical activity. Physical Best explores enjoyable and interesting activities that promote a conceptual knowledge of fitness in hopes that a child will not only have a positive experience but will be able to make better decisions about his or her own health.

Of course, designing and implementing a health-related physical fitness education program that motivates students to be active for life is easier said than done. Whitehead (1994) suggests what programs might sound like, depending on whether extrinsic or intrinsic motivation is used (see table 2.5). Begin to listen to and monitor your own attitudes and see if you are more intrinsic or extrinsic in approach.

To help you start or improve a program that cultivates intrinsic motivation, these guidelines may prove useful (Sallis 1994):

1. Pay attention to typical physical activity behaviors based on age. Encourage young

What Is "Fun"?

Throughout this book we emphasize the importance of making physical activity "fun". It's important to note that fun is not a goal or objective of a quality physical education program. Rather, fun is a means to achieving the ultimate goal of having students adopt physically active, healthy lifestyles (see National Physical Education Standard #7, page 140).

We know people are more likely to participate in activities they enjoy and there is no reason why being physically active can't be enjoyable. Of course, what is fun for one person may not be fun for others. Some people like competition (e.g., playing team sports), some like cooperative social activities (e.g., participating in an aerobics class), while still others prefer individual activities (e.g., running on a treadmill at home while watching television). The key is making physical education purposeful *and* enjoyable so as to achieve the goal of graduating students who will be physically active, healthy, productive adults.

Table 2.5   Meanings and Expressions of Intrinsic Versus Extrinsic Motivation

Words that connote or promote feelings about motivation

Intrinsic	Extrinsic
Play	Work
Excitement	Tension
Challenge	Pressure
Interest	Disinterest
Curiosity	Boredom
Importance	Irrelevance
Mastery	Incompetence
Success	Failure
Improvement	Deterioration
Choice	Coercion
Freedom	Constraint

Expressions of motivational mind-sets

Intrinsic	Extrinsic
"Let's help kids get fit."	"We must make kids fit."
"Let's help kids motivate themselves."	"We have to motivate kids."
"Let's make exercise fun for kids."	"We must make kids work harder."
"These are your exercise choices."	"You should/must do these exercises."
"This information will help you set goals and plan your personal exercise program."	"Your goal is to achieve X fitness level in Y weeks' time."
"These are the good reasons for taking part in an exercise program."	"You have to take part in this exercise program because I say so!"

Reprinted, by permission, from J. Whitehead, 1994, "Enhancing Fitness and Activity Motivation in Children." In *Health and Fitness Through Physical Education*, edited by R. Pate and R. Hohn (Champaign, IL: Human Kinetics), 87.

children to maintain their generally high levels of physical activity and adolescents to increase their participation in physical activity.

2. Prepare secondary students to transition to adult life by helping them design and use personal fitness plans.

3. Target age-appropriate motivators. Opportunities for enjoyment, companionship, and adult approval are more likely to motivate young children. Opportunities to demonstrate self-control, improve body shape, and control stress are more likely to motivate adolescents.

4. Make special efforts to motivate and support girls as they are less likely to be active than boys.

5. Don't get caught up in gender stereotypes, however. For example, some boys and some girls may be too embarrassed to exercise in groups.

6. Give extra support to those who need it, but do so in a way that is perceived as helpful, not stigmatizing.

7. Emphasize benefits of physical activity that can be experienced now (looking

Dressed for Success

Remember the ugly old gym uniforms that used to be required? Talk about motivating students to skip physical education! Remember that students, especially at the middle school and high school level, are very concerned about how they look. Consider allowing students to choose their own physical education clothes, but with specific guidelines (e.g., no offensive language or artwork, appropriate for moving freely, purposeful, functional, appropriately fitting, safe, clean), or design a contemporary outfit that kids will like. Being able to dress in sharp workout clothes instead of really ugly uniforms can make a difference in the attitude of your students. You might work with a local sporting goods retailer to come up with a design that can be offered for a very reasonable price. Do keep in mind the attitude of students—at some schools kids fight over trendy clothes. Work with your administrators and students to find solutions.

Social interaction can be motivating to middle school students. Help students learn that fitness can be social as well as good for their physical health.

and feeling better). Have students who have successfully improved their health-related fitness (especially such achievements as improved body composition) share the benefits they've realized from physical activity with their fellow students.

8. Build in success so students feel confident enough to participate in physical activity.

9. Reduce competition and reward participation instead of performance.

10. Work with physicians to encourage youth to be physically active.

11. Involve families, for example, through homework, newsletters, volunteer opportunities, and special family events and programs.

12. Be physically active yourself and talk positively about your physical activity endeavors.

13. Teach both elementary and secondary students time management strategies to help them schedule physical activity.

Debating About Rewards and Awards

Whether or not to offer extrinsic rewards for physical activity participation or fitness test scores is a controversial topic. On the one hand, it is important to encourage students to do their best on tests and be more active overall. On the other hand, the research shows that intrinsic motivation is longer lasting. The following are some guidelines for using rewards/awards judiciously:

- Reward the performance, not the outcome.

- Reward students more for their effort than for their actual success.

- Reward little things on the way toward reaching larger goals.

- Reward the learning and performance of emotional and social skills as well as health-related fitness endeavors.

- Reward frequently when youngsters are first learning to apply new concepts.

- Once physical activity and health-related fitness habits are well formed, you only need to reinforce them occasionally. In other words, you can use extrinsic rewards to change students' physical activity habits, then slowly "wean" them onto intrinsic appreciation of physical activity.

- Use rewards that have meaning to the recipients. Ask students what they might find reinforcing. Be age appropriate in your choices.

- Don't forget that rewards can be words of praise, chances to choose from a wider variety of activities, as well as more tangible items, such as stickers and T-shirts.

Adapted, by permission, from Rainer Martens, 1997, *Successful Coaching*. (Champaign, IL: Human Kinetics), 36–38.

14. Be sensitive to factors children may have no control over, such as urban crime and parent work schedules limiting physical activity opportunities.

15. Allow students to choose lower intensity levels, which they're more likely to maintain than higher intensity activities.

16. Be sensitive to income, race, and ethnic background differences among students. Promote inexpensive, low-equipment physical activities that do not require special facilities.

Specific Strategies for Promoting Physical Activity and Fitness

Remember, children and adolescents are not mini-adults. Look for age-appropriate ways to tailor the general strategies described in the previous section to the realms of home, school, and community. Table 2.6 offers several specific suggestions that the Physical Best program endorses.

Finally, don't forget one of the most important keys: Emphasize enjoyment! If a child remembers nothing else from your class, it should be that being physically active is enjoyable and interesting. This is surely an important key to a lifetime of fitness.

Goal Setting

Goal setting is a mechanism that helps students understand their potential and feel satisfied with their accomplishments. Using goals created from personal assessments establishes their ownership and fosters pride in the process. Written action plans help to establish a pathway to the destination that has been set. Then the types of behaviors (goals) students require for improving health-related fitness can be determined from a pretest. Establishing goals is a good way to encourage changes in behavior leading to improved

Provide individualized motivation and support, but do so in a way that is perceived as helpful rather than stigmatizing.

Table 2.6 Strategies for Promoting Physical Activity in Children

Setting	Objectives	Strategies
Home	Presentation of physically active parental role model	Parents are physically active at home in presence of children.
	Joint parent-child physical activity participation	Parents and children are physically together after school and on weekends.
	Parent facilitation of child activity	Parents supervise child activity and, if necessary, transport children to activity settings and programs.
	Limitation of TV watching	Parents limit TV watching by children, particularly at times when physical activity is an option.
School	Provision of significant amounts of physical activity	Physical activity time in physical education and during other available time is optimized.
	Promotion of lifelong physical activity	Physical education provides enjoyable exposure to developmentally appropriate physical activities.
	Promotion of motor skill acquisition	Physical education provides basic mastery of motor skills that are applicable to lifetime fitness.
	Promotion of physical activity via after-school programming	School provides after-school physical activity programs that give priority to the needs of the majority of children.
	Presentation of physically active teacher role models	School provides employee health promotion program and encourages on-site teacher/staff physical activity.
Community	Provision of physical activity programs for all children and youth	Community recreation programs and private youth organizations offer and promote a wide range of physical activity programs, including those that are noncompetitive.
	Provision of safe and attractive physical activity facilities	Communities provide parks, playgrounds, pools, gymnasia, and bike/jogging trails that are safe, readily accessible, and attractive for children and youth.

Reprinted, by permission, from R. Pate, 1995, "Promoting Activity & Fitness." In *Child Health, Nutrition, and Physical Activity*, edited by L. Cheung (Champaign, IL: Human Kinetics), 143-144.

It's OK to Excel

Throughout this book, we emphasize that lifelong physical activity is for all students, and we especially need to work with low-fit students who have long been ignored. We don't, however, want to forget about the highly motivated students who want to achieve a high level of fitness for a variety of reasons. Just as we want to provide opportunities for excellence to students interested in science or math, we should also provide the same types of opportunities to students who are interested in achieving excellence in fitness. For example, creating an individualized plan for a student who wants to compete at an elite level in tennis or track, or having a student serve as a mentor to other students could help a student decide if he or she would enjoy a career as a physical educator or personal trainer. The first key, of course, is that this is voluntary on the students' part. We should explore ways of individualizing programs for these students to help them safely achieve their goals. We provide examples in later chapters.

health and fitness. This process is invaluable to physical education—as well as to other areas of life.

Goal setting, however, must be done carefully to successfully enhance motivation. It takes experience and practice for both students and educators. Many factors should be taken into consideration: gender differences, current fitness level, information about fitness improvement, and growth and maturation. The criteria-level (Healthy Fitness Zone) charts provided in the *FITNESSGRAM* assessment reflect both gender and age differences. In general, the less fit an individual, the greater the gains may be. For the more-fit individual, smaller gains are more realistic to expect. Finally, remember to focus on personal improvement—and encourage students to do so as well—rather than on comparisons to others.

Adapted, by permission, from AAHPERD, 1998, *Physical Best Activity Guide—Elementary Level*. (Champaign, IL: Human Kinetics), 18-22.

Basic Strategies for Successful Goal Setting With Students

Encourage students to set goals based on their current fitness status rather than to compare personal status with others. Motivation is related to competence or perceptions of success in a particular area, so basing success on current physical fitness levels allows students the potential for improvement and thus to experience success at goal setting. This positive experience will influence

the student's motivation and behavior. Following several goal-setting guidelines will help motivate students and positively influence their behavior toward physical activity.

Involve the Student in the Goal-Setting Process

Involving students enhances their commitment to achieving their goals and encourages self-responsibility for personal fitness. Scores should be their own, not norm-based. Consider the age, maturity level, and knowledge level of each student, which should influence the amount of input a student will have. And, of course, an individual's interests and needs should be part of establishing fitness goals.

Start Small and Progress

Start with a small class. Begin the goal-setting process with one grade level and continue to set goals with this class as its members progress through the school system. In a few short years, they will be experienced in setting goals in all areas of fitness.

Focus on Improvements Relative to an Individual's Past Behavior

Take into account the student's initial level of performance. The lower the level of performance, the greater the potential for improvement. The higher the level, the less improvement is possible. If a student has problems with motivation, set the individual's goals at

Leaving Behind America's Physical Activity Myths

For years Americans have heard the message that they should exercise vigorously for at least 20 minutes per day, three times per week. They believed that nothing less would do. Even though many people today might be able to recite the recommendation from memory, the vast majority of Americans have not successfully carried out the advice. And in the process, it is likely that a good many have given up trying.

Previous efforts by public and private organizations to promote physical activity have emphasized the importance of high-intensity physical activities. As a result, many people are convinced that they must engage in vigorous, continuous activity for at least 20 minutes three times a week to achieve any health benefits. Rather than do less than this, many people choose to do nothing at all. As people's perception of the effort required to perform an activity increases, their participation in physical activity seems to decrease (Dishman and Sallis 1994).

Therefore, if people with little confidence in their ability to be physically active were convinced that moderate-intensity activity counts and that "it's easier than you think" to fit activity into the course of a busy day, perhaps the number of people who were willing to adopt and continue a physically active lifestyle would increase. . . . Perhaps if Americans felt more comfortable with their own ability to fit physical activity into their lives, they'd be more likely to spread the word and really get the ball rolling for a "fitness revolution." After all, studies show that people who have confidence in their ability to be physically active and who receive support from family members and friends are more likely to begin and continue exercise programs (Dishman and Sallis 1994).

From USDHHS 1999.

lower increments than you might for a student who is already highly motivated. For example, you may need to cajole the less motivated student more than you would others.

Set Specific and Measurable Goals

Specific and measurable goals have been found to be more effective than vague goals (such as "I'll run faster"). For example, if a student wants to run faster and had completed the mile in a 12:05, you can help the student set a more specific, measurable goal of running the mile in an 11:50. Students need some instruction, direction, and practice in identifying specific, measurable goals. If the goals are not measurable, it is impossible to determine if the student has been successful at achieving them, which defeats the purpose of goal setting.

Set Challenging and Realistic Goals

When you assist students in setting physical fitness goals, take into consideration the student's initial fitness level. Also, plan the time carefully between the pretest (to estab- lish the goal) and the posttest (to measure the achievement). The lower the student's initial fitness level and the longer the student has between testing periods, the greater the potential for improvement. The higher the student's initial fitness level and the shorter the time the student has between testing periods to work on fitness, the less the potential for improvement. It is important that the goal not be so easy that it does not challenge the student. Most students make the goal too difficult, and their motivation suffers when they cannot attain their goals. It may be helpful to have students practice setting goals and making intermediate goals until they learn more about themselves and their physical fitness levels.

Write Down Goals

Written goals hold more meaning for students and help them focus on what they need to accomplish. If you work with preliterate or dyslexic students, it can help to use alternative methods such as pictures. Appendix B contains a sample contract form for recording specific goals. You will also need to spend

Sample Goals for Aerobic Fitness

- I will reduce my mile run by ___ seconds by performing aerobic activity ___ times per week for at least ___ minutes each session.

- I will exercise aerobically ___ times a week, running the one-mile distance at least ___ times a week, timing and logging the results.

- I will perform aerobic activity ___ times a week, recording the amount of time, type of activity, and intensity of the activity.

- I will walk briskly ___ times a week for a total of ___ blocks. Each week I will increase my distance ___ blocks.

- I will replace sedentary (inactive) habits with active habits at least three times per day.

more time with students who have special health conditions. These students usually need extra guidance or incentives and may have health concerns.

Provide Students With Strategies

Students must understand *how* to change behaviors that are detrimental in improving or maintaining physical fitness. You can suggest examples of strategies, such as having students ride their bikes three times per week, do 25 curl-ups each night before bed, or stretch every day using a series of stretches that you provide. In other words, provide strategies for improvement. It would be better, of course, if students develop strategies on their own with your guidance. Learning how to develop goals based on the FITT principle (frequency, intensity, type, and time) and nutrition is a crucial part of the lifelong-fitness process.

Support and Give Feedback About Progress Toward Goals

An important aspect of goal setting that many teachers disregard is giving positive reinforcement and encouragement. Verbal encouragement (such as "I see you have been running one mile every other day. Keep up the good work!"), written encouragement (such as a note saying, "John, I was glad to see you practicing modified pull-ups today at recess"), and verbal recognition (such as "Susan has set a great example for all of us by doing her flexibility exercises daily!") can assist in keeping students committed to positive fitness behaviors.

Create Goal Stations

Setting up goal stations for students helps instill a sense of ownership as they write their own goals. The students can rotate in small groups to work on particular goals. Students can be placed in groups that received similar scores on their assessments. They will likely have similar goals and provide one another extra motivation and encouragement in achieving the goals. As they enter the class, students can also work individually at stations to improve (instant activity). Allowing them to choose work areas places the responsibility for improvement on them.

Provide Opportunities for Periodic Evaluation

Periodic reassessment of fitness behavior helps students assess how they are progressing toward their personal goals. Assessment opportunities should occur regularly throughout the year. These reassessment opportunities can include informal testing and self-testing, both in school and at home. Use the information gained through reassessment to evaluate and adjust existing goals where necessary. You and the students will also have the opportunity to change their goals and determine if the goal was perhaps too difficult or too easy.

Building a Fitness Program Around Student Goals

The Physical Best program is a model for establishing goals in physical fitness levels, activity participation, and the affective and cognitive domains. The Physical Best program recognizes the achievement of goals set by students, an important reinforcement for student motivation.

Using goal-setting techniques and strategies helps students have positive experiences through movement activities, feel good about themselves in physical activity, and carry positive fitness habits for a lifetime. Physical educators can support the students' use of goal setting to enhance their lives and fitness abilities.

Table 2.7 provides some guidelines for setting fitness goals, but the numbers in the chart are simply guidelines. Initial level of fitness is already built into the table:

- Low—initial level is far from reaching the criteria levels
- Moderate—initial level is close to the criteria levels
- High—initial level is at or above the criteria levels

Nevertheless, each of the other unique circumstances each student presents must be considered for establishing that student's goals. For example, two moderately fit students might establish upper-body strengths that fall at the extremes of the range. One might have class only two times a week, not get much encouragement at home, and be somewhat overweight. The other student might have an hour-long class five times a week.

Table 2.7 is based on reasonable estimates. Pursuing further research will provide more objective informational guidelines, and thus the standards will be adjusted. You and your students will improve in the ability to set goals as you practice setting more goals and observing the outcomes.

Summary

Summarizing the research, the Physical Best program offers the following suggestions for

Table 2.7 Guidelines for Goal Setting (Amount of Change to Consider a Reasonable Goal)

Fitness component	If pretest score is far from criteria levels	If pretest score is near criteria levels	If pretest score is equal or better than criteria levels
Aerobic endurance (1-mile run)	Decrease time 1–4 min	Decrease time 1–2 min	Decrease time 30–60 s
Flexibility	Increase reach 2–8 cm	Increase reach 2–5 cm	Increase reach 1–3 cm
Body composition	Decrease skinfold sum 1–10 mm	Decrease skinfold sum 1–5 mm	Maintain, or possibly decrease, 1–2 mm
Upper-body muscular strength and endurance	Increase by 4–5 reps	Increase by 2–3 reps	Increase by 1 rep
Trunk muscular strength and endurance	Increase by 5–10 reps	Increase by 3–7 reps	Increase by 2–5 reps

Reprinted, by permission, from AAHPERD, 1998, *Physical Best Activity Guide—Elementary Level.* (Champaign, IL: Human Kinetics), 22.

motivating students to be physically active for life:

1. Award the process of participation, rather than the product of fitness.
2. Set goals that are challenging yet attainable.
3. Develop basic skills so that students feel competent and confident in physical activity.
4. Use bulletin boards and visual aids to publicize items of interest in fitness.
5. Emphasize self-testing programs that teach children to evaluate their own fitness levels.
6. Do not use fitness-test results for grading.
7. Involve the parents by creating a comprehensive approach to health promotion.

Throughout this book, we offer more specific suggestions for developing the desire within students to be physically active for life.

Chapter 3

Health-Related Physical Fitness Education

Life isn't a sprint; it's a marathon, so prepare for the long haul.

—Anonymous

Too often in education, we teachers try to "sprint"—hurry and fill students with as much knowledge and skill as possible, without giving them the problem-solving tools to continue the journey after they leave us. In addition, many students simply are not allowed the time they need to master the essential knowledge and skills—whether through administrative decisions that limit physical education time or unsatisfactory teacher choices. In this chapter, we outline our philosophy on how to give students the tools they need to be fit for life.

Philosophy of Health-Related Physical Fitness Education

Health-related physical fitness education seeks to produce graduates who view physical activity as a worthwhile, pleasurable, lifelong endeavor; who have discovered where their physical activity interests lie through experiencing an individualized and varied curriculum; and who know how to design and implement a personal health-related fitness plan, given the opportunities and constraints faced (such as individual abilities, available community facilities and activities, and cultural interests). In short, the quality physical education program includes fitness education, which teaches students how and why to engage in lifelong, individualized, health-related physical activity *and* inspires them to do so.

"Health-related physical fitness education" can also be considered a curricular model in itself. Ennis (1996) describes this approach as a "personal fitness" curriculum: "Students learn to test themselves and to set realistic personal goals. They interpret the scores and use the test results to develop a fitness program that is right for them within realistic . . . guidelines." Such programs are "most successful when they blend an emphasis on the fitness knowledge base with an emphasis on the individual's concerns for an enjoyable, interesting program."

A quality health-related physical fitness education program mirrors the Physical Best philosophy and approach:

- Individualized—meeting each student's needs and abilities and helping them set realistic personal goals
- Fair—assessing students based on personal improvement, not by comparing them to others

Curriculum Models

There are many different approaches that can be used in teaching quality physical education. Examples of different physical education curriculum models include sport education, skill-themes approach, movement education, interdisciplinary, and personal fitness. The connection between Physical Best and the personal fitness curriculum model is obvious, but Physical Best is designed to also be used to provide the health-related fitness component of any physical education curriculum model. Physical Best is important to all curriculum models because fitness education is essential physical education content.

- Health oriented—emphasizing the components of health-related fitness
- Educational—teaching the "whys" and concepts behind physical activity
- Enjoyable—interesting, fun, social experience because, ultimately, many people will choose to be active for a lifetime when they find physical activity can be fun and social
- Realistic—focusing on accessible lifetime activities applicable to real-life settings

Health-related physical fitness education must be tailored to the age group and individual to which it is taught. For example, it is more appropriate to integrate the teaching of basic general motor skills (particularly gross motor) at the elementary level than at the middle or high school level. Middle school students should concentrate on combining skills and strategies that enhance physical activity performance. And actually developing a detailed personal fitness plan is appro-

Biking is a lifetime activity that is accessible in most communities.

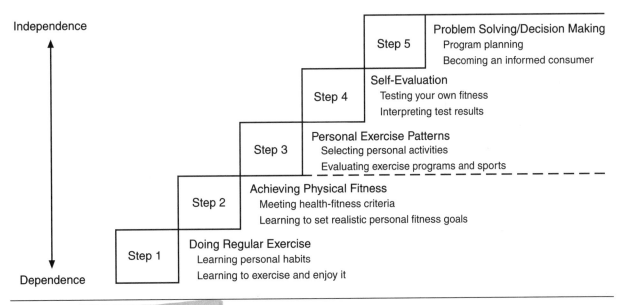

Figure 3.1 Stairway to lifetime fitness.

From *Fitness for Life: Teachers Annotated Edition* by C.B. Corbin and R. Lindsey. © 1993 by Scott Foresman. Used by permission.

priate for high school students. Overall, the K–12 program should build progressively toward the ultimate goal: producing members of society who take lifelong personal responsibility for engaging in health-related physical activity, not only because they know it's good for the body and why, but also because they know how intrinsically rewarding it is to move in ways they enjoy.

Naturally, when it comes to a child assuming total responsibility for her own health, she will have to "crawl" before she can "run." Health-related physical fitness education focuses on this *process* of having students assume progressively more responsibility for their own health, fitness, and well-being. With his well-known "Stairway to Lifetime Fitness," Corbin (Corbin and Lindsey 1993) succinctly outlines the process through which we must guide our students (see figure 3.1). The younger the student, the more likely he is to be on a lower, more dependent step. Conversely, the older the student, the more he needs to be operating on a higher step—and the more responsible you are for facilitating this.

The CDC suggests that we "implement physical education curricula and instruction that emphasize enjoyable participation in physical activity and that help students develop the knowledge, attitudes, motor skills, behavioral skills, and confidence needed to adopt and maintain physically active lifestyles" (Human Kinetics, *Active Youth* 1998, p. 14). This includes the following:

- Providing planned, sequential physical education curricula for all grades that encourage enjoyable, lifelong physical activity. These curricula should emphasize settings and activity parameters for lifetime activity over those for competitive sport. Physical fitness testing should be integrated into the curricula, but results should not form the basis for report card grades.

- Using the NASPE national standards for physical education to develop the curricula. These standards are designed to develop the physical, cognitive, and affective domains in children through physical education.

- Promoting enjoyable participation by using active learning strategies; developing students' knowledge, confidence, and motor and behavioral skills; and providing a significant opportunity for regular physical activity. Ultimately, this will promote participation in enjoyable physical activity both in and out of class.

Guidelines on Physical Activity for Children

The Council for Physical Education for Children (COPEC) has issued the following guidelines for educators. (The following list is reprinted from *Physical Activity for Children: Statement of Guidelines* (1998) with permission from the National Association for Sport and Physical Education (NASPE), 1900 Association Drive, Reston, VA 20191-1599.)

- Provide time for activity in the school setting—daily physical education and other chances to move, such as recess.
- Individualize activities—let students determine their own workload to foster interest in lifelong activity.
- Expose youngsters to a variety of activities—help them (regardless of ability or skill) find activities they enjoy through variety.
- Focus instructional feedback on process, not product—don't worry about "how fast" or "how difficult"; give feedback to those who are participating and doing their best.
- Continue to teach physical skills—students are more likely to be physically active and therefore maintain their health and fitness as adults if they feel competent in the skills of physical activity. Students should leave the physical education curriculum with basic skills in a variety of activities.
- Be an active role model—don't just teach it, live it. Share your personal strategies for staying physically active.

- Care about the attitudes of students—make the physical education experience a positive one, pulling students toward a lifetime of physical activity, rather than pushing them relentlessly toward temporary fitness.
- Teach positive approaches to lifetime activity—help students succeed in a variety of lifetime activities and develop personal fitness plans so they can "coach" and encourage themselves after leaving the program.
- Promote activity outside the school environment—encourage activity at home and in community recreation settings.
- Consider lifetime activities that endure—individuals are more likely to become positively addicted to physical activities that are noncompetitive, not mentally taxing, possible to do alone, seen as valuable by the individual, and easier and more meaningful as the individual persists in the activity. Examples include walking, jogging, hiking, biking, and the like.

To this list, Physical Best adds: Celebrate activities already done outside of school with parents and friends in community and home settings. Encourage students to share such activities with the rest of the class, sparking interest in others.

Age-Appropriate Practical Applications

Corbin (1994) offers age-appropriate practical pointers for facilitating students' progression up the Stairway to Lifetime Fitness. Use

Teaching Tip: Motivating With Knowledge

When I was teaching at the University of Illinois (Chicago) in 1967–69, I developed a conceptual approach to teaching fitness, complete with slides, programmed text, and audiotapes. As director of conditioning programs, I selected 8 of 40 classes to which I taught these concepts. Although these 8 classes were not graded on fitness, these students' fitness levels improved more than the students' in the traditional conditioning classes. When I asked why—since they exercised only half the class time the students in the traditional classes did—they said they had exercised at home. It was the first time that they realized they should. When I asked the traditional class students, they said that they were in better condition than they had ever been, they felt great, but now that the class was over, they never wanted to go near a gymnasium again!

Dr. Ron Feingold
Adelphi University, Long Island, New York

and adapt them to help you apply the philosophy of health-related physical fitness education in real-life settings.

Elementary School Fitness Education

Elementary school children are often quite active. You can help them carry that activity forward for a lifetime by following these guidelines. (The following list is adapted, by permission from C. Corbin, 1994, "The Fitness Curriculum—Climbing the Stairway to Lifetime Fitness." In *Health and Fitness Through Physical Education*, edited by R. Pate and R. Hohn (Champaign, IL: Human Kinetics), 62-63.)

1. Focus programs of fitness education for young children on activities that both promote fitness and teach a love of activity.
2. Accompany fitness education for young children with a quality program of skill education.
3. Do not use exercise as punishment.
4. Do not deny children fitness or skill education because of inadequate performance or behavior in other subjects.
5. Do not overemphasize fitness test performances.
6. Place special emphasis on helping those who are low fit to reach appropriate health fitness standards.
7. Take special care not to undermine self-esteem in fitness education programs.
8. Expose upper elementary school and middle school children to the many activities of our culture.
9. Focus fitness testing on meeting health criteria (healthful levels of fitness), rather than performance criteria, based on arbitrary normative standards.

Middle School Physical Education

Middle school students exhibit a wide range of intellectual, physical, psychological, social, and ethical development levels. At this time in their lives, students are going through many changes and are making the transition from childhood to young adulthood. They tend to be very self-conscious, especially about their appearance and physical growth. Unfortunately it is during this time period that many students "turn off" to physical activity for a variety of reasons. It is very important to teach children that physical activity can enhance appearance as well as health, that it can

© Photophile/Ed Gohlich 1993

Encourage students to be physically active before and after school and on weekends. Help your students move toward self-responsibility for their personal fitness.

Problem Solving

Through its core philosophy, Physical Best and the health-related physical fitness education that stems from it promote problem solving as a way of life. While other curriculum models espouse problem solving as an important component, most of these add problem solving as just another ingredient in the recipe—not a basic philosophy. Physical Best believes, however, that problem solving must arise from the core of a program, not be tacked on almost as an afterthought. When students learn to design and implement personal fitness plans and leave physical education programs prepared and empowered to modify these plans to suit their individual needs over the course of their lifetimes, they have truly learned problem-solving skills that will transfer to and apply in a variety of life's situations.

be social (fun to do with peers), and that it is for adults, not just children (middle school students want to be viewed as adults, not children). Some basic guidelines for middle school fitness education include the following:

1. Remember your students' dignity. Do not place them in situations where they will be embarrassed while participating in physical activity.
2. Connect lessons to student interests and help them understand the reasons for the lessons. Middle school students want to know why they have to do things.
3. Use students' names. Middle school students often have low self-esteem, so make them feel important by calling them by name.
4. Do not post fitness test scores or compare students to each other. Make testing individualized and personal.
5. Be aware of social circles at school and help all students be included in meaningful physical activity.

High School Fitness Education

By the time students reach high school, many elements of their lives have become well established, including regular patterns of activity—or inactivity. Students will have skills in some activities, but not in others. They will have definite preferences about physical activities. Some will feel competent in physical activity, but many will not. The following recommendations are not final solutions to problems of fitness education, but are possible aids in helping youths reach the top of the lifetime-fitness stairway. (The following list is adapted, by

permission, from C. Corbin, 1994, "The Fitness Curriculum—Climbing the Stairway to Lifetime Fitness." In *Health and Fitness Through Physical Education*, edited by R. Pate and R. Hohn (Champaign, IL: Human Kinetics), 63-65.)

1. Avoid threatening the self-esteem of teenage students in fitness education.
2. Recognize that physical appearance is critical to teenagers [but not all in the same way].
3. Offer students a variety of activities from which to choose.
4. Provide a class for all secondary school students that teaches the facts about fitness and exercise, including fitness self-evaluation and program planning.
5. Require all students to participate in an elective physical activity program based on Point 4.

The SPARK Program

The Sports, Play, and Active Recreation for Kids (SPARK) program is an example of a proven program that teaches fourth- and fifth-grade children behavioral and cognitive skills that will help them stay physically active (McKenzie and Sallis 1996). The program emphasizes self-management of behavior and includes a general session on self-management, goal setting, positive reinforcement for meeting activity goals, and parental involvement. Self-management helps students understand their ability in physical performances and take responsibility for their own health-related fitness levels (Hichwa 1998).

Teach lifetime skills at the elementary level—it is more difficult to learn skills later in life.

6. Modify school facilities to accommodate sound fitness education programs.
7. Design fitness testing largely for self-evaluation.

Defining "Lifelong, Individualized, Health-Related Physical Activity"

Let's turn now to examining each element of Physical Best's ultimate goal:

- Lifelong—possessing the knowledge, skills, and self-motivation to regularly engage in one or more physical activities as an ongoing lifestyle choice.
- Individualized—having the opportunity and freedom to choose activities that are

interesting to oneself as well as the knowledge and freedom to modify an activity to suit one's needs, goals, and abilities, without losing its health-related effectiveness.

- Health-related physical activity—engaging in activities that maintain or improve any of the components of health-related physical fitness (aerobic endurance, muscular strength and endurance, flexibility, and body composition). Skill- or performance-related fitness components (agility, balance, coordination, power, speed, reaction time) may also be involved if the focus is using skills or sports to enhance health-related fitness, as, for example, the person who plays basketball as a fun way to maintain aerobic endurance and a healthy body composition.

Why Change?

Making the change from a traditional "skill-only" physical education program might seem like a difficult task, but it's proven to be very rewarding to many teachers. Here's what a couple of veteran physical educators from Naperville, Illinois, had to say about their change from a traditional physical education program to a health-related physical fitness education program. These quotes are taken from interviews conducted for the Physical Best *Instructor's Video*.

> ...to the older physical education teacher, change is not easy...nobody likes to change but I guess I would relate it to the medical field ...would you want to go to a doctor who says I want to teach medicine the same way I did 25 years ago, because I feel comfortable doing that? Do you want your children going to that doctor?
>
> —Phil Lawler, Middle School Physical Education Teacher, Naperville, Illinois

> For a change I'm glad to see the shift going away from athletics and sports for the elite to involve more kids. I got into this profession to educate kids and for the first time in my life I feel like I'm actually doing it.
>
> —Paul Zientarski, High School Physical Education Teacher, Naperville, Ilinois

Help! A Lot of My Middle Schoolers Never Acquired Basic Skills

Perhaps you teach in a middle school and many of your students never acquired basic skills because your district does not support physical education at the elementary level, or they simply weren't taught in a progressive, developmentally appropriate program. You know they might be insulted and disruptive if you use activities that are too basic, so what can you do? Possible solutions include the following:

- Modify popular games to focus more on basic skills; seeing where they'll need the skills to enjoy the games can be very motivating. Have students use a basic skill in several different ways in various games.

- "Review" the skills you think will give them what they need to pursue the physical activities they're most interested in (you might survey students to determine this) by asking the students to design their own games to use the skills.

- Occasionally, arrange to have classes of elementary students visit your classes to motivate your students to train as "student teachers." They have to know the basics to teach them. Students learn skills better when they teach the skills to someone else. This has the added benefits of reaching younger students before they come to your program and networking with their teachers.

- Use peer tutors; students of equal ability can help each other learn, and highly skilled students will feel more challenged. Give partners critical element checklists to guide their teaching.

The bottom line is that the strategy or activity to teach the basic skill must be developmentally and age appropriate. Be creative and network with other teachers to brainstorm activity ideas with them.

Integrating Skill Development

In our zeal to focus on health-related physical fitness as the core of our program, however, we must not neglect the importance of crucial basic motor skill and concept development (Schmidt and Wrisberg 1999). Corbin (1994) writes, "Basic skills . . . are very difficult to learn later in life; they must be taught and learned in elementary schools" (p. 62). He also warns, "Skill education is not a substitute for fitness education and vice versa" (p. 62).

Students benefit from skill education in many ways. For example, "People who are skillful and feel competent in physical activity are more likely to enjoy and benefit from it" (Corbin 1994, p. 62). Performance at adult levels requires higher-order thinking and combinations of elementary skills and concepts. Students (and, ultimately, adults) need to be skillful enough to obtain fitness benefits without needless injury or frustration. For example, if an individual develops an interest in

tennis, he or she will not realize health-related or social-emotional benefits from playing it if he or she is unsuccessfully picking up the ball most of the time. Another reason to ensure students develop basic skills is that the *perception* of competence encourages individuals to engage in physical activity.

As students get older, you should continue to push them toward mastery but offer them choices as to the type of skills they focus on. Help them find what they like and master those skills necessary to enjoy that physical activity. Be careful, however, not to emphasize that if you're not highly skilled you shouldn't be out there moving. Instead, encourage each student to be the best he or she can, but to *keep moving*. At the middle school level and beyond, we have to begin to loosen our control over student choices and empower students to make personal choices. If a student simply cannot seem to master a physical skill despite repeated instruction, help the individual find other ways to stay involved. For example, someone who has trouble learning the latest dance can still reap aerobic endurance benefits from dancing. Thus, such a person can still reach the ultimate goal—that of lifelong, individualized, health-related physical activity—despite lacking a highly developed motor skill.

Summary

Health-related physical fitness education produces individuals who view physical activity as a worthwhile, pleasurable, lifelong endeavor; who have discovered where their physical activity interests lie; and who know how to design and implement a personal health-related fitness plan that suits their needs and situations. These goals do not, however, mean you should ignore skill development, because reasonably skillful individuals are more likely to pursue and enjoy physical activity. It is the job of physical educators to give students the tools they need to meet these goals.

Chapter 4

Managing Health-Related Physical Fitness Education

The quality of health-related physical fitness education is greatly enhanced when physical education teachers are able to effectively organize and administer their programs and successfully collaborate with others in the wider school and local communities. In this chapter, the basic organizational and administrative details of offering a safe and effective health-related physical fitness education program are outlined.

Scheduling

Physical education should be scheduled in a way that provides the best opportunity for effective teaching to take place. Unfortunately, too often a physical education program schedule ends up being the result more of available facilities and other schoolwide priorities than of sound pedagogical thinking. Advocate for your program so that it does not get relegated to leftover time slots and pigeonholed into a format that works for every subject but physical education. One way to prevent these problems is to take an active role on school committees that make these type of decisions, or at least to discuss your concerns and goals with your administrator. Be willing to be part of the team that helps make school more productive for all students, and you may find your program also takes a more central role in helping the school achieve its overall mission. AAHPERD and NASPE have materials available to help you advocate for your physical education program.

Extending Physical Activity Time

The amount of time that physical educators have with their students varies widely from state to state, school to school, and level to level. But whether you see your students just once a week (as, unfortunately, some elementary physical education teachers do) or every day, you should take advantage of a number of proven strategies for extending physical activity time beyond your program. Remember that the goal is to get students into the habit of being physically active on their own; keeping activities personally enjoyable is important so students don't view these extra activities as drudgery. Adapt these suggestions to fit your students' age range, your school's facilities, and other pertinent factors. Note that these ideas should all serve as *extensions* of physical education, not replacements. In other words, they serve in a sense as physical education homework and are meant to enhance what is taught during physical education class. It is important that your administrators and colleagues understand this so that they don't think it would be OK to cut back on physical education classes since students can participate in these activities outside of class.

- Fitness breaks—The Surgeon General's report (1996) guidelines assert that physical activity can be accumulated throughout the day in short bouts, making this an increasingly popular and beneficial option in some districts. As you train classroom teachers to conduct these breaks, offer concrete reasons that are important to them, such as exercise increases blood flow to the brain, helping a person think better. The trained and certified physical educator must take responsibility for this

information. Perhaps offer a five-minute summary of several possible activities at each staff meeting and help teachers solve any problems they're having.

- Recess—Ensure students have ample equipment and input for fun and beneficial physical activities during recess. Don't hesitate to teach fun physical fitness activities during physical education that students can easily use during their free times—then point these out. After all, this can form the beginning of self-responsibility for physical fitness. In addition, you should advocate for proper facilities and adequate supervision during recess. Re-

Parent volunteers can be used to help with innovative after school physical activity programs.

cess, of course, isn't available at middle and high schools, but many of these same ideas could be used for nonclass times during the day.

- Lunchtime—Lunchtime free play is simply a longer recess in most schools, but you can make it so much more. Consider making yourself available as a personal fitness consultant to interested students, or train student volunteers to conduct fun fitness activities during free play times or to assist you with younger students in physical education class. You can even start a fitness club and offer incentives for participating.

- Intramurals—These are physical activity programs conducted between teams of students or individual students from the same school. Adapt a program to augment your fitness curriculum in specific, stated ways, then work to ensure the program is fun and friendly, welcoming all who wish to participate. When creating teams, be sure to make them as even as possible. Then insist that participants focus primarily on skill, fitness, and social development, not cutthroat competition. Consider having students keep track of minutes of activity or calculate calories burned as a way of keeping activity and fitness as the focus. You might also consider allowing students to add points for using encouraging words to classmates to keep the focus on social development and fun. Think of other inno-

vative ways to "keep score" to encourage student development toward program goals.

- After-school programs—Consider creating a new program or working to enhance an existing after-school child care program. If you cannot commit the time to after-school activities, train others who can, such as parent or senior volunteers or child care workers.

- Home-based activities—Send home interesting assignments and have families design 10-minute routines they can do together first thing in the morning or last thing at night (Virgilio 1997) or at another workable family time. Encourage families to make physical activity a fun and regular family event. They can even create ways to work out while watching television (such as jumping rope, stretching, or doing sit-ups). (See the next section, discussing South Carolina's student performance standard.)

- Cross-curricular events—Work with other teachers in your school to design events that incorporate physical activity and academic and arts learning. For example, ask the music teacher to help you stage a show that demonstrates how, for example, dancing can build aerobic endurance. Or work with the social studies teacher to have students "run" through the geographical area they're studying, awarding mileage

Ride for Life

Renee McCall, preschool adapted physical education specialist in North Syracuse, New York, shares how she adapted the Hoop/Jump Rope for Heart events sponsored by AAHPERD and the American Heart Association to fit her students' special needs (McCall 1997):

"I wanted to actively involve all the children in something they love and could succeed at, so our department held the first ever 'Ride for Life,' a preschool tricycle riding event to promote the importance of cardiovascular fitness for children of all abilities.

"We chose to have the children ride their tricycles during a 25-minute period by class (12–15 children each) with therapists and classroom staff helping as needed. Our gym was set up to look like a large oval race track with decorative banners, balloons, and so on.

"To raise funds, we asked family and friends to donate $1 or more in support of the children who pedal during the designated time. We gave the children certificates of participation for their efforts. We promoted the event by contacting local media, decorating bulletin boards, and sending home fliers. We raised over $1,250!"

Adapted, by permission, from "Ride for Life" by Renee McCall, 1997, *Teaching Elementary Physical Education* 9(3):12, 27.

for minutes spent outside of class on physical activity (such as biking, playing sports, roller skating).

- Community events—Family nights, health fairs, Jump Rope/Hoops for Heart (American Heart Association and AAHPERD) events involve the wider community, from parents and siblings to senior citizens. Not only are such events ways to help students become more fit and healthy, they also provide good public relations for your program (see also Collaboration and Public Relations and Program Advocacy sections later in this chapter).

South Carolina's Approach

In 1995, South Carolina established a student performance standard for high school students that requires health-enhancing physical activity outside the physical education class. We have reproduced this standard here:

Criterion Three: Participate regularly in health-enhancing physical activity outside the physical education class.

Description of the criterion: The intent of this standard is to help the student make a transition from physical education class to a physically active lifestyle and *real-life* opportunities. The high school student should participate regularly in physical activity outside the physical education setting if patterns of participation appropriate for a physically active lifestyle are to be established. Two dimensions of participation are critical. The first is the student should be *exploring* opportunities both in the school and in the community and surrounding areas for participation in a wide variety of physical activities. The second is the student should be developing the ability to make wise choices about how he or she spends time both in terms of the structured activities chosen to participate in as well as choosing more active alternatives in daily living (e.g., taking the stairs rather than the elevator). The student should independently seek opportunities for activity and design activity programs as a lifestyle issue. This criterion can be

met through opportunities in the school and community as well as through independently designed programs of physical activity.

Definitions:

- **Regularly:** weekly over a nine-week period
- **School activities:** sport teams, intramural, club activities
- **Community activities:** church sponsored, parks and recreation programs, YM(W)CA, commercial companies
- **Health-enhancing physical activity:** moderate to vigorous exercise (consecutively and/or totally) for 20 minutes or more a day, three times per week
- **Components of health-related fitness:** cardiovascular endurance, muscular strength, muscular endurance, body composition, and flexibility
- **Independent programs:** family-designed structured programs and independently designed structured programs (the term "structured" here means designated time and place with planned regularity)

Critical aspect of performance: The student provides evidence of regular participation for a minimum of nine weeks in an activity normally producing moderate levels of physical activity.

Examples of student performance meeting the criteria:

1. The student participates in a youth baseball league in the community.
2. The student sets up a walking club with several other students during the lunch hour.
3. The student sets up a personal fitness program consisting of weight lifting and aerobic exercise on a regular basis.
4. The student participates in a folk dance or cycling club in the community.
5. The student successfully participates as a member of a school athletic team.

Assessment examples:

1. The student keeps a daily journal of par-

ticipation in his or her outside activity recording each day of participation and what he or she does each day. The student evaluates his or her participation every three weeks indicating the extent to which he or she is meeting the health-enhancing aspect of the criterion; the personal benefits of their participation; and the difficulties they have encountered in participating regularly in the activity. The journals are shared and discussed in the physical education class. Assessment criteria:

- The student participates in the activity regularly for a period of at least nine weeks.

- The student evaluates the level of his or her participation appropriately.

- The student appropriately identifies both the advantages and disadvantages of participation.

2. The student submits a signed form from a responsible adult describing the participation in an independent project. Assessment criterion:

- The student meets the criterion for type of activity and regularity of participation.

Block Scheduling

Many high schools are moving away from the traditional schedule in which classes meet each day for 45 to 50 minutes and students attend six to eight classes a day. Some of the complaints about traditional scheduling include lack of time to explore a topic in depth, use more involved teaching styles, or apply higher-level thinking skills; too much time spent on transitions between classes and administrative chores; and difficulty getting to know each student personally. Block

MOVING TO SUCCESS

Physical education at Woodland Heights Elementary School (Spartanburg, South Carolina) develops both skillfulness and health-related fitness. The move toward integrating the two began with Physical Exercise Revives Kids (PERK), a five-minute daily early-morning activity conducted in classrooms. While music is broadcast over the school's public address system, pairs of trained fifth-grade leaders guide students through choreographed routines that include a variety of motor skills, fitness concepts, and musical experiences. Every student and teacher participates in a warm-up, vigorous movements, and cool-down.

PERK demonstrated to classroom teachers, students, and parents the value of physical activity. This small beginning became part of a larger effort called "Moving to Success." Activities added include expanded PERK routines conducted in physical education classes called PERK Too, and Discover and Understand Communities, Kids, by Walking (DUCK Walking); other morning activities for students; PE Club (running and sport performance troupes); and additional family and community events. A major consideration is planning activities that are positive, fun, innovative, and developmentally appropriate and safe for elementary children. Moving to Success provides a framework within which activities are coordinated to most benefit students' motor skill development and health-related fitness levels.

Reprinted from J. Steller and D. Young, 1994, "Moving to Success: A Comprehensive Approach to Physical Education." In *Health and Fitness Through Physical Education*, edited by R. Pate and R. Hohn (Champaign, IL: Human Kinetics), 177-178.

scheduling attempts to resolve these problems by extending class periods to 80 or more minutes, reducing the number of courses a student takes in one time period, and reducing the number of class preps a teacher must deal with in one time period.

A big advantage of block scheduling is that it allows physical educators to get students out of the gymnasium and into physical activity settings in the community. For example, it allows the time to take trips to the local health club, wall-climbing facility, mountain-biking course, ice-skating arena, dance club, hiking trails, and so on. It also allows for more in-depth instruction on how to get involved in these lifetime activities.

Of course, we'd like students to get used to regular bouts of physical activity. Thus a disadvantage of block scheduling is that physical educators don't see their students every day or every semester and therefore can't ensure that they're participating in physical activity as often as they should (although using physical activity logs outside of class time might help solve this problem; see chapter 19).

Equipment

It is essential to have enough equipment to maximize student time on task. Certainly,

Block Scheduling Example

There are many different ways that block scheduling can be used to enhance your physical education program. Here is an example of how a modified version of block scheduling could be used at a high school that allows for five hours of physical education per week. In this example the instructor has two sections of senior (grade 12) physical education. The instructor wanted to give these seniors plenty of opportunities to experience different ways of being physically active in the community, but an hour class just did not afford enough time to take these field trips. The solution was to schedule one 2-hour class for each section per week that would be dedicated to field trips. Examples of these field trips include a visit to a local health fitness club, a cross-country skiing trip, a hike at a state park, a mountain biking trip on a local trail, and so on. Here is how the schedule was modified to accommodate the need for a longer class.

Old schedule		Block schedule	
Mon. 8–9 a.m.	PE 12 Sec. 1	Mon. 8–9 a.m.	PE 12 Sec. 1
Mon. 9–10 a.m.	PE 12 Sec. 2	Mon. 9–10 a.m.	PE 12 Sec. 2
Tue. 8–9 a.m.	PE 12 Sec. 1	Tue. 8–9 a.m.	PE 12 Sec. 1
Tue. 9–10 a.m.	PE 12 Sec. 2	Tue. 9–10 a.m.	PE 12 Sec. 2
Wed. 8–9 a.m.	PE 12 Sec. 1	Wed. 8–9 a.m.	PE 12 Sec. 1
Wed. 9–10 a.m.	PE 12 Sec. 2	Wed. 9–10 a.m.	PE 12 Sec. 2
Thur. 8–9 a.m.	PE 12 Sec. 1	Thur. 8–10 a.m.	PE 12 Sec. 1
Thur. 9–10 a.m.	PE 12 Sec. 2		
Fri. 8–9 a.m.	PE 12 Sec. 1	Fri. 8–10 a.m.	PE 12 Sec. 2
Fri. 9–10 a.m.	PE 12 Sec. 2		

no one ever developed health-related fitness waiting in line for a turn with a piece of equipment. Yet for many programs, obtaining and maintaining enough equipment to run a viable program is an ongoing headache.

Finding More Equipment

There are many sources of free or inexpensive equipment. For example, you can make equipment from free or inexpensive materials. The following lists a few of the many ideas physical educators have used successfully:

- Sit-and-reach box made from plywood scraps
- Rackets made from nylon stockings stretched over reshaped hangers
- Balls made from socks, yarn, or scrap paper
- Mats made from sleeping bags (not for tumbling)
- Jump ropes made from woven plastic bread bags (find a volunteer to put in the time here)
- Cones made from plastic milk jugs or pop bottles

Block Scheduling at Portage High School

At Portage (Indiana) High School the block 4 scheduling format is used to provide freshmen a daily one-and-a-half-hour physical education class for a nine-week term. The advantage of this schedule is the longer class time, which allows for each class to experience fitness (aerobics, weight lifting, jogging, etc.) and discuss fitness concepts as well as to develop skills and participate in sports and individual physical activities. Since the class meets daily and allows for both fitness and skill development, students are able to see significant gains in their health-related fitness over the course of the nine-week term.

The disadvantage of this schedule is that after the nine-week term, students rotate to other classes and thus don't have physical education at all for the next nine weeks, so it's good to encourage independent projects during these "off" terms.

As an example, below is the schedule for Ruth Aydelotte-Parks, physical education teacher at Portage High School:

Daily Schedule
(eight-minute passing time between classes)

Block 1	7:25–8:55 a.m.	Planning
Block 2	9:03–10:33 a.m.	Freshman PE Sec. 1
Block 3	11:11–12:41 p.m.	Freshman PE Sec. 2
Block 4	12:49–1:05 p.m.	Announcements and Channel One
	1:05–2:35	Freshman PE Sec. 3

Class Schedule

10 min	Dressing out and attendance
10 min	Warm-ups and stretching
15 min	Fitness activities MWF: Aerobics and weight training
	Tues.: Jogging
	Thurs.: Fitness stations
45 min	Skill development and participation in team and individual sports
10 min	Change and shower time

Station Learning and Equipment

Stations arranged on a circuit are a good way to stretch the equipment you have a little further while also providing variety. For example, if you only have four stationary bikes, you can place these in one station on a circuit and divide the class into groups of four. The other stations can also feature aerobic endurance activities, such as rope jumping, step routines, and aerobic dance. If you have plenty of steps and jump ropes, arrange more than one station using each of these so that groups alternate activities. See chapter 13 for more information on using station learning.

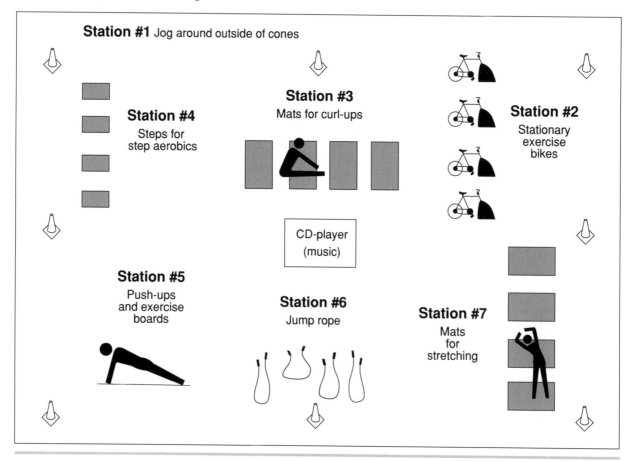

- Older equipment from fitness clubs (might be given away as the clubs purchase new equipment)

See *Creative Physical Activities & Equipment: Building a Quality Program on a Shoestring Budget* (1998) by Bev Davison for more elementary-level ideas for making equipment.

You can also obtain fitness and game equipment from garage sales and classified ads. One teacher even went so far as to call and tell sellers that she could not pay anything for the equipment, but that if it didn't sell, she'd be happy to take it off their hands in exchange for a receipt for a tax deductible charitable donation. She was able to fully equip a fitness center for her middle school students in this way (Williams 1997). Parents may also be willing to donate used equipment, so let them know what you're interested in. In South Carolina, many schools have worked with their PTAs to publicize the need for equipment and have received a great response in obtaining fitness equipment that wasn't being used. Brainstorm other ideas, based on your needs. The point is to not let a low budget stop you from providing the equipment your students need.

Insist that students wear proper shoes and recommend loose-fitting clothing for fitness testing. It is not necessary to require uniforms for physical education as long as standards for clothing appropriate for participation in physical activity are set and followed. Uniforms, however, can be a nice touch if you show some creativity (see also the sidebar entitled Dressed for Success in chapter 2). In addition, they could be a money-raising idea: You might work out a deal with a local company to have uniforms designed and sold specifically for your program. If you can get the shirts for $5 each from the company and then you sell them for $10 each, you'll have $5 per student to be able to purchase additional equipment to further enhance your program. However, be sure to work out the details with your administration so you follow the proper procedures for this. Make sure you allow for students who cannot afford uniforms (make "scholarships" available to purchase them or have extra uniforms from the company avail-

Physical education uniforms can be designed to look good and be functional.

Creating a Complete Collection

The following is a basic list of items that would greatly enhance your ability to run a quality health-related physical fitness education program. Ensure you have enough of each to maximize student time on task.

- Sit-and-reach boxes
- Skinfold calipers
- Tape or CD player and music brought in by students (preview for appropriateness)
- Heart rate monitors (see sidebar on ways to raise money to purchase these)
- Cones for marking boundaries
- Tubing, light dumbbells, or small water bottles filled with water or sand for strength training
- Mats
- Manipulatives for physical activities, such as balls, jump ropes, and the like
- Steps (for step aerobics)
- Medicine balls

Reprinted, by permission, from AAHPERD, 1999, *Physical Best Activity Guide—Elementary Level.* (Champaign, IL: Human Kinetics), 45.

able to low-income students). Be sensitive to how you handle this, remembering that physical education should be a class in which all students are welcome.

Fund-Raising to Buy More Equipment

Of course, there will be times when your program will be best served by purchasing new equipment. This is where fund-raising can really help fill the empty spaces in your storage closet. There are many ways to raise funds: going after school budget funds and applying for mini-grants your district might offer are good places to start. Look, too, for technology and drug-free school grants. Don't forget about your colleagues in other disciplines, either. You could pool your funds, for example, with the science department to purchase heart rate monitors. AAHPERD and the American Heart Association also provide funds for physical education programs as part of the Hoops for Heart and Jump Rope for Heart events.

You can also design your own special fundraisers. If you make them fun and visible, not only will you make more money, you'll also advertise your program to the community. So

The Jog-a-Thon: A Healthy Fund-Raiser for Physical Education

To conduct a successful elementary or middle school jog-a-thon, several components are necessary. Beginning four weeks before the event, encourage classroom teachers to "buy into" the event by fully informing them of the details and offering them an incentive in the form of a share of the profits (e.g., $100 each to use for field trips, learning materials, and so on). They are needed for distributing and collecting student pledge forms and discussing sponsor-gathering procedures with their classes.

Three weeks before the event, send a letter to parents requesting volunteers to run the event. Use this forum to inform parents of past uses of fund-raiser money and this year's goals. Request written confirmation of volunteers' willingness to help. Simultaneously, send information home with event time line and information about the event and pledge collection. [For safety reasons, discourage students from collecting pledges from strangers.] Offer incentives to students as well.

On event day, mark off a course on the playground or nearby field or use a nearby track or running trail. Participants can run during morning, noon, or afternoon recesses, or the last hour of the school day on one or two school days. Assign a volunteer to each group of runners and post these personnel around the perimeter of the running course so they do not interfere with each other. As students complete a lap, they should shout out their last name when they pass the checker to ensure accuracy. The checker then marks a lap on the student's lap sheet.

This event encourages classroom teachers and parents to become more involved in the physical education program—all while encouraging health-related fitness among students!

Adapted, by permission, from "The Jog-A-Thon: A Fundraiser for Physical Education" by Bud Turner and Sue Turner, 1998, *Teaching Elementary Physical Education* 9(3):5–8.

adhere to the following guidelines to ensure an efficient and successful fund-raiser:

1. Obtain administrative support—Make sure your supervisor agrees with and supports your efforts. Share your goals for your program and outline how a fund-raiser may help you attain these goals. (Remember, obtaining administrative support is much easier if you've done a good job of advocacy, that is, if your administration is already aware of your program.)

2. Form a fund-raising committee—You need help pulling this off and input as to what may be feasible. Call on parents, fellow teachers, students, community members, and administrators to join your efforts.

3. Set goals and parameters—Decide as a committee what you want to gain and what the time and activity limits are (e.g., ask, Is this worth the effort? Will our goal of promoting lifetime physical activity also be met through the fund-raiser? How exactly will we spend the money we make?).

4. Plan ahead—Allow plenty of time for plotting out the actual event, advertising it in advance, and troubleshooting any prob-

lems. Establish a time line for each step of the way through assessing the event afterward.

5. Call in the troops—The committee members can't do everything, so ask other parents, students, colleagues, and community members for help in actually implementing the fund-raiser. Obtain local business sponsors by offering to share their advertising with the school community in exchange for their support.

6. Let everyone know—Advertising through flyers sent home with students and local media is essential.

7. Relax and have fun—Let the fund-raiser be an enjoyable (if hectic) extension of your health-related physical fitness education program.

8. Assess the fund-raiser's effectiveness—As a committee, ask, Was this worth our time and effort? What can we do better in the future? How is the money best allocated (especially if the total is above or below the goal)?

9. Move on to another idea—Using fresh ideas for each fund-raiser, perhaps in a

three- to five-year rotation, keeps students and volunteers interested and involved.

Other ways to raise funds include applying for grants and soliciting business sponsorship separate from other fund-raising efforts. Be sure you can offer some intrinsic reward for agency and business support, such as visible thank-yous (such as banners prominently posted, mentions in newsletters, and the like), making parents and students aware of the help you have received.

Caring for Equipment

Once you have a piece of equipment, take good care of it. The primary ways to extend its life are to provide regular maintenance, teach students proper usage, and store it properly when not in use. Consider providing official "certification" programs to students who have demonstrated they know how to use certain pieces of equipment (e.g., weight training, heart rate monitor) properly.

Maintain your equipment by regularly inspecting it and repairing or replacing items as needed. File the owner's manuals and other manufacturer information carefully so you can refer to it as needed. Before using secondhand equipment, be sure you know how to ensure it is in full working order. You may have to contact the manufacturer or talk to personnel at a local sporting goods outlet.

Take the time to teach students proper use of each piece of equipment as you introduce it. Regularly monitor how students are treating equipment and insist on proper procedures not only for the equipment's sake but also for safety's sake (see also sidebar Equipment and Facility Safety). In addition, you are preparing your students to be responsible for their own equipment, so help your students become knowledgeable consumers of fitness equipment.

Appropriate storage saves time, trouble, and needless wear and tear on equipment. See-through bins, baskets, and bags for small items; hanging bags; organized shelves; and labeled storage containers keep equipment safe and accessible. Secure exercise equipment, such as treadmills and stationary bikes, so that it cannot be used without adult supervision. Install a sign-out procedure and carefully oversee timely and accurate returns, if you share equipment with other teachers.

Technology

Although not essential to a good program, advanced technology can help you teach health-related physical fitness education. From heart rate monitors to computer databases to state-of-the-art exercise equipment,

Fund-Raising Can Be Fun!

Fifty physical educators in Jacksonville, Florida, decided to jump on the advocacy bandwagon to promote physical education and make their programs more visible. One such effort involved selling bright yellow bumper stickers that read, "Physical Education . . . Knowledge to Last a Lifetime."

Their goal was to use the stickers to remind families and individuals of the value of exercising and making healthy choices. Purchasing a bumper sticker was an easy way for parents to get involved and show their support, especially after they realized that many physical education programs were in jeopardy following district budget cuts.

The bumper stickers were sold for $1 each during school, community, statewide, and regional events. Organizers were also able to gain support from a large local amusement center, which gave them coupons for its entertainments with each bumper sticker sold. The schools used the money raised to purchase much-needed equipment. Most importantly, however, this fund-raiser generated a great deal of positive publicity for physical education within the community.

Adapted, by permission, from "Fund-Raising Can Be Fun!" by Jan S. Tipton and Susan L. Tucker, 1998, *Teaching Elementary Physical Education* 9(3):14.

spark interest in health-related fitness with a few carefully chosen and applied investments.

If possible, tap into equipment your non-physical education colleagues already have. For example, schedule time in the school's computer lab for students to learn to log physical activity time or convince the language arts teacher to make your physical education writing assignment idea his class assignment. The science department may have items you can use, such as interactive CD-ROMs that teach about the human body. (*Note*: Technology can provide an efficient and interesting medium for team teaching and cross-curricular learning.) For example, the new *FITNESSGRAM* software (see chapter 17) not only provides teachers with functions such as the ability to print out reports and keep information organized, it also provides a mode through which individual students (using passwords) can keep track of their own progress on the computer. Another new feature is the *ACTIVITYGRAM*, which allows teachers and students to monitor activity levels.

Before deciding to purchase a new technology, try to borrow it from a colleague or see a demonstration given by a salesperson to determine if the item is right for your program and student population. Then decide how many you need and can afford.

One final point: Remember, high-tech can help you teach, but it is no substitute for a solid program. So don't turn technology into expensive toys. Make sure your reasons for using each item are sound and that your applications of the technology are relevant, both to your students and your program goals.

Facilities

Some physical educators use purpose-built, up-to-date facilities dedicated exclusively to physical education, whereas others use facilities that double as cafeterias and auditoriums. Although a good facility does not a good program make, certain basic features are essential: At a minimum, a facility (or field) should be clean, maintained for safety, and large enough for the class sizes you teach.

Using Space Efficiently

If you must share your gymnasium with the lunch staff because it doubles as a cafeteria, work with these personnel to make transitions smooth for both programs, minimizing lost instructional time. At the secondary school level, you may need to work with coaches with whom you share facilities (gymnasium, track, and playing fields) to make sure everyone is able to use these facilities to their fullest. At the elementary level, if classroom teachers use your equipment and facility on the days you don't teach their classes, work with these colleagues to ensure both the equipment and facility are treated with respect and care. Try to look at these potential irritations as opportunities to network with other school staff—as a stepping-stone to more significant interactions such as cross-curricular units.

If you share facilities with other physical educators, strive to coordinate units so that each teacher can meet his or her objectives in

---

Teaching Tip: Technology as a Teaching Tool

More and more, technology is becoming a necessity in education. Having access to technology is an everyday occurrence at Trace Crossings. It is not unusual to see students working on computers to develop their own personal fitness programs or assessments. Students use interactive programs to reinforce fitness concepts. Teachers use computer programs as teaching tools to introduce new concepts. Other technology-driven items, such as digital cameras and laser disc players, provide information and help teachers and students analyze student performance.

Robin Litaker
Trace Crossings Elementary School
Hoover, Alabama

Equipment and Facility Safety

Ensure that each piece of equipment you acquire is safe or can be made safe to use before allowing students access to it. In addition, elementary schools may "inherit" equipment from secondary schools as long as it is not too large so as to be unsafe or otherwise developmentally inappropriate for younger students.

Facilities (gymnasiums, locker rooms, bathrooms, racket courts, fields, bleachers, playgrounds, and so on) must be inspected for hazards, debris, and cleanliness on a regular basis. Find out who is responsible for performing and documenting this function, and make sure this person knows the standards the school is expected to uphold. Ensure that proper procedures have been established for dealing quickly and effectively with problems so that no one is endangered or hurt. Mike Sutliff of California Polytechnic University at San Luis Obispo lists some dangerous conditions that are sometimes found in school settings:

- Unstable bleachers
- Slippery floors
- Poor heating or ventilation
- Unlit water fountains
- Debris or unused equipment lying around a field or gymnasium
- Ungroomed fields, hiding debris
- Holes on fields, cracked blacktop surfaces, and dangerously loose gym floorboards
- High flood areas and deep water on playing fields
- Sports fields too close to playgrounds
- Unsafe traffic conditions, such as classes walking through the instructional area because it is the only route available

Warning! The following may lead to lawsuits: holes on auxiliary fields, cracked blacktop surfaces, and dangerously loose gymnasium floorboards.

Give your students instructions on how to properly select and use equipment for various physical activities.

a logical sequence. The department head should set up a yearlong schedule of facility usage in consultation with all involved staff. This person should then oversee this schedule throughout the school year and mediate any problems that arise. Equipment sign-out and facility reservation sheets may be helpful to prevent problems.

Finally, insist that facilities are kept in good repair so that instructional time is not lost due to hazards.

Finding More Space

Although many schools are "bursting at the seams," a little creative thinking may help you "discover" an underused area of your school that you could put to better use. For example, don't waste space on improper equipment storage. Perhaps you can consolidate two storage areas into one by getting organized, then create a mini-fitness center in the other one. This is a good way to protect larger pieces of exercise equipment, such as rowing machines, from unsanctioned use. Just ensure the area is well lit, adequately ventilated, that you can supervise both this room and the larger activity area simultaneously, and that students cannot inadvertently be locked in.

Perhaps there's a classroom that has become a dumping ground for unwanted school supplies. Ask your administrator for permission to reorganize the room so you can hold classes in it. Set it up so it's safe to do physical activities in. Keep audiovisual equipment handy for concept and skill lessons. This may allow you to expand the time you have with your classes, as you will not be totally dependent on the availability of a multipurpose room or the state of the weather. You could also use such a classroom to provide an optional before- or after-school, lunchtime, or recess fitness club for students and teachers alike. Remember, however, you must ensure adequate adult supervision of such alternative areas.

At the elementary level, don't overlook the playground. Climbing equipment can help develop muscular strength and endurance, and a blacktop area can be painted to suit your program (such as game grids, "track" for

aerobic endurance activities, station numbers). It is wise, however, to avoid regularly scheduled recess times and to explain to students the goal of the lesson (as opposed to recess) before arriving at the activity site.

Collaboration

Helping students make healthy life choices is the job of the entire school and the community, not just the health-related physical fitness education program. A school should educate the whole child in a coordinated effort through developing a comprehensive school health and wellness program and otherwise tapping into parent and community resources. An atmosphere of cooperation and collaboration among those most interested in students' well-being creates a nurturing and supportive school atmosphere, thereby facilitating learning.

A Comprehensive School Health and Wellness Program

One way to collaborate is to develop and implement a comprehensive school health and wellness program. (Such a program can be considered a curriculum model, but it can also be organized and administered to support existing physical education curricula, which is why it is addressed here.) A comprehensive school health and wellness program involves working with staff, parents, administrators, and community agencies to provide the health and wellness support and services your students need and deserve. The following lists the components of such a program. (List adapted, by permission, from B. Mohnsen, 1997, *Teaching Middle School Physical Education.* (Champaign, IL: Human Kinetics), 28-29.):

- Health-related physical fitness education— Naturally, the knowledge and physical activity time students gain through your program are an important part of a health and wellness program. Teach concepts and skills to promote pleasurable participation in physical activity in order to create a desire in students to be physically active for life.

- Health education—Work with the health educator to coordinate your curricula so that each component reinforces the other. As a team, strive to sharpen critical thinking and problem-solving skills so students can make healthy choices throughout their lives.

- Health services—While the school nurse may be several schools' nurse in some districts, other communities are seeing the value in bringing formal health care into the school to better serve the student population, particularly at the secondary level. Thus, school-based medical clinics are becoming more common. Your school's health and wellness program should tap into whatever health services may be available to both treat and prevent health problems that interfere with learning. Health services should also help educate students as to healthful choices and screen systematically for medical problems. Health services personnel might consider working with a local hospital to arrange for health screenings to be available at your school.

- Nutrition services—Make healthy meals the norm in your school's cafeteria by working with school administrators and cafeteria staff. This may be the only place students see a model of a balanced and healthful diet, low in fat, salt, and sugar.

- Counseling and psychological services— Many children need help developing emotional, social, and mental health. Counselors should offer group sessions to guide all students in healthy emotional and social development and provide services and links to services for troubled students.

- Parent and community support—A comprehensive school health and wellness program is more visible than a physical education program that stands alone, so garnering parent and community support may be easier. Use the team approach to inform parents and the community of your goals and efforts and to ask for the support you need.

- A safe school environment—Children must feel psychologically and physically safe to learn to their full potentials. Develop and implement a school philosophy that treats students with respect, demands that students treat each other with respect, and insists upon clean and well-maintained facilities.

- Staff health and wellness—Staff should strive to set good examples of healthy lifestyles and should receive the support they need to do so, perhaps, for example, in the form of an on-site fitness club and health-related issues in-services (such as weight control, stress management, health screening).

Maybe your school is already providing most of these services but in an uncoordinated way. Work to install missing services and coordinate all services for the benefit of students and staff.

How S.W.E.E.T. It Is

I started a group a few years back called S.W.E.E.T. Walkers from Sweetwater County, Wyoming. S.W.E.E.T. stands for Students Walking for Education and Environment. We "connect" to the community by walking to a business and doing a project, sharing a lesson we are learning, or the like. We have cleaned up along a river, built projects to earn "Greenbelts" (beaver houses, bird houses), and visited senior and child care centers and read to the seniors and children—anything to get out and walk! After each walk, we return to school and process through writing and discussion what we have experienced and learned.

Nancy Raso-Eklund
1996 NASPE Elementary Physical Education Teacher of the Year
Washington/Roosevelt School, School District #2, Sweetwater County
Green River, Wyoming

Parents and Community Members as Resources

As you organize a physical education program that is health-related, it's important to remember that an overriding goal is to keep fitness programs individualized. Getting as much help as possible with this endeavor is essential. To this end, parents and community members can make excellent volunteers in your program. They can work one-on-one with students who need remediation or enrichment and can also work to carry out cross-curricular units. Be sure to provide the training they need, however, so that your program philosophy is respected and program goal attainment is enhanced. Parents and other volunteers can also visit your classes to talk about a physical activity they're involved in, or if your insurance and school policy allow, teach the activity to the class. (Remember, however, you are still responsible for each student's safety and well-

Help your students get involved in community programs that promote participation in lifetime physical activities.

being, so remain present at all times, assisting the volunteer.)

Ask community businesses and agencies to volunteer their services in exchange for free publicity. Here are some suggestions. Adapt them to fit your students' needs, interests, and age level:

- **Local restaurant**—Sample heart-healthy foods and discuss how to prepare them.
- **Health club**—Visit for equipment demonstrations.
- **Dance studio**—Take a jazz dancing lesson.
- **Nurse**—Request blood pressure screening.
- **Nutritionist**—Discuss healthy snack habits.
- **University health and physical education department**—Have an expert perform body composition testing.
- **Sports apparel store**—Learn how to select the correct athletic shoe.
- **Exercise physiologist**—Dispel myths about exercise.
- **Grocery store**—Take a tour and allow students to "purchase" foods with play money. If you can get the store to ring the purchases up, students can take the receipts back to school to analyze their choices according to the Food Guide Pyramid.
- **Park district**—Conduct a "Fun Run" with awards for all participants in each age division.
- **Food bank**—Organize a canned foods drive, emphasizing foods low in fat, salt, and sugar. Teach students how to read the labels accurately. Perform arm curls holding a can in each hand.
- **Senior citizen center**—Pair students and seniors to walk, exercise, and visit together once or twice a month. Encourage participants to share their feelings and experiences regarding exercise. These same partners can be pen pals, enhancing language arts and social studies learning.

Adapted, by permission, from S. Virgilio 1997, *Fitness Educational for Children: A Team Approach*. (Champaign, IL: Human Kinetics), 75-77.

Public Relations and Program Advocacy

Both your school and local community need to know what you're doing to make your physical education program health-related. This helps you find the volunteer and fund-raising support you need as well as educates the community as to the good you're doing. This can be a "life or death" situation for some schools in this era of budget slashing. All too often, physical education is seen as a "frill" that the school can do without. It's your job to see that parents, other voters, and policy makers view physical education as an essential component of a top-notch education. Also, it's important to work with AAHPERD, NASPE, and your state and local organizations, as there is strength in numbers. Contact AAHPERD, NASPE, and your state AHPERD to learn more about advocacy opportunities (see appendix C).

Offer an Excellent Program

The single most important factor in good public relations and program advocacy is to provide an excellent program. The following lists the components of a top-notch health-related physical fitness education program:

- Developmentally appropriate
- Positive learning atmosphere
- Emphasis on enjoyment and personal success
- Individualized
- Integrated curricula (across subject areas and affective, cognitive, and physical domains)
- Meets national and state standards and guidelines
- Provides a logical scope and sequence to its curriculum
- Inclusive
- Parent and community involvement

Seek Professional Development

Another factor in providing a quality health-related physical fitness education program as well as in creating good public relations is ongoing professional development. Teaching is as much about learning as it is about teaching, so don't stop learning after you've earned your degree. The following is a list of ways you can become the best instructor possible:

- Pay close attention to the plan-teach-assess cycle explained in chapter 16. Use affective, cognitive, and physical assessment results to improve your program.
- Network with other physical educators in your school, district, region, and state.
- Seek in-service training: Travel to conferences and workshops and get your administration to bring in speakers.
- Review current related research regularly in books and journals.
- Dress professionally and keep yourself fit and healthy.
- Earn certification as a Physical Best Health-Fitness Specialist.
- Seek other advanced certifications in health-related fitness.
- Seek advanced education, such as a master's degree in a health-related fitness field.
- Join AAHPERD/NASPE and your state AHPERD, and get involved.

Let Your School and Parents Know

Maybe you and your students know you're offering a top-notch health-related physical fitness education program, but if this awareness stops at the gymnasium door, your program may suffer. Use the tips listed here to help you "blow your own horn" effectively.

- Hold family fitness events and shows to share your program and to model ways to have fitness fun as a family and to spread the good news about what you're doing to help each child develop to his or her potential.

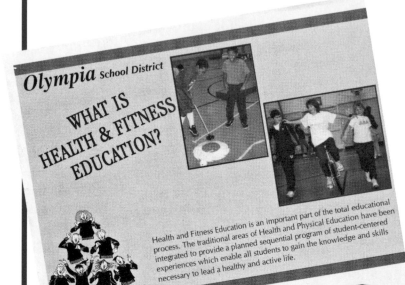

Olympia School District

WHAT IS HEALTH & FITNESS EDUCATION?

Health and Fitness Education is an important part of the total educational process. The traditional areas of Health and Physical Education have been integrated to provide a planned sequential program of student-centered experiences which enable all students to gain the knowledge and skills necessary to lead a healthy and active life.

It is important that you let parents and the community know about your program. The Olympia (Washington) school district does it by distributing a brochure explaining the basics of their program in a very professional manner.

Contributed by Jeff Carpenter, coordinator of Health and Fitness Programs at the Olympia School District in Olympia, Washington.

The major objectives of Health and Fitness Education are the development of:

1. Good health and physical fitness.
2. Knowledge and skills in a variety of leisure and sport activities.
3. Positive self-esteem and confidence leading to healthy life-style decisions.

THE PROGRAMS:

Component I: Physical Education/Fitness

The purpose of Physical Education/Fitness in the Olympia School District is to provide a varied program of instructional activities which allow all individuals to enter adult life with the skills, knowledge, and attitudes necessary to enjoy a healthy and physically active life-style.

Pre K - 5:

The focus of the elementary program is to provide age-appropriate movement experiences for each child on a daily basis.

The curriculum is sequential in nature and provides basic movement and manipulative skills at the primary level. At the intermediate level, the basic skills are refined and expanded through application in individual, team, and recreational game activities.

Health-related physical fitness is a major component of the program beginning at the primary level. Students are taught the importance of developing and maintaining

an appropriate level of fitness and the recognized components of health-related physical fitness. By presenting lessons related to nutrition and physiology along with the development of skills and a positive attitude toward being active, a solid foundation is developed for maintaining a healthy life-style.

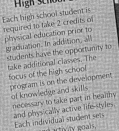

Middle Level:

Students at the middle level continue to progress through a pre-planned sequence of age-appropriate activities. At this level, students participate in a variety of challenging activities presented in short units. Activities include racquet sports, individual and partner/team activities, dance and alternative leisure activities such as juggling, golf, and bowling.

High School Level:

Each high school student is required to take 2 credits of physical education prior to graduation. In addition, all students have the opportunity to take additional classes. The focus of the high school program is on the development of knowledge and skills necessary to take part in healthy and physically active life-styles. Each individual student sets fitness and activity goals, monitors their own progress and refines their personal program. It is at this level that the previously learned skills are combined with nutrition, risk reduction, and life-style design through the analysis of the individual needs and goals.

In addition, numerous activities help each student to refine previously learned skills while focusing on activities which are meaningful to them.

Component 2:
Health Education

Pre K - 5:

At the primary level (Pre K - 2), the focus of health education is to provide information related to health practices including prevention of communicable disease, oral health, and the need for proper nutrition and exercise. In addition, initial lessons on personal safety and substance use and abuse prevention are presented.

The focus at the intermediate level (3-5) is on a review of the basic health principles, conflict resolution skills, decision making, alcohol and other drug prevention education and HIV prevention.

Middle Level:

At the middle level, health education is presented as part of the "block" program, and elective "wellness" classes.. The major areas of focus are alcohol and other drug prevention education, disease prevention, safe living, consumer health, nutrition, body systems, human sexuality, consumer health, and social interaction/self esteem. Lessons are presented in each of these "strands" in a progressive and sequential manner allowing for both review and the introduction of new material.

High School:

At this level, health education is a requirement for all Freshman. The program is designed to integrate basic knowledge into the development and maintenance of a healthy life-style. In presenting a review of basic health knowledge, students are asked to develop practical skills for implementing this information into their daily lives.

INNOVATIVE HEALTH AND FITNESS PROGRAMS:

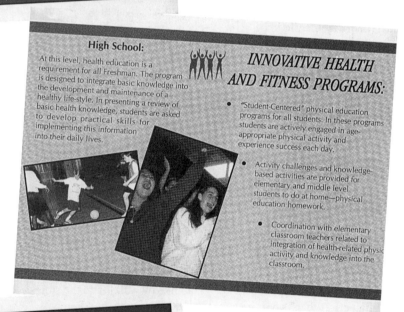

- "Student-Centered" physical education programs for all students. In these programs students are actively engaged in age-appropriate physical activity and experience success each day.

- Activity challenges and knowledge-based activities are provided for elementary and middle level students to do at home—physical education homework.

- Coordination with elementary classroom teachers related to integration of health-related physical activity and knowledge into the classroom.

- Use of "alternative" equipment and teaching methodologies to motivate and involve all students in daily activity.

- Middle level physical education programs which provide a variety of activities designed to give each student a broad base of knowledge and skills to be used both in the school and community setting.

- High school physical education programs designed to assist students in the development and implementation of a healthy and active life-style.

- Planned sequential health education instruction presented as part of all elementary programs and middle level block classes.

- Health education instruction which is student-centered and focuses on knowledge and skills which lead to maintaining a healthy and active life-style.

- High school health education programs designed to focus on life-style development and the setting of personal goals.

- Direct community in instructional programs: "MEDs" is a program in which local physicians develop and teach high school classes related to their area of specialty.

A Newsletter for the RISD Physical Education Program

How Parents Shape a Child's View on Physical Activity

Children learn many important social behaviors through day-to-day interactions with their parents. Recent research suggests that parents also play an important role in socializing their child to be physically active. Socialization processes are influenced by the parent's values and expectations regarding physical activity and physical fitness. If a parent <u>values</u> physical activity and <u>expects</u> their child to be regularly active, they will demonstrate and reinforce this behavior in their children. Through these continual parent-child interactions, children come to view physical activity as an important part of their daily life.

Socializing your child to be physically active requires a consistent and concerted effort but no more of an effort than is required to teach your child other important behaviors, (i.e. proper manners and morals). The most important thing is to send consistent messages about physical activity on a regular basis.

Parents who participate in physical activity with their children, organize activities, or transport children to places for activity provide the most effective support. Time spent outdoors is also highly related to activity levels. By providing access to a safe outdoor play area your child will have more opportunities to develop regular habits of physical activity.

Parents also shape their child's attitudes and beliefs about the importance of an active lifestyle through their own behaviors. For example, by walking to the store instead of driving, children will see that you value an active lifestyle and will come to value activity as well. Look for ways to be a good role model.

In general, parents underestimate the impact they have in shaping their child's attitudes toward physical activity and physical fitness. By regularly participating in activities with your child and encouraging them to participate, you can socialize your children to adopt an active lifestyle.

Ideally, children will come to see physical acitivity as an important part of their daily routine-just like brushing their teeth before they go to bed!

Tips to Get Your Child Active

- Provide a safe play area for your child and opportunities to be active.
- Provide equipment and supplies for your child to be active.
- Encourage your child to play outside instead of watching TV or playing computer games.
- Participate in physical activity with your child or as a family.
- Work with your child on his/her physical skills so they can feel competent.

> *This week take a walk with your child or go to a park!*

Published by:
The Cooper Institute for Aerobics Research, Dallas, TX 75230

Distributed by:

Human Kinetics Education Foundation

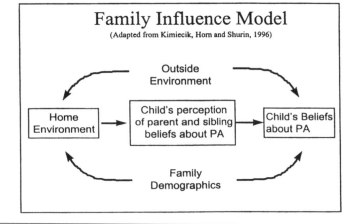

Figure 4.1 Sending a newsletter like this one home with your students is an excellent way of communicating with parents and gaining their support.

Prepared for the Cooper Institute for Aerobics Research by Gregory J. Welk, PhD, Director of Childhood and Adolescent Health. Reprinted by permission.

- Regularly send a newsletter with physical education news and health-related fitness tips. Produce a very professional-looking newsletter with the help of computer technology and volunteer support (see figure 4.1 for an example).
- Invite parents to attend classes.
- Volunteer for schoolwide committees to give physical education the voice it deserves.
- Send *FITNESSGRAM* and *ACTIVITYGRAM* reports home to parents.

Let Your Community Know

Many of the ways you communicate with parents will also help you communicate with the larger community in which your school operates:

- Invite community leaders to attend classes.
- Use the local media: Write press releases, contact television stations when you're putting on an unusual or big event, and invite local media personalities to a special breakfast or fund-raiser.
- Form partnerships with area businesses and religious and service organizations.

Always offer something in return, such as free publicity, for the support you receive.

- Set up or support a mentoring program to provide health-related fitness and academic support for at-risk youth.
- Organize a communitywide health fair or set up a demonstration booth at an already-established event.
- Elect yourself or a physical education colleague to attend all school district board meetings (Bell 1995).

Summary

Yes, it's more work to provide a superior physical education program that is health-related than a mediocre one. It takes more effort to let everyone know about it. But you will find your endeavors will be well worth the effort as you see your students thrive and health-related fitness become not only important to your "captive audience" but also to their parents and the wider school and local community. Over time, you can have a tremendous impact on the health of your entire community and therefore your students' futures.

Part II

Components of Health-Related Fitness

Chapter 5

Basic Training Principles

A big part of reaching the goal of producing adults who are physically active as a way of life is to teach the basic training principles to our students. These are the *hows* of physical activity that empower our students to construct and tailor workouts that meet their individual health-related fitness needs. Understanding that many instructors are likely to be familiar with this information, we have included this chapter as a quick reference to make the job of teaching this information easier. You may also wish to share this concise summary when including colleagues, administrators, and parents in schoolwide physical activity events.

Overload and Progression

Overload refers to the load or amount of resistance for each exercise, providing a greater stress, or load, on the body than it is normally accustomed to in order to increase fitness. *Progression* is the way in which an individual should increase overload. It is a *gradual* increase in either frequency, intensity, or time, or a combination of all three components (see next section). Emphasize that all progression must be gradual to be safe. Progressing too quickly can lead to injury or unnecessary fatigue, both of which can discourage or prevent an individual from participating. Thus, for each component of health-related fitness, take the time to outline and model appropriate progressions. Emphasize that improving your fitness level is a continual, ongoing process. Hinson (1995) suggests giving students opportunities to track their progress.

The FITT Principle

The FITT principle describes how one safely applies the principles of overload and progression:

> Frequency
> Intensity
> Time
> Type (specificity)

Frequency

Frequency is how often a person performs the targeted health-related physical activity. For each component of health-related fitness, beneficial and yet safe frequency is three to five times a week. However, the exceptions are activities intended purely for increasing muscular strength. Most experts believe these activities should be limited to three nonconsecutive days per week, unless different muscle groups are exercised on alternating days (see chapter 7).

Intensity

Intensity is how hard a person exercises during a physical activity period. Intensity can be measured in different ways, depending on the health-related component involved. For example, monitoring heart rate is one way to gauge intensity during aerobic endurance activities but gives no indication of intensity during flexibility activities. Appropriate intensity depends on the goals of the activity. For example, higher intensity is often appropriate when training for competition, whereas lower intensity still gives basic health-related benefits. Monitor children to ensure intensity

does not reduce the quality of performance. In other words, teach students that trying too hard can cause technique to suffer, increasing the likelihood of injury. Instead, teach students the appropriate range of intensity for each type of activity. In addition, the more intense the activity, the shorter the bout should be for younger or less-fit children (see next section).

Time

Time is the duration of a physical activity. As with the other aspects of the FITT principle, time varies depending on the health-related fitness component targeted. For example, appropriate time for flexibility (stretching) exercises is 10 to 30 seconds each stretch multiplied by the number of times an individual performs each stretch (three repetitions is optimal). The minimum time an individual should perform aerobic activity is 20 minutes of continuous activity in the target heart rate zone in one session or 30 minutes of "huff-and-puff" activity accumulated throughout the same day in no less than 10-minute segments. In muscular strength and endurance activities, we measure time in terms of the number of sets and repetitions.

Younger children are less able than older children and adolescents to perform intense physical activities all in one time period. In a landmark position paper developed by the Council for Physical Education for Children (COPEC), Corbin and Pangrazi (1998) summarize time guidelines for children:

- The normal activity patterns of children are intermittent. Alternating bursts of energy followed by recovery may persist for long periods of time. This pattern of activity is normal and may be a necessary condition for stimulating optimal growth and development. Some moderate to vigorous activity periods should last from 10 to 15 minutes or more, alternated with *brief* rest periods.

- Elementary school children should accumulate *at least 30 to 60 minutes* of age- and developmentally appropriate physical activity on all, or most, days of the week.

- An accumulation of *more than 60 minutes, and up to several hours per day*, of age- and developmentally appropriate activities *is encouraged* for elementary school children.

- It is recommended that adolescents participate in at least 20 minutes of continuous moderate to vigorous physical activity on at least three days of each week.

Therefore, in terms of time, be sure to construct lessons and workouts that take into account age-appropriate expectations as well as your particular students' current fitness levels. In addition, keep in mind that younger children usually do not have a very firm grasp of time lengths.

Type

Type, or specificity, refers to the specific physical activity chosen to improve a component of health-related fitness. Specificity is directly related to the energy system's demand to perform an activity (Arthur and Bailey 1998). If, for example, your students are performing aerobic activity or exercise, the energy system that is providing the fuel for that activity is the oxygen system (figure 5.1). Students engaged in activities or exercise that develop

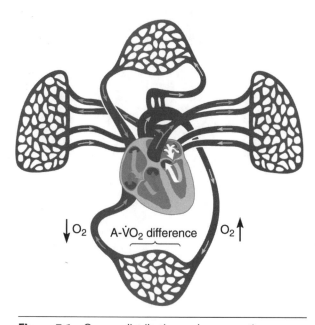

Figure 5.1 Oxygen distribution and consumption.

Reprinted, by permission, from A. Jackson, 1999, *Physical Activity for Health and Fitness*. (Champaign, IL: Human Kinetics), 175.

muscular strength or muscular endurance draw energy primarily from the ATP (adenosine triphosphate) energy system, found in the muscle cells. Teach students to select physical activities that specifically target their personal goals. For example, an individual wishing to increase arm strength must exercise the triceps and biceps, whereas an individual wishing to increase aerobic endurance needs to walk, run, swim, or perform another aerobically challenging activity.

FITT Age Differences

Most of the research we have into the FITT principle is based on adult physiology. Young children, however, do not experience physical activity in all the same ways as adults. So if you teach at the elementary level, you need to be especially aware that you're not dealing with "mini-adults." If you teach at the secondary level, keep in mind that the closer your students are to adulthood, the more like adults they will react to these training principles.

Be especially careful to take self-concept into consideration when working with adolescents. For example, since percent body fat increases may occur at a higher rate in girls than in boys (especially during adolescence), it is important to help them understand that training methods can assist in maintaining a healthy body composition. However, also teach students that girls should naturally have more fat than boys to help students set realistic and healthy body composition goals. Both boys and girls begin to experience hormonal growth changes during puberty, and therefore helping them understand the importance of health-related physical activity can lead to improved self-confidence. While natural growth and maturation will occur in students, it is important to teach even very young children that health-related fitness habits, along with sound nutritional practices, are important ways to provide lifelong healthy benefits. This approach will help combat today's media, which overemphasizes the need for outward appearance over inner health and wellness. Students will be exposed to this at many times during their development. So teach your students the values and benefits associated with health-related physical activity.

Components of a Workout

Every workout or physical activity should incorporate a systematic approach to ensure not only safety but also to prepare the body for the rigors of the workout. Properly warming up before and cooling down after a workout is vital to preventing injuries and returning the body to a more rested state, respectively. The main part of the physical activity must also be conducted appropriately for students to feel and understand, through participation, the importance of being physically active.

Warming Up

Explain to students that warming up properly allows the heart to gradually increase the rate at which it is pumping blood to the body. This process prepares the muscles and other tissues for functioning fully during the main phase of physical activity. Gentle stretching and walking or slow jogging for about five minutes are common and safe warm-up activities.

In age-appropriate ways, discuss with students why you have chosen a particular warm-up for a particular activity. Ensure students understand that an appropriate warm-up prepares the muscles, joints, and other tissues they will use during the main physical activity phase. For younger children, to help prevent discipline problems, plan and lead warm-ups that provide "instant activity" as they arrive at the lesson site (Graham 1992). For older students, post the warm-up in the locker rooms or at the lesson site and make them responsible for carrying it out independently. Finally, work to make warm-ups interesting, challenging, varied, and fun. For younger children, this may mean, for example, a chance to play a quick game; for older children, this may mean, for example, a chance to chat and socialize while warming up.

Walking or slow jogging—followed by gentle stretching—are common and safe warm-up activities.

Main Physical Activity

This is the core of the lesson or workout intended to improve or maintain one or more health-related fitness components. The type of activity and time and intensity of the workout depends on the goal(s), length of the class period, and the current fitness level of individual students. Whether you're teaching kindergarteners or high school seniors, share with students your goal(s) and how the day's activity will help them reach the goal(s) so that, ultimately, they will be able to design their own beneficial workouts as adults.

Cooling Down

A proper cool-down allows the body to slow down and return to a more regular pace or rate of functioning. Ensure that students understand that the body needs this chance to recuperate after vigorous activity by explaining that cooling down properly helps prevent muscle stiffness and soreness and, possibly, lightheadedness. Teach them to resist the urge to simply sit or lie down after physical activity; instead, they should gradually slow down their activity by walking for three to five minutes, or until their heart rate returns to a rested state.

Training Differences

The overload, progression, and FITT guidelines in this chapter outline the minimum amounts of physical activity that individuals should engage in to reap the basic health-related benefits as recommended by various entities, including the CDC, NASPE, and ACSM. And while it is crucial that students understand that these minimums are sufficient for a lifetime of health, wellness, and fitness, you will have certain students who are interested in achieving higher levels of health-related fitness. Perhaps they wish to further condition themselves in order to enjoy recreational sports more. Or perhaps they are serious competitors who wish to reach maximal levels of fitness. Note, however, that striving for

higher fitness levels should be the personal choice of the individual, not that of a teacher, coach, or parent. Throughout the remainder of part II, we refer to the overload, progression, and FITT guidelines for three main levels of fitness:

- Base health-related fitness—the minimum level of fitness required for health benefits to occur.

- Intermediate health-related fitness—the level of fitness required for optimally enjoying recreational sports, activities, and good health.

- Athletic performance fitness—the level of fitness required to succeed in formal interscholastic sport competition.

The best way to increase health-related fitness is to begin with the base level of health-related fitness. Building a solid base, or foundation, will allow the student to progress to the next level more prepared physically and with more confidence (figure 5.2). (See chapters 6 and 7 for a detailed discussion of progression.) To prevent the student from losing interest, or to keep him or her from losing the desire to become more physically fit, help each student explore other recreational activities so that variety itself creates interesting ways to increase total physical activity time. In addition, point out ways a student can vary workouts and act as a liaison between the student and the community, pointing out the various recreational programs available in your community (such as leagues, health clubs, park district activities).

A student wishing to train for higher levels of competition may seek your advice, whether or not you are also his or her coach. First, ensure this student has a firm grasp of the overload, progression, and FITT principles and how they apply to his or her chosen sport. Then, you may choose to work closely with this student, helping him or her set reasonable goals and plan how to reach them in a realistic time frame. Or you can simply offer him or her the latest information regarding specialized training by pointing out websites, books, magazines, and other relevant sources.

Figure 5.2 The three primary levels of fitness are base health-related fitness (the minimum for health benefits to occur), intermediate health-related fitness (the level required to participate in recreational sports and activities), and athletic performance fitness (the level needed to succeed in high-level sport competition).

Take care not to offend a coach who may be offering contradictory advice, but don't hesitate to pass on current research. It is also critical to establish a health history on the student seeking this level. Take note of such problems as joint injury, broken bones, concussions, and hospitalizations and surgeries.

Depending on age, ability, and the particular sport, the serious athlete will of course need to understand the principle of specificity as it applies to the particular sport. Much has been written on the improvement of athletic performance. If a student is pursuing athletic performance development, you might want to suggest that the student meet with a certified strength training specialist, or refer to books that focus specifically on the development of athletic performance.

Balancing the Components of Health-Related Fitness

Children, like adults, will express and act on preferences among the many physical activities available. We strongly encourage you, the teacher, to provide a wide variety of activities and to allow a wide range of personal choice in your program. However, you must ensure

your students understand that they need to address each component of health-related fitness. In short, choice is available within each component, but each component is important. So the student who elects to swim laps, instead of going cross-country skiing, is addressing aerobic fitness appropriately, but still needs to work on flexibility, muscular strength and endurance (not addressed by the activity), and body composition. We will further explain how the overload, progression, and FITT principles apply to each component of health-related fitness in coming chapters. Heyward's (1998) Exercise and Physical Activity Pyramid is an effective tool for teaching students how to weigh each component of health-related fitness as well as inactivity against each other component (figure 5.3).

Safety Guidelines for Health-Related Fitness Activities

Encourage the student seeking any level of health-related fitness to listen to his or her body and slow down if feeling overtired, losing weight too rapidly (more than two pounds per week), or suffering soreness that is in-

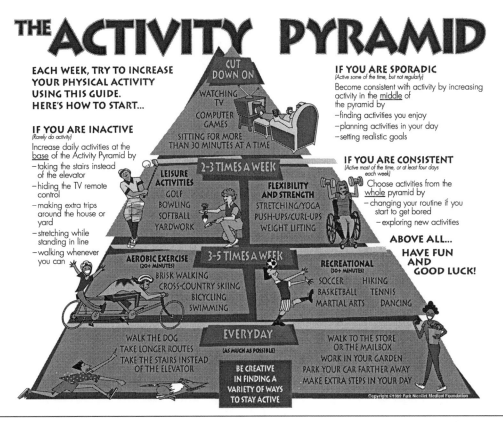

Figure 5.3 The Exercise and Physical Activity Pyramid is a tool that will help your students understand how to address each component of health-related fitness.

Copyright © 1996 Park Nicollet *HealthSource*® Institute for Research and Education. Reprinted by permission.

tense or lasts more than a day or so. Take care to teach students that increasing the intensity of workouts can be the hardest to do gradually. Beginners, especially, tend to not recognize they are overdoing it until it is too late to prevent injury or excessive fatigue.

In regard to flexibility and muscular strength and endurance, students need to understand that concentrating on only a few muscle groups and neglecting others can make an individual more susceptible to injury. For example, only working on leg strength and leg flexibility, but playing a sport that involves the arms, such as basketball, can lead to shoulder or back injuries. What actually causes an imbalance in a particular individual depends on that individual's needs. So encourage students to take a whole-body approach to health-related fitness.

Summary

Remember, we're talking about health-related physical *activity*—not Olympic training. Students, no matter their ages, should be presented with reasonable choices of how intensely they will work during a given workout, based on their personal goals. Keep in mind that fitness is a journey, not a destination. We all want to see our students develop lifelong health-related physical activity habits. Moreover, it is vital that students understand the overload, progression, and FITT principles of training so that, ultimately, they can choose to increase their performance and fitness levels as they desire—and know how to do so safely.

Chapter 6

Aerobic Fitness

To many people, *aerobic* fitness is synonymous with *health-related* fitness. While aerobic fitness is just one component of health-related fitness, it is generally considered the most important physiological indicator of good health and physical condition. There are a number of other terms that can be used to describe this important component of health-related fitness. Terms commonly used include: aerobic endurance, aerobic capacity, aerobic power, cardiorespiratory fitness, cardiorespiratory endurance, cardiovascular fitness, and cardiovascular endurance. Although the terms cardio (heart), vascular (blood vessels), respiratory (lungs and ventilation), and aerobic (working with oxygen) differ technically, they all are closely related (Howley and Franks 1997).

Sharkey (1997) explains the varied terminology: "Years ago, as I began my career in exercise physiology, we used the term cardiovascular to define fitness . . . . The changes in terminology reflect insights derived from several decades of research, based on a clearer view of the effects of training. We used cardiovascular when the best documented effects were on the heart and circulation. Cardiorespiratory became popular when we began to

Figure 6.1 Sample activities that can help students improve aerobic fitness.

understand the importance of oxygen intake as well as transport. Aerobic was adopted to indicate that oxygen intake, transport, and utilization were all improved with training" (p. 86).

It is important that your students understand how all these terms are related so they will not be confused when they receive information using varying terminology. Also, in the interest of helping your students become lifelong learners, a discussion of how terminology changes through the years could be a helpful exercise.

Defining and Measuring Aerobic Fitness

Aerobic fitness is a measure of the heart's ability to pump oxygen-rich blood to the rest of the body and the ability to adjust to and recover from physical activity. Aerobic fitness is measured by gauging maximum oxygen uptake, known as $\dot{V}O_2max$, which is how efficiently the body uses oxygen during moderate to vigorous physical activity. The mile-run, PACER, and walk tests are common field tests used to measure aerobic fitness. These tests are available through the *FITNESSGRAM* assessment program (see chapter 17). The Cooper Institute for Aerobics Research (creators of *FITNESSGRAM*) uses the term *aerobic capacity* instead of aerobic fitness in their program because the tests and standards are based on a direct prediction of $\dot{V}O_2max$. However, it is clearly used synonymously with aerobic fitness. The following excerpt from the FITNESSGRAM *Test Administration Manual* (Second Edition) helps clarify the use and interpretation of these tests for the assessment of aerobic fitness (p.11):

Aerobic capacity is perhaps the most important area of any fitness program. Research clearly indicates that acceptable levels of aerobic capacity are associated with a reduced risk of high blood pressure, coronary heart disease, obesity, diabetes, some forms of cancer and other health problems in adults (Blair et al. 1989, Blair et al. 1992).

Aerobic capacity relative to body weight is considered to be the best indicator of a person's overall cardiorespiratory capacity. Many terms have been used to describe this dimension of physical fitness, including cardiovascular fitness, cardiorespiratory fitness, cardiorespiratory endurance, aerobic fitness, aerobic work capacity, and physical working capacity. Although defined somewhat differently, these terms can generally be considered to be synonymous with aerobic capacity. A laboratory measure of maximal oxygen uptake ($\dot{V}O_2$max) is generally considered to be the best measure of aerobic capacity. The field tests used for aerobic capacity have demonstrated strong reliability and validity against measured $\dot{V}O_2$max.

In addition to the achieved test score, the estimated $\dot{V}O_2$max adjusted according to kilogram of body weight per minute is also reported on the *FITNESSGRAM* program output. It is possible to compare results between different measures such as the PACER, the one-mile run, and the walk test. These are the three aerobic capacity test options. The PACER is the default item for all students and is strongly recommended for participants in grades K-3. The emphasis for testing in grades K-3 should be on fun, allowing the students to participate in a pleasant experience.

Throughout this chapter and text, we will use the term *aerobic fitness* to reflect a person's aerobic capacity.

Teaching Guidelines for Aerobic Fitness and Aerobic Capacity

In a school setting, measuring heart rate before, during, and after physical activity is a practical way to monitor this component of health-related fitness. Focusing on aerobic fitness is appropriate for all age groups, kindergarten through 12th grade and, of course, throughout adulthood. Students need to understand not only what aerobic fitness is but also how maintaining or improving it helps us lead more active lives. Moreover, students need to know that a wide variety of enjoyable and accessible activities are appropriate for maintaining and improving aerobic fitness. Aerobic fitness activities form a large segment of Heyward's (1998) Exercise and Physical Activity Pyramid (figure 5.3) because aerobic fitness is so important to overall good health. Help students explore practical applications such as logging free-time aerobic fitness activities in a journal, learning to take their pulses, or organizing a school fitness night for their families and friends. See the examples of lifetime and class activities described in chapters 11 and 12 for maintaining or improving aerobic fitness.

Be sure students new to aerobic activity start out cautiously. Better for these individuals to limit intensity and time at first and slowly progress to more intense and longer workouts than to overdo it initially and become discouraged. You should also require parents to fill out a health history on each student to help you screen for students who should use extra caution when engaging in aerobic fitness activities.

Overload, FITT, Progression, and Specificity Principles

The CDC's guidelines for aerobic fitness training are sufficient for a lifetime of good aerobic health. Yet, as mentioned in chapter 5, you will most likely encounter students who wish to achieve higher levels of fitness. Provide accurate and helpful information to help interested students reach their aerobic endurance goals safely. In table 6.1, we summarize how to apply the overload, progression, and FITT principles based on fitness level goals.

Primary grade students can begin to monitor their intensity levels by placing a hand over the heart before, during, and after moderate to vigorous physical activity and noting the general speed of the heartbeat using terms such as *slow*, *medium*, and *fast* or *turtle* and *race car*. Introduce fourth- and fifth-grade students to locating their pulses (carotid artery, wrist), counting their pulses, and calculating maximum heart rate (MHR) and target heart rate zone (THRZ). Expect most students sev-

enth grade and up to be able to learn to calculate these numbers, but provide data in chart form when appropriate to save class time (see table 6.2). The point is not to produce expert mathematicians, but to familiarize students with the process so they understand where THRZ and MHR guidelines are coming from and that these numbers will change as they age. In this way, students will know it's important to seek this information as adults.

Taking the Pulse

Several methods exist for counting or assessing pulse rate. Two of the more common

Table 6.1	Training Principles Applied to Aerobic Fitness, Based on Fitness Goals		
	Base health-related fitness	**Intermediate health-related fitness**	**Athletic performance fitness**
Frequency	3 times per week	3–5 times per week	5–6 times per week
Intensity	50–60% maxHR	60–75% maxHR	65–90% maxHR
Time	30 min total, accumulated*	40–60 min total, accumulated*	60–120 min total, accumulated*
Type	Walking, jogging, dancing, games, and activities that require minimal equipment demands**	Jogging, running, fitness-based games and activities, intramural and local league sports***	Training programs, running, aerobics, interscholastic, and community sports programs
Overload	Not necessary to bring child to overload during base level.	Be creative with activity to increase tempo or decrease rest period; 1–3 times per week.	Program design should stress variable intensities and durations to bring student into overload; 2–3 times per week.
Progression and specificity	Let student "get the idea" of movement. Progression is minimal.	Introduce program design and incorporate variation.	Specific sets, repetitions, and exercises to meet desired outcomes

*Activity can be accumulated throughout the day in segments of at least 10 minutes each (for students in grades three and above).
**Refer to *Physical Best Activity Guide — Elementary Level.*
***Refer to *Physical Best Activity Guide — Elementary Level* and *Physical Best Activity Guide — Secondary Level.*

Table 6.2   Calculating Maximum Heart Rate (MHR) and Target Heart Rate Zone (THRZ)

Age	MHR	THRZ (60% to 75% of MHR, rounded to nearest whole number)
9	211	127 to 158
10	210	126 to 158
11	209	125 to 157
12	208	125 to 156
13	207	124 to 155
14	206	124 to 155
15	205	123 to 154
16	204	122 to 153
17	203	122 to 152
18	202	121 to 152

Calculating Maximum Heart Rate and Target Heart Rate Zone

Explain to students that maximum heart rate (MHR) is calculated by subtracting one's age from 220. To calculate target heart rate zone (THRZ), find the lower and higher percentages of the MHR. For example, a student who is 14 years old seeking a basic level of fitness (at 60–75 percent MHR) would find his THRZ as follows:

$$220 - 14 = 206 = MHR$$

Calculate the THRZ by changing the percentages to decimals and multiplying them with the MHR:

$$.60 \times 206 = 123.6$$

$$.75 \times 206 = 154.5$$

Rounded to the nearest whole numbers, this student's THRZ for maintaining or improving basic fitness in aerobic endurance training is 124–155 heartbeats per minute.

Pulse Math

To promote interdisciplinary learning, you can easily create math problems around calculating heart rate by having students count their pulse for different intervals. To add interest, make up word problems such as the following:

- Sam counted 35 heartbeats in 30 seconds. What is his heart rate?

$$60 \text{ s} \div 30 \text{ s} = 2$$

so you multiply 35 by 2:

$$35 \times 2 = 70 \text{ heartbeats per min}$$

- Lan counted 27 heartbeats in 10 seconds. What is her heart rate?

$$60 \text{ s} \div 10 \text{ s} = 6$$

so you multiply 27 by 6:

$$27 \times 6 = 162 \text{ heartbeats per min}$$

- Which person is more likely to be jogging, Sam or Lan? (*Lan*) Which person is more likely to be sitting in class? (*Sam*)

Because this is a practical way to integrate math across the curriculum, fourth-, fifth-, and sixth-grade classroom teachers may be willing to help you construct similar problems or provide math class time for students to learn and complete this type of work. Some students may also be able to design problems for themselves or peers to complete.

methods or sites used are the carotid artery (on the neck) or the wrist. Teach students to first locate the pulse by placing the first two fingers of the right hand lightly on the right side of the neck, below and to the right of the Adam's apple (figure 6.2a). Be sure each student is capable of feeling his or her heart beating. (Make sure they don't press too hard or they'll slow down blood flow.) Teach students the wrist method by placing the first two fingers of either hand on the opposite wrist (palm facing up), just below the base of the thumb (figure 6.2b). Have students move their fingers around until they locate the pulse.

Teach students that they may count their pulse (starting at zero) for either 6 seconds and multiply by 10 (or simply add a "zero" to the number they counted), count to

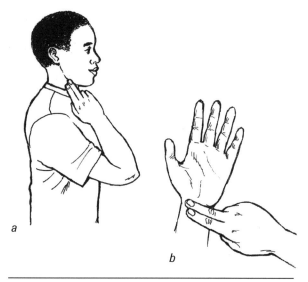

Figure 6.2   Two methods of taking a pulse: *(a)* the carotid artery (neck) method and *(b)* the wrist method.

10 seconds and multiply by 6 (see table 6.3), or count for 15 seconds and multiply by 4. Generally, the method of counting for 6 seconds, then adding a "zero," works best.

Using Heart Rate Monitors

While heart rate monitors are not necessary, they are a popular and exciting way to teach students about aerobic fitness concepts. Heart rate monitors provide accurate information, whereas manual pulse counting may not be done accurately by some students. In their book *Lessons From the Heart* (Human Kinetics, 1997), Kirkpatrick and Birnbaum advocate the use of heart rate monitors for the following reasons, among others. Heart rate monitors

- allow instructors to monitor and document effort, making it easier to reward effort instead of physical prowess;
- make it easier for low-fit students to experience success because the focus is on staying in the THRZ, rather than on competition against classmates or unrealistic standards;
- encourage personal responsibility for aerobic endurance fitness;
- help instructors teach students how to individualize a fitness program, allowing students to gain fitness benefits safely; and

- are fun to use, leading to increased interest in physical activity.

Training Methods for Aerobic Fitness

There are four main training methods to maintain or increase aerobic fitness: continuous, circuit, interval, and Fartlek training. You must adjust how you apply these methods, depending on the age, ability, and fitness level of each individual. Building personal choice into each activity can do some of this individualizing for you. For example, offer a longer rest option during interval or Fartlek training. Having students frequently monitor their heart rates (with or without the help of a heart rate monitor) also helps individualize a workout; if a student's heart rate goes above or below the THRZ, he should slow down or speed up, accordingly.

Continuous Training

This is simply the same activity or exercise performed over an extended time period. Three to five minutes of continuous activity at a moderate intensity level may be the limit of very young or low-fit students, whereas 10 minutes at a time is a good limit for older (intermediate grade) elementary students.

Table 6.3 Heart Rate Based on a 10-Second Count			
Beats	**Heart rate**	**Beats**	**Heart rate**
10	60	22	132
11	66	23	138
12	72	24	144
13	78	25	150
14	84	26	156
15	90	27	162
16	96	28	168
17	102	29	174
18	108	30	180
19	114	31	186
20	120	32	192
21	126	33	198

Table 6.4 Duration of Aerobic Activity

Students	Duration
Primary (K–2) and low-fit students	3–5 min
Intermediate (3–5) students	10 min
Middle school and high school students	20 min and more

Twenty minutes or more continuous activity, depending on fitness level and goals, is appropriate for middle and high school students (table 6.4). With continuous training, monitoring of students' active heart rates becomes important, as precautions must be taken to not overdo the level of exertion. To accentuate the principles of overload and progression, increasing the pace or duration of the activity will provide positive health benefits to your more-fit students. Active, low-organization games are fun ways to provide continuous physical activity. Teach students games and activities they'll want to also play on their own in their free time. Middle and high school students may find that a mix of aerobic activities that will sustain a target elevated heart rate for a designated period of time will be more enjoyable and therefore more beneficial to their overall fitness level.

Circuit Training

This type of training involves several different exercises, allowing you to vary the intensity or type of activity as children move from station to station. You can also adjust intensity by changing the amount of time groups spend at each station or the amount of rest or activity between stations (for instance, stretching between stations versus running once around the activity area). An example of circuit training appropriate for elementary age children is shown in figure 6.3. Secondary students might, for example, lift light weights to music, changing the

exercise performed at each station and using a step in between stations. Circuit training is an excellent way to create variety in aerobic endurance activity, as the possible combinations of stations are endless. Older elementary and secondary students can even design the stations for you as a practical application of the fitness knowledge they're learning. Like continuous training, circuit training should be aerobic in nature, depending on the intensity and duration of the activity in relation to the individual's fitness level. Use task cards and arrow signs to direct the activities (see also sidebar in chapter 13 titled Using Learning Stations Effectively).

Interval Training

This type of training involves alternating short bursts of activity with rest periods. Young children naturally engage in this type of activity; simply ensure they rest a safe amount of

Have a Heart—A Healthy One

The Healthy H.E.A.R.T. (Habits of Eating, Activity, and Reducing Risks Together) Program and Heart Lab at Ellisville (Missouri) Elementary School concentrates on teaching students how to maintain cardiovascular health. Developed by Ron Ramspott, physical educator, and his colleagues, fourth and fifth graders use the Heart Lab once a week for six weeks of every nine-week quarter. Each week, they visit a different station: step aerobics using heart rate monitors, step machines, stationary bikes, nutrition using a computer program, fitness tests, and a rotating educational activity. Funds for equipment were raised from community sources, such as raffles and an Exercise-a-Thon.

Younger students take part in several Healthy H.E.A.R.T. activities that introduce them to cardiovascular fitness concepts. Plans to include parents and school staff more are in the works.

The program won the Missouri AHPERD Gold Star Award in 1995, but Ramspott asserts he will be most pleased if it can be shown that the effects last after students leave the school.

Adapted, by permission, from "Have a Heart—A Healthy One," by Sara Lipowitz, 1997, *Teaching Elementary Physical Education* 8(2):16–17.

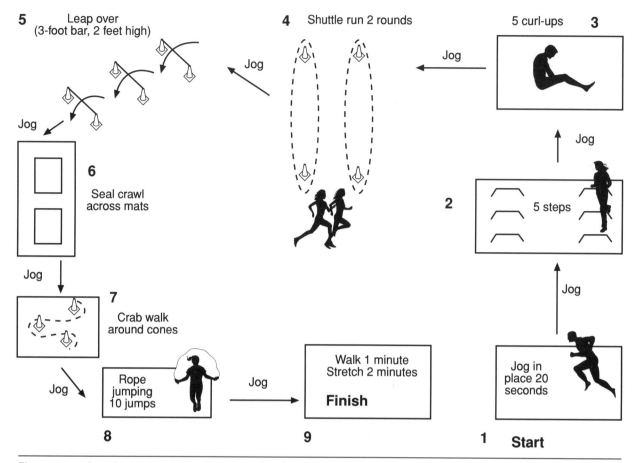

Figure 6.3   Sample circuit training plan appropriate for elementary age children.

Reprinted, by permission, from S. Virgilio, 1997, *Fitness Education for Children*. (Champaign, IL: Human Kinetics), 149.

time between bursts (enough for heart rate to slow to the low end of the THRZ). Older students are capable of engaging in more structured interval training. The trick is to make this type of training interesting. Leave running wind sprints for the track coach and have your students, for example, pass a soccer ball between partners, running as fast as they can downfield. Interval training can be more *anaerobic* (without oxygen, or performing physical activity without the presence of oxygen as the primary energy source) in nature as the individual focuses intensely on the short bursts of activity. However, if the rest periods are shortened to allow the training heart rate not to lower to a point that full recovery of the energy system occurs, the net outcome will be aerobic in nature. Interval training is based on the concept that more activity can be performed at higher exercise intensities with the same or even less fatigue compared to

continuous training (figure 6.4). The key to increase his or her speed in a particular sport such as basketball. At the elementary level, Fartlek training simply involves placing stress on different muscle groups by changing levels and direction frequently (Virgilio 1997).

Line Change

Virgilio (1997) offers a continuous aerobic fitness activity. This could also be considered a Fartlek training activity (see Interval Training section), as students may have to speed up temporarily to take over the lead:

Arrange students in straight lines of seven or eight, facing the same direction. Have them begin jogging or walking in any direction, staying in lines. At the signal, have the last student in line jog to the front to become the leader. Continue until everyone has had a chance to lead the line.

Figure 6.4 Interval training is more than wind sprints. Here a student jumps rope to an audiotape that alternates faster and slower music.

Effective interval training is to be sure that your students are actively engaged in physical activity at a rate of one part activity to one part rest and recovery.

Fartlek training is a form of interval training in which intensity is controlled, for example, by running hills for 200 to 600 meters at a time. Hill running develops technique, strength, endurance, general aerobic endurance, and mental fitness (Greene and Pate 1997). Reserve it for the serious athlete who wants to increase his or her speed in a particular sport such as basketball. At the elementary level, Fartlek training simply involves placing stress on different muscle groups by changing levels and direction frequently (Virgilio 1997). Figure 6.5 shows a sample Fartlek training course appropriate for older, reasonably well-conditioned elementary students. As with circuit training, use task cards and arrow signs to direct the activities.

Addressing Motor Skills Through Aerobic Fitness Activities

Address motor skill learning during aerobic fitness training to help make these activities more enjoyable and interesting. For example, add a manipulative object or vary the form of locomotion. This approach demonstrates to students how aerobic fitness applies in the real world of physical activity. So add motor skills to aerobic fitness activities and incorporate aerobic fitness training into motor skill learning. Either way, address both whenever possible. The following lists several specific ways to integrate motor skills with aerobic fitness activities and vice versa:

- Cross-training
- Obstacle courses
- Soccer keep-away
- Cycling
- In-line skating
- Swimming

Teaching Tip: Sounds Like Fun

Many students, particularly young children, will understand and monitor their heart rates more effectively when you provide some extra context. For example, you might use a metronome for teaching about heart rate. Students will better understand what 200 beats per minute sounds like. Then they can focus on what their target heart rate zones sound like.

Another fun method to reinforce how hard the heart works is to ask the students to calculate how many beats their hearts have made since birth. Figure out how many heartbeats per minute, then per hour, per day, per week, per year, and then years since birth. Encourage students to be as exact as their ages and abilities allow.

Carolyn Masterson
Physical Education Specialist
Elizabeth Morrow School
Engelwood, New Jersey

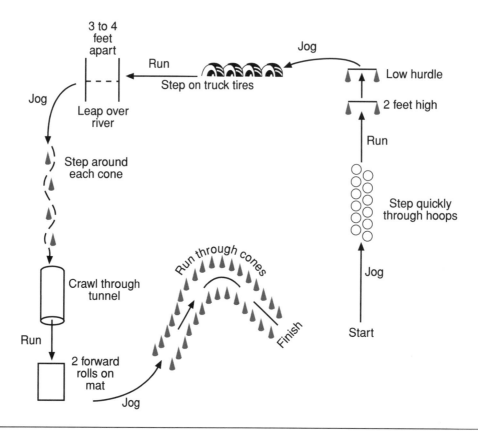

Figure 6.5   Sample Fartlek training course. Students who use a course like this one should be older elementary age and reasonably well-conditioned.

Reprinted, by permission, from S. Virgilio, 1997, *Fitness Education for Children*. (Champaign, IL: Human Kinetics), 149.

Safety Guidelines for Aerobic Fitness Activities

Research has shown that children respond to exercise differently than adults (Bar-Or 1993, 1994; Zwiren 1988). When helping children increase their aerobic fitness, keep the following information regarding physiological responses in mind, in addition to taking the principles of overload, FITT, and progression into consideration (Harris and Elbourn 1997):

- Children's bodies produce more heat than adults' bodies do.
- Given the same speed, children's bodies use more oxygen than adults'.
- Children's heart and breathing rates are higher on the average for the same intensity.
- Children cannot get as much oxygen out of the air as adults because their lungs work less efficiently. Thus, their bodies have to work harder to get the oxygen they need.
- Having to breathe harder means children's bodies lose water more quickly than adults.
- Children aren't able to cool as efficiently as adults.

Therefore, build in frequent rest periods for younger students, and regardless of age, provide water before, during, and after physical activity. Also, for safety reasons, make rest periods an option for older students: Although you don't want them to waste the activity period, you must empower them to choose what feels safe to them so they can do so outside your program. Avoid very hot and humid weather conditions altogether with elementary age children and, using your best judgment, slow down or cancel the activity with secondary students.

Although most students in your classes will be able to handle aerobic fitness activities safely, you will encounter a few who will need

Alaskan Teacher Takes Physical Education to Heart

Teaching quality middle school physical education can often be frustrating. Despite the long hours spent designing meaningful assignments, some students—and even some parents—still consider "gym" to be a waste of time, a bother. But Alaska physical education teacher Martin Niemi has never let frustration get in the way of his dedication to providing quality programs, and at least one student and her parents couldn't be happier about that fact.

Martin has been teaching physical education for the past 10 years at the State Department of Education's Alyeska Central School in Juneau, a correspondence school for students who live in isolated areas of the state ("out in the bush"), take part in high-level training (as did Olympian Tommy Moe), or are home-schooled.

The five or six courses Martin teaches each semester (by mail, phone, and computer) allow 415 students in grades 6 through 12 to increase their knowledge and skills about fitness and physical activities relative to their specific lifestyles and circumstances. His duties typically include creating and sending out assignments, grading them, and then determining if students have met the requirements of their particular class.

Molly Meeham, 12, of Eagle River is one of Martin's students. Molly, a seventh grader who is being home-schooled, has always been a normal and active kid: hiking, biking, swimming, horseback riding, jumping on the backyard trampoline with her friends. She had never shown any sign that might lead one to think she had a potentially fatal heart condition. That is, until she met up with Martin. That's right, Martin Niemi, her physical education teacher.

Molly was enrolled in Martin's physical education contract course, the purpose of which, Martin says, is "to get students participating in activities that enhance their lifestyles and help them develop proper exercise habits." As part of the course Molly had to participate in

at least 65 hours of approved activities (most students, Martin says, end up with 90 to 200 hours). Students also complete such assignments as fitness challenges, a written paper on the benefits of health-related fitness, a pulse graph activity, and a daily log of participation time.

Molly's mom, Sandy, thought doing all this would be "a bother. After all, my husband [Mike] and I knew she was physically fit. Why did we have to document it for someone else?" Although they didn't know it at the time, Molly's pulse graph would not just help her pass the class—it would save her life.

For the pulse-graph activity, students take their pulses on seven different occasions over a given period (for example, while completely rested, after doing chores, and after aerobic and anaerobic exercising); then they graph them and send them in. When he looked at Molly's graph in March, Martin saw that all seven of her heart rates were between 100 and 125 beats a minute—making "the strangest pulse graph I had ever seen."

Given that Molly had completed her assignment, Martin could have stopped right there. Instead, he drew in red on her graph what a "normal" pattern should look like and sent it back to Sandy, expressing his concern that either the assignment had not been completed properly or that there was possibly "some sort of a health problem."

Upon receiving the assignment back, Sandy Meeham was a little peeved at first, she recalls. "We were just getting ready to go on a family vacation; the PE course was the last one Molly had to finish. We had figured that because it was just PE, the class would be a piece of cake—no big deal. And here we were getting an assignment back because it may not have been completed properly?" Once Sandy thought about it over the course of the day, however, she felt that perhaps there really was something to

Martin's comments. "I started thinking, how could we have counted that many pulses wrong?"

Now concerned, Sandy contacted her pediatrician, who assigned her to take Molly's pulse that night while Molly was sleeping. It turned out to be 120 beats a minute, compared with a normal rate of 80 beats or less. The next day, with the help of an EKG, it was determined that something was indeed wrong with the electrical impulses of Molly's heart. She was taken immediately to a specialist in Portland, OR, for testing, and a few weeks later, after 5 hours of exploratory surgery, Molly's condition was diagnosed—she was born with an extra pacemaker in her heart, which caused it to beat much faster than normal.

Sandy credits Martin with alerting their family to Molly's condition. "Had Martin not been so thorough and adamant in his concern over her graph, it is likely I wouldn't have paid it immediate attention. If I hadn't, there is no doubt Molly would be one sick little girl right now. I can only say, I believe it's all part of a big plan. We are thankful that Martin has been part of that plan."

Martin, who received a commendation from Alaska's Governor Walter Hickel for his action, says, "I feel really proud and happy that I got to play a part in Molly's having a chance to live a healthy, happy life. This has helped remind me that we as physical educators do a lot of things day in and day out, and it's important not to trivialize them. Each child we teach is important and has important things to say."

And what about Molly? A week after her surgery, she was playing the piano at church. She's recently completed a 12-mile hike; a 27-miler is in the works. Thanks to the dedication and persistence of her physical education teacher, Molly can again be just like her friends. "We will be forever grateful," says Sandy. "The bottom line of this all is that I saw the PE course as the least significant class Molly had, but it turned out to be, literally, a lifesaver."

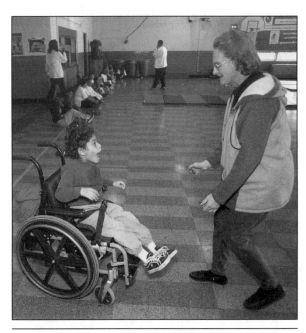

Teach the overload, progression, and FITT principles to students with special needs through carefully planned and modified activities.

special guidance and modified activities. Be sure you know who has any form of asthma, orthopedic concerns, heart anomalies, and the like. Not all of these conditions will be obvious, so review school records, talk to the school nurse or classroom teachers, survey parents, and carefully follow school or district policy to ensure you're fully informed. Ask for input on what each child in question can handle and advice on how to apply the overload, progression, and FITT principles safely. If in doubt, obtain written parental permission to talk to the student's health care provider (see also chapter 15 on inclusion).

Summary

Use the information in this chapter as a quick reference when teaching aerobic fitness concepts. In addition, refer to the aerobic fitness activities described in chapters 11 and 12 and in *Physical Best Activity Guide—Elementary Level* and *Physical Best Activity Guide—Secondary Level* to show students how to apply the concepts in practical ways. Review the teaching guidelines outlined in this chapter periodically to ensure your expectations are reasonable based on your students' ages, abilities, fitness levels, and interests. Always adjust your program to meet individual needs.

Chapter 7

Muscular Strength and Endurance

Two of the most important components of health-related fitness are muscular strength and muscular endurance, as they are important to preventing health problems such as backaches, weak and porous bones, and muscle injury and excessive soreness. Improving muscular strength and endurance benefits the body in many ways, including increasing stamina, improving circulation, and assisting in body balance and coordination. In addition, strong muscles help a person look better through facilitating good posture; and muscle cells burn more calories than fat cells do, helping an individual reduce excess fat, thereby improving body composition. Athletes will also find that improved strength enhances performance (Arthur and Bailey 1998). In this chapter, our goal is to provide a solid, scientifically proven overview of an approach to teaching the principles of muscular strength and endurance to your students. The Recommended Reading list, at the back of this book, lists several books on this topic for those interested in more in-depth information.

Teaching Tip: Teaching About Muscular Strength

Elementary students need to learn how different weights feel. Have different types and sizes (2 to 10 pounds) of weights available at a station so the students can learn about using weights and learn how each weight feels.

There is more than one way to do a push-up, but they all require keeping the back stable. Place a beanbag or tennis ball on the backs of students to help them understand the correct form of a push-up. Challenge the students to keep the beanbag or tennis ball on their backs, which will indicate good technique.

Carolyn Masterson
Physical Education Specialist
Elizabeth Morrow School
Engelwood, New Jersey

Defining Muscular Strength and Endurance

Muscular strength is the ability of a muscle or group of muscles to exert a maximal force against a resistance. Technically speaking, it is one maximum effort, often denoted as "1RM," which stands for "one repetition maximum." *Muscular endurance* is the ability of a muscle or muscle group to exert force over a period of time against a resistance less than the maximum an individual can move. Muscular endurance training involves submaximal muscle contractions extended over a high number of repetitions with relatively little rest, or "recovery," between each exercise (figure 7.1). The Physical Best program groups them together, because in practical application of activities and exercises, they are difficult to separate.

Teaching Guidelines for Muscular Strength and Endurance

You can teach muscular strength and endurance concepts and conduct training sessions whether you have state-of-the-art equipment or not. Surgical tubing for resistance bands is inexpensive and readily available. Collect and use cans of food for small weights, then donate them to a local food bank. You can use balls, too, which incorporate balance and

strength. There are always body weight and partner-resisted exercises. If you are planning to purchase equipment, focus on buying items that will meet the primary needs of your students. Remember that using traditional weight-training equipment represents only a small segment of exercises and activities. It's important to first manage one's own body weight before lifting increased weights. We have included many activities and exercises in the *Physical Best Activity Guide—Elementary Level* and *Physical Best Activity Guide—Secondary Level* to teach muscular strength and endurance concepts.

Overload, FITT, Progression, and Specificity Principles

The principle of overload—progressively placing greater-than-normal demands on the musculature of the body—suggests that individuals involved with activities designed to improve muscular strength and/or muscular endurance will need to increase their workload periodically throughout the course of the program. Specifically, to develop muscular strength, the overload principle dictates increasing the resistance against the muscles involved to a level greater than that used before. To develop muscular endurance, the overload principle dictates increasing the number of repetitions, increasing the length (time) of the repetition, decreasing the rest interval between activities, or a combination of two or three methods. Keep in mind

Figure 7.1   Sample activities that can help students improve muscular strength and endurance.

that the amount of increase must be appropriate for the age and fitness level of the students.

The principle of progression refers to incorporating a systematic approach to increasing frequency of exercise, the volume of repetitions, and/or the intensity of the activity. To avoid injury, however, students must understand appropriate progression and set goals accordingly. For example, they should know that adding only a couple pounds at a time is safer and more realistic than increasing by an excessive amount. There may be instances in which one component may be increased, whereas the other components may actually be decreased. For example, as intensity increases, volume will decrease, and vice versa. Make sure that you develop a plan of health-related fitness activities that will lead the student to an improved level of fitness in a safe but progressive manner. The *Physical Best Activity Guide—Elementary Level* and *Physical Best Activity Guide—Secondary Level*

provide many activities that have been developed with this principle in mind.

The principle of specificity technically states that the "type of demand placed on the body controls the type of adaptation that will occur" (Baechle 1994). For our purposes,

Caution!

While safety is a concern in any aspect of physical education and health-related physical fitness, it is especially critical to closely follow safety guidelines as outlined later in this chapter. You should also seek additional training specific to working with children and adolescents in developing muscular strength and endurance in a safe and effective manner. Furthermore, use common sense when designing and implementing curricula and activities in this area, paying careful attention to the ages, developmental readiness, abilities, maturity levels, past experiences, and fitness levels of your students.

Table 7.1	Training Principles Applied to Muscular Strength and Muscular Endurance, Based on Fitness Goals		
	Base health-related fitness	**Intermediate health-related fitness**	**Athletic performance fitness**
Frequency	2–3 times per week; allow for minimum one-day rest between training sessions	3–4 times per week; alternating upper- and lower-body segments will allow for consecutive training days	4–5 times per week; training activities are specific to sport participation
Intensity	Very light, less than 40% of a "projected" maximal effort	Light to moderate, 50% to 70% of "projected" maximal effort	Specific load adaptation required for sport participation
Time	1–2 sets of 6–12 repetitions	1–3 sets of 6–15 repetitions	3–5 sets of 5–20 repetitions
Type	Body weight, single and multijoint activities involving major muscle groups*	Resistance exercises such as leg press, bench press, pull-ups, additional presses and pulls**	Advanced sport-specific, multijoint lifts (clean pulls, power presses, Olympic style lifts)
Overload	Not necessary to bring child to overload during base level	Introduce one of the components of overload; 1–2 times per week.	Program design should stress variable intensities and durations to bring student into overload; 2–3 times per week.
Progression and specificity	Let student get the idea of correct movement. Progression is minimal.	Introduce program design and incorporate variation.	Specific sets, repetitions, and exercises to meet desired outcomes

*Refer to *Physical Best Activity Guide – Elementary Level.*
**Refer to *Physical Best Activity Guide – Elementary Level* and *Physical Best Activity Guide – Secondary Level.*

specificity suggests that the activities you select should provide the outcome represented by that day's class objectives (see Physical Best activity guides for examples). The previous principles of overload and progression provide the foundation for establishing specificity in your teaching plan.

Your students need to know that engaging in muscular strength and endurance training twice per week is sufficient for a lifetime of good muscular health. Yet, as mentioned in chapter 5, you will most likely encounter students who wish to achieve higher levels of fitness. It is your job to provide accurate and helpful information to assist interested students in reaching their muscular strength and endurance goals safely. In table 7.1, we summarize how to apply the FITT (frequency, intensity, time, and type) principle, based on fitness level goals.

Calculating 1RM

Javier wants to learn his current 1RM value for the bench press. He lifted 125 pounds 10 times during testing. His 1RM for the bench press is:

$$(10 \text{ repetitions} \times .03 = .30) + 1 = 1.30$$

$$1.30 \times 125 \text{ pounds} = 162.5 \text{ pounds}$$

Griffin (1998) defines intensity as the "power output of an exercise and [intensity] is dependent upon the resistance and speed of movement." In regard to muscular strength and endurance, we can gauge intensity by calculating the percentage of one repetition maximum (1RM), much like we figure a target heart rate zone based on percentages of maximum heart rate. To determine a "projected," or calculated, one repetition maximum without subjecting your students to unsafe testing of actual one repetition maximums, have the student perform the resistive exercise at a safe weight for no less than 6 and no more 12 repetitions. Multiply the number of repetitions lifted by .03, then add 1. Finally, multiply by the original amount of weight lifted. This will provide a safe and effective way to determine maximal efforts using a submaximal load. (See "Calculating 1RM".)

An individual can develop either muscular strength or muscular endurance with the same total load. To develop muscular strength, increase intensity by increasing the weight lifted and reducing the number of reps. For example, bench-pressing 100 pounds for 6 reps would be appropriate. To develop muscular endurance, increase intensity by decreasing the weight lifted and increasing the number of reps. For example, bench-press 50 pounds for 12 reps instead of 100 pounds for 6 reps.

As defined earlier by Griffin, speed of lifting also influences intensity. If an individual takes 90 seconds to lift a weight 12 times, the intensity is lower than if the same individual takes 60 seconds to lift the same weight the same number of reps. However, be aware that especially with weight machines, lifting too fast creates momentum that aids the lifting, thereby reducing intensity. Lifting too fast (4 seconds or faster per rep) also increases the likelihood of injury. Westcott (1996) recommends 6-second reps (2 seconds lifting and 4 seconds lowering), but asserts 8- (4 lifting and 4 lowering) to 14-second (10 lifting and 4 lowering) reps are also effective. Moderate to slow exercise speeds, Westcott reports, have several advantages over fast exercise speeds, including a "longer period of muscle tension, a higher level of muscle forces, a lower level of momentum, and a lower risk of tissue injury."

Training Methods for Muscular Strength and Endurance

According to the National Strength and Conditioning Association (NSCA), a 5 to 10 percent increase when guiding a student to progress from base development to intermediate to advanced development in overall load is appropriate for most children. Help each child begin slowly, then gradually increase frequency, intensity, and/or time, according to individual needs and goals. Table 7.2 offers general progression guidelines, based on age group. A training log such as the one shown in figure 7.2 can help a child see individual progress and feel a sense of accomplishment.

Body Weight Training

Although it is difficult to quantify intensity, sit-ups, curl-ups, push-ups, and flexed arm hangs all help build muscular strength and endurance with little or no equipment. This type of resistive training is appropriate for the very young (K–4) or the student who is just beginning resistance training activity. These activities can be presented in a fun and safe way, providing very positive health-related benefits to the student. Add interest to them by playing music or creating games such as "Around the World" from *Right Fielders Are People Too* (Hichwa 1998). (See sidebar on page 105.)

Body weight training isn't only for young children, however. It has the advantages of not requiring equipment, which means it's an inexpensive part of a strength and endurance training program throughout adulthood. It is

Table 7.2 Basic Guidelines for Resistance Exercise Progression in Children

Age (years)	Considerations
7 or younger	Introduce child to basic exercises with little or no weight; develop the concept of a training session; teach exercise techniques; progress from body weight calisthenics, partner exercise, and lightly resisted exercises; keep volume low.
8-10	Gradually increase the number of exercises; practice exercise technique in all lifts; start gradual progressive loading of exercises; keep exercises simple; gradually increase training volume; carefully monitor toleration of the exercise stress.
11-13	Teach all basic exercise techniques; continue progressive loading of each exercise; emphasize exercise techniques; introduce more advanced exercises with little or no resistance.
14-15	Progress to more advanced youth programs in resistance exercise; add sport-specific components; emphasize exercise techniques; increase volume.
16 or older	Move child to entry-level adult programs after all background knowledge has been mastered and a basic level of training experience has been gained.

Note. If a child of any age begins a program with no previous experience, start the child at previous levels and move him or her to more advanced levels as exercise toleration, skill, amount of training time, and understanding permit.

Reprinted, by permission, from W. Kraemer and S. Fleck, 1993, *Strength Training for Young Athletes*. (Champaign, IL: Human Kinetics), 5.

Name ____________________

Week ____________________

Day ____________________

Weight ____________________ lb

	Set 1		Set 2		Set 3	
Exercise	Weight	Reps	Weight	Reps	Weight	Reps

Figure 7.2 Sample training log.

Reprinted, by permission, from W. Kraemer and S. Fleck, 1993, *Strength Training for Young Athletes*. (Champaign, IL: Human Kinetics), 23.

also less likely to cause injury—and the easiest program to take along on vacation! So teach proper form for a variety of body weight alternatives to students of all ages even if your high school is lucky enough to have a state-of-the-art weight room.

Partner-Resisted Training

This training method is an extension of basic body weight exercises. Although it is difficult to gauge the intensity of this type of training, it is helpful for starting a program or living with a tight budget. Using simple equipment, such as a towel, or no equipment, partners can better isolate individual muscles or muscle groups than solo body weight exercises, much as weight machines do. They are useful with all age groups from upper elementary grades through adulthood, but especially so to those too small to fit standard exercise machines. Figures 7.3 and 7.4 show two such exercises.

When selecting partners, match height, weight, and strength levels as closely as possible to ensure safety and ease of working together. Encourage good communication and demand mature, safe behavior: Partners should also help each other maintain correct technique and high motivation through monitoring and encouraging each other.

Resistance Band Training

This training method, appropriate for upper elementary and older students, involves using either surgical tubing, rubber cords, or bands manufactured specifically for muscular strength and endurance training, such as the Exertube, Dyna Band, Flexi-Cord, or Thera-Band. Use thicker tubing for greater resistance and thinner tubing for less resistance. In addition, a student can adjust resistance by prestretching the cord more or less. Although a user cannot measure intensity precisely, this is an inexpensive, effective way to expand

Partner-Resisted Hamstring Curl

Figure 7.3

Starting Position. The trainee lies on the floor on his or her stomach, with knees flexed at about a 45-degree angle. A partner kneels facing the soles of the trainee's feet, grasping the lower leg just below the heels of the trainee (figure 7.3a).
Movement. The trainee flexes at the knees until the heels touch the buttocks (figure 7.3b). The partner resists the trainee but allows completion of the movement in approximately 6 seconds. The trainee and partner reassume the starting position and perform the next repetition.
Spotting and Safety. No spotting is needed. The partner must have a secure grip on the trainee's ankles in order to supply sufficient resistance.
Muscles Strengthened. The hamstrings group located on the back of the upper leg.

Art and exercise descriptions reprinted, by permission, from W. Kraemer and S. Fleck, 1993, *Strength Training for Young Athletes*. (Champaign, IL: Human Kinetics), 59.

Partner-Resisted Triceps Extension

Starting Position. The trainee stands erect with the feet approximately shoulder-width apart, the back straight, and the head upright. The arms are overhead with the lower arms parallel to the floor and the elbows flexed. The trainee grasps the middle of a towel, which hangs behind the trainee's head. A partner grasps the towel at both ends (figure 7.4a).
Movement. Keeping the upper arms perpendicular to the floor, the trainee straightens the elbows. The partner supplies resistance by pulling on the towel but allows the trainee's elbows to become completely straight (without locking the joint) in approximately 6 seconds (figure 7.4b). The motion is then reversed, with the trainee resisting movement and the partner supplying resistance so that the starting position is reassumed in approximately 6 seconds.

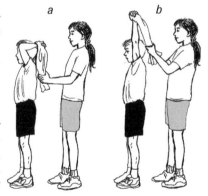

Figure 7.4

Spotting and Safety. No spotting is needed. The towel needs to be strong enough to withstand the forces encountered in the exercise.
Muscles Strengthened. Extensors of the elbow (triceps) located on the back of the upper

Art and exercise descriptions reprinted, by permission, from W. Kraemer and S. Fleck, 1993, *Strength Training for Young Athletes*. (Champaign, IL: Human Kinetics), 58.

your muscular strength and endurance training program. An added advantage is that spotting is rarely required for such exercises. Figures 7.5 and 7.6 show two resistance band exercises.

Weight Training

A program may use free or machine weights or both, depending on goals, equipment availability, and space in which to safely conduct a weight-training program. Introduce exercises one at a time by discussing each one's purpose, demonstrating correct technique, and outlining ranges of appropriate weight loads, repetitions, and speed. In addition, relate these factors to intensity, program goals, and individual goals. Follow the safety and health guidelines provided earlier in this chapter to ensure a safe and effective weight-training program. While you may opt to use weight training in addition to or in place of other forms of training, as discussed in the body weight training section, also teach students

alternative exercises that target the same muscle or muscle group. Likewise, if your program relies heavily on machine use, demonstrate the corresponding free weight exercises to broaden the chances that students will use the exercises outside of and after your program. Figure 7.7 shows the preacher bench curl as performed on a machine, and figure 7.8 shows its free weight alternative.

Addressing Motor Skills Through Muscular Strength and Endurance Activities

Simply put, a stronger, more-enduring muscle can do what it's called on to do more reliably and accurately. So increasing muscular strength and endurance enhances performance. But by the same token, you can have students perform motor skills to increase muscular strength and endurance. For example, young children enjoy playing tag games using various locomotor skills, which increase

 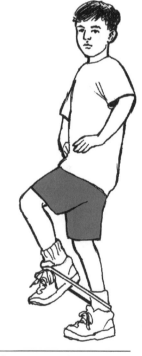 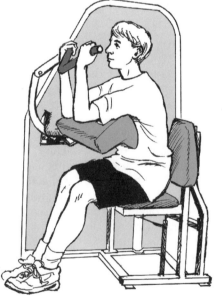 

Figure 7.5 A resistance band exercise.

Figure 7.6 A resistance band exercise.

Figure 7.7 Preacher bench curl performed on a machine.

Figure 7.8 Preacher curl performed with free weights.

Figures 7.5–7.8 from W. Westcott, 1996, *Building Strength and Stamina* (Champaign, IL: Human Kinetics).

the muscular endurance of the leg muscles. Students from fourth grade on up may enjoy team-building activities that require arm strength to conquer, such as the "circle of teamwork." This activity requires a group of students to stand in a circle, interlock their arms, stretch the circle out by walking backward, then at the tightest point, the students simultaneously lean backward. Such activities help students see how specific strength-building activities (e.g., calisthenics and weight lifting) help a person enjoy real-life as well as practical ways enjoyable activities build muscular strength and endurance in themselves. Help students see the connections among the many physical activities in your program as well as among community-based physical activities.

Safety Guidelines for Muscular Strength and Endurance Activities

In the past, many fitness and health experts as well as parents have feared strength training for children was dangerous. They pointed to the possibility of harming bone development, stunting growth. However, the research does not support these fears—as long as the child strength-trains in an age-appropriate program that emphasizes safe limits and includes adequate adult supervision. The American Or-

Around the World

Build upper-body strength and reinforce math skills with this activity. Divide students into groups of four to six students. Have them each get into push-up position and form a circle with their feet in the center and their heads facing outward. Direct the students in each group to pass a beanbag from one person to the next around the circle. Have each group count the number of passes they can make in 30 seconds, then rest 30 seconds. Conduct up to three 30-second rounds.

Adapted, by permission, from *Right Fielders Are People Too*, Hichwa 1998, p. 106 (HK).

thopedic Society for Sports Medicine, the American Academy of Pediatrics, and the NSCA have all taken the position that children can "benefit from participation in a properly prescribed and supervised resistance training program" (Kraemer and Fleck 1993). Specifically, the NSCA asserts that even in the very young child, strength can be improved through training, and strength training can begin at any age (NSCA 1996). This can include using the child's body weight in calisthenics (such as sit-ups, push-ups, and the like) or high repetitions with light weights or resistance bands. Lifting maximal weights, however, should be delayed until all the long bones have finished growing at about 17 years

Position of the National Strength and Conditioning Association on Youth Resistance Training

It is the current position of the NSCA that:

1. A properly designed and supervised resistance training program is safe for children.

2. A properly designed and supervised resistance training program can increase the strength of children.

3. A properly designed and supervised resistance training program can help to enhance the motor fitness skills and sports performance of children.

4. A properly designed and supervised resistance training program can help to prevent injuries in youth sports and recreational activities.

5. A properly designed and supervised resistance training program can help to improve the psychosocial well-being of children.

6. A properly designed and supervised resistance training program can enhance the overall health of children.

From A. Faigenbaum, 1996, "Youth Resistance Training: A Position Paper and Review of Literature," *Strength & Conditioning* 18(16):62. Reprinted by permission of the National Strength and Conditioning Association.

NSCA Youth Resistance Training Guidelines

1. Each child should be physiologically and psychologically ready to participate in a resistance training program.

2. Children should have realistic expectations. Remind children that it takes time to get in shape and learn a new skill.

3. The exercise environment should be safe and free of potential hazards.

4. The exercise session should include 5 to 10 minutes of general warm-up exercises (e.g., low intensity aerobic exercise and stretching) followed by one or more light to moderate specific warm-up sets on the chosen resistance exercises.

5. The exercise equipment should be in good repair and properly sized to fit each child.

6. All training sessions must be closely supervised by experienced fitness professionals.

7. Careful and competent instruction regarding exercise technique, training guidelines, and spotting procedures should be presented to all children.

8. Weight room "etiquette" (e.g., returning weights to proper place and respecting physical differences) should be taught to all children.

9. Start with one set of several upper and lower body exercises which focus on the major muscle groups. Include single-joint and multijoint exercises in the training program. Begin with relatively light loads (e.g. 12-15 RM) to allow for appropriate adjustments to be made.

10. The resistance should be gradually increased as strength improves. A 5 to 10% increase in overall load is appropriate for most children.

11. Progression may also be achieved by gradually increasing the number of sets, exercises, and training sessions per week. Depending upon the goal of the training program (i.e., muscular strength or local muscular endurance), 1 to 3 sets of 6 to 15 repetitions performed 2 to 3 nonconsecutive days per week is recommended. Throughout the program, observe each child's physical and mental ability to tolerate the prescribed workout.

12. Each child should feel comfortable with the prescribed program and should look forward to the next workout. If a child has concerns and/or problems with a training program, the fitness professional is expected to make the appropriate modifications.

13. Specific multijoint structural exercises (bench press, squats, leg press) may be introduced into the training program based upon individual needs and competencies. When performing any new exercise, start with a relatively light weight (or even a broomstick) to focus on learning the correct technique while minimizing muscle soreness.

14. Advanced multijoint structural exercises (e.g., Olympic lifts and modified cleans, pulls, and presses) may be incorporated into the program provided that appropriate loads are used and the focus remains on proper form. The purpose of teaching advanced multijoint lifts to children should be to develop neuromuscular coordination and skill technique. Coaching guidelines and instruction regarding resistance training and weight lifting exercises are available through the NSCA.

15. If a child seems anxious about trying a new exercise, allow the child to watch a demonstration of the exercise. Teach the child how to perform the exercise and listen to each child's concerns.

16. Incorporate the concept of periodization into the child's training program by systematically varying the resistance training program throughout the year.

17. Discourage interindividual competition and focus on participation with lots of movement and positive reinforcement.

18. Make sure that each child enjoys resistance training and is having fun. Do not force a child to participate in a resistance training program.

19. Instructors and parents should be good role models. Showing support and encouragement will help to maintain interest.

20. Children should be encouraged to drink plenty of fluids before, during, and after exercise.

21. Encourage children to participate in a variety of sports and activities.

Age-specific training guidelines, program variations, and competent supervision will make resistance training programs safe, effective, and fun for children. Instructors must understand the physical and emotional uniqueness of children and, in turn, children must appreciate the potential benefits and risks associated with resistance training. Although the needs, goals, and interests of children will continually change, resistance training should be considered a safe and effective component of youth fitness programs.

From A. Faigenbaum and W. Kraemer, 1996, *A Position Paper and Literature Review of Youth Resistance Training* (Colorado Springs, CO: National Strength and Conditioning Association, 1996), pp. 16–17. Reprinted by permission of the National Strength and Conditioning Association.

of age. In his book *Kid Fitness* (1991), Dr. Ken Cooper also recommends alternating sets of basic calisthenics with 30-second rest periods. To figure the number of reps per set, have the child count how many total reps can be done with correct form, then use half of that number as the set size. As this becomes easy, work up to two sets, then three, conscientiously applying the principles of progression and overload. Retest for maximum reps when performing three sets becomes too easy. Kraemer and Fleck (1993) recommend no less than two minutes' rest between weight-lifting sets if strength is the goal, unless an older student (middle school and above) is ready for more specialized training, depending on maturity and fitness levels.

Elementary age children from kindergarten through fourth grade should begin their resistance training program by performing body weight training only. Properly instructed and supervised older elementary age children can use resistance bands and light free weights safely. Older elementary age children can also learn how to perform partner-resisted exercises such as the partner-resisted lateral arm raise shown in figure 7.9. Make sure this age group understands that they will not necessarily build the large muscles some older adolescents and adults are able to build; this is simply not a realistic goal. Secondary students (7th–12th grades) can and should participate in resistive muscular strength and endurance activities that involve the use of free weights if they are able to do so. You do not, however, need to be restricted to dumbbell and barbell weight room activities, although, if available and proper instruction and supervision exists, incorporate them. Just

Figure 7.9 Partner-resisted lateral arm raise.

Reprinted, by permission, from W. Kraemer and S. Fleck, 1997, *Strength Training for Young Athletes*. (Champaign, IL: Human Kinetics), 57.

don't forget resistance bands, body weight exercises, homemade equipment (e.g., plastic milk jugs filled with sand), and so on.

One of the most important safety considerations is to individualize your resistance training program. In addition, encourage children to compete against themselves and not each other in terms of how much they can lift. Helping all children—kindergartners and high school seniors alike—set realistic goals and focus on correct technique are important safety precautions. To satisfy the competitive spirit in some children, however, Kraemer and Fleck (1993) suggest holding correct technique contests in which weight load plays no role in the final calculations (see figure 7.10).

Training a Student to Spot a Partner

Spotting techniques vary according to whom is reporting on the subject; however, one very important common denominator exists among everyone in the weight-training community: Proper spotting is vital to the overall safety of the individual lifting the weight and the effectiveness of incorporating the FITT principles. Although this chapter is not geared specifically to weight training, but rather to health-related physical activity that suggests weight training merely as one of many methods, suffice it to say that proper execution of spotting must be used when training your students with resistive weights. Several good books exist on weight training that incorporate spotting techniques, in particular, *Steps to Success: Weight Training Instruction* (2nd edition) by Thomas Baechle and Barney Groves (see the Recommended Reading list, at the end of this book).

Bench Press Technique

Resistance Use	40 to 50 percent of body weight.
Starting Position	Elbows are straight; feet are flat on the floor or flat on end of bench or platform; buttocks and shoulders touch bench; back is not excessively arched; bar is over upper chest; bar is horizontal.
	Points Available: 0-6 Points Earned: _____
Lowering (Eccentric) Phase	Descent of bar is controlled; elbows are out to side; forearms are perpendicular to the floor; bar touches chest at nipple level; there is no bounce on chest touch; bar is horizontal; feet stay flat on floor; back is not excessively arched; head stays still.
	Points Available: 0-7 Points Earned: _____
Up (Concentric) Phase	Back is not excessively arched; elbows are out to sides; bar is horizontal; both arms straighten at same speed; motion is smooth and continuous; head stays still; feet stay flat on floor.
	Points Available: 0-9 Points Earned: _____
Finishing Position	Same position as starting position.
	Points Available: 0-3 Points Earned: _____
	Total Points Available: 0-25 **Total Points Earned:** _____

Figure 7.10   Correct technique is vital for weight training, so focus on technique during instruction and during assessment. Reprinted, by permission, from W. Kraemer and S. Fleck, 1993, *Strength Training for Young Athletes*. (Champaign, IL: Human Kinetics), 30.

Before having an individual child begin a resistance training program using any type of equipment, ask yourself the following questions (Kraemer and Fleck 1993):

- Is the child psychologically and physically ready to participate in a resistance training program?
- What program should this particular child follow?
- Does the child know the proper lifting techniques for the chosen exercises?
- Does the child understand the necessary safety spotting techniques?
- Does the child know the safety considerations for each piece of equipment to be used?
- Does the equipment fit the child properly?
- Does the child participate in a balanced physical activity program in which resistance training is only one part?

Obviously, you will have to train and assess students systematically to ensure you can answer "yes" to all these questions for each child.

Finally, if you have one, ensure the weight room is set up so that traffic can flow through it efficiently and that there is enough room between stations. Kraemer and Fleck (1993) recommend a minimum of five feet between machines and adequate room for free weights to be dropped suddenly if need be. If possible, use machines instead of free weights for overhead movements such as those required in the bench press. Always use spotters for all but the lightest free weights, no matter the exercise. Students can work in pairs, spotting each other and monitoring correct technique.

Above all, to provide a safe and beneficial muscular strength and endurance program, do *not* use a program meant for adults with children—even with adolescents. Modify and individualize, progress slowly, and reassess your program's safety and effectiveness frequently.

Summary

By following the guidelines outlined in this chapter, you can teach students the importance of muscular strength and endurance

Your ultimate goal is that your students will take personal responsibility for health-related fitness, so give them opportunities to practice planning and implementing their own programs.

training in safe and effective ways. It is important to remember that the best way to keep each child safe is to build in individual choices and help each child to set realistic goals. Never push a child to lift a heavier weight than he or she has trained for or to perform "just one more rep." Instead, motivate children to participate and progress through creating an enjoyable and supportive class atmosphere and rewarding effort and correct technique rather than physical prowess. Chapters 11 and 12 offer a variety of muscular strength and endurance training activities as do the Physical Best activity guides for elementary and secondary levels. Resistance training can be extremely interesting and rewarding, so keep in mind as you select and adapt activities that suit your students' needs that the ultimate goal of health-related physical fitness education is to produce graduates who take personal responsibility for each area of health-related fitness as a way of life.

Chapter 8

Flexibility

Your students may have little or no knowledge of flexibility principles or practices, or they may have picked up unsafe or unhelpful information in sport or recreation settings. Thus, yours may be a task of either education or re-education so that students know correct stretching techniques and that good flexibility provides many health-related fitness benefits. Specifically, a well-designed flexibility training program (stretching on a regular basis in a progressively intense manner) can help muscles relax; improve overall health-related fitness, posture, and body symmetry; relieve muscle cramps and soreness; and reduce the risk of injury—all of which make physical activities of all types easier and safer to do (figure 8.1). In addition, stretching can relieve emotional stress and otherwise increase feelings of well-being, and can help prepare the body to move from resting to exercising more smoothly. This chapter covers the basic information regarding flexibility fitness and stretching techniques that your students should know before leaving your program, so they can apply this information to improve and maintain good flexibility for life.

Figure 8.1 Sample stretches that can help students improve flexibility.

Defining Flexibility

Flexibility is the ability of a joint and the muscles and tendons surrounding it to move freely and comfortably through its intended full range of motion (ROM). Simply put, it is the "range of motion available in a joint or group of joints" (Alter 1996). Optimal flexibility, then, allows a joint or group of joints to move efficiently. Flexibility—and the stretches that foster it—can be classified as follows (Alter 1996):

- Static—using the ROM of a joint slowly and steadily in a held position
- Dynamic—moving (quickly or slowly) in a ROM necessary for a sport movement
- Ballistic—quickly and briefly bouncing, rebounding, or using rhythmic motion in a joint's ROM (usually to mimic sport movements)
- PNF (proprioceptive neuromuscular facilitation)—using the body's reflexes to relax a muscle before stretching it, so it can be stretched farther

Note: We discuss the pros and cons of the stretches associated with ballistic and static flexibility later in the chapter.

Laxity refers to the "degree of abnormal motion of a given joint," and *hypermobility,* sometimes known as "double-jointedness," refers to excess ROM, both of which may predispose an individual to injury (Alter 1996).

Teaching Guidelines for Flexibility

Establish a regular practice of flexibility fitness and stretching in your classes. This will not only teach your students the importance of flexibility and stretching but also will allow for integration of flexibility concepts into all other aspects of health-related fitness components. Two major advantages of teaching about flexibility are that it does not require much in the way of equipment, and many activity spaces are appropriate for conducting the program. For example, you can have

Genetics and Flexibility

Although, according to Franks and Howley (1998), flexibility is limited by genetics, it is still necessary to use the joints regularly to develop and maintain the flexibility you are capable of. If this is not done, you will not be as flexible as you could be. For example, if a person breaks an arm at the elbow, when the cast is removed, the person will have to reteach the joint to move through its normal ROM. This is because, while the arm was immobilized in the cast, fibrous connective tissue, called "adhesions," began to cling to the ligaments, tendons, and bones in the elbow, impeding its ROM. In addition, because the cast held the arm at a fixed angle, the tendons and muscles in the upper arm shortened, preventing the arm from straightening after the cast is removed. Both the condition of the connective tissues at the joint and the ability of the muscle to stretch affect flexibility. This is true even without the problems caused by wearing a cast. Stretching helps maintain the proper muscle-tendon unit length while helping prevent adhesions. Stretching is an important part of both warm-ups and cool-downs because, along with other gentle activities, stretching helps get the joints ready for more strenuous activity by encouraging the body to release fluids that lubricate the joints and increasing the size of the soft cartilage around the joint to help absorb the shock of impact.

students stretch in a gymnasium, on a field, on blacktop, in a classroom, or, if there's little through traffic, in a hallway. Use mats or parachutes laid on the ground to protect cloth-

THE FAR SIDE   By GARY LARSON

The Vikings, of course, knew the importance of stretching before an attack.

ing outdoors. Visual aids such as posters, task cards, and pictures of schoolmates performing stretches help guide students working independently at stations.

Stress safety and gradual, individualized progression when teaching children about flexibility. Never make flexibility training competitive; instead, as with muscular strength training, emphasize correct technique and personal bests. Younger or less-experienced students need to learn basic static stretches that increase the flexibility of the major muscle groups. Older or more experienced students may be ready for a greater variety of muscle- and activity-specific stretches. Above all, dispel the "no pain, no gain" notion (see section titled Safety Training Guidelines for Flexibility Activities later in this chapter). See *Physical Best Activity Guide—Elementary Level* and *Physical Best Activity Guide—Secondary Level* for further guidelines and activities for teaching flexibility fitness and stretching.

Overload, FITT, Progression, and Specificity Principles

All your students need to know how to apply the overload, FITT, and progression principles to achieve the basic level of health-related fitness in the area of flexibility. Note that flexibility intensity involves how the stretch

Elastic and Plastic and When to Stretch

The argument for warming up indicates that muscles and other tissues are easier to stretch when they are warm. The connective tissues are easier to stretch when they are warm. The connective tissues of the muscle-tendon unit have both "elastic" and "plastic" properties. The elastic property allows the tissue to return to its normal length following stretching; the plastic property is what establishes its normal length when at rest. The stretching routine is aimed at changing the plastic property, so that the joint can move through its normal range of motion. It is easier to lengthen the connective tissues while minimizing tissue damage if the muscle-tendon unit is already warm. The contrasting argument suggests that muscles are normally "warm," and light warm-up activities don't increase that very much. We recommend that you have the participants do some light stretching activities at the beginning of an exercise session and a more thorough program of stretching during the cool-down when body temperature is elevated and greater flexibility gains can be made.

Reprinted, by permission, Franks and Howley 1998, p. 92.

feels; time is the length of time a stretch is held multiplied by the number of times each stretch is performed; and type is the specific muscles the stretch addresses. That is, you must stretch leg muscles to have more flexible legs and arm muscles to have more flexible arms. Table 8.1 outlines these principles applied to flexibility, based on fitness goals.

As with other areas of health-related fitness covered thus far in this book, some students will seek additional information and guidance from you regarding flexibility. Keep in mind that each individual should gradually progress to a higher level of fitness in this component, depending on his or her goals, abilities, and interests. Make sure, too, that the athlete knows that ballistic stretching should only be added in a closely supervised, sport-specific situation (see Training Methods for Flexibility).

Intensity is an extremely important factor in a safe and effective flexibility training program. A static stretch that goes beyond the point of mild discomfort to pain merely increases the likelihood of injury. When it comes

to intensity and flexibility, overloading is moving just beyond the existing ROM (Alter 1996). Overloading may also involve one or more of the other parts of the FITT principle: stretching more often (frequency), holding a stretch longer (time), or stretching specific muscles (type). Naturally, safe overloading involves increasing all aspects of the FITT principle in a gradual, progressive manner. Indeed, as with other aspects of health-related physical fitness, overloading without pain is the only way to increase flexibility.

Training Methods for Flexibility

The two main types of flexibility of interest to physical educators are also the names of the two main types of training: static and ballistic. Which is "better" or more appropriate in which situation is the subject of much debate among sport scientists, laypeople, physical educators, coaches, and participants.

Static Stretching

Static stretching is generally most appropriate for physical education settings. Its advantages include proven effectiveness in enhancing ROM and ease of implementation. A program of static stretches (like those shown in figure 8.2) does not take much class time, and it is generally easier to ensure each individual in a large group of students is performing them correctly. Some researchers believe that static stretching makes it easier to stretch

Physical Best's Position

Despite Franks and Howley's (1998) recommendations, many other experts caution that participants perform at least five minutes of low-intensity aerobic endurance activity before performing any stretching. Thus, Physical Best recommends you have students take this simple precaution.

Table 8.1   The FITT Principle Applied to Flexibility Training, Based on Fitness Goals *

	Base health-related fitness	Intermediate health-related fitness	Athletic performance fitness
Frequency	Before and after each activity/exercise session (minimum of 3 times per week)	Before and after each activity/exercise session (daily)	Before and after each training session
Intensity	To mild tension, or slight muscular discomfort	To mild tension, or slight muscular discomfort	To mild tension, or slight muscular discomfort, at a level appropriate for sport participation
Time	10–15 s; 2 times per stretch	10–15 s; 3 times per stretch	Dependent on static, dynamic, or ballistic (usually conducted by qualified trainer/coach)
Type	Static; major muscle groups	Static; major muscle groups, introduction of dynamic stretching	Usually dynamic and/or ballistic; major muscle groups and sport-specific stretches
Overload	Not necessary at base level	Ask student to identify level of stretch intensity; if appropriate for activity, have student stretch slightly farther than previous same stretch	As dynamic and ballistic stretches dominate advanced level, overload is not appropriate to ballistic stretching
Progression and specificity	Start very easy into stretch; slow movements with minimal applied resistance to muscle involved	Stretch major core muscles first, then move to extremities; begin introduction of dynamic flexibility	Start with easy multi-joint dynamic movements, progressing to more resistive dynamic movements, followed by moderate static and/or PNF stretching

*A warm-up of full body movement, such as walking, jogging or stationary bicycle must precede any flexibility training activities. Generally, five minutes is sufficient; however, age appropriateness and level of current fitness of students should be considered.

Be sure the student has sufficiently had time to warm up all muscles, primarily those muscles involved in the flexibility activities.

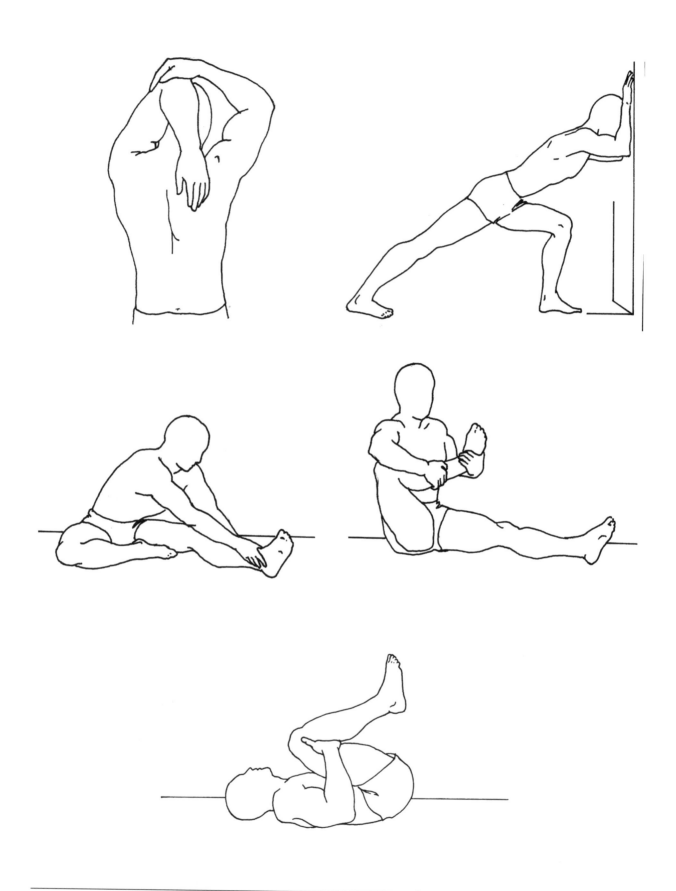

Figure 8.2 Several examples of static stretches.

Reprinted, by permission, from M. Alter, *Sport Stretch*. (Champaign, IL: Human Kinetics), 30-31.

A static stretch to improve hamstring flexibility.

specific muscles (that is, *type* in the FITT principle; Thigpen 1984). Others believe static stretching is better than ballistic stretching because it takes less energy, generally results in less muscle soreness, and can relieve muscle distress (de Vries 1966, 1986).

The arguments against static stretching include that it's boring and that it isn't specific enough, that is, it doesn't replicate sport movements well enough to do much good. In addition, stretching used as a complete warm-up does nothing to actually warm up the body. Some question whether static stretching helps prevent injury (Murphy 1991).

Ballistic Stretching

Also known as *dynamic*, *fast*, *isotonic*, or *kinetic* stretching, ballistic stretching usually involves bouncing, bobbing, rebounding, and rhythmic motion. Often maligned as dangerous, some experts argue it has its place in certain situations. According to Alter (1996), major arguments in favor of ballistic stretching are that it develops dynamic flexibility (needed during actual movements) and team camaraderie (because it can be done in cadence as a group) and is generally more interesting.

Arguments against ballistic stretching include inadequate time for tissues to adapt to the motion, increased likelihood of soreness,

The Ballistic Stretching Controversy

There are many exercise scientists, coaches, and personal trainers who believe ballistic stretching, used appropriately, can be helpful in improving a person's skill-related fitness. However, there are many physical educators who believe that ballistic stretching should not be taught in physical education because (1) static stretching is more important to maintaining good health and (2) ballistic stretching is more likely to be harmful if not performed properly. It is the opinion of the Physical Best Steering Committee that ballistic stretching not be taught in an elementary, middle, or high school physical education program. However, if a student athlete asks about ballistic stretching to help his or her sport performance, physical educators should provide appropriate information.

Guidelines for Safe Ballistic Stretching

Ballistic stretching can be performed safely to enhance sport-specific movements. Teach interested student athletes the following guidelines (Arthur and Bailey 1998; Baechle 1996):

- Warm up first with a whole-body activity.
- Perform static stretching before ballistic.
- Do quick movements that duplicate specific sport movements.
- Keep movements gentle and controlled despite speed.
- Choose movements that isolate individual muscles or muscle groups needed for the targeted sport-specific movements.
- Avoid overstretching (overloading too aggressively).
- Increase ROM and speed gradually and progressively.

initiation of the stretch reflex, and inadequate time for neurological pathways to adapt to the movement (Alter 1996). In short, some believe ballistic stretches are too fast and that the stretch reflex will actually cause the tissue involved to contract rather than relax.

The Physical Best program recommends that physical educators focus on teaching the principles, practices, and specific exercises of static stretching as part of a safe and effective lifelong health-related fitness program.

Addressing Motor Skills Through Flexibility Activities

Naturally, an individual who can move through a full range of motion (ROM) in the joints involved in a movement is more likely to be ready to learn to perform the movement correctly. Likewise, a student with limited ROM will have a harder time mastering the same motor skill. Good flexibility, then, enhances the possibility of motor skill development. Address motor skills through flexibility activities and vice versa by pointing out the connections between the stretches you're teaching students and the motor skill activities they're practicing in class. When students see the connections between flexibility and the physical activities they're engaging in, they are more likely to continue working on enhancing flexibility as a lifestyle choice. In short, you create a deeper awareness of the need for flexibility.

Safety Guidelines for Flexibility Activities

The three main keys to safe stretching in the physical education setting are using slow, controlled movements (static stretches), warming up with whole-body activity first, and encouraging students to individualize their efforts. Beyond these points, be aware that several factors may limit flexibility in an individual, the primary factor being lack of regular participation in an adequate flexibility training program. In addition, research shows that females and individuals under 6 and between 12 and young adulthood are generally more flexible than males or individuals between 6 and 12 years of age and older adults (Alter 1996). Although it is widely believed that excess body weight may impede flexibility around certain joints, the research does not seem to support this belief (Alter 1996). No matter the general trends, however, most people can improve their flexibility through appropriate and regular stretching.

A number of factors may limit flexibility. Take each possible limit into account for each

The trunk lift measures trunk extensor strength and flexibility.

Teach students the concepts of flexibility and how to individualize their efforts to improve.

individual when designing a flexibility training program (Alter 1996):

1. Connective tissues in joints or muscles that lack elasticity
2. Tension in muscles
3. Poor coordination and strength during active movement
4. Limitations caused by bone and joint structures
5. Pain

Although most of these can be overcome in a well-designed, appropriately progressive flexibility program, pain should never be ignored, and limitations caused by bone or joint structures may require special attention and individualization. Teach your students to use static stretching, moving slowly and steadily only to the point of mild tension, not pain—regardless of what they've been told in the past. They should hold the stretch 10 to 15 seconds, depending on what is comfortable for them, not what a classmate can do. In these ways, you empower students to individualize

each stretch—and the flexibility training program—for themselves. Teach students that ballistic stretching is only appropriate in certain sport situations and then only if done correctly.

If you believe a student is too flexible (displays hypermobility of the joints), has abnormal ROM (laxity), severely lacks flexibility, or has other unusual bone or joint structural limitations, and such an anomaly seems to cause serious performance or safety problems, refer the student to trained health care professionals, such as a certified athletic trainer, physical therapist, or an orthopedic medical specialist. Then have the student and parents ask this professional for specific recommendations for safe participation in physical education. Meet with the student and parents to discuss and document these recommendations.

Summary

Flexibility is just as important to health-related fitness as other components, so resist the temptation to always relegate it to warm-ups and cool-downs. When appropriate, feature it as the core activity of a lesson to give you the time to demonstrate how important, relaxing, and pleasurable it is. See *Physical Best Activity Guide—Elementary Level* and *Physical Best Activity Guide—Secondary Level* for model flexibility training lessons. Then you can refer to the basic concepts and principles of flexibility as you use it to enhance performance in other areas of the physical education curriculum. Finally, remember that, while ballistic stretching can be effective in some circumstances, it is more appropriate to use static stretching in a health-related physical fitness education program.

Chapter 9

Body Composition

Few physical educators would deny that teaching about body composition is one of the most sensitive areas of health-related physical fitness education. Certainly, cultural, social, and personal beliefs and attitudes make this a difficult topic, making the temptation to avoid the subject great. Yet understanding body composition, what affects it, and the benefits of a healthy body composition is critical to overall health-related fitness. Note, too, that while it is not important to calculate exact body composition indicators with very young children, these children still need to explore the related concepts and understand how physical activity affects body composition. Older children need this information, too, as well as tools to monitor and positively affect body composition throughout life.

Defining Body Composition

Body composition is the ratio of lean body mass (all tissues not fat, such as bone, muscle, organs) to body fat, usually expressed in terms of *percent body fat*. There are several common ways to gauge whether or not body composition is healthy, with a range of what constitutes a healthy body composition. Table 9.1

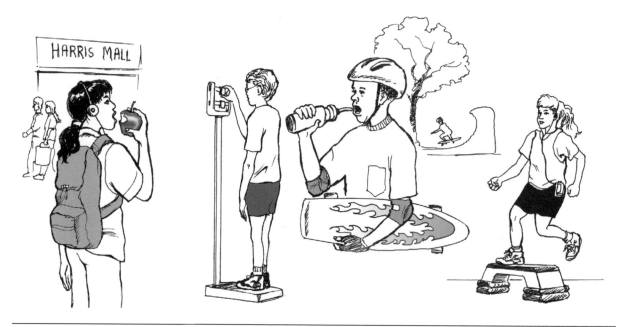

A thorough understanding of body composition, what affects it, and the benefits of a healthy body composition is critical to overall health-related fitness.

gives recommended ranges for body fat (Franks and Howley 1998).

Teaching Guidelines for Body Composition

There are four main aspects to teaching students about body composition in a sensitive and professional manner:

1. Project an attitude of acceptance toward individual differences and demand that students follow your lead with their peers.

2. Respect each individual's privacy.

3. Relate body composition to the other three components of health-related fitness in meaningful ways.

4. Acknowledge whether or not you can help an individual who is over or under an appropriate body composition, and refer the student or parents to professional help if you cannot.

Accepting Individual Differences

Avoid asserting that there are absolute indicators of good and poor health related to body composition. Remember, experts cannot even agree completely as to what constitutes a healthy body composition or how this is best measured.

Approach body composition as an individual and personal issue that everyone should try to be compassionate about. Never use a student as a positive or negative role model of body composition. Also discuss that heredity plays a role in body composition. Make it a point to openly discuss how various cultures view and influence body fatness. For example, eating disorders are more common in the industrialized world than in developing nations, as the media has "taught" us that thinness equals "attractiveness." At the same time, high-fat food is readily available in oversized portions from fast-food restaurants and other outlets such as snack machines. Adding to the problem is an overemphasis on sedentary recreational activities such as TV, video

Table 9.1 Recommended Body Fat		
	Males	**Females**
Minimum healthy body fat	10%	17%
Maximum healthy body fat	25%	32%

games, and spectator sports. Contentment with body weight varies among ethnic groups as cultural differences influence perceptions. For example, white women are more likely to express dissatisfaction with their body weights than are black women of the same weight. Not surprisingly, then, African American women are less likely to develop eating disorders than white women (Wilfley 1996 in Walsh and Devlin 1998; Pike and Walsh 1996 in Walsh and Devlin 1998).

As a physical educator, encourage individuals to find personal satisfaction with their overall health, wellness, and physical activity habits, rather than struggling to measure up to scientific methods of calculating body composition or cultural expectations.

Respecting Privacy

Never publicize a student's measurements or percent body fat and be sure to secure the information where it cannot be accessed by other students. Conduct skinfold caliper testing and any other measuring in private as a

All students can benefit from being physically active, regardless of their body composition.

voluntary activity. Obtain help with testing or with conducting the rest of the class safely while you are occupied with this procedure. Explain to students that body composition is a personal matter and they should only focus on their own information. Check with your administrator to see if it would be wise to obtain parental permission for skinfold testing or at least if you should notify parents of upcoming testing and have another adult present during testing to prevent harassment issues.

Relating Body Composition to Other Health-Related Fitness Components

As with any other component of health-related fitness, an individual's body composition does not happen in isolation from the other components. Indeed, it is perhaps even more important to show students the connections among all four components so that they can clearly see how their personal choices impact this area of health-related fitness. While genetics, environment, and culture play significant roles in body composition, it is in large part a result of the individual's physical activitiy levels in the other components:

- Muscular strength and endurance—muscle cells burn (metabolize) more calories at rest than fat cells. (Keep in mind that this effect takes place over a long period of time, and it is more difficult for women to obtain because it is more difficult for women to build large muscle mass.)
- Aerobic fitness—aerobic activities burn calories and raise resting metabolism rates.
- Flexibility—a flexible body can better tolerate muscular strength and endurance and aerobic endurance activities.

Strive to point out connections among physical activity, diet, and body composition related to daily life, recreational, and physical education activities. Emphasize, too, that a student who is overfat because of genetics

Strength Training and Body Composition Management

Strength training can be a valuable adjunct to a body composition management program. A weight reduction program can cause loss of protein tissue (primary muscle) along with body fat. Strength training can prevent significant loss of lean body mass, while also preventing decreases in resting energy expenditure (REE; the energy the body uses at rest). Each additional pound of muscle tissue can raise the REE by 35 kilocalories per day (Campbell et al. 1994), which, over the course of a year, can result in weight loss.

However, students need to know that

1. although resistance training does burn calories, the effect is relatively small compared to that of aerobic exercise, and

2. it is physiologically impossible for muscle cells to turn into fat in the future, and vice versa. A combination of aerobic exercise and light resistance training is best for body composition management.

Overweight or Obese?

The words *overweight* and *obese* are often used interchangeably, but there is a difference. In fact, a person might be overweight without being obese. This is because the height-weight charts do not take into account that some people carry more muscle weight. Let's look at two women who are the same height, weight, and frame size.

Jane and Jeanette both weigh 130 pounds, are 5'6", and have medium-size frames. But tests show that Jane is carrying 45 pounds of fat, while Jeanette only has 25 pounds of fat. Jane's percent body fat is calculated as follows:

$$45 \div 130 = .35 \text{ (rounded to the nearest 100th)}$$

$$.35 \times 100 = 35\% \text{ body fat}$$

Jeanette's percent body fat is:

$$25 \div 130 = .19 \text{ (rounded to the nearest 100th)}$$

$$.19 \times 100 = 19\% \text{ body fat}$$

Jane's percent body fat is nearly twice Jeanette's even though they are the same weight! In fact, Jane is obese because she is over 32 percent body fat, the guideline fo adolescent female obesity. So although height-weight charts can narrow down who has potential body composition problems, they do not tell the whole story.

can still greatly reduce health risks by being physically active. In fact, one study revealed that overfat people who exercise regularly are at no greater health risk than thin people who don't exercise (Blair 1995).

Helping the Overfat or Underfat Student

You most likely will have students who, either through formal testing or informal observa-tions, appear to be over or under appropriate percent body fat. While it is beyond the scope of a physical educator to treat serious prob-lems such as eating disorders or extreme obe-sity, you may be able to point such students or their parents toward professional help. If you are concerned about a particular student, use the following guidelines to approach the situ-ation in a professional manner:

• Always maintain student and family pri-vacy.

- Approach the student and/or parents diplomatically.

- Respect parental wishes unless you believe, as in the case of suspected anorexia nervosa, the child is in danger. (See chapter 10 for more about eating disorders.)

- Work with other school personnel such as the school nurse, and seek written permission to share your observations with the child's health care provider. At the same time, seek advice as to how you can tailor your program to meet the child's needs.

- Ensure your program is interesting and promotes physical activity as a lifestyle choice for all students. Avoid unreasonable expectations. For example, obese children are more likely to maintain and therefore benefit from mild physical activity than moderate-to-vigorous physical activity (USDHHS 1999).

- Deal with only less serious problems; know when you're in over your head and refer such students to a professional qualified to treat the problem.

Methods of Measuring Body Composition

Experts do not agree on what the best method for measuring body composition is. Elementary students should be taught the basic concepts of body composition and what affects it, while secondary students should be taught specific methods of assessing body composition and their pros and cons.

Skinfold Caliper Testing

This is the most commonly used method for determining body composition in the physical education setting. It involves using calipers to take skinfold measurements at specific sites on the body (figure 9.1).

This is the most accurate way of measuring body composition generally available to the physical educator, and it is relatively inexpensive to implement. However, a tester must be well-trained to take reliable measurements, the measuring takes a great deal of class time

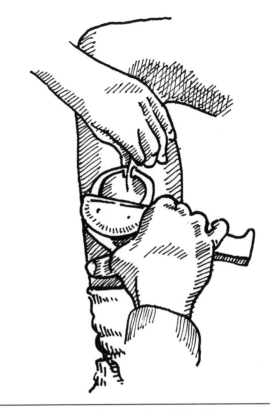

Figure 9.1 Using calipers to take a calf skinfold measurement.

Reprinted, by permission, from The Cooper Institute for Aerobic Research, in press, *FITNESSGRAM Test Administrator's Manual, 2nd Ed.* (Champaign, IL: Human Kinetics).

and teacher attention, and concerns about potentially being accused of sexual abuse are greater than with other common methods, as it involves actually touching a student. If you do not feel comfortable with or qualified to perform this testing method, obtain further training or arrange for more qualified personnel to help you (perhaps the school nurse or someone from the physical education department of a local university). High school students can learn to take a partner's skinfold measurements, but these will not provide reliable data. However, this approach introduces this technique in a meaningful way. (See chapter 17 for proper protocols for administering skinfold caliper testing.)

Body Mass Index

Although attention paid by the media to body mass index (BMI) has recently risen, this method of determining body composition is nothing new. Even so, researchers do not agree on what the exact range for a healthy

BMI is, but, in general, BMIs under 25 are safe. BMI is a ratio between weight and height. It is a mathematical formula that correlates with body fat. Some argue that BMI can drop too low, but others disagree.

BMI provides a quick body composition check a person can self-administer, especially using a chart such as that shown in table 9.2. This method takes little class time and teacher attention and is easy for a student to use outside a physical education program. Its primary disadvantage, however, is that it is a vast oversimplification of the body composition picture, as it does not take into account percent body fat. For example, any two individuals at the same BMI and fitness level may have differing fat-to-lean mass ratios, based on genetic and nutritional factors such as bone size and density (see example in the Overweight or Obese? sidebar earlier in the chapter). Or any two people with the same BMI may have vastly differing percents body fat. In short, a person can be fit and healthy or unfit and unhealthy at any of the BMIs within the extremes of clinical obesity and severe underfatness. Even so, BMI gives us one indicator of health and wellness. Look closely at students with BMIs at the extremes for causes and solutions (see Helping the Overfat or Underfat Student earlier in this chapter).

Height-Weight Charts

Height-weight charts arose in the late 1950s as insurance companies attempted to scientifi-

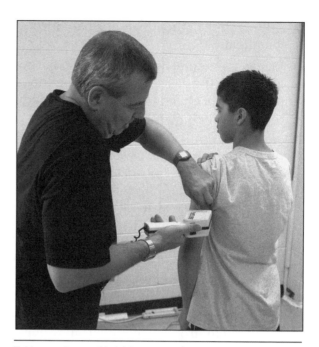

Taking a triceps skinfold measurement.

cally predict which clients were lower or higher risks. As with BMI, they are oversimplifications of body composition data, as they do not take into account percent body fat. While using wall charts may make teaching progression simpler, it does not provide accurate results, and it has often led to public posting of comparisons of students' body compositions (something that must be avoided at all costs!).

Waist-to-Hip Ratio

Because some research shows that where body fat is distributed may affect how unhealthful it is, scientists have investigated the correlation between waist-to-hip ratios and health risks. The findings indicate that it is better to be pear-shaped than apple-shaped; that is, it may be better to have excess weight on the hips and thighs than around the waist (Wickelgren 1998). Waist-to-hip ratio is a simple way to evaluate how pear- or apple-shaped a person is. For example, a person with a waist measurement of 28 inches and a hip measurement of 38 inches would have a waist-to-hip ratio of .74 (28÷38 = .736, rounded to the nearest hundredth). Ratios above .86 in women and .95 in men indicate "appleness"

Calculating BMI

To calculate an individual's BMI, simply find height in meters and weight in kilograms and plug that information into the following formula:

$$BMI = weight\ (kg) \div height^2\ (m^2)$$

For example, a boy who weighs 55 kg (121 pounds) and is 1.64 m (5'3") tall has a BMI of:

$$55 \div (1.64)^2 = 20.4$$

or 20, rounded to the nearest whole number. (For BMI calculations using inches and pounds, see table 9.2)

Table 9.2 BMI Chart

Weight (lb)	Height (in.)																							
	55	56	57	58	59	60	61	62	63	64	65	66	67	68	69	70	71	72	73	74	75	76	77	78
40	9	9	9	8	8	8	8	7	7	7	7	6	6	6	6	6	6	5	5	5	5	5	5	5
45	10	10	10	9	9	9	9	8	8	8	7	7	7	7	7	6	6	6	6	6	6	5	5	5
50	12	11	11	10	10	10	9	9	9	9	8	8	8	8	7	7	7	7	7	6	6	6	6	6
55	13	12	12	11	11	11	10	10	10	9	9	9	9	8	8	8	8	7	7	7	7	7	7	6
60	14	13	13	13	12	12	11	11	11	10	10	10	9	9	9	9	8	8	8	8	8	7	7	7
65	15	15	14	14	13	13	12	12	12	11	11	10	10	10	10	9	9	9	9	8	8	8	8	8
70	16	16	15	15	14	14	13	13	12	12	12	11	11	11	10	10	10	9	9	9	9	9	8	8
75	17	17	16	16	15	15	14	14	13	13	12	12	12	11	11	11	10	10	10	10	9	9	9	9
80	19	18	17	17	16	16	15	15	14	14	13	13	13	12	12	11	11	11	11	10	10	10	9	9
85	20	19	18	18	17	17	16	16	15	15	14	14	13	13	13	12	12	12	11	11	11	10	10	10
90	21	20	19	19	18	18	17	16	16	15	15	15	14	14	13	13	13	12	12	12	11	11	11	10
95	22	21	21	20	19	19	18	17	17	16	16	15	15	14	14	14	13	13	13	12	12	12	11	11
100	23	22	22	21	20	20	19	18	18	17	17	16	16	15	15	14	14	14	13	13	13	12	12	12
105	24	24	23	22	21	21	20	19	19	18	17	17	16	16	16	15	15	14	14	13	13	13	12	12
110	26	25	24	23	22	21	21	20	19	19	18	18	17	17	16	16	15	15	15	14	14	13	13	13
115	27	26	25	24	23	22	22	21	20	19	19	18	18	17	17	16	16	15	15	15	14	14	14	13
120	28	27	26	25	24	23	23	22	21	21	20	19	19	18	18	17	17	16	16	16	15	15	14	14
125	29	28	27	26	25	24	24	23	22	21	21	20	20	19	18	18	17	17	16	16	16	15	15	14
130	30	29	28	27	26	25	25	24	23	22	22	21	20	20	19	19	18	18	17	17	16	16	15	15
135	31	30	29	28	27	26	26	25	24	23	22	22	21	21	20	19	19	18	18	17	17	16	16	16
140	33	31	30	29	28	27	26	26	25	24	23	23	22	21	21	20	20	19	18	18	18	17	17	16
145	34	33	31	30	29	28	27	27	26	25	24	23	23	22	21	21	20	20	19	19	18	18	17	17
150	35	34	32	31	30	29	28	27	27	26	25	24	23	23	22	22	21	20	20	19	19	18	18	17
155	36	35	34	32	31	30	29	28	27	27	26	25	24	24	23	22	22	21	20	20	19	19	18	18
160	37	36	35	33	32	31	30	29	28	27	27	26	25	24	24	23	22	22	21	21	20	19	19	18
165	38	37	36	34	33	32	31	30	29	28	27	27	26	25	24	24	23	22	22	21	21	20	20	19
170	40	38	37	36	34	33	32	31	30	29	28	27	27	26	25	24	24	23	22	22	21	21	20	20
175	41	39	38	37	35	34	33	32	31	30	29	28	27	27	26	25	24	24	23	22	22	21	21	20
180	42	40	39	38	36	35	34	33	32	31	30	29	28	27	27	26	25	24	24	23	23	22	21	21
185	43	41	40	39	37	36	35	34	33	32	31	30	29	28	27	27	26	25	24	24	23	23	22	21
190	44	43	41	40	38	37	36	35	34	33	32	31	30	29	28	27	27	26	25	24	24	23	23	22
195	45	44	42	41	39	38	37	36	35	33	32	31	31	30	29	28	27	26	26	25	24	24	23	23
200	46	45	43	42	40	39	38	37	35	34	33	32	31	30	30	29	28	27	26	26	25	24	24	23
205	48	46	44	43	41	40	39	38	36	35	34	33	32	31	30	29	29	28	27	26	26	25	24	24
210	49	47	45	44	42	41	40	38	37	36	35	34	33	32	31	30	29	28	27	26	26	25	25	24
215	50	48	47	45	43	42	41	39	38	37	36	35	34	33	32	31	30	29	28	28	27	26	26	25
220	51	49	48	46	44	43	42	40	39	38	37	36	35	33	32	31	30	29	28	28	27	26	26	25
225	52	50	49	47	45	44	43	41	40	39	37	36	35	34	33	32	31	31	30	29	28	27	27	26
230	53	52	50	48	46	45	43	42	41	39	38	37	36	35	34	33	32	31	30	30	29	28	27	27
235	55	53	51	49	47	46	44	43	42	40	39	38	37	36	35	34	33	32	31	30	29	29	28	27
240	56	54	52	50	48	47	45	44	43	41	40	39	38	37	35	34	33	33	32	31	30	29	28	28
245	57	55	53	51	49	48	46	45	43	42	41	40	38	37	36	35	34	33	32	31	31	30	29	28
250	58	56	54	52	51	49	47	46	44	43	42	40	39	38	37	36	35	34	33	32	31	30	30	29
255	59	57	55	53	52	50	48	47	45	44	42	41	40	39	38	37	36	35	34	33	32	31	30	29
260	60	58	56	54	53	51	49	48	46	45	43	42	41	40	38	37	36	35	34	33	33	32	31	30
265	62	59	57	55	54	52	50	48	47	45	44	43	42	40	39	38	37	36	35	34	33	32	31	31
270	63	61	58	56	55	53	51	49	48	46	45	44	42	41	40	39	38	37	36	35	34	33	32	31

BMI category	Health risk	BMI category	Health risk	BMI category	Health risk
19–24	Minimal	27–29	Moderate	35–39	Very high
25–26	Low	30–34	High	40+	Extremely high

It's important to relate body composition to other health-related fitness components. For example, aerobic fitness activities burn calories and raise resting metabolism rates.

and indicate higher risk of heart disease and diabetes. These numbers have not been adjusted or validated for children, however, so the usefulness of this test is limited in the health-related physical fitness education program.

Summary

Although approaching body composition in the physical education setting can be a delicate matter, it is just as important as any other health-related component of physical fitness.

Handle body composition instruction professionally and effectively by focusing on how an active lifestyle positively impacts body composition rather than overemphasizing test results. This is where connecting this material to the other components of health-related fitness comes in. Remember, make testing voluntary and respect each student's privacy. Finally, learn to recognize when a student's body composition is a serious health concern and refer such children to qualified health care professionals. You will also find the next chapter on nutrition helpful in teaching about body composition.

Chapter 10

Nutrition

The science of nutrition defines and explains the human body's dietary need for specific chemical substances to maintain life. We all have the same general nutritional needs, but the amounts of specific nutrients that we each require vary according to age, gender, heredity, and lifestyle. Each of us has several diet options that can afford pleasurable eating while meeting individual nutritional requirements. Thus the amount of energy and the quantity of nutrients we require are best tailored individually. The challenge we each face is to obtain all the essential nutrients from our individual diets. Use the information in this chapter to teach your students about proper nutrition in age-appropriate ways. The *Physical Best Activity Guide—Elementary Level* and *Physical Best Activity Guide—Secondary Level* also provide specific activities in the body composition activity chapters to help you teach about nutrition.

What Is Diet?

Diet is the total intake of food (and supplements, if any) consumed in a five-to-seven-day period. No single food or single meal defines the diet. Over a 70-year life span, a person will eat some 70,000 meals—about

1,000 each year—plus snacks. Is it any wonder that eating is automatic?

Although all foods have nutritional value—there are no "junk" foods with absolutely *no* nutritional value—clearly some foods are more valuable than others. In making sure we take in good nutrition, the primary goals are to

- provide a variety of different foods,
- supply all the nutrients in adequate amounts, and
- supply sufficient energy (calories) to maintain an ideal body mass.

Infinite ways exist for each of us to meet these dietary needs. Taste, culture, and economics often affect what we choose. Researchers have developed broad, useful guidelines to encourage individuals to obtain the essential amounts of the nutrients they need to promote growth and development and to maintain an ideal body mass, regardless of personal preferences. The following three agencies have developed such guidelines:

- The Committee on Dietary Allowances establishes guidelines called the Recommended Dietary Allowances (RDA). The RDA cite the amount of each nutrient required on an average day to meet the needs of most healthy people under usual environmental conditions in the United States.
- The Food and Drug Administration develops standard formats for food labeling (figure 10.1).
- The U.S. Department of Agriculture (USDA) designed the Food Guide Pyramid (figure 10.2) to graphically show the most necessary nutrients within each food group, the number of recommended servings, the size of such servings, and foods within each group categorized by nutrient and density.

Behavioral Foundations of Diet

For countless generations food choices were largely determined by what people could grow (farm) or catch. Knowing and choosing what to eat was fairly easy—people simply ate what was available. Of course, we have much more choice today, making it more difficult to decide what food to eat. We must *learn* how to make healthy choices.

All people require the same nutrients, but in amounts that vary from individual to individual and from stage to stage in life. Neonatal and infant nutrition set the stage for the later interaction of home and school in influencing a child's nutritional habits. After undergoing extremely rapid growth during the first year of life, a child continues to develop and change, but somewhat less quickly. The cumulative effects over the next decade are remarkable. A child enters the school system at a critical stage of growth and development, which will continue through the elementary, middle, and high school years. To have a healthy diet, a child must eat food that provides all the nutrients (particularly iron, trace elements, calcium, protein, and vitamins) in adequate quantities over a five-to-seven-day period—all the time.

The childhood years offer the best chance for parents and teachers to influence not only

Food Labels at a Glance

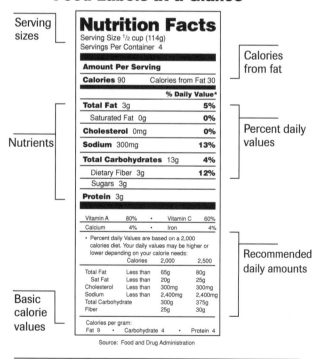

Figure 10.1 The standard format for food labeling, as developed by the Food and Drug Administration. impact.

Reprinted, by permission, from AAHPERD, 1999, *Physical Best Activity Guide—Elementary Level*. (Champaign, IL: Human Kinetics), 66.

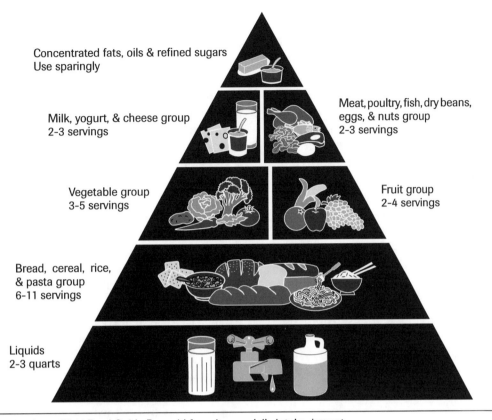

Concentrated fats, oils & refined sugars
Use sparingly

Milk, yogurt, & cheese group
2-3 servings

Meat, poultry, fish, dry beans,
eggs, & nuts group
2-3 servings

Vegetable group
3-5 servings

Fruit group
2-4 servings

Bread, cereal, rice,
& pasta group
6-11 servings

Liquids
2-3 quarts

Figure 10.2 A modified Food Guide Pyramid focusing on daily intake. impact.

Reprinted, by permission, from AAHPERD, 1999, *Physical Best Activity Guide—Elementary Level*. (Champaign, IL: Human Kinetics), 67.

current but also future food choices, and thus to help develop good eating behaviors. Parents are the gatekeepers; they control and influence the availability and choices of food in their children's environment. As a physical educator, you must actively help educate parents about nutrition. It is critical that parents and teachers help establish *good* eating habits at the elementary school level and make students aware of the relationship between nutrition and health, both now and for the future. The concept of balance and moderation to obtain and maintain an ideal body weight is crucial in preventing such eating disorders as overweight (obesity) and underweight (including anorexia).

A person's total nutrient needs are greater during adolescence than at any other time of life, except pregnancy and lactation. According to the USDA guidelines, during adolescence girls need 2,200 calories a day, whereas boys require 3,000 calories a day (Saltman, Gurin, and Mothner 1993). Nutrient needs rise throughout adolescence and then level off (or

even diminish slightly) as an adolescent becomes an adult.

Of course, adolescents make many more choices for themselves than do young children, both about their activity level and what they eat. Social or peer pressures may push them to make both good and bad choices. Children and adolescents acquire information—and misinformation—on nutrition from personal, immediate experiences. They are concerned with how diet can improve their lives and looks *now*, so they may engage in crash dieting or the latest fad in weight gain or loss. It is also common to see increased calorie consumption, especially of fats and carbohydrates, among adolescents.

Counting Calories

A *calorie* is the amount of energy it takes to raise the temperature of one gram of water one degree Celsius. The body's needs are much greater than water's, of course, so we measure energy in *kilocalories* (1,000 calories, or one kcal). Popular sources often shorten the term *kilocalories* to simply *calories,* which can be confusing. We will refer to calorie counts in this book, rather than using the less-familiar term kilocalorie. Different types of food have different energy values for equal weights (see table 10.1). *Nutrient density* refers to the amount of a given nutrient per calorie. A variety of foods with high nutrient densities should predominate in a diet. Basing a diet on foods with low nutrient densities, for example, risks either overeating to obtain adequate amounts of necessary nutrients or doing without those necessary nutrients.

When you read the labeling on a food package, you'll notice that calories are based on a defined serving size, which may or may not accurately reflect normal consumption. For example, the labels on some 12-ounce cans of soft drinks list values based on two servings per can, although many people consume a whole can as a single serving.

Of course, we don't always eat equal weights of different foods. Make sure your students know that "virtuously" eating reduced-fat and reduced-sugar foods will not necessarily lead to consuming fewer calories if you eat them in a greater volume! A boy who eats one table-spoon of peanut butter (about 45 calories) consumes fewer calories than a girl who eats a plain baked potato (about 140 calories). Even though peanut butter has more calories per gram than the baked potato, the potato weighs a lot more, and thus has more calories than the peanut butter.

Poor childhood habits in both physical activity and nutrition often lead to health problems in adulthood. For example, obese individuals seldom develop heart disease, cancer, or gall bladder diseases as children. However, childhood obesity may set the stage for adult obesity, when the threat of these and other diseases associated with obesity does increase.

The interactions of physical activity and nutrition are important in every person's life. We need physical activity as much as we need all 45 nutrients in our diets.

Six Fundamental Needs

There are six important nutritional concepts that you as a teacher should emphasize to students at all levels. This chapter focuses on them, relating the concepts to youths and integrating their present diet with their future development by promoting the development of good health habits now. Your task is to help students integrate the science of nutrition with their own social, economic, and cultural backgrounds so that they can develop and enjoy lifelong, healthy habits of nutrition and physical activity.

By applying knowledge from nutrition, medicine, and physiology and committing to physical activity, a student can achieve the ancient Greek ideal of a sound mind *and* a sound body. A balanced diet supports a healthy lifestyle by meeting the six fundamental nutritional needs to

1. ensure and maintain proper hydration and electrolyte balance,

2. develop and maintain an ideal body mass,

3. develop and preserve a lean body mass,

4. provide adequate carbohydrates to optimize metabolism,

5. maximize oxygen delivery, and

Table 10.1 Common Food Values

Food	Amount	Calories
American cheese	50 g (about two slices)	185
Fast-food fried chicken drumstick	54 g (one)	135
Hard-boiled egg	50 g (one large)	80
Breaded fish sticks	55 g (two)	100
Pork (breakfast) sausage links	50 g (three)	185
Flour tortilla	53 g (one 8-inch)	155

Reprinted, by permission, from AAHPERD, 1998, *Physical Best Activity Guide—Elementary Level.* (Champaign, IL: Human Kinetics), 68.

6. develop a high-density skeleton.

See appendix D to read more about the biochemistry of meeting the six fundamental needs.

Ensure and Maintain Proper Hydration and Electrolyte Balance

It is important to maintain proper hydration and electrolyte balance, particularly during physical activity. Water makes up 55 to 60 percent of an adult's body weight, and an even higher proportion of a child's weight. Sweating, vomiting, or urinating can cause dehydration. Conversely, excessive water intake can cause water intoxication, a temporary sluggishness and disorientation caused by excessive water retention.

The body attempts to maintain *homeostasis* (the proper level of hydration) by regulating both water intake and loss. When the concentration of *solutes* (which are dissolved chemicals, usually fairly simple compounds such as salt) in the blood is too high, receptors in the brain trigger the thirst sensation to make you want to drink. The brain regulates water loss through sweating, urination, and other mechanisms using similar signals.

Although sweating causes a loss of salt along with water, people don't usually lose enough salt to require salt supplements. Americans take in plenty of salt through their diets. In fact, excessive salt consumption, often resulting in hypertension (high blood pressure) and other ailments, is a serious public health problem.

While thirst signals the body's need for water, this signal is slow to express the need. In other words, by the time thirst is signaled, an individual is already significantly dehydrated. Dehydration leads to poor thermal regulation, loss of circulating water in the blood, and increased concentrations of sodium and potassium. Changes in electrolyte concentrations alter the performance of the heart and other neuromuscular systems. In

© Photophile/S. Dawson 1994

It is vital to maintain proper hydration during physical activity.

addition, loss of circulating water in the blood reduces blood pressure. Students must know that they need to replenish lost water by drinking fluids (of any type) before, during, and after activity, rather than only when they become thirsty.

Develop and Maintain an Ideal Body Mass

As children mature through the stages of life, they gain greater independence in creating their own lifestyles. The choices children make determine their ability to maintain an ideal *body mass*, which is defined as the sum of lean body tissue (primarily muscle and organs) and stored (depot) fat.

Obesity is now the biggest nutritional problem among youths. In our complex society, however, we cannot focus only on obesity. In fact, psychological and social pressures to look thin have driven many youngsters to the extremes of anorexia and bulimia, which pose serious health risks. Helping your students achieve and maintain an ideal body mass requires teaching them the right combination

Females tend to have a greater percent body fat, with the *ideal* ranging from 18 to 23 percent body fat (compared with 16 to 19 percent for males). The body uses sex hormones to regulate its body fat. The *minimum* recommended healthy body fat for females is 17 percent and for males is 10 percent. The *maximum* recommended body fat is 32 percent for females and 25 percent for males.

Dietary Disorders

Obesity is an all-too-common consequence of poor dietary habits. While some individuals may be genetically predisposed to becoming obese, everyone can positively impact their weight through a healthful diet. Obesity results from one dietary factor: excessive caloric intake. Remember, all calories are equal. Those excess calories commonly come from eating too much fat, but they could come just as easily from simply eating too much. Obesity can have serious consequences, such as heart disease, diabetes, joint and bone injuries, and kidney disease. Limiting or eliminating excess weight is a matter of reducing the excessive caloric intake. The best way to reduce the excess is through a combination of healthier eating—consuming fewer calories—and greater physical activity, which burns off calories through both the activity itself and raising the resting metabolic rate (RMR).

An obsession with obesity—or the perception of being obese—can also result in serious harm, however. An individual who is seriously underweight is also unlikely to be fit. The most common eating disorders associated with underweight are anorexia and bulimia. Advertising showing all body and dietary fat as "bad" only complicates the issue. Once again, a healthful diet, appropriate physical activity, and fitness knowledge are the best defenses against eating disorders.

---

of caloric intake, caloric expenditure, and behavior modification. Behavior modification includes the frequency of eating, the portion sizes of food, and commitment to physical activity (see also chapter 9).

Develop and Preserve a Lean Body Mass

Exercise both builds up and breaks down muscle protein. Maintaining and increasing muscle mass requires optimal protein synthesis. Efficient production of new muscle mass results only when the diet provides all the amino acids, particularly the essential amino acids. A healthful diet includes enough high-quality protein to support muscle growth and sufficient energy sources to preserve amino acids for building muscle. This is particularly important during the growth years.

Provide Adequate Carbohydrates to Optimize Metabolism

All dietary sugars, complex and simple, are metabolically equal. The body breaks down starches and sucrose into simple sugars for absorption. Sugar is both a fuel and an essential intermediate for burning fats and amino acids. For most individuals, young and old, the diet should supply enough carbohydrates to store glycogen in the muscles and liver as fuel for activity. However, excessive carbohy-

drate consumption can lead to weight gain, just as can excessive fat consumption.

Maximize Oxygen Delivery

The diet must provide certain trace elements, particularly iron and copper, in order to synthesize hemoglobin, which is critical for carrying oxygen to the tissues. The rate of metabolism, and thus the generation of energy, is a direct function of oxygen utilization. Maximizing the delivery of oxygen to the red blood cells requires developing an optimal lung capacity for gas exchange. Physical activity greatly enhances the capacity of the lungs and the circulatory system's functioning.

Iron-deficiency anemia prevents the body from synthesizing hemoglobin. Anemia, therefore, is a special concern in children during their fast growth spurts, because their growing bodies need to supply the new tissues, and therefore need more iron to make more blood. It also is important to avoid anemia in early adolescence as girls approach menarche.

Develop a High-Density Skeleton

Throughout a life, the body continuously builds and breaks down bone. Humans turn over their skeleton every 7 to 10 years. The bone is built from minerals (primarily calcium) and an organic matrix, much like reinforced concrete (see figure 10.3). Bone development depends on physical activity, nutrition, and heredity. Nutritional factors affecting bone density include calcium, vitamin D, and fluoride to build the mineral matrix and trace elements to build the collagen of the organic matrix. Dairy foods are the primary source of calcium for children and adolescents. The synthesis of bone is stimulated by weight-bearing exercises and hormone production.

In females very low body fat can limit the body's ability to respond to female hormones, thus leading to brittle bones and osteoporosis—even in children. Maintaining an ideal body mass (ensuring that the body has enough fat) and performing weight-bearing activity to stimulate bone production will help prevent osteoporosis and brittle bones.

Consequences of Unhealthy Diet

We all want to believe in magic when it comes to nutrition and physical activity. Students must be taught, however, to separate magic and myth from reality. The belief that you can get something for nothing and achieve success without effort does not stand up to the First and Second Laws of Thermodynamics. No single diet or supplement is magical for losing or gaining weight, maintaining beautiful skin or hair, or imparting strength or agility.

Remembering the First Law of Thermodynamics (we can neither create nor destroy energy), we can extend the principle to calories: All of them are equal, no matter what food source they come from. Consider some of the fashionable diets. Low-fat diets can provide pleasure in eating along with fewer fat calories. Consumed in large amounts, however, the reduced-fat items actually provide excessive calories. High-protein, moderate-fat, and low-carbohydrate diets suppress the appetite and lower calorie consumption, but such regimens may have toxic side effects. High-carbohydrate diets, which are low in fat and protein intake, restore carbohydrate de-

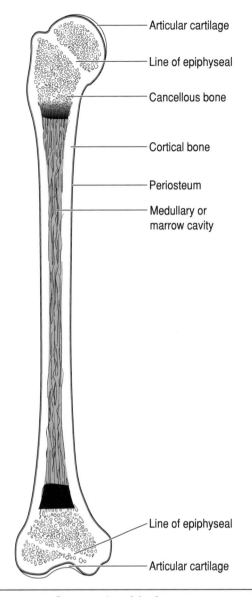

Figure 10.3 Cross-section of the femur.

Reprinted, by permission, from AAHPERD, 1999, *Physical Best Activity Guide—Elementary Level*. (Champaign, IL: Human Kinetics), 71.

pots for athletes, but this style of eating may compromise overall energy intake and provide too little protein.

If the diet provides inadequate levels of specific vitamins and minerals, nutritional supplements such as vitamin pills can make up the difference. There is little proof, however, that supplementing the diet with vitamins and minerals *beyond* the RDA significantly benefits performance or enhances nutrition.

There are plenty of strategies you can use to help youngsters learn good eating habits. Remember as you plan your activities with

To become their physical best, students must be physically active *and* eat a healthful diet.

students that strategies for good eating should include the following:

1. Individual eating habits should respect family lifestyles.
2. Begin the day with breakfast to provide energy and nutrients.

3. Control calorie consumption by spacing meals throughout the course of the day.
4. Most nutritional needs should be met with regular meals, supplemented by snacks.
5. Find pleasure in food while being aware of the nutrient and caloric content in food.
6. Practice balance, variety, and moderation. Understand that there are no health foods and no junk foods—only foods with higher or lower nutritional value.
7. Enjoy good food. Enjoy good health. Enjoy life.

Summary

The most serious consequence of a person's poor diet is an ongoing failure to achieve his or her physical best. The diet provides both energy and building blocks for everyone, regardless of activity level. A fit individual eats a healthful diet. It's impossible to build aerobic endurance without having the energy to keep the heart rate elevated. Muscular strength and endurance require building new muscle tissue with nutrients. Good flexibility requires a healthy skeleton, also built up from nutrients. And an ideal body composition clearly depends on an appropriate diet. Good diet alone cannot create fitness; neither can activity alone. Use the information in this chapter to teach students these connections.

Part III

Curriculum and Teaching Methods

Chapter 11

Curriculum Development for Health-Related Physical Fitness Education

A well-written *health-related physical fitness education curriculum* provides the framework within which students learn the necessary health-related physical fitness concepts, so they can apply them in real life. It integrates these concepts with motor skills and actual physical activity in a developmentally appropriate K–12 progression. The progression reinforces prerequisite skills and knowledge through their use and application.

For example, you might have first graders put their hands on their chests to feel their hearts beating fast and talk about how being active causes this to happen. Third graders might practice counting how many times they feel their hearts beat and discuss more specifically how this relates to physical activity. Fifth graders can be taught to find their pulse two different ways (wrist and carotid artery) or use a heart rate monitor and then graph their rates based on different activities. Seventh graders might be asked to monitor their

Disclaimer

It would take an entire book to cover curriculum development in detail but, in this chapter, we offer an overview that will enable you to work with district and state physical education directors to ensure that a curriculum is developed that meets the health-related fitness needs of all your students.

heart rates for a week doing different activities, graph the results, and write a paper that compares the various rates and offers reasons for the differences. A high school student might be asked to calculate target heart rates, develop an exercise plan based on their target heart rates, carry out the plan, and record the results (which requires knowing how to take their own pulse). Unfortunately, however, we still find some programs in which students do the same lesson year after year, with no applications or extensions. For example, asking third graders, fifth graders, seventh graders, and high school students to simply find their pulse without asking them to apply this information in a progressively more complex or varied manner does little to prepare students for managing personal lifelong physical activity plans.

Of course, at every level you will have students who lack the prerequisite skills, knowledge, and motivation to move forward. In these cases, the use of peer tutors, stations, teaching assistants (including volunteers), and other teaching strategies will allow you to "catch up" some students while not boring the rest of the class.

General Strategies for Developing a Curriculum

All curricular plans—no matter what the subject area—should be based on the desired outcomes, that is, what you want the student to know and be able to do. So before planning your curriculum, identify the exit outcomes you want students leaving your program to have achieved. *Exit outcomes* are the ultimate desired achievements of students who graduate from a K–12 curriculum (e.g., the national

standards). Then set intermediate outcomes that students should achieve at each stage in your program as well as on completion of each unit and lesson.

The Physical Best program uses the national standards developed by national organizations, including NASPE (AAHPERD), for physical education, health education (AAHE), and dance education (NDA) and their corresponding standards are also supported and reinforced by Physical Best programs. Collectively, these standards help determine exit outcomes and developmentally appropriate curricula that will help students achieve the ultimate goal of becoming adults who value and pursue active lifestyles. Tables 11.1–11.3 list the standards set by the national governing bodies for each discipline. Remember, Physical Best is not intended to replace exist-

Table 11.1 National Standards for Physical Education

Standard 1	Demonstrates competency in many movement forms and proficiency in a few movement forms.
Standard 2	Applies movement concepts and principles to the learning and development of motor skills.
Standard 3	Achieves and maintains a health-enhancing level of physical fitness.
Standard 4	Exhibits a physically active lifestyle.
Standard 5	Demonstrates responsible personal and social behavior in physical activity settings.
Standard 6	Demonstrates understanding and respect for differences among people in physical activity settings.
Standard 7	Understands that physical activity provides opportunities for enjoyment, challenge, self-expression, and social interaction.

Reprinted from *Moving Into the Future: National Standards for Physical Education* (1995) with permission from the National Association for Sport and Physical Education (NASPE), 1900 Association Drive, Reston, VA 20191-1599.

Table 11.2 National Health Education Standards

Standard 1	Comprehend concepts related to health promotion and disease prevention.
Standard 2	Demonstrate the ability to access valid health information and health-promoting products and services.
Standard 3	Demonstrate the ability to practice health-enhancing behaviors and reduce health risks.
Standard 4	Analyze the influence of culture, media, technology, and other factors on health.
Standard 5	Demonstrate the ability to use interpersonal communication skills to enhance health.
Standard 6	Demonstrate the ability to use goal-setting and decision-making skills to enhance health.
Standard 7	Demonstrate the ability to advocate for personal, family, and community health.

Reprinted by permission of the American Cancer Society, Inc. A work of the Joint Committee on National Health Education Standards. Copies may be obtained through the American Health Association, Association for the Advancement of Health Education, or the American Cancer Society, Inc.

Table 11.3 National Standards for Dance Education

Standard 1	Identifying and demonstrating movement elements and skills in performing dance.
Standard 2	Understanding choreographic principles, processes, and structures.
Standard 3	Understanding dance as a way to create and communicate meaning.
Standard 4	Applying and demonstrating critical and creative thinking skills in dance.
Standard 5	Demonstrating and understanding dance in various cultures and historical periods.
Standard 6	Making connections between dance and healthful living.
Standard 7	Making connections between dance and other disciplines.

Adapted by permission from National Standards for Dance Education developed by the National Dance Association, an association of the American Alliance for Health, Physical Education, Recreation and Dance. © National Dance Association. Complete copies may be purchased from NDA/AAHPERD, 1-800-321-0789.

ing curricula, but rather to complement and support other programs. Appendix A also lists the Centers for Disease Control and Prevention's Guidelines for School and Community Programs to Promote Lifelong Physical Activity Among Young People (1997).

Basic Principles

Allow several basic principles to guide every curricular decision you and your colleagues make (figure 11.1). Curriculum designers take care to (Hopple 1995)

- stay focused on the exit outcomes for each grade level, which are the goals toward which you should teach and assess;

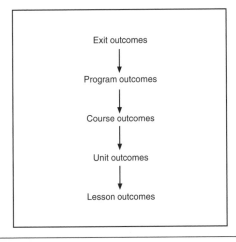

Figure 11.1 Designing down helps you create lessons that contribute to your overall curriculum goals.

Reprinted, by permission, from C. Hopple, 1995, *Teaching for Outcomes in Elementary Physical Education.* (Champaign, IL: Human Kinetics), 6.

- plan for ample opportunities for students to master the desired outcomes, including ensuring students have mastered prerequisite skills and knowledge before progressing to higher levels;

- set high expectations within reason, planning how each student will receive the support he or she needs to reach program goals; and

- design down, working backward from exit outcomes so that, ultimately, each unit and lesson enhances each student's chance of achieving those outcomes. See *Moving Into the Future: National Standards for Physical Education.*

Plan from the earliest stages for integrating related disciplines into health-related physical fitness education. For example, at the elementary level, plan to keep physical activity levels high while teaching basic motor skills and fitness knowledge. A visual way to describe this is displayed in the Exercise and Physical Activity Pyramid (see figure 5.3). Ensure that your curriculum includes a balance of types of activities in the middle two levels *and* teaches the skills needed to perform these activities safely and competently. Then teach to ensure that your students know how lifestyle activities and rest and inactivity fit into the picture.

Next, when possible, coordinate your curriculum concepts with colleagues in other disciplines. A cross-curricular approach helps students see and understand the real-life connections among subjects. They will ultimately learn more as the various curricular areas reinforce each other. For example, math instructors can teach students to calculate the target heart rate zone. Geography classes can use students' mileage or laps to "run" or "walk" across a topographical map while they also study the terrain. English classes could write about the historical sites students are "running" through. (See also the discussion about learning styles and Gardner's Theory of Multiple Intelligences in chapter 12.)

Designing Down

To create a curriculum that produces students who have achieved the set standards, work backward from those standards all the way down to day-to-day lesson plans. Plan to include all essential content.

Choose and Educate a Committee

Select a committee of physical educators (K–12), adapted physical educators, administrators, parents, community members, and students to work together to establish exit outcomes for each grade, representing a cross-section of the population that will be served. Each committee member should be or become knowledgeable about the best teaching practices currently in use as well as the local, state, and national standards relevant to health-related physical fitness education. (If you find you must operate on the building level only, at least consult with other physical educators in the district to ensure your program meshes as well as possible with other programs.)

Determine Exit Outcomes

The national standards provide appropriate expectations of achievement by the end of the program. The Physical Best activity guides provide the means to help students meet these standards lesson by lesson. However, every good teacher modifies his or her program where appropriate to meet the needs of the population served. Therefore, determine whether or not the national standards meet your students' needs. If not, modify your approach to them to better fit your situation. Simply be sure your approach is relevant, broad-based, demonstrable, and challenging (Mohnsen 1997). For example, the NASPE standard, "Demonstrates competency in many and proficiency in a few movement forms," may be nearly impossible to achieve for the majority of students if your physical education lesson time is severely limited. You might, then, list ways to help more students reach the standard despite time limitations. This same situation will ultimately dictate that

Standards for Teaching Students With Disabilities

The Adapted Physical Education National Standards (NCPERID 1995) provide teaching standards focusing on adapting to meet the needs of people with specific disabilities. We recommend that you consult those standards or an adapted physical education specialist if your program involves working with students with disabilities.

fewer movement themes are explored through the years of the program. In contrast, if students spend ample time in physical education classes in your district throughout their school careers, you might modify this standard to read, "Demonstrates competency in many and proficiency in *several* movement forms." The curriculum design committee should also consult state and local standards, if they have been established. Note, however, that some states set standards, so you will need to find out how much flexibility you have to interpret the state standards according to the local student population's needs.

Identify Program Standards

Program standards should specify what you expect "students to have learned and be able to do with that learning in physical education by the time they complete high school" (Hopple 1995). Develop these cooperatively as a committee so that each "piece of the puzzle" works with the next, meaning that students are taught along a logical and progressive continuum.

First, examine how each level (elementary, middle, and high school) must help students meet the exit outcomes (e.g., the national standards). Next, look closely at NASPE's benchmarks for the relevant grade levels as well as state and local guidelines. (Appendix E includes South Carolina's guidelines.) Then set reasonable goals for each program level.

Outline Course Standards

A *course* may simply be the curriculum taught at an elementary grade level or a semester of health-related fitness education at the secondary level or any other distinct group of units taught as part of the overall health-related physical fitness education program. Whatever the case, design each course to meet one or more desired program standards. For example, if an elementary program standard is to be proficient in locomotor skills that can be used to enhance aerobic endurance, the kindergarten course standards might include, "Students will become familiar with several forms of locomotion, for example, walking, running, hopping, skipping," and the second grade course standards might include, "Students will become proficient in several forms of locomotion, for example, walking, running, hopping, skipping, galloping, leaping, chasing, dodging, fleeing, faking, jumping and landing, sliding."

Organize Learning Into a Progressive Scope and Sequence

Courses should take place within a logical scope and sequence so that students learn the requisite psychomotor, cognitive, and affective skills they need to succeed in future courses. Table 11.4 provides one example of such a progression, the K–12 program in Corvallis, Oregon. Appendix F includes two additional examples of scope and sequence progressions: NASPE's 1995 guidelines for grades K–12 and the Olympia, Washington, school district's plan for grades 1–10.

Determine Unit Outcomes

Units and their outcomes are the "nuts and bolts" of a solid health-related physical fitness education program. Look more closely at specifics relevant to your local situation. When selecting and designing units, take into account the facilities, equipment, community opportunities, and student ages and interests. For example, if youth and adult soccer leagues are popular in your area, you might

Table 11.4 Sample K–12 Progressive Scope and Sequence

Beginning Grades K–1 Level 0	Developing Grades 2–3 Level 1	Capable Grades 4–5 Level 2	Fluent Grades 6–8 Level 3	Accomplished Grades 9–10 Level 4	Mastery Grades 11–12 Level 5 EXIT
Active lifestyle					
Explores moderate to vigorous physical activity in a physical education setting	Demonstrates sustained moderate to vigorous physical activity in a physical education setting	Maintains moderate to vigorous physical activity levels in a variety of activity settings that utilize the skills learned in a physical education setting	Participates regularly in health-enhancing physical activities in both school and nonschool settings	Maintains a consistent pattern of participation in games, sports, dance, outdoor pursuits, and/or other physical activities that contributes to a physically active lifestyle	Continues to maintain a consistent pattern of participation in games, sports, dance, outdoor pursuits, and/or other physical activities that contributes to a physically active lifestyle
Choice/preference					
Shows preference in physical activity choices	Identifies and regularly participates in a variety of physical activities	Makes personal choices to develop skills and engage in more formal participation in physical activities	Explores a variety of new physical activities for personal interest in both school and nonschool settings	Seeks and selects physical activities from a variety of movement forms based on personal interest and capabilities	Understands that preferences for activity participation patterns change throughout life and develops and explores strategies to deal with those changes

(continued)

144

Table 11.4 *(continued)*

	Beginning Grades K–1 Level 0	Developing Grades 2–3 Level 1	Capable Grades 4–5 Level 2	Fluent Grades 6–8 Level 3	Accomplished Grades 9–10 Level 4	Mastery Grades 11–12 Level 5 EXIT
Adequate level		Understands that to be physically active, one needs adequate levels of fitness	Identifies the health-related fitness component(s) necessary to pursue selected physical activities	Describes how varying fitness levels can inhibit or enable participation in physical activities	Discusses how maintaining health-related fitness and pursuing physical activity are reciprocal (e.g., health-related fitness is necessary to pursue physical activity, and increased physical activity contributes to attaining health-related fitness)	Discusses the long-term physiological, psychological, and social benefits of physical activity on the individual and society
	Demonstrates awareness that physical activity is both fun and good for you					
Assessing levels of fitness		Begins to measure performance of health-related fitness (e.g., flexibility, muscular strength, cardiovascular endurance)	Participates in formal assessments of health-related fitness and interprets results as an indicator of personal health status	Achieves or demonstrates improvement toward the age/gender criterion-based fitness standards	Continues to achieve or demonstrate improvement toward the criterion-based fitness standards	Continues to achieve or demonstrate improvement toward the health-related, criterion-based fitness standards
	Explores the tasks that evaluate health-related fitness (e.g., curl-ups, push-ups, running, stretching)					

(continued)

Table 11.4 (continued)

	Beginning Grades K–1 Level 0	Developing Grades 2–3 Level 1	Capable Grades 4–5 Level 2	Fluent Grades 6–8 Level 3	Accomplished Grades 9–10 Level 4	Mastery Grades 11–12 Level 5 EXIT
Setting goals	Explores fitness challenges and purposefully practices tasks to gain greater success	Begins to understand that formal measurements of health-related fitness are important/significant	Begins to develop, with teacher assistance, goals and strategies for improvement/maintenance of selected fitness components based on fitness assessments	Continues to develop and pursue fitness goals with some teacher guidance	Continues to set personal health-related fitness goals and designs and implements a personal fitness program	Demonstrates the skills and knowledge to monitor and adjust activity levels to meet personal fitness needs (e.g., motivation, obstacles, lifelong)
Fitness principles	Demonstrates awareness of perceived exertion (e.g., "high," "medium," "low" energy output)	Recognizes the physiological indicators that accompany moderate to vigorous physical activity (e.g., sweating, increased heart rate, heavy breathing)	Monitors intensity of exercise (e.g., recognizing target heart rate and recovery time). Explores the principles of fitness training (e.g., frequency, intensity, duration, and mode of exercise)	Understands and applies basic principles of training to improve physical fitness (e.g., frequency, intensity, duration, and mode of exercise)	Uses and interprets principles of training for the purpose of modifying levels of fitness (e.g., frequency, intensity, duration, and mode)	Develops a personal fitness plan that reflects knowledge and application of principles of fitness training (e.g., frequency, intensity, duration, and mode)

Submitted by Aleita Hass-Holcombe, Corvallis, courtesy of Corvallis School District 509J (Corvallis, Oregon).

Pride in Physical Education: Take Ownership of New Curriculum

At Ontario High School (Ontario, California), there is no more picking teams, no more nonsuits, and no more making physical education a negative, embarrassing experience. The staff has changed their teaching methods to focus on the whole student, not just his or her body. The curriculum enhances the development of self-esteem, social skills, cooperative learning, and the ability to succeed in lifetime activity skills.

Students are taught in a sequentially planned program, not only specific psychomotor skills and physical activities, but also how to talk in a positive manner and not to embarrass their fellow classmates. Students also teach each other how to perform skills. Winning and losing don't matter; the goal is for each student to succeed and have a good time.

In accordance with the state guidelines, freshmen participate in several physical activities, learning in sequential patterns that help them become successful participants. Tenth graders begin to analyze the skills used for effective movement and choose physical activities that they want to pursue. They also continue to learn new physical activities. Juniors and seniors generally are gaining proficiency in their chosen physical activities and have laid the groundwork for lifelong fitness. Students at this level learn to set up and implement their own health-related fitness programs.

From an article by the same name by Richard Smith, 1995, *Teaching High School Physical Education* 1(5):1, 4–5.

Locomotor and manipulative skills learned at the elementary level prepare students for advanced activity lessons in middle and high school.

opt to include several progressively advanced units from kindergarten through 12th grade to build student skills so that they can choose to enjoy this physical activity at a proficient level after they leave your program. Plan unit outcomes that make the connections between being fit and enjoying playing soccer more, such as "Students will recognize the value of flexibility to playing soccer and other sports." Build, then, on local interests and opportunities, while helping students see the connections between these and health-related physical fitness so they can turn it into a beneficial lifetime activity. Meanwhile, however, introduce students to other physical activities to "broaden their physical activity horizons." Another example is a locale that offers many winter physical activities such as cross-country skiing and snowshoeing. Here, unit outcomes might include developing an appreciation for each of these lifetime physical activity options.

To this Physical Best adds, a learning experience should have the potential to improve health-related fitness and/or health-related fitness knowledge.

Identify Lesson Outcomes

At the lesson level, plan exactly how you will help students achieve the unit outcomes you

Making Final Content Decisions

Tailor the specific content you choose to your unique situation so as to maximize learning for all students, given the parameters you must work within. Take the following factors into consideration before making your final selection of specific units and activities:

- Number of students in your class
- Developmental levels of your students
- Cultural orientation(s) of your school
- Facilities
- Equipment
- Amount of time per physical education class period
- Number of physical education class periods per week
- Safety issues
- Overall value to exit outcomes

Then ensure that each component of a lesson meets the following criteria (Rink 1993). The learning experience

- must have the potential to improve the motor performance and movement skills of the students (*Note*: in some situations with students with special needs, you might need to change *improve* to *utilize*);
- must provide maximal activity or practice time for all students at their individual ability levels;
- must be appropriate for the experience level of each student; and
- should have the potential to integrate physical, affective, and cognitive educational goals whenever possible.

set. For example, you might plan a field trip to allow students to explore snowshoeing as you guide them toward the unit outcome of appreciating this physical activity and its health-related fitness value. A specific lesson outcome might be "Students will calculate how many calories they burned in a half-hour of snowshoeing." Another outcome of the same lesson might be "Students will recognize the value of snowshoeing in developing aerobic

Career Paths and Physical Education

Physical education credits, while counting toward high school graduation, are not counted when it comes to getting into college. Thus, in the limited time available, most college-bound students opt to take electives that will enhance their transcripts, such as extra science or math courses. College-bound students in the Murrieta Valley Unified School District (Murrieta, California), however, no longer have to choose between producing a "strong" transcript instead of a strong body. This district has developed a creative solution (instead of mandating more physical education credits, which college-bound students may get waived). Physical educators designed new classes that meet college entrance requirements, while at the same time giving students a wider range of movement experiences. These courses include—among others—Dance Choreography and Production, Athletic Training, and Sports Media. In so doing, these innovators have sparked new interest in physical education participation as well as taken a more central role in the overall school curriculum.

From an article by the same name by Guy Romer, 1995, *Teaching High School Physical Education* 1(5):5.

Teaching Tip: Student Needs Versus Teacher Interests

Most physical education teachers love sports, and we design our programs to teach what we like. Most of us were involved in sports during high school. Many continued to participate in college, and a few have continued for a time after graduation. We have gained the necessary skills to become highly proficient and have experienced the thrill of victory more often than the agony of defeat. As we have matured, our bodies are no longer able to perform as they did when we were younger. The sports we loved in high school and college no longer offer the opportunities they once did when we were young. For our students, who may not enjoy competition and who do not have the talent necessary to develop skills, a competitive team sport approach to physical education is not at all appealing. Today's physical education teacher must recognize that competitive team sports are not lifetime in nature, that developing a high level of skill is not possible for all individuals, and that not all students are athletes. A healthy lifestyle that includes regular physical activity should be the objective of our programs. Our programs must emphasize fitness and physical activity not just skill and competition. Our objectives are to teach our children to enjoy physical activity and what it takes to stay fit so they can continue to enjoy physical activity as much in adulthood as they did when they were 12 years old.

Bane McCraken
Cabell Midland High School, Ona, West Virginia
1997 NASPE Secondary Physical Education Teacher of the Year

From *Teaching High School Physical Education for Lifetime Activity* (in press, Human Kinetics).

endurance as evidenced by a journal entry." Or, "Students will understand how and where to select and purchase snowshoes and appropriate clothing as well as where in the community they can go to snowshoe, as evidenced by completing a shopping list and planning and participating in an outing." Note how the same lesson integrates a fitness concept, actual physical activity, and a psychomotor skill as well as a practical application all into one integrated package.

Delivering Up

Delivering up is simply another way to say "teaching." As illustrated in figure 11.2, implementation of a curriculum occurs lesson by lesson to reach the ultimate goals identified as exit outcomes.

Develop lesson plans in which each activity helps deliver up one element or another toward producing students who achieve the exit outcomes. If you're not sure an activity will enhance this process, think about it, consult with colleagues, and modify it to ensure its value to the overall program. A major advantage of this process is that you can rest assured you're not wasting valuable lesson time going off on a tangent.

Another key to planning lessons that enhance the chances of achieving exit outcomes is to always strive to integrate two or more aspects of physical education into each lesson. When you teach a fitness concept (e.g., incorporate moderate to intense physical activity, and target a psychomotor skill or

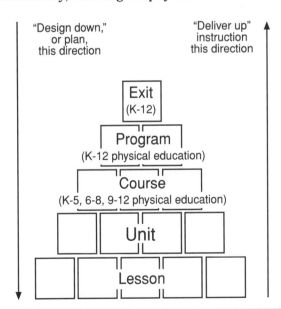

Figure 11.2 Carefully plan lessons that will help students achieve their long-term goals.

Adapted, by permission, from C. Hopple, 1995, *Teaching for Outcomes in Elementary Physical Education*. (Champaign, IL: Human Kinetics), 16.

Lifetime Physical Education (Eaton High School, Eaton, Ohio)

Penny Portman and Rick McCollum saw a need: stress in high school students. The answer: an elective Lifetime Physical Education course. Its goals include offering students a variety of physical activities in which to participate under school supervision, helping students develop the skills they need to participate successfully, offering physical activity as a stress reduction option, and involving community resources in supporting the course. Activities include a 50/50 balance of traditional and nontraditional lifetime sports [for their locale].

Many community volunteers shared their "loves" with the students from fly fishing to skiing to scuba diving, to name a few. Community resources also helped provide funding. Administrative, student, and parental support were elicited as well. Field trips have included an 11 p.m. to 4 a.m. snow-skiing jaunt.

Portman shares, "The Lifetime Physical Education program [offers] students a broader perspective on life and the opportunity to learn new activities that otherwise would be unavailable to them—activities that they can continue long after graduating from high school."

From "Eaton High School Lifetime P.E." by P. Portman and R. McCollum, 1995, *Teaching High School Physical Education* 1(2):9.

concept all in one integrated lesson), you make the connections among these aspects so that students learn how to do so on their own. In short, you provide a model for effective real-life approaches to physical activity. Try consciously identifying these aspects in each lesson as shown on page 151 until this process becomes second nature. Refer to the *Physical Best Activity Guide—Elementary Level* and *Physical Best Activity Guide—Secondary Level* for further examples.

A complete lesson plan includes an appropriate introduction, the main activity, and an appropriate closing. To introduce a lesson, create a *set induction*, also known as *cognitive set* or *anticipatory set*, which involves "priming the pump"—helping students see how and why the current lesson's learning fits into the unit's content, encouraging students to want to learn through today's activities. The *core lesson content* includes explanations, demonstrations, and student activities. Remember, each component of the core lesson content must pass the criteria we have outlined, so you don't waste precious instructional time. And just as an entire curriculum builds unit upon unit, course upon course, the activities within a lesson must build one upon another. A *closure activity* summarizes the day's learning and allows you to quickly assess understanding. It solidifies student learning by reminding students of the lesson's purpose within the context of both the unit and everyday life. You can also use closure time to prepare students for the next lesson, making it a "pre-set induction." Insist that students be especially quiet during cool-down so you can conduct brief but effective closure discussions at the same time. (See chapter 13 for more information on effective lesson delivery.)

Integrating Across the Curriculum

In the past, many have viewed physical education and "academics" as being on opposite sides of the educational fence. But "body, thought, and emotion are intimately bound together through an intricate nerve network, and function as a whole unit to enrich our knowing" (Hannaford 1995). Therefore, integrate other subjects into health-related physical fitness education curricula whenever possible.

Given the limited time we have with our students, compared to the demands placed on us, it simply makes sense to work together on a schoolwide basis to reinforce learning. For example, a physical education lesson on spatial awareness for kindergartners could

Developing Activities for Teaching Lifelong Fitness

Activities that help students learn while doing are the most successful for teaching lifelong fitness. The Physical Best activity guides provide a wealth of activities designed specifically to help students learn through doing. These are a great start to developing an excellent program, but you'll want to add more activities especially suited for your students. Following is a step-by-step procedure for developing your own activities.

Carefully consider the **level** of the students for which you're developing the activity.

Write out the **concept** you wish to teach, using language appropriate for the level you are teaching.

Spell out the **purpose** of the activity. What do you want your students to learn?

Determine what **equipment** you'll need.

Define the relationship of this activity to the **national standards**. This helps you keep your curriculum focused.

Write a **set induction**. How will you prepare students to learn?

Develop a step-by-step **procedure** for leading the activity. You might modify this after you've done the activity a few times and worked the "bugs" out.

Think about what **teaching hints** you'll need to be aware of. Write this down so when you have a substitute, the sub can take advantage of your experience.

Remember to include a **closure and an assessment** for the activity. Check for student understanding.

Finally, plan for ways of **extending the lesson**. If the activity goes well, you'll want to challenge your students to take it to the next level or further assimilate the learning.

---

3   My Body

Primary Level

Growth and developmental influences on body composition: Your body is made of billions of cells that need all type of foods to live. Your body shape, type, and size are influenced by many factors, some of which you can control and some which you cannot control. The uncontrollable factors are your genetics (family history), age, and gender. Controllable factors are how much you eat, what you eat, and how much physical activity you do.

Purpose

Students will understand the factors that influence their body shape, type, and size and understand the uniqueness of each person and how each person is different in his or her nutrient and physical activity requirements.

Equipment Needed

- Variety of balls, such as, playground, Nerf, tennis
- Hula hoops

Relationship to National Standards

Physical Education Standard 3: Student exhibits a physically active lifestyle—Student will identify the benefits derived from regular physical activity.

Health Education Standard 1: Student will comprehend concepts related to health promotion and disease prevention—Student will describe relationships between personal health behaviors and individual well-being.

Set Induction

If time allows, use an ink pad and fingerprint each child. Have student compare the fingerprint with everyone else's to show how everyone is different. The fingerprints are all different just like the bodies are all different and come in all different sizes, colors, and shapes.

Explain that each student will choose the ball they will use for this activity. Explain that their choices are similar to their fingerprints and bodies, in that everyone has their own and that they are not always the same as the other classmates.

Procedure

1. Place a variety of types and sizes of balls about the activity area in hoops and allow students to use any size ball they are comfortable with.
2. Take students through a series of manipulative skills (e.g., toss and catch, ball handling, bounce and catch, roll and catch, dribbling, partner skills, and so on), offering students two or three challenges in each of the skill categories.
3. Explain that we are not all the same size. Many factors influence our size and shape, such as what we do and eat and the family we come from (our parents).

Teaching Hints

Be sure to allow each student to select the ball he or she is comfortable with. Add claps, turns, and so on to the skills you're using to increase the level of challenge.

Make sure that there are more than enough balls for every student in order that the majority get their choice.

Closure and Assessment

Written and Oral

- Ask "What lesson did I want you to learn about body composition by participating in today's activity?"

Project

- Direct students to do the following: "Ask your mom or dad for the following recent photos: of you, of your mom or dad, and of that parent's parents. Try to get photos that are of each person's whole body. Paste the photos side by side on a sheet of paper. Compare body shapes, types, and size." (Note: You may choose to make a sample photo array to use for comparison, rather than having all students bring in photos.)

Extending the Lesson

- Have each student draw a picture of her family involved in physical activity.
- Have each student draw a picture of himself doing his favorite activity or something he likes about himself.

Reprinted, by permission, from AAHPERD, 1999, *Physical Best Activity Guide—Elementary Level.* (Champaign, IL: Human Kinetics), 204.

It is important to take into account student interest when designing courses. If, for example, a version of swing dance is popular with teenagers in your community, it might be a good choice for a dance unit.

include having the students form letters with their bodies, thereby integrating prereading skills, or a lesson on aerobic endurance can reinforce a science unit on the cardiorespiratory system. Likewise, movement can be integrated into other subjects. For example, classroom teachers can use movement to check for academic understanding (e.g., have students divide the class into thirds, fourths, and so on) or to reinforce learning (e.g., moving through a simulated nervous system to understand how the brain and nerves work together to send and receive messages). Encourage older students to integrate fitness and movement skills and concepts into academic projects, such as creating and implementing a health-related fitness program appropriate for senior citizens as part of a service learning project.

Make logical and natural connections between subject areas; however, don't force them. They must make sense to everyone, especially the students. This will better simulate real-world approaches to problems, deepening student understanding.

Selecting Appropriate Lifetime Activities

Lifetime activity refers to activities that are accessible and enjoyable throughout one's life, especially those that adults are most likely to engage in regularly for recreational and health-related fitness reasons over the course of a lifetime. What constitutes "accessible" and "enjoyable" will vary from individual to individual, of course, depending on an individual's interests, locale, and skills. Career and financial constraints may also play a role in an individual's choice of lifetime activities.

Taking an Age-Appropriate Approach

Effective lifetime activity curricula is vastly different for a primary grade (K–3) student than a high school student. Thus, unit and activity selection should occur along a continuum from completely childlike to as adultlike in nature as possible. To select specific age-appropriate lifetime activity curricula, work on a districtwide basis and design down from high school, ensuring appropriate progression and minimizing unnecessary duplication. Then the elementary and middle school teachers can see what they need to focus on so that students are academically and physically prepared for the high school program. Figure 11.3 shows a sample continuum for aerobic endurance activities that proceed from very childlike activities in the early grades to very adultlike activities in high school.

But how can you call a tag game a "lifetime activity?" It is not, but a kindergartner would almost certainly find a more adultlike activity, such as jogging for 20 minutes, boring (and maybe dangerous). In addition, tag is an activity children engage in when they are playing on their own, so it makes sense to validate it in health-related physical fitness learning. Keeping our ultimate goal in mind, tag is one of the more appropriate ways to develop a love for aerobic endurance activity in the early grades, thereby feeding into the middle and high school programs. In short, students who enjoy aerobic endurance activities in the early grades are more likely to be open to developing themselves in this area in later school years and on into adulthood. The same is true for any component of health-related fitness. As another example, a high school student who has set a personal goal of playing more forcefully on her roller hockey team may find lifting weights interesting, while a second grader will benefit more physically and psychologically from developing muscular strength and endurance on playground equipment.

At the same time, remember to individualize so that, within a developmental level, you are providing a range of appropriate challenges, giving the low-fit or low-skilled student a chance to enjoy your program as much as the average to high-fit or highly skilled student (see also chapter 13).

Another way to think of a lifetime activity curricula continuum is to consider a diamond-shaped framework such as that shown in figure 11.4. Within the diamond curriculum framework, elementary level students develop the basic skills and concepts (both fitness and movement related) they need to ultimately be able to enjoy lifetime activities (see Don't Forget Skills Development). Middle school students then use these skills to sample a wide variety of physical activities. This gives students the opportunity to form personal opinions about various activities and sports. Then high school students select a few physical activities in which to specialize and around which they may build personal physical activity plans. The foundation of basic skills in elementary school and development of proficiency in self-selected areas in high school forms a continuum that is likely to lead to positive adult health-related fitness behaviors.

Elementary Health and Wellness School

In Wichita, Kansas, a magnet school program is used to provide educational alternatives and at the same time sustain a desegregated school system. Woodland Magnet Elementary parents and faculty designed a health and wellness theme to address parental concerns about overweight and unfit children (Kuntzleman and Reiff 1992). Innovators saw the plan as a way to improve children's education while promoting healthy lifestyles and not compromising basic academic skills. The Woodland philosophy believes that it makes more sense to set good health habits early in life than to try to change bad health habits later. Woodland represents the imagination of Wichita parents to tailor education to their children's needs.

Each school year is divided into thematic quarters: growth and development, diet and nutrition, physical fitness, mind and body. The health and wellness theme pervades every curricular area. A special event, such as a fair or open house, culminates each quarter. A health profile is compiled at the beginning of the school year so that faculty can accurately track success relative to each child's starting point.

Adapted, by permission, from "The K–5 Health and Wellness Magnet School," by Todd T. Russell, 1992, *Teaching Elementary Physical Education* 3(6):14–15.

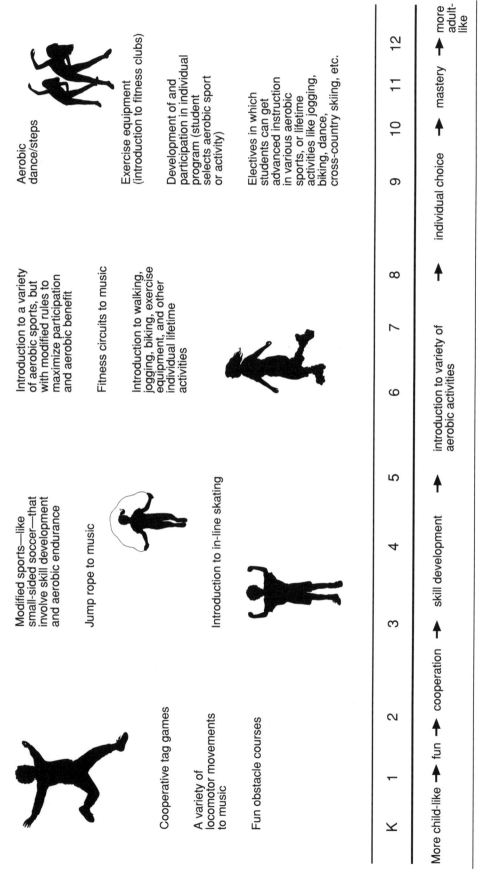

Aerobic dance/steps

Exercise equipment (introduction to fitness clubs)

Development of and participation in individual program (student selects aerobic sport or activity)

Electives in which students can get advanced instruction in various aerobic sports, or lifetime activities like jogging, biking, dance, cross-country skiing, etc.

Introduction to a variety of aerobic sports, but with modified rules to maximize participation and aerobic benefit

Fitness circuits to music

Introduction to walking, jogging, biking, exercise equipment, and other individual lifetime activities

Modified sports—like small-sided soccer—that involve skill development and aerobic endurance

Jump rope to music

Introduction to in-line skating

Cooperative tag games

A variety of locomotor movements to music

Fun obstacle courses

| K | 1 | 2 | 3 | 4 | 5 | 6 | 7 | 8 | 9 | 10 | 11 | 12 |

More child-like → fun → cooperation → skill development → introduction to variety of aerobic activities → individual choice → mastery → more adult-like

Figure 11.3 Your activity selection should occur along a continuum that moves students from child-like activities to adult-like activities. This example describes a possible continuum for teaching aerobic fitness.

Exploring the Opportunities

Most communities offer at least some recreational and fitness opportunities that students can choose to pursue as adults. Share the information in this section with older students as you explore the various activities in physical activity and lecture settings (see also chapters 13 and 14). The bottom line is, your program should reflect what people actually do in real life to stay fit. For example, since walking is such a common adult health-related fitness activity, find enjoyable ways to explore this option in your program.

Overcoming Barriers to Participating in Lifetime Activities

Adults list many barriers to participation in physical activity as excuses not to exercise (see also chapter 2). Show students how to overcome these barriers through your health-related physical fitness education curriculum:

1. **Fear of the unfamiliar**
   Curriculum decision guidelines: Allow middle school students to sample a wide variety of activities.

2. **Expense**
   Curriculum decision guidelines: Respect economic diversity by helping students explore equipment and facility options (e.g., the YMCA is cheaper than an upscale fitness club and provides financial aid to those who qualify) as well as physical activity options that do not require equipment or special facilities at all. Point out the benefits of lifestyle activities to health and fitness (e.g., mowing a larger lawn with a push mower or walking briskly to school are certainly workouts).

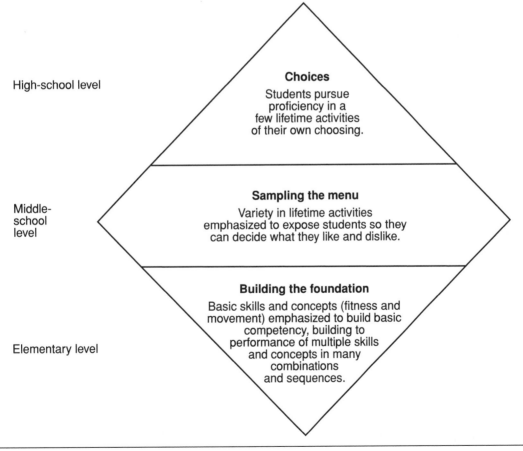

Figure 11.4   This diamond-shaped framework provides another way of describing a lifetime activity continuum.

Reprinted, by permission, from C. Himberg, in press, *Teaching Secondary Physical Education in the 21st Century*. (Champaign, IL: Human Kinetics).

3. **Fear or dislike of competition**

   Curriculum decision guidelines: While people may naturally compete, physical education programs need not emphasize it. Instead, emphasize cooperation and intrinsic motivation over competition and extrinsic rewards. Make competition simply one choice for those who enjoy it.

4. **Lack of skill or the perception one must be good at something to benefit from it**

   Curriculum decision guidelines: Help students learn to recognize the need for skill utilization (e.g., dribbling competently with the feet to play better and to gain more aerobic endurance benefits in soccer), rather than think they have to master them completely. Teach students to analyze their skills. Individualize skill development instruction. Allow older students to specialize more to develop feelings of competence. Emphasize enjoyment can be had with competent but not excellent skills.

5. **Lack of knowledge**

   Curriculum decision guidelines: Integrate the *whys* of health-related fitness pursuits into the fun activities that develop health-related fitness components.

6. **Time**

   Curriculum decision guidelines: Work on a districtwide basis to develop time management skills in students. Show students ways to make time for fitness in their lifestyle routines (e.g., taking stairs instead of elevators). Emphasize that the new health-related fitness guidelines validate the effectiveness of several short bursts of activity; that is, you don't have to block out one large amount of time per day to achieve basic health-related fitness benefits. Invite guest speakers (e.g., parents, community leaders) from many different walks of life to share how they keep fit within the framework of their responsibilities, resources, and interests.

Competitive Sports as Lifetime Activities

Certainly competitive sports can be an appropriate way to stay physically active. Many

Fitness Rules!

According to a recent participation study by the Sporting Goods Manufacturers Association, health club–related activity represents more than half of the 25 most popular sports in the United States. Health club–related activities are in *italics*.

1. Bowling
2. *Basketball*
3. *Free Weights*
4. Billiards
5. Freshwater Fishing (other than fly)
6. Tent Camping
7. *Treadmill Exercise*
8. *Stationary Cycling*
9. *Fitness Walking*
10. *Running/Jogging*
11. *In-line Skating*
12. *Golf*
13. Fitness Bicycling
14. *Exercise to Music*
15. *Volleyball (court)*
16. *Resistance Machines*
17. *Swimming*
18. Softball (slow pitch)
19. Hiking/Backpacking
20. (tie) Touch Football
20. (tie) Soccer
22. *Tennis*
23. Table Tennis
24. *Stairclimbing Machines*
25. Shooting (target)

Reprinted, by permission, from Fitness Rules, 1998, *Club Industry*, 14(6):16.

communities have full leagues for sports such as basketball, volleyball, and softball. Most of these sports provide appropriate activity, but this isn't always the case, especially with softball, for example, where sometimes a participant may get less activity from playing in a game than he or she would from raking the leaves or going on a moderately paced walk. However, even though many adults do participate in competitive sports throughout their entire lives, the majority of older adults do *not*

Teaching Tip: Skills and Fitness

Developing sport skills has been the main element of traditional physical education, and skills should still be an element in a comprehensive lifetime approach. However, students should not be led to believe that it is always necessary to have a high level of skill. Overemphasis on skill development may lead students to believe that if they can't be highly skilled, they can't participate. Physically immature students, with poor coordination, low strength and endurance, need to develop good physical activity habits even more than the gifted athlete. Placing more emphasis on teaching students to learn to recognize skills and improve them to the best of their ability is a much better strategy.

Bane McCraken
Cabell Midland High School, Ona, West Virginia
1997 NASPE Secondary Physical Education Teacher of the Year

From *Teaching High School Physical Education for Lifetime Activity* (in press, Human Kinetics).

choose competition as a means for developing and maintaining health-related fitness. Thus, while it is important to provide support to the student who currently values athletics, it is even more important to make it clear to the rest of your students that participating in sports is not necessary to achieving or maintaining health-related fitness—it is simply one option for those who are interested. Help your students set realistic competitive and noncompetitive expectations for themselves, based on interest, time, and other factors. Point out that adults who do compete generally do so for fun, not glory, status, or money. Invite local adult sport league participants to share with your students the various sports available in your community.

Essential Fitness Skills

There are many skills students need to develop to become self-sufficient in health-related fitness activities. Besides learning the basic skills and concepts common to all movement forms, students should learn skills

Everyone Can Benefit

Recognize—and help students recognize—that it is not necessary to be highly skilled in order to receive the fitness benefits of participating in an activity. Weekend golfers with high handicaps receive the same fitness benefits from a round of golf as professionals. In fact they receive more. They usually don't use a caddie, so they carry their own clubs, take a lot more swings, and walk farther chasing their errant shots. When our programs overemphasize skill development, our students perceive that they must have high levels of skill, or they can't participate. Therefore, many never try. To make activities more attractive to all students and not just the gifted athlete, we must do more than teach skill.

From *Teaching High School Physical Education for Lifetime Activity* (in press, Human Kinetics).

Don't Forget Skills Development

In the past many physical education programs placed their entire focus on the development of sports skills. In this book we emphasize the need to focus on health-related fitness. However, we want to make it clear that learning skills remains an important part of a quality physical education program. All students can improve their skills to some degree, which is an important factor in preparing them to lead physically active lives. The key is not to overemphasize skill develop so as to discourage those students who, due to any number of factors, will never be as highly skilled as the top athletes in your school. Not all students can be highly successful competitive athletes, but all students can lead physically active, healthy lives.

The Twin Cities Twosome

The Twin Cities Twosome, sponsored in Champaign-Urbana, Illinois, by Human Kinetics, is an excellent example of using a community activity to involve students in physical activity. The entry fees from this event are donated to local women's and men's shelters.

The Twosome is a 5K race in a local park that is divided into several divisions. Two of these divisions form the School Duel—one for elementary schools and one for secondary schools. The "winner" of each division is the school with the most participants (students and teachers) from that school. This past year (1998), each participant from the winning schools received a certificate good for two free slices of pizza, while the school itself received a $200 gift certificate for athletic equipment from a local sporting goods company, a $100 gift certificate from a local bookstore, and a trophy.

According to Julie Rhoda, who has helped coordinate the Twosome for

The Twin Cities Twosome encourages family participation.

several years, the winning schools have always had a teacher actively promoting the School Duel. All participants in the School Duel can enter the Twosome at a reduced entry fee and receive a free Frisbee.

The race itself emphasizes family participation. It includes a variety of divisions—walking and running, relays with mothers and daughters, and so on. Participation in any race division counts toward winning the School Duel.

The Twosome has two mass starts—one for runners and one for walkers. There is a pre-race 100-meter "fun run" for preschool kids, too. The emphasis on family participation is a goal shared by a sound health-related physical fitness education program.

necessary to facilitate health-related physical fitness. Pacing while running, for example, saves precious energy to go the distance. Thus, students need to learn to judge their effort and speed. Students should also master basic running biomechanics and other techniques (e.g., proper stretching and weight-lifting safety) to prevent injury, ensuring they can participate safely and efficiently in the long term. Students must be able to not only identify but also use specific strategies for measuring frequency, intensity, and time of their participation in physical activity. Other relevant health-related fitness skills include ability to accurately monitor and interpret heart rates, ability to apply basic injury prevention and treatment strategies, and evidence of physical activity participation or, for older students, of employing a self-designed personal fitness plan. You must design a developmentally appropriate, progressive curriculum for teaching these skills from K–12. Refer to the many content suggestions and teaching tips in chapters 13 and 14.

Inexpensive Lifetime Fitness Activities

Because the cost of an activity can be the most prohibitive factor for an otherwise enthusiastic individual, here we list less costly physical activities and curriculum guidelines for elementary and secondary levels. Not surprisingly, generally the lower the equipment and facility requirements, the lower the expense of the activity. Note that this means lower expense for your program as well as the student or adult participant.

Walking, Jogging, Running

Elementary curriculum decision guidelines: Ensure that walking and running gaits are correct. Discuss safety in terms of where to run, watching out for traffic, and so on. Also discuss appropriate shoes, clothes, safety in weather conditions (heat and cold), and reflective clothes/shoes when running or walking at night. Devise fun run events and geography scenarios (e.g., log miles from your school to a fun or historical site such as an amusement park or a national park). Establish a walk/jog club before and/or after school. Set limits on number of laps allowed to encourage honesty and participation. Reward milestones (e.g., 10, 20, 25 laps) with participation certificates.

Secondary curriculum decision guidelines: Include units on hiking, backpacking, and orienteering. Get involved with local running and walking clubs. Have students get involved with local runs/walks for charity.

Jumping Rope

Elementary curriculum decision guidelines: Make jumping rope fun. For example, include jumping to popular music. Have your students learn unique ways to jump. Have students help you design jump rope games. Organize jump rope demonstrations. Contact a Jump Rope for Heart coordinator for new ideas (see appendix C).

Secondary curriculum decision guidelines: Emphasize how easy it is to store and use a jump rope for cardiorespiratory fitness. Hold voluntary contests for displaying skills and endurance. Make it clear that the demonstrations are just for fun, and that they are not required and are not for grading purposes. Use jump rope stations in circuit training programs—it's a great individual warm-up activity.

In-Line Skating

Elementary curriculum decision guidelines: Teach students the basics, especially safety and equipment.

Secondary curriculum decision guidelines: Use peer tutors to help those students who don't already know how to skate. With advanced students, have them keep logs of distance or time per week on their own. Take students to local areas where it is safe to in-line skate.

Dancing

Elementary curriculum decision guidelines: Emphasize fun and the basic steps. Point out that dancing can be a great way to stay in shape and have fun. Dancing is a great creative activity. It is excellent for processing basic skills and movements in a non-competitive way.

Secondary curriculum decision guidelines: Also emphasize dance as a fun way to be physically active. Work on dances that are currently "hot." Point out appropriate places for teenagers to go to dance in the community.

Bicycling

Elementary curriculum decision guidelines: Teach basic skills and emphasize safety and appropriate equipment. Discuss the fitness benefits of biking. Don't forget fun as well.

Secondary curriculum decision guidelines: Discuss opportunities in local community— bike trails, off-road opportunities, local bike clubs, local races, and so on. Talk about equipment and clothing. Have students develop training logs for their cycling pursuits.

Harvest Scavenger Hunt

In this elementary level seasonal walk/run activity, students in groups go to six or seven locations at which you have posted a cue card with directions to the next station and a letter written on a 3 × 5 card, which they will unscramble and use to spell a fall food item or holiday.

To organize this event, if, for example, you have six groups, create six stations and direct each group to begin at a different station. Give each group a number and place that number on each of that group's letter cards. Give each group a list of the order in which they should visit the stations to try to prevent having more than one group at a station at a time. When the groups have collected all their letter cards, have them return to the start and act out their food item or holiday for the rest of the class.

Jennie Gilbert
California State University
San Bernardino, California

Summary

A quality physical education curriculum provides the framework within which students learn the necessary health-related physical fitness education concepts. It integrates motor skills (see *Moving Into the Future: National Standards for Physical Education* for details on sequencing motor skills within a curriculum) and actual physical activity in a developmentally appropriate K–12 progression as well as other subject areas to create a well-balanced, meaningful approach. Students should graduate from a well-designed and expertly implemented health-related physical fitness education curriculum empowered and inspired to lead physically active lives. Use the strategies outlined in this chapter to design your own curriculum.

Chapter 12

Effective Teaching Principles for Lifelong, Individualized Health-Related Fitness

Teaching is a process, and because it is a process, teaching behavior is interactive and, to a large degree, context specific. Not only must teachers have the technical skills of teaching, they must also be able to use those skills appropriately for particular situations. . . . The goal is not the acquisition of discrete, effective teaching behavior, but effective, context-specific practice.

—Judith E. Rink (1998)

No matter how well-conceived a curriculum plan is, it is two-dimensional: It might look good, but it's flat and lifeless. Effective teaching brings a three-dimensional learning environment to life out of the plan. Through appropriate learning experiences, it affects student behaviors as evidenced by actual behavioral changes in students. Effective teaching takes many forms.

Create an Enjoyable and Active Learning Environment

Students might not remember the details of your program when they're in their 50s, but chances are they will remember how they felt about it and physical activity. Work to make good memories for tomorrow's adults, while providing a balanced health-related physical fitness education program.

> The goals related to the development of self-esteem, self-direction, and a sense of responsibility for self and others, which we share with all educational programs in the school, may actually have more of an impact on maintaining an active lifestyle than our unique contribution in motor skills and fitness.
>
> —Judith E. Rink (1994)

Set a Positive Tone

Run your program in a positive manner:

- Create an attractive learning environment—Get rid of the torn, faded, and outdated posters and take the time to create bright and interesting bulletin boards and other wall displays that teach. Integrate

Provide students with both general and specific positive feedback.

student work and pictures of your students in action whenever possible. Older students, parents, and other volunteers can help create these displays. Make sure your activity areas, locker rooms, and classroom are clean, freshly painted, and safe. Grass in outdoor areas should be cut regularly and free of debris and "potholes" (see chapter 4).

- Play music—Music can welcome students, signal station changes, and provide a stimulating background. Within the bounds of good taste, allow students to bring tapes or CDs from home (screen before using in class).

- Know your students—A person's name is very precious to him or her, and knowing each student's name is the beginning of developing true rapport as well as an essential factor in managing behavior. At the elementary level, request that classroom teachers send students to class wearing name tags until you know everyone's name. Devise physically active games that help both you and students learn everyone's name. For both younger and older students, take or obtain class or individual pictures and practice identifying students at home.

- Make all students feel welcome—Greet each student as an individual at the door as he or she enters the class site. A nod, smile, or high-five means a lot to students, especially those who may not feel successful in other school settings. Seek out the quiet student while circulating among students during class and work to find common interests with the difficult student.

- Give general and specific positive feedback—It's only natural: Focus on the positive and kids will, too. Offer both general praise such as "Good job!" or "Keep up the good work!" and specific positive feedback such as "I like the way you paced yourself during the mile run." When giving corrective feedback, serve a "praise sandwich" by offering a positive comment, then the corrective feedback, and finally another positive statement. For example, say, "I see

Praise Phrases

Praise and encouragement are two ways we can all feel good about ourselves and each other. Here are 71 ways to say "Very good!"

1. "Good for you!"
2. "Superb."
3. "You did that very well."
4. "You've got it made."
5. "Terrific."
6. "Couldn't have done it better myself."
7. "You're doing fine."
8. "You're really improving."
9. "Now you've figured it out."
10. "Outstanding!"
11. "Incredible!"
12. "Good work."
13. "You figured that out fast."
14. "I think you've got it now."
15. "Tremendous!"
16. "You did well today."
17. "Perfect!"
18. "Nice going."
19. "Now you've got the hang of it."
20. "Wow!"
21. "Wonderful!"
22. "You're getting better every day."
23. "You're learning fast."
24. "You make it look easy."
25. "Super!"
26. "You did a lot of work today!"
27. "Keep it up!"
28. "Congratulations."
29. "Exactly right!"
30. "Nice job."
31. "Excellent!"
32. "Sensational!"
33. "You've just about mastered that."
34. "That's really nice."
35. "That's the best ever."
36. "That's great!"
37. "Way to go!"
38. "That's the way to do it!"
39. "That's quite an improvement."
40. "Good thinking."
41. "You're really going to town."
42. "Keep up the good work."
43. "That's better."
44. "You nailed that one."
45. "You haven't missed a thing."
46. "Fantastic!"
47. "You're doing a good job."
48. "That's the right way to do it."
49. "Good try."
50. "Right on!"
51. "That's the best you've ever done."
52. "That's RIGHT!"
53. "You must have been practicing!"
54. "Great!"
55. "Keep working on it—you're getting better."
56. "You remembered!"
57. "That kind of work makes me very happy."
58. "You're really working hard today."
59. "I knew you could do it!"
60. "One more time and you'll have it."
61. "Fine!"
62. "That's good."
63. "Good job."
64. "You really make this fun."
65. "Nothing can stop you now."
66. "You are doing much better today."
67. "Keep on trying."
68. "You are really learning a lot."
69. "You've just about got it."
70. "I've never seen anyone do it better."
71. "You are very good at that."

Create a learning environment that students want to be in and therefore set the scene for fun and fitness.

Reprinted, by permission, from D. Glover and D. Midura, 1992, *Team Building Through Physical Challenges*. (Champaign, IL: Human Kinetics), 9.

you are pacing yourself better while running. Now try to see if you can finish stronger. You've really come a long way since school started!"

Run Classes Efficiently

It's vital to effective class management, safety, and a good learning atmosphere to establish routines and otherwise facilitate smooth lessons. In short, chaos is not fun, so be organized and efficient:

• Set up equipment before class. If this is not possible, have it ready to go in your storage area. Test audiovisual equipment and computer programs before trying to use them in class. Train students to help with setup and cleanup.

• Establish routines for taking attendance, signaling stopping and starting, keeping equipment still during instruction, and dealing with emergency situations.

• Ensure you have enough equipment to minimize time wasted waiting for turns, from having enough jump ropes in the gymnasium to having enough pencils in the classroom (see also chapter 4).

• Keep your instructions short and to the point, returning students to the physical activity as soon as possible.

Always be thinking of other ways you can make your classes run more smoothly in your particular situation.

Supervise Actively

Circulate among students during each physical and classroom activity, giving feedback while still keeping an eye on the entire class. Move closer to students who are straying off task. Often you won't even have to say anything to them. Simply communicate in a firm but friendly manner that you know what is going on in your class, that you are "with it," and that you expect cooperation (Graham 1992). You don't have to use words; for example, a slight smile can say "Come on, let's get back to business" without being threatening or confrontational. Find what works for you and short-circuit behavior problems—before they escalate or spread to other students.

Keep Students Focused

Carefully plan the focus of each lesson and stick with it. As described in chapter 11, a complete lesson begins with a set induction, continues with the core lesson content, and concludes with a closure activity. Use each of these parts to focus and refocus student attention as necessary on the key lesson objectives. Work at communicating this focus clearly; for example, put critical directions and information in writing (posters, handouts, student folders, and the like) both to place the responsibility for learning back on students and to avoid repeating yourself. Then check for understanding as you circulate among students during the core lesson con-

Avoid Being Negative

Lavay, French, and Henderson, authors of *Positive Behavior Management Strategies for Physical Education* (1997) suggest you avoid the following practices:

• Comparing children to each other—this is a form of putting down.

• Making idle threats—say what you mean, mean what you say, do what you say you're going to do.

• Being sarcastic—hurting feelings is never a positive action to take.

• Humiliating students—never make fun of students or use anyone as a negative example (e.g., "Look at the way Sue runs. Boy, that's how *not* to do it!").

• Using physical activity as punishment—need we say more?

• Overreacting—don't say something you can't, won't, or shouldn't follow through on.

tent. Ask yourself, Do students seem to understand what they're supposed to be doing? Can they answer my questions quickly and confidently? Finally, use informal assessment strategies as part of each closure activity to give you input into how to shape the next lesson (see also part 4 on assessment).

Ensure Developmental Appropriateness

First, study guidelines set by experts in the field such as the Council on Physical Education for Children (COPEC) and Middle and Secondary School Physical Education Council (MASSPEC) of the National Association for Sport and Physical Education (NASPE). Then use experience as the best teacher: Learn by trial and error what each particular group of students can handle. Perhaps three of your fourth-grade classes do well with an activity, for example, but one class simply cannot handle it. Instead of bemoaning this fact (especially to the students), "think on your feet," modifying the activity to ensure all students can benefit and feel successful, or change to another activity that will help meet the same objectives.

Initially target developmental appropriateness on a grade-level basis. One important key to ensuring you have time to break down concepts into learnable pieces based on student ability is to not try to do too much in too short a time. Rink (1994) suggests that "targeting grades for particular goals allows time to develop those goals avoiding the use of all the K–12 time for one aspect of the program [e.g., calculating heart rate]." Rink (1998) also recommends that physical educators "choose several grades throughout the curriculum that will focus primarily on fitness [e.g., fourth, eighth, and tenth grades]" and that teachers "design a large part of the year to meet [fitness] objectives."

Once developmentally appropriate grade-level curriculum is set, look closely at each student. Planning individualization into each lesson helps ensure developmental appropriateness and therefore, success and benefits

Recommended Reading

The COPEC and MASSPEC pamphlets listing developmentally appropriate practices by age group are recommended reading for all teachers of physical education. Order by calling NASPE. See appendix C.

- COPEC. 1992. "Developmentally Appropriate Physical Education Practices for Children." Reston, VA: NASPE/AAHPERD.
- MASSPEC. 1995. "Appropriate Practices for Middle School Physical Education." Reston, VA: NASPE/AAHPERD.
- MASSPEC. 1998. "Appropriate Practices for High School Physical Education." Reston, VA: NASPE/AAHPERD.

for each child. This may mean making a task easier or more difficult for one individual or small group. For example, for a flexibility task, it may mean you have some students perform the sit-and-reach touching their knees, whereas others reach for their toes or beyond their toes. For an aerobic endurance activity, you might have students use the PACER tape for an activity called "Beep and Turn." In this activity, a child turns at whatever point she is on her way to the endline and travels in the opposite direction until the next beep, at which point, she turns and runs toward the opposite endline, and so on. Graham (1992) calls this process *intratask variation,* which, simply put, is selecting a way to make a task easier for a lower skilled student or more difficult for a higher skilled student. Appropriate adjustments motivate students to keep practicing because the task meets the individual's needs better and is therefore more interesting.

Another way to individualize is *teaching by invitation,* which is "simply a way of allowing children to adjust the task so they can be successful—and challenged" (Graham 1992). In health-related physical fitness education, this approach allows students to make personal choices regarding intensity and duration of an activity. For example, allow students to choose to practice for the PACER test of aerobic endurance from a list of choices.

Students enjoy making choices. Allowing students to make choices helps them learn self-responsibility. For example, you might let your students select either the PACER or the mile-run as their aerobic endurance test.

Remember, the point is to make the task both learnable and enjoyable, and simply having a choice greatly increases motivation and interest levels. Just as importantly, offering choices simulates real life better. After all, students will choose their training methods as adults and should have practice doing so beginning in kindergarten.

Use Appropriate Teaching Styles

How you actually teach can greatly affect student interest and enjoyment, and therefore student attitudes toward physical activity.

Summary of Teaching Styles

Each of the 11 styles Mosston and Ashworth (1994) describe in their "Spectrum of Teaching Styles" can enhance the health-related physical fitness education program. As you review this summary of the information, think about which styles will work with which lessons in your own teaching situation.

- Command—Teacher makes all the decisions and gives step-by-step instructions that all students follow at the same time. This style is appropriate for teaching a new

skill and for managing a class that needs a high degree of structure. For example, the command style is probably appropriate when teaching students how to properly take their pulse or how to properly put on heart rate monitors.

- Practice—Teacher decides what to teach, demonstrates or uses task sheets to introduce the skill, mandates the amount of time students will practice, and circulates among students giving feedback. Students determine number of practice trials and the order in which they will practice skills (if more than one is part of the lesson). This style is appropriate for teaching a new skill and affords students more latitude than in the command style as to how much practice they think they need. For example, you might ask high school students to bring their heart rates into their target heart rate zones, but allow them to choose from many different activities to do so.

- Reciprocal—Teacher chooses the task, but students give each other feedback during practice times. Teacher should introduce the task by demonstrating it and having students practice giving feedback to the teacher. Teacher helps observers give their partners helpful feedback by providing a task sheet and by monitoring student interactions. This style is appropriate for reviewing previously introduced skills and for enhancing social development. For example, to prepare for taking the *FITNESSGRAM* tests, have students practice the tests in pairs, giving each other feedback on technique.

- Self-check—Teacher determines task, but each student gives himself feedback. This style is appropriate for building self-reliance, but limits interaction with the teacher and fellow students. This style is appropriate for some in-class practice sessions (especially with older students) and for homework assignments that encourage skill practice. For example, ask students to log aerobic endurance activity time performed outside of class. Allow students to select the appropriate activities for themselves and to monitor their own progress, giving themselves feedback through self-assessment of their aerobic endurance fitness.

- Inclusion—Teacher chooses task (as in intratask variation), but allows students a range of performance levels to choose from (as in teaching by invitation). The student takes responsibility for deciding when to move to a more difficult level of performance. This style helps the teacher both individualize lessons and empower students to move closer toward health-related physical fitness activity independence. For example, give students the choice of jogging or walking briskly as a warm-up activity or between a variety of push-ups (with hands on a bench or on the floor, for example) when working on mus-

cular strength and endurance. Express the expectation that students will increase the difficulty when they judge they are ready.

- Guided discovery—Teacher determines the task and then designs a sequence of questions or problems that will lead students to one right answer. Teacher may also need to respond with an activity through which students may test their responses. Student success depends on the teacher's ability to arrange questions or problems in a logical sequence posed at the right time in the learning experience. Although time consuming for both teacher and student, this style helps students remember the answer better than less involved approaches, as students must take more responsibility for discovering the answer. An example of a guided discovery lesson might be assigning students to write a report answering the following questions:

1. One way to maintain good aerobic endurance is to go jogging. What is one jogging route in your community that allows you to jog for 20 minutes starting from school or home?

2. What should you wear? How might this change with the time of day and weather?

3. What are the safety issues to which you have to pay attention? Do these change with the time of day or weather (figure 12.1)?

- Convergent discovery—This style extends the guided discovery style. Teacher poses a problem or question, but students go through the discovery process to converge on the one right answer without teacher

Who's in Charge?

The teacher chooses how to alter an activity when using intratask variation, then directs certain students to make those changes as the teacher deems appropriate, based on observation and past experience. A sequence of small tasks can help accommodate the student having trouble mastering a task. The teacher strives to be diplomatic and to approach individuals privately when employing intratask variation.

When teaching by invitation, the teacher controls what the acceptable choices are, and the students make personal choices from this list. The teacher refrains from ranking choices (i.e., as better or worse) and from pressuring students to make other choices.

guidance. Teacher provides the setting in which students may discover the answer through a process of trial and error. This style is appropriate for students who have become proficient at finding answers through the guided discovery approach. For example, ask high school students to complete a report on what it would take to begin participating in a beneficial aerobic endurance lifetime activity in their community. Have them research the aerobic endurance benefits of various activities, find ones that can be done in the community, and find out the costs for equipment, where to do the activity, and what prerequisite skills are necessary, and so on.

- Divergent production—Teacher poses an open-ended problem for students to problem-solve and find answers to. Students learn that many physical activity situations have multiple solutions. This style is appropriate for students who are ready to work more independently of the teacher to meet health-related fitness challenges. For example, pose a situation to students: You have broken your ankle, but you want to maintain good aerobic endurance fitness while the cast is on. Devise an aerobic endurance fitness plan to meet this challenge.

Figure 12.1 An example of a guided discovery assignment might be assigning students to write a report that answers questions such as, "What safety concerns should you address when jogging in your neighborhood?"

- Individual program-learner's design—Teacher chooses the general subject area, but student determines the task and possible solutions. This style encourages students to design their own learning programs, based on their abilities, interests, and learning styles and so more closely simulates real-world situations, for example, the adult who designs her own health-related fitness program.

- Learner initiated—Similar to previous style, but student chooses general subject area as well and approaches the teacher on his own, not in response to teacher prompting. This style evolves in some older students who, for example, may have specific sport interests that compel them to seek teacher input.

- Self-teaching—The extreme opposite of the command style, this style empowers students to make virtually all the learning decisions. This style is appropriate for high school students who have proven, through the learner-initiated style, that they can pursue their own interests independent of a teacher, and for adults engaging in physical activity on their own.

Work to incorporate several different teaching styles into your program to create variety and give students opportunities to practice greater independence. Keep in mind, too, that, although the styles described form a continuum from teacher dependence to independence, a student does not fully "graduate" from any one approach. For example, the command and practice styles will be appropriate at times for most students all the way through high school—at least for part of a lesson. Even a highly motivated adult will benefit from these more teacher-dependent styles when learning a new physical activity or perfecting a familiar physical activity, such as learning to swim for the first time. However, give students more and more practice farther along the continuum as they grow older and more experienced. This broader experience in self-directed approaches to physical activity will serve them well as adults.

Teaching Tip: Varying Your Teaching Style

Most effective teachers have a variety of teaching styles in their repertoires. Different classes, skills, and concepts will benefit from using different styles, and it is a challenge for teachers to find which styles they find produce the most learning in various situations. The better grasp you have of the different styles, the more likely you will be to try to use them. It can be compared to learning carpentry. If you only have a hammer and a saw in your tool belt, you will be limited as to what kinds of work you will be able to produce. Likewise, if you as a teacher only have two teaching styles in your repertoire, you will be limiting the possibility of reaching all your students—and the opportunity for them to learn more.

Cathrine Himberg
Professor of Physical Education
California State University
Chico, California

From *Teaching Secondary Physical Education in the 21st Century* (in press).

Teaching Styles and the Stairway to Health-Related Lifetime Fitness

Whenever possible, consciously emphasize teaching styles that promote independence to reach the goal of producing adults who independently pursue health-related fitness as a way of life. Indeed, the continuum from the command style to the self-teaching style is the pedagogy behind Corbin and Lindsey's (1993) Stairway to Lifetime Fitness (figure 3.1).

Another way to look at teaching styles is that the ones that facilitate learner independence also, quite naturally, encourage students to use higher levels of thinking (e.g., synthesis, analysis, evaluation). This, in turn, enhances the development of life skills, such as problem solving and making accurate judgments and wise decisions, which can be used both within and outside of the realm of health-related fitness. This is an important consideration when tying your curriculum into a school's overall mission of producing independent learners and doers.

Gardner's Theory of Multiple Intelligences

Just as students learn through different teaching styles, they also possess differing learning styles. One way we can examine this aspect of teaching, take a cross-curricular approach, and individualize our approach further is to look at Gardner's Theory of Multiple Intelligences. Gardner (1983; 1993) asserts that different individuals are strong in different "intelligences." In other words, each of us learns and produces best through various avenues. Each of our students needs to have opportunities to develop weak avenues and to excel through strong avenues. Do this by developing an interdisciplinary team of colleagues or by expanding your own approach.

Bodily-Kinesthetic Intelligence

Individuals strong in bodily-kinesthetic intelligence solve problems or create with their bodies. Mime, crafts, hands-on science, dramatics, physical education, and other creative movement opportunities interest them. Skilled actors, dancers, athletes, surgeons, and craftspeople are likely to be high in bodily-kinesthetic intelligence. To address this intelligence in health-related physical fitness education, be sure to have students actually apply health-related fitness concepts. For example, don't just talk about designing a personal fitness plan: Have students actually design and use such plans.

Spatial Intelligence

Understanding how objects orient in space is the strong suit of individuals with high spatial intelligence. A strong sense of direction and the ability to visualize end products accurately are evidence of this intelligence. Skilled architects, sculptors, and navigators are most likely strong in spatial intelligence. Sketching ideas; using charts, graphs, maps, diagrams, and graphics software; and through building models are the preferred modes of learning. Assign these forms of conveying ideas as project options. In addition, incorporate teacher and student demonstrations into your teaching as much as possible. For example, have students show and analyze each other's running technique.

Interpersonal Intelligence

Ability to understand and relate well to others, as in the cases of psychologists and social workers, indicates strong interpersonal intelligence. Group brainstorming, cooperative activities, peer tutoring, simulations, and community-based activities interest these individuals. Incorporate cooperative learning approaches to foster interpersonal intelligence. A health-related physical fitness education example may be having students work in small groups to develop an aerobic endurance circuit.

Musical Intelligence

Fascination with sound and the ability to interpret, transform, and express musical forms indicates strength in musical intelligence. Skilled musicians and dancers are strong in musical intelligence. Use raps, chants, songs, rhythms, and musical concepts to reach these students.

Music and movement are almost impossible to separate. Consider allowing students to report on health-related fitness research through music. Use music to enliven and set the pace for physical activities as well.

Linguistic Intelligence

Linguistic intelligence involves using words very effectively. Skilled writers, poets, and public speakers are displaying linguistic intel-

ligence. Opportunities to read, tell stories, listen to lectures, and participate in small- and large-group discussions, debate, and writing activities interest these students. To speak to this intelligence, require students to keep a written log of their health-related physical fitness education activities.

Logical-Mathematical Intelligence

A strong ability to reason and use numbers very effectively indicates high logical-mathematical intelligence. Scientists, mathematicians, and engineers are good examples of people high in logical-mathematical intelligence. Science demonstrations, math problems, sequential presentation of subject matter, critical thinking activities, and problem-solving exercises are preferable ways to learn for these individuals.

Challenge secondary students to solve health-related fitness problems, for example, calculating target heart rate zones or the percent of calories (kcal) of fat provided in a serving of a food, how much work is done climbing a flight of stairs, or how many kcals are expended walking versus running a mile. Elementary students can create movement sequences and patterns, such as a jump rope routine or counting reps of selected skills to

Cooperative activities interest students with strong interpersonal intelligence.

repeat a pattern, while developing muscular strength and endurance or aerobic endurance.

Intrapersonal Intelligence

Those who know both their strengths and weaknesses well can be said to be strong in intrapersonal intelligence. They are self-reliant and independent, preferring to learn through making personal connections, using interest centers and self-paced activities, reflecting, and goal setting. A health-related physical fitness education program should guide all students toward becoming more independent through, for example, self-testing and reflective journal writing opportunities.

Naturalistic Intelligence

People who are adept at identifying flora and fauna are strong in naturalistic intelligence. Address this intelligence in health-related physical fitness education by using themes from nature as well as stories and poems about nature to encourage movement experiences that develop health-related physical fitness. For example, performing the crab walk, bear walk, and seal crawl helps young children study movement in nature, while devel-

oping muscular strength and endurance (figure 12.2). At the secondary level, ask science teachers, for example, to create a study of how plants and animals live at high altitudes, and what the physiological implications of performing at high altitude are for humans (i.e., What adaptations have plants and animals made at high altitude? What are the acute changes humans face performing at high altitudes, and what are the chronic adaptations to high altitude?). Secondary students can also consider the value of physical activity in natural settings, such as hiking, canoeing, rafting, and so on.

Summary

Bring your curriculum plan to life by creating an effective learning environment. Use the basic teaching principles we have described in this chapter to encourage students to pursue lifelong health-related fitness. Work to create a fun and active learning environment, use appropriate teaching styles, apply Gardner's Theory of Multiple Intelligences, and truly individualize a curriculum, through addressing each form of intelligence. The next two chapters provide more specifics to help you implement your program.

Figure 12.2   Performing the crab walk and seal crawl helps children study movement in nature while developing muscular strength and endurance.

Chapter 13

Teaching Through Physical Activities

Students should be kept as physically active as possible as they learn necessary movement concepts and skills. In addition, it is ideal to cover cognitive material while students are actively engaged in physical activity. For example, discuss how to stretch safely, while having students stretch as part of a warm-up or cool-down. Sometimes, however, you will need to go into greater depth and use teaching aids not practical in the physical activity setting (e.g., gymnasium, field, or pool). This is where a classroom lecture can greatly enhance your program, as student understanding of the cognitive aspects of health-related physical fitness education is critical (see next chapter).

Most physical educators are already comfortable teaching in gymnasium or outdoor settings, especially when teaching physical skills. You will find as you study this chapter that most of the teaching skills you've honed, while teaching a skill-based curriculum, will carry over well to teaching health-related fitness.

Selecting Activities

When selecting physical activities, emphasize enjoyment, individual choice, and full and active participation. Remember, the ultimate goal is for our students to be physically active for their entire lives. A "boot camp" approach (e.g., regimented calisthenics) does not serve this goal. Instead, instill in your students that physical activity is enjoyable by keeping several aspects in mind when selecting activities.

Developmentally Appropriate

When planning, you tried to choose activities that seemed developmentally appropriate (see chapters 1 and 12). But now, as you're teaching a lesson, you notice that students are confused and some are straying off task even though the lesson is well organized and you're supervising actively. You signal for everyone's attention and explain the activity in different terms and demonstrate once again. But most students are still confused. In such a situation, while perhaps age appropriate, it's possible that the activity is not developmentally appropriate. In other words, it's either too difficult, too easy, or otherwise unreasonable for a particular group of students, and therefore, not beneficial. To state positively, *developmentally appropriate* activities are those that are appropriate based on a student's developmental level, age, ability level, interests, and previous experience and knowledge.

For example, a teacher modified official softball rules to limit team size according to the COPEC (1992) guidelines regarding number of children on a team. He also changed the game to increase intensity and time spent moving actively by having all members of the batting team run the bases when the ball was hit and requiring that all members of the fielding team touch the ball before the batter could be tagged out. However, students were still not enjoying the game, nor were they meeting the lesson's objectives through playing it. Why? In this case, the class consisted of first graders who did not possess the prerequisite skill to strike a pitched ball (the teacher should have used a batting tee) or the fielding skills to field a regulation softball (the teacher should have used a softer ball). Of course, all these conditions would most likely be developmentally appropriate at the secondary level, provided the goals of health-related fitness education are met (i.e., active participation by all students that enhances one or more components of health-related fitness). Modifying activities to meet student needs is a never-ending but extremely important facet of teaching.

Of course, take age into consideration, regardless of ability. For example, if a high schooler lacks aerobic endurance, tag is not an appropriate activity to offer as a choice, but riding a stationary bike while reading a favorite magazine is.

Sequential

Doing the same activities with the same students year after year for no clear pedagogical reason will not only bore students, it will also fail to equip them with the tools and experiences they need to be successful in physical activity.

Review, rather than reteaching, of fitness and movement concepts and skills over

What's Really Important

Even the best health-related fitness education program can only do so much to influence personal fitness levels. Factors such as genetics, parental attitudes, and past experiences also play a major role. But you can greatly influence the process of students' being active for life in appropriate and enjoyable ways. Remember, simply "getting kids in shape" during class may not be the best way to ensure students become active for life; fitness is temporary, and students must want to stay fit. For example, there have been cases of former star athletes who died in middle age of heart attacks because they did not continue to eat well and stay physically active after their playing careers ended, while there are also many people, who could not play sports well in school but walk every day, and, in their 70s, are more healthy and fit than most people half their age.

Competition and Cooperation

Neither competition nor cooperation is inherently good or bad: They are simply two different approaches. On the other hand, competition is best when cooperation is at the highest level. Each can be used in health-related fitness education either to create a positive class atmosphere—or to make students miserable. Consider the following parameters for choosing which approach is most appropriate in a situation:

- Age—primary grade students (K–3rd grades) should experience cooperative situations almost exclusively. Older students (4th–6th grades) can begin to experience competition in limited ways and at carefully selected times. Many secondary students may benefit from and enjoy having more opportunities to compete; but some may not, so keep it as only one choice.

- Choice—competition should be one choice, not the mandated mode of play. For example, set up several basketball games, one in which score is kept between teams, one in which a collective score is kept (adding both teams scores together), and one in which score is not

Some students enjoy competitive activities.

kept at all. Allow students to choose the game in which they'll participate.

- Attitude—focus on affective development by teaching fair play. Teach competing students to cooperate with teammates and to demonstrate respect, such as shaking hands and complementing the opposition after a contest (Clifford and Feezell 1997). Teach students playing cooperative games to be supportive of and positive with each other.

- Goals—students needing to work on social skills may gain more from cooperative activities, but competitive situations can also enhance social skills in older students, particularly if having a good attitude is emphasized. For fitness testing, never encourage competition between students. Rather, encourage each individual to compete with his or her own past performance to improve over time.

Cooperative activities are a great way of teaching social skills and teaching students that physical activity does not have to be competitive to be beneficial.

the years is important to learning. In addition, sequential patterns should take into consideration individual readiness to progress. The key is to build upon the topic over the years so that students progress to adulthood with the knowledge, skills, and experience they need to be physically active in meaningful ways. Table 13.1 shows examples of topics as they develop from age group to age group.

Table 13.1   Sample Activity Progressions by Topic

	Primary (K–3)	Intermediate	Middle/junior high school	High school
Corbin and Lindsey's Stairway to Lifetime Fitness (1993)	Step 1—Doing regular exercise	Step 2—Achieving physical fitness	Step 3—Personal exercise patterns	Step 4—Self-evaluation Step 5—Problem solving/decision making
Heart rate	Place hand on heart before and after vigorous activity and compare speed of HR	Count pulse; learn math to find HR based on partial count; use HR monitors to help stay in THRZ	Practice math to find HR based on partial count; graph HR monitor data; assess effort based on graphed data	Design workouts based on knowledge of HR and THRZ
Running	Learn correct stride; run in low-organization games	Analyze running strides of peers, using rubric; design low-organization games that incorporate a high amount of running	Teach peers to run more efficiently; report on how running efficiently helps one succeed in a favorite sport	Design interval workouts that alternate high- and low-intensity effort as determined by heart rate; make the workout fun for a friend to do
Upper-body strength training	Play on the monkey bars on the playground	Play fun push-up games (see Hichwa 1998); learn tubing exercises	Learn more tubing exercises; design games that increase muscular strength without equipment	Learn how to lift weights safely; design a personal weight-training program; explore community options for weight training and do cost analysis
Throwing/ catching	Learn basic skills; apply in low-organization, small-sided games	Design low-organization, small-sided games to practice the skills; self-analyze what makes a throw stronger	Modify a physical activity that involves these skills to include a stronger aerobic endurance component	Apply skills in more complex games; analyze similarities in the skills' uses among several sports

Keep in mind that the ideas in table 13.1 are only a few of the many ways each topic can be taught. Have students apply the same information in a variety of ways from unit to unit and year to year to keep interest high, and to provide more meaningful experiences that will transfer to real life better.

Enjoyable

Learning is the goal, of course, but it cannot be stressed enough that enjoyment is an essential part of a quality health-related physical fitness education program. Without interesting and enjoyable activities, a program lacks one of the greatest intrinsic motivators. Enjoyment, or "fun," is a by-product of effective teaching.

Naturally, what's enjoyable for an adult may not be enjoyable for a child. For example, a busy parent may seek physical activity as a way to make time for him- or herself, while a middle schooler may seek physical activity as a way to socialize with peers. Another student may find a highly competitive basketball game enjoyable, whereas still another may prefer jumping rope to music. So pay attention to the psychological makeup of each class as you select activities and teaching styles to use (more on teaching styles later).

Many factors affect how enjoyable your program is, some of which follow.

Variety

Variety allows you to show students several different ways they might apply what they learn in real life. For example, when you vary warm-up activities, depending on the main physical activity, available equipment and facilities, weather, and other factors, you model this approach to students (see also chapter 5). Even given the same factors, vary the warm-up just for the fun of it. A change of music, a change of scenery (e.g., walk to a nearby park for the lesson), a change of leader (e.g., students or adult volunteers instead of you), can all make your lessons more interesting. At every level offer choices. Station teaching and elective courses can help. For example, design a high school curriculum that offers electives such as aerobic dance, volleyball, fitness walking, softball, and strength training instead of offering "9th," "10th," "11th," and "12th grade" physical education classes. The heart doesn't care if it is getting in shape through in-line skating, swimming, dancing, or whatever. You'll also find that appropriate choices can increase participation and decrease discipline problems.

Using Learning Stations Effectively

Grineski (1996) asserts that a "learning station circuit is a series of activities, usually centered around a particular theme or skill." He offers several hints:

- Reinforce what students have already learned—do *not* introduce new skills or concepts.
- Pictures, diagrams, and written description cards help students learn and remember.
- Let students help design some of the activities.
- Focus on one specific skill, concept, or fitness component at each station.
- Alternate the intensity or specificity of the physical activity from station to station.
- Post signs to direct traffic flow.
- Instruct younger students to use different locomotor skills to move from station to station. Music can cue students to move to the next station or serve as a background.
- Designate a peer coach for each group. Brief these students during the class warm-up.
- Insist on responsible behavior.
- Individualize: build skill and intensity choices into instructions.

Adapted, by permission, from S. Grineski, 1996, "Improving Practices in Elementary Physical Education," *Teaching Elementary Physical Education* 7(5):14-15.

Lifetime of Tennis

Tennis is an example of a physical activity that can be enjoyed throughout a person's life. It is important to prepare your students for lifetime activities by carefully planning appropriate sequential progressions.

The key to teaching lifetime activities is to build on them over the years so that students will progress to adulthood with the knowledge, skills, and appreciation they need to be physically active in meaningful ways.

© CLEO Photography

Encourage students to make suggestions for variations, perhaps as a homework assignment. Poll high school students as to what physical education electives they would like to see offered. This approach brings the cognitive domain into play in a relevant way.

Safety

A safe learning environment is the foundation of learning and fun. After all, no one can learn about or enjoy physical activity if he or she is afraid of physical or emotional pain. Be positive with students and individualize instruction (see chapter 12). Ensure proper physical conditions (e.g., temperature, humidity levels, clean facilities in good repair), appropriate equipment, and developmentally appropriate activities. Match up students in group and partner activities to avoid size mismatches that can lead to injury.

Inclusion

Although this term is generally used as a philosophical and programmatic descriptor relating to students with special needs or disabilities, we are broadening this to target every student. Simply put, being included in a positive way is fun; being excluded intentionally or by default is not. Figure 13.1 lists components you can focus on in the physical activity setting to

---

You can offer choices of one or more components of an activity to teach by invitation or designate changes to employ intratask variation.

- Equipment—size, type (e.g., hard or soft ball)
- Distances—from target, between bases, of endlines from each other, of sidelines from each other
- Rules—cooperative or competitive, child designed or teacher designed, participate alone or with a group or partner
- Movement—speed, type (e.g., form of locomotion), effort
- Time (duration)—increase or decrease time allowed for a task

---

Figure 13.1 By offering choices and modifying components of activities, you can create physical activity opportunities inclusive of all student.

teach by invitation and employ intratask variation effectively (see also chapter 12).

Model for students how to modify activities to include their peers. In fact, assigning a task that involves designing an inclusive physical activity is another excellent way to encourage cognitive development in physical education. In turn, this process provides additional practice for modifying physical activities to better suit oneself and therefore to include oneself in physical activity outside the physical education setting (see also discussion on games design in chapter 15).

In keeping with the philosophy of inclusion, remember that elimination games and long waits for turns are the opposites of inclusion. Usually the child who most needs to practice the skill is the first to be eliminated. Likewise, the child who waits in a long line gains little or nothing and can even keep slipping to the back of the line to avoid physical activity altogether. In general, you can reduce waiting time and eliminate elimination by

- supplying enough equipment (e.g., one ball per child),
- setting up small-sided games so turns are more frequent,
- running several games at once so an eliminated player simply rotates to another group and continues to play,
- altering rules to keep everyone playing (e.g., in a tag game, have "helpers" who "unfreeze" taggers quickly; "Steal-the-Bacon Baseball" in which everyone receives a pass before the ball is put up for a goal), and
- having baseball batting teams perform a locomotor task while the base runner runs the bases so all are active.

Many teachers have worked hard to change games and other physical activities to be more inclusive. See chapter 15 on including students with special needs and games design.

Purposeful

Yes, we want our students to enjoy themselves, but there's no time to waste. Always be sure you screen each activity according to the parameters discussed in chapter 11. Ask yourself, Does this activity enhance students' chances of reaching a program goal? If not, modify it or choose another activity.

Practice times are essential but easily squandered. It is too easy to lose sight of their purpose and simply pass the time. Someone once said, "Practice doesn't make perfect, perfect practice makes perfect." For our purposes, this means skill practice (both fitness and motor) is only helpful if it is organized and carried out in effective ways. Selecting and giving appropriate cues are two aspects of using this time wisely (see later in chapter). Organizing the learning environment properly is another (see chapter 12). Then make sure students receive helpful and frequent peer and teacher feedback.

Connected

Another way to ensure an activity serves Physical Best's purpose—the ultimate goal—in health-related physical fitness education is to connect it to real life wherever possible. For example, let primary students know that playing small-sided games of soccer now will help them get in better shape and do better in "real" soccer and other physical activities when they are in middle school. Help older students see the connections between being physically active and looking and feeling better.

As students move from middle to high school, it's especially important to select activities that are relevant to them both now and in their futures. Show them what is available in your community for young adults. Are there bike paths, volleyball leagues, cross-country skiing, walking paths, health clubs, and so on? Take field trips to introduce students to the many options available. Have community members (e.g., health fitness instructors, league directors, running club leaders, and sport facility owners, and the like) come to class to demonstrate new activities and tell students how they can get involved. Assign homework that relates to the real world, such as consumer education assignments. For example, have them price ski equipment, lift

ticket cost, and other expenses so they can plan a ski trip. Or have them select the health club they would join as an adult and write a paper about why they chose the particular club. In short, the older students are, the more authentic the activities you choose should be. Certainly, having 12th graders who, for example, have no interest in track and field practicing the discus and shot put is a waste of time.

Teaching Principles for Physical Activity

Here, we look more closely at the day-to-day issues that will affect your program.

Professionalism

Help parents, students, administrators, and the general public remember you're not a playground supervisor; you're a well-trained educator, ready to give the students your best. Accomplish this primarily by staying current on educational topics and instructional techniques. As an aside, dress to be active, but do so professionally. Nice sweats with a polo shirt would be appropriate at most schools. A ragged T-shirt and cut-off shorts clearly are not appropriate.

The deeper, lasting impression you make, however, must come from a positive attitude and energetic approach. Don't sit on the sidelines reading the newspaper or planning the basketball team's practice. You may laugh at these stereotypical images; unfortunately, however, some physical education teachers still behave in these unprofessional ways. Instead, use and adapt the ideas described in chapter 12 for creating a positive learning environment in which students want to participate fully.

> No one is angrier and more offended by a bad teacher than a good teacher.
>
> —Dave, teacher

Finally, continue to seek professional development throughout your career. Always

Should Physical Educators Be Fit?

Physical activity should be an integral part of your life. You should be a walking, talking advertisement for fitness and healthy living. Remember, fitness is a pursuit, a process, a lifestyle. It's about making the right choices for living a higher quality life.

As teachers, we have an enormous responsibility to be role models for youngsters. Because our profession deals with healthy, active living, it is imperative that we convey such a lifestyle to our students. We can't reach children in today's society by telling them: Do as we say, not as we do. We have to lead by example. If we want to create healthy, active, self-responsible adults, then we have to be healthy, active, self-responsible adults ourselves. Think of it this way: You wouldn't ask an illiterate person how to read, and you wouldn't ask a poor person how to make money. So why would you expect your students to ask an overweight, out-of-shape, inactive person to help them become fit? If we're not passionate about practicing what we preach, how can we expect to excite our students?

True, not everyone is going to have the perfect body, no matter how much they exercise. But everyone can live active, healthy lives, allowing them to lead by example. It's never to late to become a positive role model. That's part of being an effective educator in any discipline.

Adapted, by permission, from C. Hinson, 1998, "Should Physical Education Teachers Be Fit?," *Teaching Elementary Physical Education* 9(3):23.

strive to learn more and do better for all your students. Teaching is as much about *learning* as it is about *teaching*.

Presenting Information Effectively

Presenting information effectively is a cornerstone of good teaching. Rink (1998) describes four aspects of task presentation, which we will explore from the health-related physical fitness education perspective. *Task presentation* can be defined as the method(s) through which a learning experience is presented for maximal learning.

Get the Students' Attention

Students cannot learn if they are not paying attention to your explanations, demonstrations, and discussions. Therefore, set a protocol for gaining and regaining students' attention, such as a drumbeat, whistle blow (outdoors only), or other signal that saves your voice. Teach students exactly what you expect them to do upon hearing the signal.

For example, stop talking and manipulating equipment, sit or stand still in self-space, or gather in a designated area (e.g., around you, a particular corner, or the like). Make sure your protocols allow for all students to see and hear you clearly. It may seem like a waste of time to have students move closer to you when they're fully engaged in, for example, practicing the back-saver sit-and-reach test, but, if they don't understand you simply because of distance from you, you will waste far more class time on redirecting student activity. Also, ensure students are not blinded by sunlight in outdoor settings. Try to minimize distractions and noises over which you have no control, such as workmen in the class area, as much as possible. A final note: Do not attempt to shout over the noise of the class, such as social talking or the sound of jump ropes hitting the floor during an aerobic endurance session. Keep your instructions as brief as possible, but gain and insist on full attention at all times. Use multiple resources (visual aids, posters) to reinforce critical protocols.

Present the Content in a Logical Sequence

Rink (1998) asserts, "How the teacher [sequences] the content and organizational aspects of the task can determine how successful the student response to the task will be." Students need to know what task they are to perform and how they will practice the task—in that order, without mixing the two parts of the information. In other words, describe the content first, then discuss exactly how the practice will be organized. Otherwise, students, who know too soon that they need, for example, to find a partner, will be focusing on that aspect instead of listening to the content.

For example, first explain to students how to help a partner practice correct curl-up form. Only then direct students to find a partner and move to a free space and begin. You can also reverse this process by giving organizational instructions first, waiting for students to carry them out, and then giving the content information. Simply be sure that students can still hear and see you. Some classes may need to have organizational instructions broken down into smaller individual steps than others. Wait until each step is completed before stating the next step. Use your judgment and experience to determine which approach and what level of task breakdown you must employ with each particular group of students.

Communicate Clearly

Many factors affect how well students receive what you are trying to communicate. Although you cannot control every factor all the time, you can greatly enhance the likelihood that students will understand you clearly by following the guidelines outlined here. (The following list is adapted, by permission, from J. Rink, 1998, *Teaching Physical Education for Learning*, 3rd ed. (New York, NY: McGraw-Hill Companies), 89-94. Reproduced with the permission of the McGraw-Hill Companies.):

- **Set induction.** As discussed in chapter 12, students learn better if you orient them toward what they will be learning. This "priming the pump" prepares them for the lesson to come.

- **Logical sequencing of information.** In general, students need to learn how to perform a task in the order they will actually do it. For example, teaching correct push-up form should begin with showing students the start position as described in the *FITNESSGRAM Test Administration Manual (Second Edition)* and proceed step-by-step, until the body has returned to the start position.

- **Examples and nonexamples.** Help students understand what the concept or skill is and is not. For example, demonstrate a flexed arm hang correctly and incorrectly, and discuss the differences in form.

- **Getting personal.** Use student names and draw on student experiences to enhance everyone's attentiveness and understanding. For example, invite individuals to share their muscular strength and endurance training experiences when introducing a new related exercise.

Well-organized activities enhance student learning.

- **Repetition.** While you should not circulate repeating instructions (because you did not originally have the class's attention), recognize that few learners initially understand instruction completely. Use multiple sources of information so students can get it in different ways and many times. Be patient and re-explain new and difficult concepts during and after practice sessions. For example, students may have more articulate questions to ask about developing good aerobic endurance after employing a personal fitness plan for a week.

- **Determining understanding.** Double-check student understanding before students begin practicing by asking pointed questions. For example, have the entire class demonstrate for you where to find their pulse by touching the site(s) you have introduced. Then excuse them to begin the activity.

Choose How to Communicate

Both verbal and nonverbal communication play vital roles in health-related physical fitness education. Media, such as a VCR, can enhance both these forms of communication.

With verbal communication, be careful that students know what you are talking about; it is easy to assume students understand more than they do (Rink 1998). Verbal communication of a new skill or concept should be coupled with demonstration so that students can see for themselves how any new vocabulary and actions are connected.

Rink (1998) suggests many tips for effective demonstrations. Demonstrations need to be accurate; use student demonstrators as much as possible. Present demonstrations in the same organizational format as you will require the students to practice the task. For example, if you will have students practice the curl-up in groups of three, use a group of three to demonstrate. While demonstrating, focus on the most important aspects, and explain why a task should be performed a certain way. Finally, check to ensure students understood the demonstration, either by asking questions or having the students demonstrate for you to observe and offer feedback.

Preview any media you use to ensure it will do what you need it to do. Set up the computer or VCR and monitor ahead of time, and test to ensure it's functioning properly—before 35 students are staring at a blank screen. Adapt use of any media to *your* students' needs (Rink 1998).

Give Effective Cues

The following tips will help you cue student performance more effectively:

1. Offer only one idea at a time (Graham 1992). Decide what the most important aspect of a skill or concept is, then focus on and communicate it clearly to students.

2. Be accurate (Rink 1998). Know the content in order to select the most important features of a task. Use the Physical Best materials to help familiarize yourself with the content of health-related fitness education.

3. Keep it brief (Graham 1992; Rink 1998). Don't overwhelm students with too much information (see Tip 1) and don't bore students and lose their attention. Repeat yourself during practice sessions as described in the next tip.

4. Use a reminder word or phrase (Graham 1992). Pick a cue word or short phrase appro-

---

Surf for Teaching Tips

The World Wide Web on the Internet has become an excellent source of teaching tips shared by physical educators around the country. Because sites are always changing, you can start by visiting the American Fitness Alliance site (**www.americanfitness.net**), which maintains current links to physical education sites. The AFA site will serve as a gateway to health-related physical fitness education information.

priate to the age and ability of the class to remind students to focus on the desired component (e.g., "target" to remind students to stay in their target heart rate zones during a step routine). This keeps everyone focused on the target skill or concept without having to stop the action.

Class Management

Class management involves maintaining appropriate control of students and the teaching environment to ensure that all students are safe and can learn. Such issues can make or break all your good intentions. In fact, stress caused by this area is the single greatest reason physical education teachers leave the profession, making its intricacies essential to master. Know the options for dealing with students who do not respond appropriately to your efforts to prevent problems (as discussed in chapter 12), that is, those who misbehave for whatever reason.

Focus on establishing and practicing varying methods to maintain class control, make the activities engaging to students, lessening the chances of misbehavior occurring, and use stations to allow for variety while managing large classes, and so on.

If a student persists in misbehaving, in spite of your efforts to prevent problems, you can try several strategies. Less serious interventions might include the following:

- Making positive eye contact with the student as a quiet reminder (this should *not* be a "dirty look," however).

- Moving closer to the student without saying anything; both Graham (1992) and Rink (1998) call this *proximity control*.

- Privately asking an individual student to stop the behavior.

- For widespread misbehavior, regaining the class's attention and having students share what the class is supposed to be doing to help them refocus, then returning the class to the activity.

Discuss a student who persistently disrupts class or displays off-task and/or dangerous

behavior with colleagues and administrators. They may have insights into how to deal with a particular student. It is also especially important to present a consistent approach to such a student. More serious interventions might include the following:

- Time out used judiciously with younger students can be effective. Invite the student to return to the activity after a set time or when he or she is able to state what he or she *will* do that is appropriate.

- Loss or delay of a privilege, such as being allowed to use special equipment during a free time. Student must complete the main task appropriately first.

- A note or phone call to parents outlining the student's behavior and asking for support.

- Behavior contract developed in a private conference with student and, possibly, parents.

- Detention. Student may return to class when he or she has agreed to a plan for improved behavior, including consequences and rewards for behavior.

Ensure that you are in tune with your school's policies and that you use serious interventions with caution. Overuse can weaken their effectiveness. At the same time, examine your efforts to prevent problems to ensure you are doing all you can to make each student's time in your class positive and beneficial. The opposites of some of these interventions make good reinforcers of positive behavior, for example, a positive note or phone call to parents or a chance to use a special piece of equipment.

Finally, it may be a cliché, but an ounce of prevention *is* worth a pound of cure. Be positive and upbeat in your approach and reach out to those students whom you perceive are likely to present behavior problems. Don Hellison's *Teaching Responsibility Through Physical Activity* (1995) is a great resource for handling behavior problems. A positive action, instead of a negative reaction on your part, can turn a student around. As Ambrose Brazelton says, "Teach them all." (See sidebar on the next page.)

Teach Them All

Teach them all! Teach them all!
The thin, the stout, the tall;
The shy and the others, the sisters
and brothers,
The handicapped, the awkward, the small.

Teach them love, teach to their speeds,
Balance, endurance, and needs;
Respect and good manners, three Rs
and the grammars,
The ethics, the principles, the creeds.

Let them search and explore,
Their space, the walls, the outdoors;
The science of motion, the creative notion,
Decisions and problems galore.

Our task, our main goal
Is to guide and develop the whole;
Not merely athletics! Nor alphabetics;
Teach them all,
Teach it all, that's our role.

—Ambrose E. Brazelton, W.G.B.

Reprinted, by permission, from *I May Be Little but I'm Big Inside*, Great Activities Publishing Co., Durham, NC, 1991, p. 20.

Teaching Fitness Skills in the Gymnasium or Outdoors

Basic fitness skills are essential to providing students with the knowledge they need to independently participate in physical activity. Although students may benefit from having skills introduced in a lecture setting, in this chapter, we focus on those that are best taught mainly through physical activities conducted in the physical activity setting. We discuss other fitness skills that generally require more lecture time to teach in chapter 14.

Injury Prevention

Create a safe learning environment for all instruction and practice. Teach students specific safety information so that they can participate safely in physical activity throughout their lives.

- Proper warm-ups and cool-downs—The body needs time to prepare for and recover from moderate to vigorous physical activity. So don't just have students warm up and cool down; make sure they understand why. Have secondary students design their own warm-ups and cool-downs appropriate for their chosen physical activities and their physical condition. Some take longer to warm up or cool down, and all students need to "feel" warmed up or cooled down.

- Proper progression—You cannot emphasize enough the importance of increasing frequency, intensity, and time gradually. Nothing good is gained by doing too much too soon.

- Accurate specificity—Injuries can occur when the principle of specificity is ignored or undervalued. For example, a flexibility routine that isn't specific enough to the particular physical activity can lead to muscle and joint soreness or injury. A strength-training program that fails to strengthen the muscles used most by a physical activity may lead to injury.

- Effective body control—Students need to learn that they are responsible for their movements, both how these affect themselves and others. Learning to travel through general space safely and stay in self-space are important keys here.

- Facilities inspection—Conduct regular inspections of gymnasiums, pools and decks, locker rooms, fields, and so on to ensure that physical activity areas are safe. Teach students what to be on the alert for, so they can help with this ongoing process (see also chapter 4).

- Basic biomechanics—Teach proper manipulative, nonlocomotor, and locomotor skill form, and point out to students why proper form is important.

Practicing Strategies for Monitoring Frequency, Intensity, and Time

Your students not only need to understand what you mean by overload, progression,

Organizational Strategies for Teaching Large Classes

Large classes (40–60) students are a sad fact of life for some secondary physical educators. Professor Allan Sander of the University of North Florida in Jacksonville offers the following field-tested strategies:

1. Alternative activity—Split large classes into two manageable groups and alternate them between an instructional and recreational/fitness activity (figure 13.2). For safety's sake, be sure you can still observe the alternative activity and that space is sufficient for both groups to work without interfering with each other.

2. Teaching stations—Organize the "alternative activity" strategy into two sets of stations (one set for the instructional activity and one set for the alternative activity). Rotate subgroups through stations on a signal. Have groups switch circuits on alternating days.

3. Modified team teaching with combined classes—Form ability-based groups from two classes (about 80 students). One teacher works with a small group (about 20) that needs extra help, while the other teacher uses Strategy 1 or 2 to teach the remaining students. One day a week, combine everyone for an activity, such as intramurals.

Efficient management skills and sufficient space are vital to safety, no matter what your strategy.

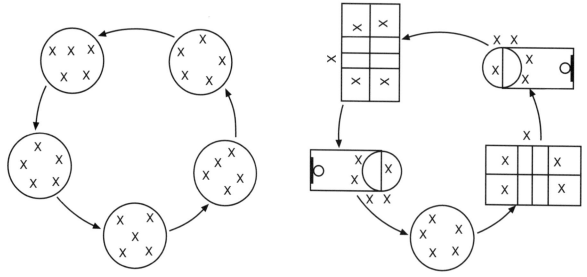

Figure 13.2 Consider splitting large classes into two manageable groups. Within each group, rotate students through fitness, recreational activity, and instructional stations.

Adapted, by permission, from A. Sander, 1996, "Organizational Strategies for Teaching Large Classes," *Teaching Secondary Physical Education* 2(1):11.

frequency, intensity, time, and type, they also need to be able to actually monitor them. Choose the methods that are appropriate for your students' ages and abilities.

- Overload—Teach students to follow the guidelines for each part of the FITT acronym, increasing only one aspect at a time.

  - Frequency—Teach students to keep accurate logs and journals. Or have each student mark a monthly calendar to provide frequency information and motivate students to engage in more physical activity. You can use a blank calendar on which you make several physical activity suggestions, such as that shown in figure 13.3. Remind students that they should engage in moderate to vigorous activity on most days of the week.

May: FITNESS MONTH

Monday	Tuesday	Wednesday	Thursday	Friday	Saturday	Sunday
	May 1–7 PHYSICAL EDUCATION WEEK **GET PHYSICAL . . . . EDUCATION**					Try a day without television. Do something outside instead. **1**
To be totally fit, nutrition is important also. Eat from all levels in the food pyramid each day. **2**	Go for a 30-minute walk with a friend. Yes, the dog can count as your friend. **3**	When you choose a snack today make it a healthy snack. *Suggestion:* **Ants on a Log** Celery with peanut butter in the groove and raisins on that. **4**	Ride your bike for 30 minutes. Tell a parent where you are going. Make sure you use hand signals and follow the laws of the road. **Be safe!** **5**	The heart pumps about 7 quarts of blood per minute. Plug the sink and dump in 7×4 cups of water to see how much volume is 7 quarts. **6**	Make up an exercise routine & put it to music. Pump up your muscles, not the volume. **7**	**8**
Jump rope during recess. Try a new trick today or make up a routine with several tricks. **9**	Always warm up when exercising. Start slowly then stretch. Warm muscles work better. Cool down also. Do not stop suddenly. **10**	When going to the grocery store have your parent park in the parking space far away from the store. **Walk!** **11**	The best time to drink liquids is *before* you get thirsty. Sip some water before you exercise. **12**	Fitness is being the best **you**. Competing against others has nothing to do with fitness. Do it for yourself. **13**	Try a carryover (lifetime) sport this weekend. Go to the driving range & hit some golf balls. Go to the tennis court & hit some tennis balls. Fitness comes in all shapes & sizes just like us. **14**	**15**
Exercise helps you to fall asleep more easily at night. Sleep tight. **16**	Organize a neighborhood running & tagging game. Play for 20 minutes. Include everyone. **17**	How many bones make up your skeleton? If you said 207 you were right. It takes a lot of muscles to move around 207 bones. **18**	Go to the nearest basketball hoop & play **Around the World, "21"**, or try 25 free throws. **19**	All exercises are not created equal. Some build strength. Some build stamina. Some build flexibility. **20**	Rake the yard for 30 minutes. Wear gloves & watch out for blisters. Jump in & over the leaf piles. Bag the leaves. **21**	**22**
Play catch with a (1) football, (2) softball, (3) frisbee, (4) dog. Don't throw the dog, throw something to the dog. **23**	Exercise helps you do better in school. Yes, you still have to study but you are less stressed & more relaxed & ready to learn. **24**	Set up a game of 4 square during lunch recess. While you are waiting for a turn, do trunk twisters, jumping jacks, or any exercise of your choice. **25**	When you are physically fit you have more energy for work and play. **Exercise = Energy.** **26**	Create a fitness rap or poem. Give it to your physical education teacher. **Look out Will Smith!** **27**	Try walking up & down the stairs for 10 minutes without stopping. **Use the handrail & keep a slow steady pace.** **28**	Children need 10 to 12 hours of sleep to remain healthy. **This is per day not per week.** Try it you might like it. **29**
Memorial Day Celebrate the holiday with the fitness activity of your choice. **30**	You should drink lots of water (8 glasses) especially when the weather is warm. Pop or soda does not count as water. **31**		Take care of your body, it is the only one you will get.			

Figure 13.3 Keeping calendars is a motivating way to help students track and plan the frequency of their participation in physical activity.

Reprinted, by permission, from AAHPERD, 1998, *Physical Best Activity Guide—Elementary Level.* (Champaign, IL: Human Kinetics), 43.

Teaching Suggestions for Integrating Fitness Concepts Into Floor Hockey

Richard Hohn of the University of South Carolina offers the following creative field-tested activities and demonstrations to bring health-related fitness concepts to life—even when teaching a floor hockey unit!

- Wear a backpack on the front containing 10 pounds of extra weight while doing drills (using a can of Crisco demonstrates clearly that this is fat). Students find out how excess weight slows them down and tires them out faster.

- Shoot to a Food Guide Pyramid outlined in masking tape on the floor. Try to hit specified spaces. Students review nutrition and the food groups (give points for shooting from various distances).

- Demonstrate the flexibility of cooked and uncooked spaghetti to show the difference warming up and working on flexibility makes in muscles' performance. Break the uncooked spaghetti really dramatically!

- Take the pulse before and after vigorous drills and games.

- Use six different colors of balls with each color representing a food group. Have each student "prepare" a plate of food by stick handling one of each "food," until they have one of each food group (color) on a paper plate. Use different size balls to provide practice in handling different size balls. Discuss what it means to eat a balanced diet.

- Take an empty round tape roll or three-quarter-inch PVC pipe, and slowly fill it with butter to show how arteries can become clogged with cholesterol.

- Use a nasal aspirator to show how veins, arteries, and the heart work to create systolic and diastolic blood pressure.

Teaching Pacing With the Borg Scale

Also known as the rating of perceived exertion (RPE), the Borg Scale is a valid method for self-measuring intensity of aerobic endurance activity with conditioned, experienced exercisers (Brehm 1998). For the purposes of teaching health-related physical fitness education, consider using it with older students or students who have had enough physical activity experience on which to base their perceptions.

To use this tool, students rate themselves on a scale of 6 to 20, according to how the exercise feels (figure 13.4). Initially, use the RPE alongside heart rate monitoring so students can learn to feel what exercising in the target heart rate zone (THRZ) feels like according to the RPE. Experienced RPE users can monitor heart rate occasionally to ensure they're still in the THRZ. Advanced RPE users can learn to choose and hold an intensity that allows them to complete a lengthy aerobic activity, such as a distance run.

Although the RPE is subjective, it is an important method to learn, as it transfers well to real-world settings. It does not require equipment, such as a clock with a second hand or a heart rate monitor, and it is less disruptive than pausing to take the pulse, as many less-experienced exercisers must do.

6	No exertion at all
7	
8	Extremely light
9	Very light
10	
11	Light
12	
13	Somewhat hard
14	
15	Hard (heavy)
16	
17	Very hard
18	
19	Extremely hard
20	Maximal exertion

Borg RPE scale
© Gunnar Borg, 1970, 1985, 1994, 1998

Figure 13.4   The Borg RPE scale.

Design developmentally appropriate activities that teach fitness concepts and skill development while making use of available equipment and space.

may in fact be working harder than someone who is exercising at a faster rate. However, discourage students from comparing themselves to others and to simply do the best they can. With the Borg scale, ask students to give the number *they* think is the correct one without regard to others' performances.

- Time—As with frequency, logs, journals, and blank calendars can help students learn to monitor this aspect of the FITT principle.

- Type—An accurate log or journal should include information about exactly what a student is engaging in to reach set goals. Check for understanding of the principle of specificity, which asserts that the type of physical activity must speak directly to the area of health-related fitness the individual desires to improve.

- Progression—Again, keeping an accurate and detailed log or journal is an excellent way for a student and instructor to monitor whether or not progression is appropriate and safe.

- Intensity—Monitoring and recording heart rate and target heart rate zone is a common way to monitor intensity (see chapter 6). The Borg Scale of Perceived Exertion (Borg 1998) can also help students understand and monitor intensity, especially in regard to pacing (see sidebar earlier in this chapter titled Teaching Pacing With the Borg Scale). The *FITNESSGRAM* PACER test also helps students develop a sense of pacing. All these methods can help students recognize that even someone who is slower

Summary

Use the many suggestions in this chapter to help you refine your teaching skills in the gymnasium or outdoor setting. Select a variety of appropriate learning experiences by ensuring each is developmentally appropriate, sequential, fun, safe, inclusive, serves a purpose, and can be connected to real life in meaningful ways. Then make sure your students not only understand basic fitness skills, but also how they can apply and monitor them in real-life situations.

Chapter 14

Teaching Through Lecture Activities

It is best to teach health-related fitness concepts in an integrated manner. That is, discuss fitness concepts and fitness skills while students are actually applying them, and work with teachers in other disciplines to create a cross-curricular approach whenever possible. But, although we want students to be involved as much as possible in physical activity, there are times when we need to teach concepts in greater depth than we can in the physical activity setting, to be sure students truly grasp the information.

Personal Lifetime Health-Related Fitness Courses

A *personal lifetime health-related fitness course* is a course that teaches the basic training principles of health-related fitness, fitness safety, nutrition, fitness consumer awareness, benefits of physical activity, and that lifelong physical activity is individual and can be enjoyable. Beginning in 1983 with Florida, the trend in secondary education is to require students to take and pass a personal lifetime health-related fitness course. Several states already require such a course for high school graduation, and many more are considering

Course Textbooks

A good textbook can be a useful tool in teaching a personal lifetime health-related fitness course. It provides a foundation of basic knowledge as well as learning activities, interesting facts, test questions, assessment tools, and so on. An instructor may elect to assign readings from the text as homework so more time in class can be used on discussion, lab activities, and so on. There are several good texts available, including:

- Charles Corbin and Ruth Lindsey, *Fitness for Life* (4th ed.) (Scott, Foresman, 1997)
- Werner Hoeger and Sharon Hoeger, *Fitness and Wellness* (3d ed.) (Morton, 1996)
- Don Rainey and Tinker Murray, *Foundations of Personal Fitness . . . Any Body Can Be Fit!* (West/ITP, 1997)
- Roberta Stokes, Sandra Schultz, and Barbara Polansky, *Lifetime Personal Fitness* (Hunter Textbooks, 1997)
- Charles S. Williams, Emmanouel G. Harageones, Dewayne J. Johnson, and Charles D. Smith, *Personal Fitness: Feeling Good, Looking Good* (4th ed.) (Kendall/Hunt, 1998)

making it mandatory. Also known as Foundations of Personal Fitness, Personal Health and Fitness, Lifelong Physical Activity for Health and Fitness, Fitness for Life, Health-Related Fitness and Wellness, and a host of other titles, some schools (or states) allow students to choose when they will take the course (9th–12th grades). Sometimes it is required at a certain level. For example, some schools (or states) require students to take the course in 9th or 10th grade so that they may apply the knowledge to a variety of elective courses or self-initiated activities (e.g., strength training, aerobic dance, sports) during the rest of their high school careers.

Naturally, how you choose to offer this course and what you designate as its content will depend on your state requirements and curriculum. Physical Best recommends, however, that certain components be offered in any such course.

Recommended Core Course Content

Include each of the following areas in a personal lifetime health-related fitness course.

- Basic knowledge of health-related fitness and physical activity principles—Students need concrete knowledge about the principles of progression and overload as applied to each component of health-related fitness, including proper nutrition, safety, and how the body adapts to exercise. This course should help students prepare for FitSmart, the national fitness knowledge test (see chapter 18), which assesses whether or not students have the basic knowledge needed to make appropriate decisions about their own activity levels, fitness, and health. Include training techniques specific to each component of health-related fitness.

- Consumer education—Students need to know the truth about fitness, weight control, and nutritional supplements and other products, especially how to discern fact from fiction in advertising. They also need experience comparison shopping for the fitness facilities, equipment, and activity opportunities that suit their interests and resources.

- Knowledge of the benefits of physical activity—Students need to know how they will benefit from physical activity today (e.g., look and feel better) and in the long term. Remember, teens don't relate well to problems they might have at 50 or 60. So, while it's vital they know this information, emphasize immediate benefits to maintain their interest.

- Understanding of the personal nature of fitness—Students need to know they can

Sample Problem-Solving Activities

The following are sample problem-solving activities appropriate for applying health-related fitness knowledge in a personal lifetime health-related fitness course.

- Discuss how there are times when the heart rate increases, not in response to physical activity, but rather due to caffeine, stress, or other stimulants. Have students research this topic.
- Compare and contrast the health-related benefits of in-line skating with lap swimming.
- Case study: Read aloud to students a true personal story from a fitness magazine, sharing only the description of the person's fitness and health dilemma. Have small groups work together to design a realistic, beneficial, and interesting fitness plan for this person. Have groups share and discuss their plans with the rest of the class. Read the rest of the true story aloud. Discuss the person's actual choices in light of the small groups' plans and the principles of safe and effective health-related fitness plans students are learning to apply.

find what works for them. Not everyone needs to do the same activities, but they do need some sort of physical activity to gain the health benefits. Curriculum should, therefore, emphasize the many choices available to be physically active.

- Knowledge that physical activity can be fun—The course should include lab/physical activity days for students to apply what they're learning in the classroom in an enjoyable learning environment. For ex-

Students need to learn basic knowledge of health-related fitness.

ample, some schools offer the course as two days per week in the classroom and three days per week in the physical activity setting.

The details of what you include to fulfill each component depend, of course, on your particular curriculum guidelines, student population, and school and community resources. In general, however, select activities that teach students to apply health-related fitness knowledge in real-life settings, that require higher-order thinking and problem solving, and that encourage students to take personal responsibility to help them progress up Corbin and Lindsey's Stairway to Lifetime Fitness (see figure 3.1 in chapter 3). See also discussion under Teaching Principles for Classroom-Based Lessons later in this chapter.

Learn how teachers have developed and implemented meaningful and effective curricula for personal lifetime health-related fitness courses in three states.

Model Approach: Florida

Dewayne Johnson and Emmanouel Harageones (1994), then of Florida State University, share the story of how the Florida Association for Health, Physical Education, Recreation, Dance, and Driver Education (FAHPERD) successfully lobbied to make Florida the first state to mandate a lifetime personal fitness course as a high school graduation requirement in 1983.

Program Overview

The intent of the Florida legislature was to give all high school students a basic physical education course that would answer state and national calls for a more physically fit population. The course provides each student with chances to develop his or her own optimal level of health-related fitness, to understand health-related fitness concepts, and to recognize how his or her lifestyle choices impact personal health and fitness.

The Florida course follows a syllabus created by a task force made up of members of the Florida Department of Education. Instructors teaching the course receive a Personal Fitness Instructional Materials Packet containing 12 instructional units. Initially, teachers received intensive in-service training at both the district and state levels. Currently, a summer workshop and annual fall conference workshop provide ongoing training and support for involved teachers.

In general, students spend three days a week in the physical activity setting engaging in physical activity. The other two days alternate with the physical activity days and are devoted to classroom activities. However, teachers have the option of spending three days in the classroom and only two on physical activity when they deem this appropriate.

Classroom Activities

The 12 instructional units provided in the packet contain a variety of learning experiences reflecting a holistic approach to lifetime physical activity learning. Following a day-by-day teaching outline, physical educators use teaching strategy suggestions, activity sheets, handouts, lab experiences, lab experience work sheets, study guides, and transparency masters to teach the course. Course content includes the following topics:

- The components of health-related fitness
- Assessment of individual fitness levels
- The relationship between health-related fitness activities and stress

Students should learn that a variety of physical activities improve health-related fitness while meeting individual needs.

- Sound nutritional practices
- Health problems associated with inadequate fitness levels
- Consumer issues
- How to evaluate physical activities in terms of their fitness value
- The variety of physical activities available for improving health-related fitness
- Design of a personal fitness program
- Correct biomechanical and physiological principles related to exercise and training
- Safety practices
- Assessment of individual lifestyles as related to quality-of-life issues
- Positive attitudes toward physical activity

Tips for Implementing a Lifetime Personal Fitness Course

From the vanguard of lifetime personal fitness course legislation come the following implementation suggestions:

- Scheduling—Students should take the Personal Fitness course early in their high school careers (9th or 10th grade) so they can use what they know throughout their high school years.

- Laboratory and classroom instruction—The course should combine both approaches, remaining flexible unit by unit as to the most effective combination.

- Classroom space—Schools should provide adequate and usable classroom space for the Personal Fitness course. Teachers might share a classroom by teaching lecture activities on alternating days and time slots.

- Class size—Schools should ensure that class size is consistent with those of other academic courses.

- Fitness assessment—Students should undergo both pre- and postassessments of health-related fitness components. Teachers should provide guidance as to how each student may design a personal plan to improve each component based on individual test results. Teachers should also share test results with parents and provide special remedial programs to extremely low-fit students. *FITNESSGRAM* is recommended as a fitness test, because it provides criterion-referenced rather than norm-referenced standards, which are preferred based on many years of research.

- Homework—Both cognitive and psychomotor homework are essential elements of a Personal Fitness course. Most Florida teachers require notebooks (for logging physical activity) and assign written homework. Physical activity as homework is especially important for the extremely low-fit students.

- Student evaluation—Evaluation should serve as a diagnostic tool to help both student and teacher—not merely the basis for grades. The evaluation system should directly correspond to the student performance standards designed for the course, including the physical, cognitive, and affective domains. Students should not receive grades based on fitness test scores.

- Instructional materials—Each student should have his or her own copy of all course materials, including a textbook. If only a classroom set of textbooks is available, the school should plan to purchase additional sets (perhaps one set per school year) until all students can be assigned their own textbook.

- Mechanisms for dealing with implementation problems—Districts should provide the support teachers need to provide the best possible Personal Fitness course, including in-service training, classroom space, reasonable class sizes, and adequate staffing. Teachers and students may need time to get over initially negative attitudes toward change (e.g., "Why can't we go to the gym and play?" and "I don't want to teach this course, but the state is making me.").

Model Approach: Maryland

Mary Etta Reedy (1996), then a supervisor of Health Education and Physical Education for the Cecil County (Maryland) Schools, shares the following story of a model health-related physical fitness education program. Physical educators in the Cecil County Schools created a coalition called Partners for P.E.O.P.L.E. (Physical Education Organized to Promote Lifelong Exercise). This coalition is made up of colleagues in their schools, faculty and professionals from the University of Delaware, and local community organizations. Partners for P.E.O.P.L.E. developed a K–12 lifetime fitness curriculum and supports its implementation.

Program Overview

Based on the premise that personalized physical fitness and the development of a healthy lifestyle should be the cornerstones of curriculum, the program evolves from the following philosophy statement:

The Cecil County Public Schools' physical education program offers a comprehensive fitness-based curriculum. This program emphasizes the health-related components of fitness and the individuality of each student. It provides the daily physical activity necessary to develop and maintain a healthful level of fitness and is designed to promote self-efficacy in all students. Students will learn to monitor their physical activity, to understand its relationship to healthy lifestyles, and to include a personal fitness program as part of their lifelong endeavors.

This approach begins in kindergarten and continues through middle school with "Project SPARK," which focuses on improving the quality of physical education classes by increasing activity levels in ways that are motivating to both physical educators and their students (see sidebar in chapter 3 on p. 48). Then in ninth grade, students must take a course called "Personal Fitness," in which they assess and improve their own fitness levels, establish a healthful lifestyle, and design their own personal fitness program, moving from primarily teacher-directed activities to individually directed programs. This course is a prerequisite to all other physical fitness electives, which include Aerobic Conditioning; Cross-Training; Strength and Conditioning; Health Education; and Walking, Running, and Jogging. In this way, the program makes clear that basic knowledge and practice precede specialization.

Partners for P.E.O.P.L.E. has designed the Personal Fitness course to integrate classroom and physical activity learning to address the components of health-related fitness cognitively, physically, and affectively. Students spend three days in the physical activity setting working on aerobic conditioning, including one day concentrating on muscular endurance, alternated with one day of strength training, and one day in the classroom/lecture setting. (The muscular endurance and strength-training days may not be completed back-to-back.) In addition, parents are involved through homework assignments, fitness progress reports, and other communication that encourages them to support their children's efforts.

Classroom Activities

Cognitive content includes the basic FITT principle and how to identify and modify cardiovascular risk factors. Students evaluate case studies and develop their personal fitness plans. The course outline includes the following:

- An introduction to fitness
- A heart rate lesson
- A self-evaluation
- An introduction to goals and personal goal setting
- Guidelines and principles of training
- The components of health-related fitness
- Nutrition
- Stress
- Consumer issues
- Field trips to health clubs
- Case studies
- A re-evaluation of lifestyles and goals
- Development of a personal fitness plan
- A cognitive test

Tips for Implementing a Community-Based Physical Education Program

Mary Etta offers the following checklist to guide other physical educators (Reedy 1996):

1. Develop partnerships with businesses, hospitals, doctors, parks and recreation departments, health departments, local fitness centers, and any other groups that might share your goals. Have all parties work together to develop a philosophy. These groups can also aid in fund-raising.

2. Work collaboratively with a college or university. This relationship can be mutually valuable; the college or university can provide resources for training, access to the latest research, and a support system. Your school can offer training and subjects for study.

3. Promote the health benefits and opportunities for success your program will offer students. Be sure to involve staff, students, and community partners.

4. Provide extensive and repeated in-service opportunities for all teachers.

5. Design a curriculum that requires students to use scientific knowledge and technology to design and implement their own physical fitness programs. The program should not rely at first on expensive technology or equipment; this can be added as you go along.

6. Design a program that will
   - move progressively from dependence to independence;
   - encourage continual formative assessment, re-evaluation of goals and re-design of personal fitness programs;
   - make success visible and obvious;
   - provide students with control over their activities, both in choice and intensity;
   - remove all ego threats, especially comparisons to other students;
   - emphasize enjoyment and the development of movement self-efficacy, rather than the achievement of fitness (fitness is too transitory);
   - have students maintain a personal portfolio;
   - encourage peer and self-support; and
   - keep the long-term goals in the minds of teachers and students.

Model Approach: Texas

Tinker D. Murray and Don L. Rainey (e-mail, January 1999), authors of *Foundations of Personal Fitness: Any Body Can . . . Be Fit!*, a high school personal fitness textbook published by West/ITP Publishers (1997), share history and hints from the Texas Association for Health, Physical Education, Recreation and Dance's (TAHPERD's) quest to institute a required personal lifetime fitness course for high school students.

Program Overview

Since 1984, when the major educational reform process began in Texas, TAHPERD members have been involved in the evaluation of the essential elements and State Board of Education (SBOE) Rules for physical education and health. Like educators in other disciplines, health and physical education professionals met in annual Texas Education Agency–sponsored regional and state curriculum review meetings to identify problem areas and weaknesses for the improvement of instructional programs of health and physical education in the public schools. One of the significant needs identified by TAHPERD in 1990, as part of the TAHPERD Plan, was the need for quality school programs in health, physical education, and recreation, and a required "Foundations of Personal Fitness Course" for all high school students who must take physical education (exemptions were provided for students in athletics, band, drill team, and the like).

As a result, in 1992, the TAHPERD Foundations Committee developed a proposal for the course modeled after the Personal Fitness Curriculum Framework/Student Performance Standards, Florida Department of Education (1984). The course was designed to (1) help students understand the need for physical fitness, (2) teach them how to assess, develop, demonstrate, and maintain an acceptable level of health-related fitness, and (3) provide them with knowledge and tools to allow them to develop a personal plan for a lifestyle of active living. Specifically, the course was designed to provide each student with opportunities to develop and maintain an acceptable level of physical fitness, and to help each student acquire knowledge and experiences, reinforcing lifestyle behaviors that enhance personal health and fitness.

Changes did not happen overnight, but rather as the result of persistance and committee members' unwavering belief in the value of such a course. TAHPERD's proposal was approved in 1992 and implemented in the Fall of 1996. Four textbooks for the course were adopted by the SBOE to be used starting in the Fall of 1997. In the Spring of 1997, individual school district textbook committees were allowed to choose one of the approved texts for their district and enough individual copies were purchased so that each student could have his or her own. Students are encouraged to take the course as 9th or 10th graders, although a few students take it as 11th or 12th graders.

Classroom Activities

The content of the TAHPERD-designed course includes the following:

- Knowledge and behavioral demonstration of the importance of health-related physical fitness
- Assessment of the components of health-related physical fitness
- Knowledge of health problems associated with inadequate fitness levels
- Knowledge and behavioral application of biomechanical and physiological principles to develop, maintain, and improve the health-related components of physical fitness
- Knowledge and behavioral application of safety practices associated with health-related physical fitness
- Knowledge of the psychological value of health-related physical fitness, including stress management
- Knowledge and behavioral application of sound nutritional practices related to health-related physical fitness
- Knowledge of consumer issues related to health-related physical fitness

Tips for Implementing a Lifetime Personal Fitness Course

Murray and Rainey (e-mail, January 1999) offer a number of helpful guidelines for maximizing the course's effectiveness:

- Scheduling—This course should be used as a prerequisite to all other high school courses, giving students a strong foundation in the knowledge they will need to lead healthy, active lives. Therefore, it is recommended that students take the course in 9th or 10th grade.

- Laboratory and classroom instruction—TAHPERD takes the stand that weekly instruction should consist of daily doses of both health-related concepts and laboratory activities, rather than alternating lab and classroom days. In this way, lab activities reinforce concepts regarding healthy lifestyle behaviors on a daily basis. This blended approach helps emphasize physical activity itself while conveying important concepts.
- Classroom space—Appropriate classroom, gymnasium, and outdoor space should be provided for the Foundations Course because a variety of educational settings enhances both student understanding and physical activity participation. Unfortunately, however, many Texas high school physical educators do not have access to a classroom; therefore, the course is often taught in gymnasiums, hallways, or other available space.
- Class size—Classes consisting of no more than 30 students are recommended to ensure that the teacher can provide quality instruction as well as have enough time to provide individual attention to the evaluation process. (*Note*: Instructors should work closely with school counselors to ensure class space and class size issues are addressed appropriately.)
- Fitness assessment—Students should be taught how to pre-test (when appropriate, e.g., height, weight, percent body fat, flexibility) and postassess (required) the health-related components of physical fitness, using a valid health-related physical fitness test battery. Students should not be tested on selected tests (e.g., distance runs, max-timed sit-up tests, and the like) until they have been allowed to condition themselves for the evaluation experience. This process should only be one part of a comprehensive health-related fitness program. Students should be assisted in goal setting and selecting planned physical activity programs based on their assessment results, and should participate daily throughout the course in health-related physical fitness conditioning activities.

- Homework—Both cognitive and psychomotor homework should be viewed as essential elements in the Foundations Course. Students should track physical activities and class and homework assignments in notebooks.
- Student evaluation—The purpose of assessment should extend beyond mere collection of data for assigning grades (and fitness test scores should never be used to assign grades). Instead, teachers should view assessment as a diagnostic tool for goal setting to help both the student and the teacher. Moreover, an effective evaluation system should correlate with the desired student performance standards and behavioral outcomes, across the cognitive, affective, and psychomotor domains.
- Instructors—Instructors of the Foundations Course should actually want to teach the course and not be forced to do so. They should employ prudent health-fitness modeling techniques and regularly participate alongside students in classroom physical activities. They need to encourage and motivate their students to achieve personal goals and to incorporate healthy fitness behaviors into their daily lifestyles, thereby facilitating the transition toward establishing prudent adult health-fitness behaviors. This means not only exposing students to a variety of activities and positive fitness concepts but also actually facilitating successful experiences performing those activities.
- Conditioning protocols—Instructors should incorporate a fun, scientifically sound conditioning protocol as part of the curriculum for their comprehensive health-fitness program, particularly for preparing students for the health-related fitness assessment process. Gradual, progressive conditioning, maximizing the safety and success of each student, should take place over a period of at least eight weeks prior to assessment in order to allow the body to adapt. Students who have demonstrated basic health-related fitness should then be guided in designing a personal fitness plan to maintain fitness.

- Technology—Teachers should incorporate the latest health and fitness technology (computers, heart rate monitors, videos, and so on) into their teaching of the course.

Other Lecture Activity Approaches

Although a personal lifetime health-related fitness course can be an effective way to teach high school and even middle school students about health-related fitness concepts, most of the lecture activities you do in your career will probably not be through such a formal course. Indeed, pass on this knowledge to children beginning in kindergarten and, when possible, integrate its teaching with actual physical activity. However, there will be times when you will find you need to explore a topic in more depth.

The Rainy-Day or They-Commandeered-My-Gym Approach

We've all been the victims of spoiled lesson plans; for example, bad weather makes outdoor activity impossible on the day the entire fifth grade is using the gymnasium for a science fair. Rather than use the precious time you have in your physical activity facilities for classroom activities, develop a core of health-related fitness classroom lesson plans for each course or grade that you teach. The number you develop should depend on the content you wish to cover and the number of class periods you project you will find yourself without physical activity facilities in the course of the school year or grading period. Then use the lessons as the need for alternative plans arises.

This method, however, is not intended to relegate health-related fitness teaching to a catch-as-catch-can status. It is simply a way to maximize your students' physical activity time when you have the facilities you need and teach fitness concepts and skills when you don't—as long as this takes place within a

Have a plan ready for teaching in a classroom setting for those days when your gymnasium is not available or bad weather keeps you from going outdoors.

well-organized and well-developed curriculum. If you make sure these lessons develop basic fitness concepts and skills in an age-appropriate, progressive manner, students will receive as complete a health-related fitness education as possible before leaving your program through this method (see also chapter 11).

One efficient way to organize these lessons is to create a file folder or box for each one. Place any audiovisual materials (e.g., videotapes, prepared overhead transparencies, posters, and the like) along with handouts, written lesson plans, and any other supplies you'll need in the file. Marian Franck, retired high school physical education teacher (Lancaster, Pennsylvania) and current P.E.-L.I.F.E. Project Director, calls this an "Emergency Kit." With one for each unit or lesson, you'll be prepared at a moment's notice.

Then, when you get to school and discover that the principal forgot to tell you the gymnasium would be used for the eighth-grade class play dress rehearsal that day, you'll be ready. All you need now is a portable kit with the general supplies you'll need (e.g., one pencil per student, art supplies, overhead marking pens, tape, and so on) and a room to meet in with the audiovisual equipment you'll need. Some physical educators are fortunate enough to have such a room available full-time, but most likely, you will have to find your own space. Plan for this possibility before school starts by seeking administrative support or by finding your own reliable solution.

The Cross-Curricular, Team Approach

Another way to be sure you cover certain health-related fitness concepts in depth is to work with teachers in other subject areas. For example,

- an elementary classroom teacher can set up a learning center in the regular classroom at which students may practice taking their pulses, then rotate the center through each fourth-grade classroom;

- a math teacher can teach geometry through the angles of rebound, trajectory, angle of releases for distance, and so on when using ball games for developing health-related fitness;

- a physics teacher can show students how Newton's Laws of Motion apply to physical activities;

Beware!

The Rainy-Day, They-Commandeered-My-Gym approach can give students the message that "when there is nothing to do or everything goes wrong we do health-related fitness." In addition, this approach does not give enough time to do health-related fitness *unless* it is very carefully planned in the curriculum.

—Richard C. Hohn, Ed.D., University of South Carolina, Columbia

- a biology teacher can cover the systems of the body and how they respond to physical activity;
- a social studies teacher can explore cultural effects on physical activity and health;
- an environmental studies teacher can point out outdoor recreational activities;
- a health education teacher (who may be the classroom teacher) can cover injury treatment in detail, nutrition, risk factors for heart disease, and bike safety (elementary level);
- a social studies or classroom teacher can have students log miles traveled (run/walk/jog) on a topographical map and study changes in elevation over historic trails; and
- secondary math students can calculate energy expenditure and many other health-related fitness data already mentioned earlier in this book.

The cross-curricular, team approach not only makes it possible for you to cover more information, it also helps students see the connections among subject areas, reinforcing their learning in all disciplines. Virgilio's 1997 model is an example of a team approach to comprehensive health and physical activity.

Caution!

Do not sacrifice physical education content in the cross-curricular approach. Your main focus still needs to be upon ensuring students leave your program armed with the specific knowledge they need to design and implement effective personal health-related fitness plans.

Other Forms of Teaching Concepts

As alternatives to lecture settings, consider using one-on-one conference time arranged on a circuit to review personal health-related fitness plans and how they relate to concepts. You can also use rubrics to guide student projects and research as a way of conveying

the key concepts you wish to cover. For example, list the aspects of the component of health-related fitness you wish the student to focus on (frequency and type when exploring flexibility).

However, you do not always have to be the "direct delivery" source of information. Consider using other avenues of communication that have been proven effective:

- Refer students to a reference library or reliable Internet source.
- Display a poster at a physical activity station and direct students to answer a short list of questions based on it.
- Assign work sheets that cover concepts to complete in the physical activity setting or as homework.
- Offer information in the form of handouts.

Think of other ways you can expand your instructional time, based on your situation.

Teaching Principles for Classroom-Based Lessons

The general teaching principles described in chapter 12 are a good starting point for teaching effectively in the classroom. In this section, we share information specific to making each classroom-based lesson as effective as possible.

Positive Learning Environment

Use the tips in this section to help you create a positive learning environment in the class/lecture setting.

Create an Attractive Setting

Of course, creating an attractive lecture setting is easier if you have a classroom to call your own. You can develop effective teaching displays, such as bulletin boards and learning centers, and you can arrange the tables or desks to your satisfaction and find it the same way each time you use the room. If, however,

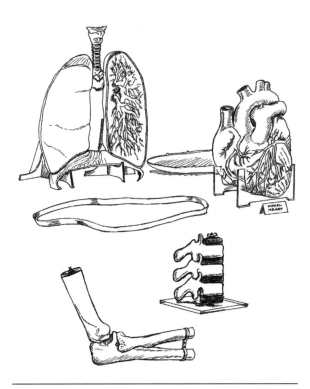

Figure 14.1 Teaching aids can provide good focal points during a lesson in a lecture setting.

you must live the nomad's life when it comes to classroom space, you can still create large posters and kits of teaching aids (e.g., models of the human heart and lungs, oversized rubber band to represent a muscle to stretch, and so on) to set up as attractive focal points during a lesson (figure 14.1). Such displays will enhance your students' chances of learning the material.

Ensure Developmental Appropriateness

For lessons involving academic skills, such as math calculations, writing assignments, technology tools, and discussion protocols, consult with colleagues to make sure students have the basic skills they need to succeed and learn in your class. Ask for ways to modify your plans to meet a wider range of abilities as well as input on the types of activities a particular student or group of students enjoys learning through. When basic skills are lacking, share student work as evidence with these same colleagues so they can continue to work with students in need.

Offer Variety

Some of the most effective ways to offer variety in the classroom setting are to use technology effectively, vary the teaching style you use, and to speak to the different types of intelligence (see sidebar on page 205) when designing activities and making assignments.

Technology can provide powerful teaching tools. VCRs, computers, and video equipment can greatly enhance the teaching of health-related fitness concepts in the lecture setting. Show videotapes about health-related fitness topics, such as the functioning of the cardio-respiratory system, training principles, false advertising, and many other areas. Students can use computers to download, analyze, graph, and store heart rate monitor data. Install one computer with a large monitor to show students how to do so or to show students how to set up a physical activity log or personal fitness plan. Have students use the Internet to research health-related fitness topics or to encourage "fitness pals" in other schools through e-mail. Divide students into small groups to develop health-related fitness reports, then videotape a "newscast" to share with peers or younger students. Some schools are equipped with in-house TV and radio stations that you may be able to use for the same purpose. HyperCard stacks for Macintosh computers are innovative tools available in some schools. Work with colleagues in other disciplines to help students learn to fully use the technology available in your school. Seek in-service training to help you fully use technology in the classroom.

Effective teaching requires a variety of teaching styles. You're sure to be the cure for insomnia if you rely solely on lecturing. Avoid always standing in front of the class and droning on about the concept of the day. Do, however, provide the basic information students need, but keep lecturing to a minimum, and get students fully involved in discussions and activities as much as possible. Employing various teaching styles is a sure way to provide the diversity that keeps students interested. The following activity ideas appropriate for the lecture/classroom setting should help you get started (refer to chapter 12 for general descriptions of each style):

- Command—Choose a fitness skill and lead students step-by-step through, for example, how to calculate a target heart rate zone. Repeat the exercise with different examples as many times as you think students need to practice.

- Practice—Choose a fitness skill and demonstrate or use a task sheet to introduce, for example, how to apply the RICES (rest, ice, compression, elevation, and support) principle to a sprained ankle. Circulate among pairs of practicing students giving feedback. Let students determine the number of practice trials until they can demonstrate competence without being prompted by you or a task sheet.

- Reciprocal—Choose the fitness skill, but have students give each other feedback during practice times. First, demonstrate the skill, for example, how to design a personal fitness plan to enhance flexibility, and then have students practice giving feedback to the teacher. Help observers give their partners helpful feedback by providing a task sheet and by monitoring student interactions.

- Self-check—Choose the task, but have each student give himself feedback, for example, by completing a task sheet on how to monitor heart rate.

- Inclusion—Choose the task, but allow students a range of performance levels to choose from. For example, allow students to choose to use a calculator or pencil and paper to calculate target heart rate zone. (See chapter 15 for further discussion of inclusion of students with special needs.)

- Guided discovery—Determine the task and then design a sequence of questions or problems that will lead students to one right answer. Use an activity through which students may test their responses. For example, ask the following in sequence and allow students to test each part. (Make sure they rest enough between each phase so results are due to extra weight, not fatigue.) First, pose a problem to solve. For example, how can we discover what the effect of added body fat is on your heart rate? Then ask the following in sequence to guide students to the solution:

  1. What is the effect of added body fat on the heart rate response to a step test?
  2. What is your heart rate response to the step test at your current weight?
  3. What is your heart rate response to the step test when you are carrying five extra pounds in a backpack?
  4. What is your heart rate response to a step test when you are carrying 10 extra pounds in a backpack?
  5. What is the effect of added weight (body fat) on your heart rate response to a step test?

- Convergent discovery—Pose a problem or question, but let students go through the discovery process to converge on the one right answer without teacher guidance. Provide the setting in which students may discover the answer through a process of trial and error. For example, you might pose the same problems mentioned earlier—How can we discover what the effect of added body fat is on your heart rate?—but let the students discover the answer without the guiding questions from you.

- Divergent production—Pose an open-ended problem for students to problem solve and find answers to. Again, use the same problem as before, but ask your students to design an experiment to find the answer.

- Individual program-learner's design—Mandate the general subject area, but let each student determine the task and possible solutions. For example, have high school students design their own health-related fitness programs.

- Learner initiated—Similar to previous style, but let each student choose a general subject area as well and approach you on his own, not in response to your prompting. This style evolves in some older students who, for example, may have specific sport interests that compel them to seek teacher input.

Students can learn to self-check themselves by monitoring their progress in a weight training unit.

- Self-teaching—This style is appropriate for high school students who have proven through the use of learner-initiated style that they can pursue their own interests independent of you.

The last two styles involve using class time to be available more as a fitness advisor than an instructor. Therefore, these approaches may only be appropriate in certain situations with high school students, perhaps with advanced placement physical education students.

Class Management

You can use the skills you've developed in the challenging, dynamic physical activity setting to create an enjoyable and productive classroom atmosphere as well.

Establishing Effective Classroom Structures

Insist that students follow the same structures required of them for other classroom courses. This includes being at their desks on time, with any needed books and materials, prepared to listen and discuss. Hands should be raised to speak, and no interruptions should be allowed. Teach students to participate in discussions respectfully, as well. Adapt procedures established in the physical activity setting to the classroom in appropriate ways. For example, whistling for attention may be appropriate on a field, but not in the confined space of a gymnasium or classroom. The same principles for gaining and keeping student attention, demonstrating effectively, and managing behavior in the physical activity setting apply in the classroom; see chapter 13.

Leading Effective Discussions

Use the positive learning atmosphere you've established to give all students a chance to exchange ideas, ask questions, and think through the content you're teaching.

- Ask open-ended questions as often as possible. This helps establish that physical activity solutions are not to be limited by the imagination (only safety and propriety considerations).

- Give students time to think about each question before calling on anyone. This encourages all to think, whereas calling on someone before asking a question, excuses the rest of the class from the thought process.

- Establish that everyone has a right to be heard and respected in a discussion. Ban put-downs and insist that students do not interrupt each other.

- To help students learn to really listen to each other, require each new speaker to briefly summarize what he or she thinks the previous speaker said (discussing the same question).

- Accept student opinions without immediately evaluating them; instead respectfully guide the discussion toward the facts students need to know by asking pointed ques-

Types of Intelligence

Challenging yourself to address each type of intelligence is another way to create variety and spark interest in the class/lecture setting when designing in-class activities.

- Bodily-kinesthetic intelligence—Moving to learn isn't just for the gymnasium! Find ways students can move in the class setting as well. Depending on age, students may enjoy miming actions (e.g., of a muscle), crafts to reinforce concepts (e.g., a valentine promising yourself to eat more heart healthy), a hands-on science lesson (e.g., capillary action shown by dropping colored water on a good brand of paper towel), drama (e.g., act out oxygen exchange in the lungs), and other creative movement opportunities. Secondary students might be asked to create a video for teaching elementary students about health-related fitness.

- Spatial intelligence—Use charts, graphs, diagrams, graphics software, and three-dimensional models to teach. Have students make their own similar items to reinforce their learning. This works well with charting heart rates, recording weight-training progress, logging physical activity, and so on.

- Interpersonal intelligence—Brainstorm solutions to problems as a class or in small groups. Use simulations to teach real-world interpersonal skills. (For instance, ask, "How would you spend $100 in this community to participate in physical activity?" Have students collect data on the cost of facilities, equipment, and so on as homework, then work in small groups to help each other make wise and satisfying choices.) Train students to participate as peer tutors or in the community on a health-related fitness service project (e.g., leading active games at a day care center).

- Musical intelligence—Allow students to give research reports in the form of raps, chants, and songs.

- Linguistic intelligence—Provide opportunities to discuss, debate, and write about fitness concepts. Show students how to keep accurate and meaningful physical activity logs.

- Logical-mathematical intelligence—Provide critical thinking and problem-solving exercises. For example, secondary students can calculate cardiac output (heart rate $\times$ SV), the relationship between METs and $\dot{V}O_2$max, resting energy expenditure, or calories and energy intake; use the Fick equation, mean arterial blood pressure, minute ventilation, and alveolar ventilation.

- Intrapersonal intelligence—Help students make personal connections to the information you're providing. For example, encourage students to research and try out various physical activities they find interesting. Provide self-paced activities and learning centers, and give students time and guidance to reflect and set goals regarding physical activity and health-related fitness.

- Naturalistic intelligence—Prepare students to get the most out of field trips to inspiring outdoor locations. For example, work with the science teacher to learn about the plants and animals you may see on a hike through a local park. Show students how fresh air, a change of scenery, and physical activity can work together to foster a sense of well-being.

In addition, keep the various intelligences in mind when creating follow-up homework assignments (in both lecture and physical activity situations).

tions. Whenever possible, act as a facilitator rather than a "fountain of knowledge." Play "devil's advocate" when you feel this will further the discussion.

- List key points as they are mentioned on a chalkboard or overhead transparency to help keep students focused on the discussion.

Help students become good fitness consumers by teaching them that they don't have to buy expensive equipment to live an active life. Dancing, for example, can be an enjoyable and inexpensive way to stay in shape.

- Before students get bored with a topic, end the line of discussion by briefly summarizing what has been said, then move on to the next question. Learn to pace discussions to keep interest high.

- Apply the same strategies in small groups within the lecture setting. For example, students trained in discussion techniques can give individual reports, then discuss the information in their group. Then as a group, they can share a group summary of the information with the rest of the class in the form of a poster, skit, or overhead transparency.

- Periodically ask students for written or oral feedback on what helps and hinders them in participating in class discussions. Work as a team to resolve problems.

Beware that you do not spend so much time on discussion that students are left with insufficient time to apply concepts under your guidance. Finally, be sensitive to individual differences in class discussions. For example, some students may be very shy or may lack the verbal skills to express themselves well.

Do not overvalue participation in class discussions as long as students are paying attention, and do not allow a few individuals to dominate.

Teaching Fitness Skills in the Lecture Setting

Certain fitness skills lend themselves to the in-depth time a lecture setting provides. Of course, all of these topics can be addressed in the physical activity setting as well, if you divide the material into small enough pieces so that you don't take away from physical activity time.

Interpreting Heart Rate Data

Even a kindergartner can understand why his or her heart beats faster after moderate to vigorous physical activity. At about third or fourth grade or so, a student can begin to understand the reasons for staying in a specified target heart rate zone (THRZ). In middle school, a student should learn to calculate heart rates and THRZs, chart heart rates in graph form, log workout results, and calculate averages.

Treating Injuries

Naturally, preventing injuries is the way to go, but students need to understand that injuries do occur at times even when you're careful. Contact the American Red Cross or the National Safety Council for more information on basic first aid and cardiopulmonary resuscitation (CPR). The following lists the injury treatment topics we recommend you cover before graduation from high school:

- RICES (rest, ice, compression, elevation, support) principle
- Heat-related problems (heat stress, heat exhaustion, hypothermia, and hyperthermia)
- Fluid intake (dehydration)
- Sunburn, skin protection

- Eating disorders
- Differences between sprains and strains
- First aid for fractures and dislocations
- Assessment of injury situations (and when to see a physician)
- Basic life support

Provide plenty of opportunities to practice treatments with teacher and peer feedback (practice and reciprocal teaching styles). Of course, much of this may be covered by your school's health education teacher. Work with this person to avoid unnecessary duplication or inadvertent omissions, or as an opportunity to team-teach.

Becoming a Good Fitness Consumer

In this age of advertising blitzes and cable shopping networks, this is an essential specific fitness skill. Students need to know how to comparison shop to get the most for their money when paying for legitimate equipment, supplies, and services, and how to discern when a product isn't worth the container it comes in. The following are suggestions for consumer education activities; adapt to fit your students' ages and abilities:

- Compare vitamin supplement claims with the research. Make recommendations to classmates based on your findings. (Have the class discuss whether they agree or not.)
- Direct students to bring in an advertisement for a fad diet or piece of exercise equipment that promises miracle results. Have them report (orally or in writing) as to whether or not the ad claim is true and why or why not.
- Discuss what might make an advertisement effective (e.g., flashy, quick "bytes" of information, enthusiastic claims, and so on). Have students in small groups develop magazine ads or act out TV commercials that advertise the benefits of a health-related fitness activity or practice (e.g., drinking plenty of water before, during, and after exercise; playing an active game instead of watching TV; and the like).

- Take a field trip to a local sports equipment store. Have students prepare specific questions to ask about the equipment they're interested in. Have the salespeople help the students compare the features of similar products; then for homework, have each student choose one of the products and explain in writing why he felt it was the best buy for his needs.

Logging Physical Activity Data

The classroom provides an ideal setting for teaching students how to set up meaningful physical activity logs. Emphasize the importance of recording data accurately. Share with students ways to make helpful and thoughtful affective comments alongside their physical activity data. Then show students the connections between keeping these records and making future plans and setting future goals. For example, if a certain activity always elicits negative comments, encourage the student to choose a different activity to meet the same goals. Finally, show students how to use technology to help them keep physical activity logs. Spreadsheet programs, computer-based calendars, and computerized log books for running and other aerobic activities are available for classroom use (see *ACTIVITYGRAM* on p. 263). Virgilio (1997) provides a sample physical activity and nutrition log.

Setting Goals

Whereas you should be able to help each student set health-related fitness goals at a station on a circuit in the physical activity setting, the classroom setting provides opportunities to explain the purpose and mechanisms of goal setting. Sample class activities include the following. As always, tailor these suggestions to fit the ages and needs of your students:

- Use the information on goal setting in chapter 2 to help a fictional person set appropriate goals (e.g., How might Jack in the Beanstalk build upper-body strength so he can climb up the beanstalk? or, Victor wants

Responding to Journal Entries

A health-related physical fitness education specialist needs to both reinforce positive physical activity behaviors and guide students toward finding solutions to physical activity problems. One way to do this is to make written responses to journal entries. Figure 14.2 shows sample entries from three students and possible teacher responses.

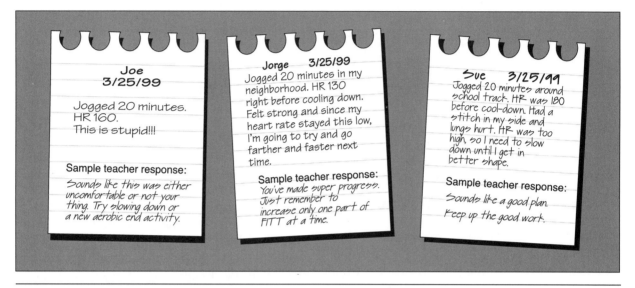

Figure 14.2   It is important to respond to students' journal entries in a positive and helpful manner—no matter what each student's attitude or level of thoughtfulness is.

Note: While it is not possible for a teacher to respond to every entry each student makes, rotating the classes you focus on will spread out the time this teaching tool takes, while still meeting this need. Even the occasional thoughtful written response from a teacher can greatly impact a student's physical activity behavior for the better. This is because the student can reread the response as many times as he or she wants, repeating the input without your repeating the effort.

to improve his body composition. What are realistic ways he can approach this?").

- Work with a friend to each set realistic goals and plan activities to reach the goals in one health-related fitness area. Help each other think of incentives you can offer each other (e.g., "If we both follow our plan, we'll buy matching workout outfits," or, "We'll walk to school together so we can have fun talking while we exercise").

- In small groups, brainstorm reasons people might not stick to their physical activity plans until they reach their goals. Then choose one problem and list ways to overcome it.

Designing a Personal Health-Related Fitness Plan

Students as young as the primary grades can begin to make choices as to how they will reach their goals in each component of health-related fitness. As an instructor, it is your task to divide the material into small enough pieces so that students can understand and apply it. How small those pieces are depends on the ages and abilities of your students. The Physical Best activity guides (*Physical Best Activity Guide—Elementary Level* and *Physical Best Activity Guide—Secondary Level*) provide examples of how to focus on one component of health-related fitness at a time in

Fitness Workout Plan

Name: _____   Date: _____

Week beginning:

Component	Activity	Mon	Tue	Wed	Thu	Fri	Weekend
	Warm-up						
Aerobic fitness							
Muscular strength and endurance							
Flexibility							
Body composition							
	Cool-down						

Figure 14.3 Sample fitness workout plan.

Reprinted, by permission, from AAHPERD, 1999, *Physical Best Activity Guide—Secondary Level*. (Champaign, IL: Human Kinetics, 223.

age-appropriate ways (figure 14.3). Following such a program means that, over time, each student will have developed his or her own personal fitness plan. You can give an overview of this procedure in a lecture setting to "prime the pump" for physical activity setting-based and homework-based personal planning activities.

Students also need to know that effective personal health-related fitness plans are dynamic, or everchanging. Illustrate this point by sharing your own or a fictitious personal plan, and showing how the goals kept being reset and specific plans changed as old goals were achieved. In this way, students see the process of tailoring a program to fit individual needs, which they can apply as adults.

Summary

While Physical Best believes it is usually ideal to integrate health-related fitness knowledge into actual physical activities, there are times when it is appropriate to share this information in greater depth in a classroom setting. But this doesn't mean you must give boring lectures! Remember to vary your teaching style and the type of intelligence you're addressing to create variety and, therefore, interest in class.

Don't be afraid to let students move and do in the classroom—interested, actively engaged students learn more. Use and adapt the tips and ideas in this chapter to help you make classroom learning more effective.

Chapter 15

Including Everyone

Effective class management, effective task presentation, and individualizing each activity help successfully include almost everyone in your program. As mentioned earlier, "inclusion" traditionally refers to the philosophy and practice of involving students with disabilities to the greatest extent possible. While this chapter explores that concept in greater depth, it also looks at how to meet the needs of each student, regardless of gender, cultural or ethnic background, disabilities, or ability level, whether or not a student has been identified as having a disability.

Inclusion used in the Physical Best program refers to the traditional meaning described, as well as to the process of creating a learning environment that is open to and effective for *all* students whose needs and abilities fall outside of the general range of those for children of similar age or whose cultural or religious beliefs differ from that of the majority group. In short, inclusion means that *all* students are included in an appropriate manner, so that *all* students can reach their maximum potential.

Relevant Laws

Although inclusion is the general trend in education and society at large (and the ethical philosophy to adopt), it is not mandated by law. The law mandates only the least restrictive environment (LRE) and civil rights. *Least restrictive environment* describes the practice of including persons with disabilities to the greatest extent possible in the situations their peers without disabilities automatically have access to. Figure 15.1 shows a continuum of placements. LRE grew out of civil rights law and the trend toward mainstreaming. *Mainstreaming* is the practice of placing students with special needs with students without special needs for classes, such as music, art, and physical education, and in the regular classroom for limited times. However, many parents and other concerned child advocates viewed mainstreaming as a basically "separate but equal" situation, similar to the separation of students based on race, outlawed in the 1950s.

More on Inclusion

For more information on including students with disabilities in health-related fitness programs, read *Physical Best and Individuals with Disabilities*. This book includes strategies for adapting the *FITNESSGRAM* test battery for use with individuals with disabilities. Also available is the Brockport Physical Fitness Test, which was developed specifically for individuals with disabilities. A package is available that includes a test manual, software, a training manual, video, and testing equipment.

The Individuals with Disabilities Education Act (IDEA) sought to change the status quo and integrate students with special needs to the fullest extent possible, based on each individual's needs and abilities. This was the beginning of educators' learning to focus first on what an individual *could* do, rather than on what he or she *could not* do. In a similar vein, Title IX of the Civil Rights Act of 1964 prohib-

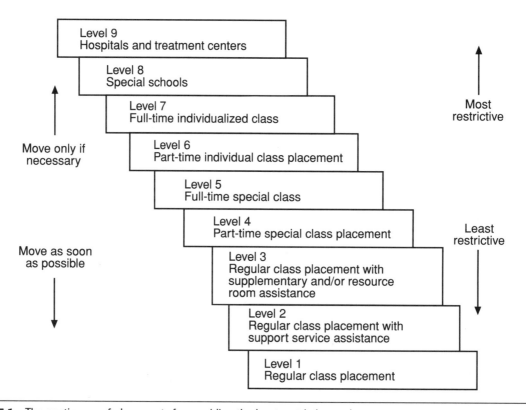

Figure 15.1 The continuum of placements for providing the least restrictive environment.

Reprinted, by permission, from J. Winnick, 1995, *Adapted Physical Education and Sport, 2nd Ed.* (Champaign, IL: Human Kinetics), 21.

ited discrimination based on gender and spelled out how public institutions should ensure an individual's civil rights regardless of gender, particularly equal opportunity to participate in sponsored physical activities. The Americans with Disabilities Act (ADA) has broadened the scope of inclusion and integration by defining a disability as *any* individual characteristic that significantly impairs a "major life activity."

Along with other civil rights legislation, this branch of law has created an acute awareness of the rights and needs of the individual. Aside from legal issues, however, offering a learning environment in which all students feel welcome and successful, achieve to the best of their abilities, and learn from diversity is simply the ethical action to take. Remember, diversity is part of our society, and it is important to simulate the society in which our students will function as adults as closely as possible—and to model appropriate behaviors toward those individu-als who appear, at least on the surface, to be unlike oneself.

Benefits of Inclusion

All students can benefit from true inclusion, from experiencing the diversity of our society, from learning from those who appear to be unlike them, and from opportunities to find common ground despite differences. Students from other cultures see a model of cultural inclusiveness that may positively influence their reactions to other cultures in the future, that validates their own culture, and that facilitates their own learning within the majority culture. Students with disabilities benefit from having peer models and from greater opportunity to participate in physical activity. Students who may otherwise suffer gender bias are free to explore all options and find their strengths and interests. All students benefit from being part of the problem solving that goes into being truly inclusive. Ultimately,

Girls and boys should learn to participate together in physical activities. As adults, men and women participate side by side in coed volleyball and softball leagues, as well as in fitness clubs, biking and running clubs, and so on.

INCLUDING STUDENTS WHO DON'T SEEM TO FIT IN

I was working with a group of teenagers, many of whom seldom dressed appropriately for physical activity and were considered by other instructors as "misfits." Instead of the prescribed activities, I introduced games analysis. We used leftover, abandoned, and broken equipment, such as broken bats and partially deflated balls. We also used as much other equipment, as possible (e.g., more than four bases, lots of balls of different sizes and shapes, large discarded orange cones from a local construction site). Gradually, as they embraced the idea of changing games, they invented a baseball-like game. To this day I don't understand all aspects of their game—but they did!

The game involved eight bases; a player could run in any order he or she chose; more than one person could be on a single base at the same time; three teams competed simultaneously; and batters selected not only the type of pitch but also the type of ball to be pitched. It was a crazy game, but it wasn't long before every player was thoroughly engaged in the process of games modification, wearing appropriate attire, and creating and completing related homework assignments. Through games analysis, ownership of the program had shifted to the players.

Reprinted, by permission, *Changing Kids' Games* (2nd ed.) by G.S. Don Morris and Jim Stiehl (Human Kinetics, 1998, pp. 41–42).

your program benefits because it is more effective for all students as you work together toward the goal of developing positive lifelong physical activity behaviors.

Methods of Inclusion

What does all this mean for a health-related physical fitness education program? For students who fall above or below the expected range of skill and ability, the answers include further individualizing, based on each student's needs; modifying the activity for all students; and/or collaborating with peer tutors, parents, other volunteers, and colleagues. The latter two suggestions are also helpful in implementing gender and cultural inclusiveness.

An example of modifying an activity for all students is to allow students to choose which test of aerobic endurance they prefer to practice and perform. That way a student with a disability can choose the test that allows him to use his abilities to their fullest, such as a blind student who chooses to perform the step test independently instead of the mile run, which would require the help of an assistant (Seaman 1995). A student with lower-body paralysis may need the activity to be changed completely, as she may benefit more from testing for the upper-body strength and endurance needed to power a wheelchair and get into and out of a wheelchair (Seaman 1995).

Changing the Activity for All

You might find that changing an activity for everyone means that more students are more actively engaged in the activity—both students who need special consideration and those who don't. Morris and Stiehl (1998) offer a model for how to change games to accommodate all play-

DISABILITIES AWARENESS FIELD DAYS

Teachers at Western Union Elementary School (Waxhaw, North Carolina) wanted to increase students' understanding and acceptance of children with disabilities. The children began learning about various disabilities at the beginning of the school year to prepare them to get the most out of a two-day field event. Immediately before the field days, students were also briefed about the activities, their purpose, and reminded they would be hosting special guests. This helped students understand that the events were for understanding what persons with disabilities *can* do, not to make fun of them. Students also raised money for Special Olympics in a Run for the Gold event held the day before the main event began.

The first day of the main event, third through fifth graders participated in six indoor activities: An Easter Seals Society representative explained the proper etiquette and preferred language to use when speaking to or about persons with disabilities; a teacher with a hearing impairment shared her daily life experiences; students taped their fingers together, arms splinted, or the like to simulate physical impairment; students wore glasses covered to varying degrees to simulate visual impairments; students wore socks on their hands and tried to perform fine motor tasks to simulate learning difficulties of people with mental handicaps; and students tried to speak with a marshmallow in their mouth to simulate speech impairment. Students were also encouraged to process what they had learned through various art and writing activities. Meanwhile, preschool through second graders enjoyed six outdoor activities (what was simulated appears in parentheses): Charades (nonverbal communication), Sit-Down Basketball (wheelchair basketball), Nondominant Hand Beanbag Throw (physical impairments such as cerebral palsy), Floor Volleyball (physical impairments experienced by persons with amputations and paralysis), and Silent 100-Yard Dash (hearing impairment). A member of the Tarwheels (a North Carolina wheelchair basketball team) also displayed his talents and spoke of never giving up. A parent shared his child's successes in judo and track and field despite a visual impairment. The second day, the two age groups followed the reverse schedules.

Adapted, by permission, from "Disabilities Awareness Field Days," by Melinda Jobe, 1998, *Teaching Elementary Physical Education* 9(1):10–11.

ers; we can adapt this model for nongame physical activities as well. Table 15.1 shows the categories and components in which a game may be changed. Table 15.2 shows how to modify degree of difficulty by changing limit and player parameters. The sidebar "Including Lenny" shows creative ways to modify the popular game of kickball to be more developmentally appropriate and inclusive.

You can teach students the game categories and components and encourage them to help you modify activities to include everyone. This problem-solving practice will also serve students well after they leave your program.

Fine-Tuning Individualization

Giangreco and Putnam (1991) have outlined two methods for including students with disabilities within the main program. Table 15.3 summarizes these two approaches.

Table 15.1   Games Design Model

Purposes	Players	Movement
Develop motor skills	Individuals	Types
Enhance self-worth	Groups	Location
Improve fitness	Numbers	Quality
Enjoyment		Relationships
Satisfaction		Quantity
Develop cognitive skills		Sequence

Objects	Organization	Limits
Types and uses	Types	Performance
Quantity	Location	Environment
Location	Quantity	

Reprinted, by permission, from G. Morris and J. Stiehl, 1999, *Changing Kid's Games*. (Champaign, IL: Human Kinetics), 18.

The multilevel approach has all students working on the same targeted area (e.g., flexibility), but each student works toward different goals appropriate for his or her abilities. For example, fourth graders without disabilities might explore stretches specific to an area of physical activity interest. At the same time, students with mild disabilities might focus on learning a new stretch, while students with severe disabilities might work on

Table 15.2   Modifying Degree of Difficulty Using Limits and Players

Category	Modification
Limits	
Physical aspects	Can you increase or decrease the size of the playing area?
	Can you use different types of equipment?
	Can teams have different numbers of players?
Activity conditions	Can you have a turn-limit game?
	Can a basket be worth five points?
	Could you add up total points of both teams, and if they equal a pre-determined score, declare a winner?
Players	
Characteristics	Could players of different ages and sizes play together safely and successfully?
Quantity	What happens if one team has more players than another?
	In soccer, could there be more than two teams on the field at the same time?

Reprinted, by permission, from G. Morris and J. Stiehl, 1999, *Changing Kid's Games*. (Champaign, IL: Human Kinetics), 35.

INCLUDING LENNY

The fifth-grade students at Adamsville School had been modifying games for quite some time when Lenny first arrived. One day, they happened to be playing a variation of kickball. Lenny had never played kickball. In fact, he had not played many games because most people agreed that a boy confined to a wheelchair could not participate in vigorous activities.

But the children immediately began to introduce themselves to Lenny and invited him to participate in the game. Lenny was frightened; he had been alone before—but never in this sense. This time he was alone in his belief that he could not participate. . . .

Lenny was assigned to the team at bat, some members of which had been deciding on a strategy for including him in a manner commensurate with his abilities. Instead of kicking the ball and running bases, Lenny had to maneuver his wheelchair through some obstacles and then squirt a water pistol at a cup that was balanced on a traffic cone. If he could get to the cup, knock it over, and return home without colliding with any of the obstacles, he was pronounced "safe."

Sometimes he succeeded, and sometimes he did not. He and his classmates determined what he *could* do, verified their strategy with us, and then agreed that this was an acceptable option. Lenny was no longer merely a spectator. His was not a case of token involvement, but of genuine participation—of inclusion.

Reprinted, by permission, from G.S.D. Morris and J. Stiehl, 1998, *Changing Kid's Games*, 2nd ed. (Champaign, IL: Human Kinetics), 10–11.

Table 15.3

	SUPPORTS	
	Supports similar to those typically available in regular education	Supports that are extended, modified, or individualized
PROGRAMS — Educational program similar to regular education	A No accommodations required	B Support accommodations required
PROGRAMS — Educational program that is extended, modified, or individualized	C Program accommodations required	D Program and support accommodations required

Reprinted, by permission, from M. Giangreco and J. Putnam, "Supporting the Education of Students With Severe Disabilities in Regular Education Environments." In *Critical Issues in the Lives of People With Severe Disabilities*, edited by L. Meyer, C. Peck, and L. Brown (Baltimore, MD: Paul H. Brooks), 247.

mastering one stretch without bouncing. Plan an activity for each level and decide which level is appropriate for which students, so that the entire class is actively involved in learning.

Figure 15.2 shows a sample form to assess the level of assistance an individual with a disability needs to perform a curl-up. Note that the task has been broken down into its component parts in a process known as *task analysis*. An individual may need a task to be broken down more or less, depending on his or her disability. A score reflecting percent-

Curl-Up

Name: _____ Date: _____

Directions:

Circle the level of assistance the individual requires in order to perform the task. Total each level of assistance column and place the subtotals in the sum of scores row. Total the sum of scores row and place the score in the individual's total score achieved row. Determine percent independence score based on the chart below. Place number of repetitions in the product score row.

Key to levels of assistance:

IND = Independent—the individual is able to perform the task without assistance

PPA = Partial Physical Assistance—the individual needs some assistance to perform the task

TPA = Total Physical Assistance—the individual needs assistance to perform the entire task

Curl-Up	IND	PPA	TPA
1. Lie on back with knees bent	3	2	1
2. Place feet flat on the floor with legs slightly apart	3	2	1
3. Place arms straight, parallel to the trunk	3	2	1
4. Rest palms of hands on the mat with fingers stretched out	3	2	1
5. Rest head on partner's hands	3	2	1
6. Curl body in a forward position	3	2	1
7. Curl back down until head touches partner's hand	3	2	1
Sum of scores:			
Total score achieved:			
Total possible points:	21		
% Independence score:			
Product score:			

Percentage of independence

7/21 = 33%	12/21 = 57%	17/21 = 80%
8/21 = 38%	13/21 = 61%	18/21 = 85%
9/21 = 42%	14/21 = 66%	19/21 = 90%
10/21 = 47%	15/21 = 71%	20/21 = 95%
11/21 = 52%	16/21 = 76%	21/21 = 100%

Figure 15.2 A sample form to assess the level of assistance needed by an individual with a disability. This sample focuses on the assistance necessary to perform a curl-up.

This material is reprinted with permission of AAHPERD, 1995, *Physical Best and Individuals With Disabilities: A Handbook for Inclusion in Fitness Programs*, page 100, a publication of the American Alliance for Health, Physical Education, Recreation and Dance, 1900 Association Drive, Reston, VA 20191.

age of independence can then be calculated, giving you valuable information as to the level and type of support that you must provide for the student. Then develop a plan to increase independence, as this enhances the "development of the fitness abilities of the participants" (Houston-Wilson 1995).

Another way to fine-tune individualization is the overlapping approach. Using this approach, all students strive for the same instructional goal, but the teacher uses different curricula to help students reach the goal, based on need and ability. For example, to reach the goal of increased aerobic endurance, a student in a wheelchair might wheel him- or herself around a "racetrack" (also increasing muscular strength and endurance of the arms), while another student runs around the racetrack dribbling a soccer ball with his or her feet (also improving this skill). To avoid collisions, teach and remind students to be aware of everyone's safety needs and to respect others in physical activity situations. Each student must take responsibility to avoid collisions on a busy track, just as they would in a park situation in which a mixture of adults and children jog, in-line skate, bike, and walk along the same paths.

Using these two approaches takes thought, foresight, and planning. Management and planning time and energy must increase; however, they really do not involve major changes. The multilevel approach is a more formal application of intratask variation (chapter 12) and will generally not require more alternative equipment than you might normally gather for a station-teaching approach. The overlapping approach allows you to use the same setup for all students, saving you time. Apply each approach as the situation warrants.

Collaborating

Creating the least restrictive environment includes organizing, training, and using other people to assist you in including a student as fully as possible. Legally, this applies to students with disabilities, but it also can help with including the motor elite and physically "awkward" as well as with eliminating gender and cultural bias. You can use these ideas in the regular class setting or in expanded opportunities, such as before- and after-school programs. These can be optional opportunities or chances to help students experiencing difficulties catch up.

You can collaborate with many different people, including peer tutors, parent and community service volunteers, paraprofessionals, and consultants (e.g., parents, medical personnel, other school staff). Choose the type of collaborator based on the student's needs, available resources, and the individualized education plan (IEP) or 504 plan (see later in this chapter).

To learn exactly the type of help a student may benefit from, first consult with the student's parents and other teachers. Maybe a parent will be willing to work with his or her child to teach the other students games from their native country. Maybe a parent will give you helpful guidance for communicating more effectively with a child with a disability. Other staff, such as classroom teachers, special education teachers, or the school nurse, may also provide insights you can use.

It is important to properly train any teaching assistants you may use. They need to know how to help a student, how not to do any harm (physical or emotional), and when to call on you for assistance. Take the time, then, to develop a specific training program before using these helpers in the physical activity setting. Discussing the student's basic needs and abilities (while ensuring privacy) and simulating learning situations are good ways to provide training. Persons with severe disabilities need assistants who are professionally trained by those qualified to do so.

Major Areas in Which to Ensure Inclusion

To ensure an inclusive learning environment, the following must be addressed: students with special needs, gender, culture, and ability levels outside the "norm."

Students With Special Needs

Each student with special needs should come to your class with either a 504 plan or an individualized education plan (IEP). An IEP will list a student's present performance; attainable annual goals and objectives; mainstreaming extent, including clear instructions as to how much time the child will spend in regular physical education class and with what support services; and the level and purpose of support services. While being part of an IEP team is a time-consuming part of teaching, it is vital to the student's learning that this process receive proper attention.

Based on the IEP or 504, adapt your curriculum and teaching methods to meet the child's interests and needs. It is important to make direct and repeated contact with involved special services staff, parents, and medical personnel. If available and appropriate, work with an adapted physical education teacher to ensure the student receives the instruction he or she needs. When designing health-related fitness plans for students with disabilities, keep in mind the following (adapted from DePauw 1996):

- Individuals with disabilities generally display the same physiological responses to exercise found in nondisabled persons. (Be careful, though, because some people with disabilities do not respond the same as those without disabilities, e.g., heat dissipation and heart rate response may be different for a person with a spinal cord injury. Ask the family to consult with their physician.)

- Although specific disabilities may affect the intensity, duration, and frequency of exercise, individuals with disabilities can benefit from training, including improving their performances.

- Wheelchairs can be adjusted or modified (by those qualified to do so) to improve physical activity performance.

- Athletes in wheelchairs play basketball, tennis, and many other sports.

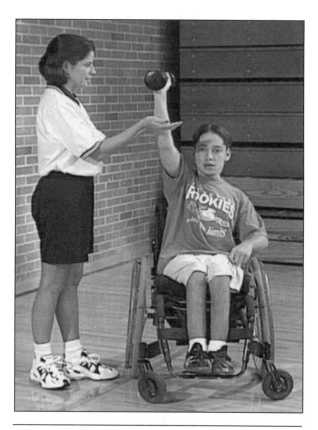

Individuals with disabilities generally display the same physiological responses to exercise found in nondisabled persons, though some factors like heat dissipation and heart rate responses may be different.

Use this information to ensure that students with disabilities are included in the class's activity to the greatest extent possible.

When deciding how best to teach an individual with a disability, focus on the *individual*, rather than the disability. In other words, refrain from making automatic judgments about an individual's condition. Look at what each child *can* do, instead of assuming he or she cannot an activity. Ask yourself, "How can I . . .

- help this child stay on task longer?
- encourage this child to keep trying?
- challenge this child's intellect?
- stimulate this child to grow in physical activity and health-related fitness?"

Design learning experiences as the answers to these questions.

Finally, apply Morris and Stiehl's (1998) Games Design Model (see tables 15.1 and

Developing a Respectful Environment

Craft (1994) suggests the following for teaching children without disabilities appropriate inclusive behavior:

- Do not allow students to show disrespectful behavior toward anyone.
- Let students know it's OK for everyone to make mistakes—including you.
- Help students understand that often people tease or put down others because they feel insecure, scared of others' differences, or unsure of their own abilities.
- Teach students to ask questions about differences in a positive manner. This helps combat ignorance.
- Have positive role models with disabilities share how they enjoy physical activity.

This list of suggestions can help encourage children to be more inclusive in regard to culture, gender, and race as well.

15.2) to your instruction, altering rules (limits), the learning environment (organization), and equipment (objects). Alter your instructional methods as needed.

Gender Inclusion

If you separate genders for activities, ensure that the activities are reasonably equivalent and not stereotypical. Physical Best recommends that you do *not* separate genders at the elementary level and try to avoid doing so at the secondary level, as well. After all, there are many activity choices that both genders can do together to reach the standards. Remember, choose activities for a purpose (i.e., meeting the national standards), not simply because they have traditionally been used. Some professionals say that there may be rare cases where privacy, size and strength differences, and safety require some *very temporary* gender separation at the secondary level, but remember, that goal-based curriculums have a plethora of choice. Therefore, focus on the idea that activity choices are not an end in

themselves. View activities as *strategies* for reaching program goals.

Remember, as adults, the majority of physical activity opportunities are not gender-segregated. Men and women participate side by side in health clubs, biking and running clubs, dancing (a great activity to build aerobic endurance), wall climbing, in-line skating, and most other physical activities. In many communities, the most popular adult sports are coed softball and coed volleyball.

Students need to experience equal opportunity within each lesson as well. Unfortunately, however, educators in general tend to inadvertently favor boys. In physical education, for example, boys are more likely to demonstrate and receive positive specific feedback or specific corrective feedback (e.g., I noticed how evenly you paced your mile run, or, Push off with your toes more). Girls are more likely to be passive observers and to receive general feedback (e.g., Good job, or, Try again). Boys are also more likely to be pushed to complete a task, whereas girls may be allowed to quit (Cohen 1993; Hutchinson 1995; Sadker and Sadker 1995).

One way to monitor your instruction for gender bias is to videotape yourself. Then watch

Both boys and girls can enjoy the benefits of a steps aerobics class.

Teaching Tip: The Educational Value of Gender Inclusion

I have found coeducational physical education to be highly successful, both for girls and boys. Certainly the skill levels of girls have improved. . . . The boys, too, have benefited from exposure to a greater diversity of activities, experienced more opportunities to be successful, and learned more social skills—with no decline in their learning of movement skills.

Jean Flemion
1990 NASPE Secondary PE Teacher of the Year
Arthur E. Wright Middle School
Calabasas, California

From *Teaching Middle School Physical Education*, 1995, 1(4).

the tape, keeping score as to the type of feedback you give boys and girls. A colleague or other trained observer could also keep score for you, if you do not have access to videotaping. Figure 15.3 shows a sample tally sheet.

Another way to fight gender bias is to ensure that the visual aids you use show both genders participating on equal terms and in nonstereotypical ways. Invite guest speakers who have crossed gender lines to play sports that are nontraditional for their gender. Finally, expose all students to a variety of activities that develop health-related fitness, regardless of gender. For example, a boy's lungs don't know that society says that dance is a "girl's thing," while a girl's muscles don't know that society says that tree climbing is a "boy's thing."

Cultural Inclusion

Cultural influences can greatly affect what an individual is interested in learning and doing. Since helping students find what physical activity is enjoyable for them is an important part of health-related physical fitness education, it is essential to be sensitive in this area. Develop a survey to help you determine student interests, then incorporate the survey results into program plans. Your obvious desire to respect other cultures will go a long way toward bridging cultural gaps. Indeed, Lowy (1995) writes, "If your students believe that their opinions and perspectives are valued and used, then you have taken the first step in setting up a culturally sensitive environment." You can take these basic steps in

tandem with teachers of other subjects to help make your health-related physical fitness education curriculum more culturally inclusive (and for that matter, more cross-curricular). Try to incorporate the physical activities, games, holidays and traditions, and music of other cultures.

Parents raised in countries outside the United States may be willing to talk to your students about the games and physical activities they enjoyed while growing up.

Girls			Boys		
Positive general feedback	Positive specific feedback	Corrective feedback	Positive general feedback	Positive specific feedback	Corrective feedback
ℋℋ ‖	‖	∣	ℋℋ	ℋℋ ‖‖‖	\\‖/

Figure 15.3   A sample tally sheet to help you prevent gender bias in your classes.

This material is reprinted with permission of R. Pangrazi and C. Corbin, 1994, *Teaching Strategies for Improving Youth Fitness*, page 5, a publication of the American Alliance for Health, Physical Education, Recreation and Dance, 1900 Association Drive, Reston, VA 20191.

Banks (1988) suggests you consider three areas when you plan your lessons and overall program:

1. Integrate content—Use activities from other cultures to achieve your program goals. For example, an active game from another country is just as good for developing aerobic endurance as a familiar game.
2. Plan how to reduce prejudice—Plan awareness activities that facilitate understanding among cultures, such as discussing different ways of dressing for exercise, based on cultural differences.
3. Employ culturally responsive pedagogy—Respect differences and learn the history

and meaning behind traditions and values.

Ask students and parents from various cultural backgrounds to share their beliefs and any individual requests with you. This process will help further sensitize you to the philosophies and sociology that may affect physical education learning and fitness attitudes. Finally, respect diversity in cultural values. For example, gender equity may be an offensive concept in certain cultures, so respect the different expectations for girls and boys within each culture you encounter. Provide equal opportunity for all, but if a student and her parents, for example, elect not to take advantage of the equal opportu-

Equity Checklist for Physical Education

- Is your curriculum gender inclusive?
- Do students participate in gender-integrated classes?
- Are teaching styles varied to accommodate different learning styles and preferences?
- Is gender inclusive language used?
- Do instructional materials portray both genders as active participants in a variety of activities?
- [Do you give] equal attention to boys and girls during classroom practices such as questioning, demonstration, and feedback?
- Are local community resources used to help erode gender barriers to sport participation?
- Is time consistently reserved for gender dialogue?
- Do you hold high expectations for both boys and girls?
- Is gender equity a pervasive schoolwide goal?

Reprinted, by permission, from L. Nilges, 1996, "Ingredients for a Gender Equitable Physical Education Program," *Teaching Elementary Physical Education* 7(5):28-29.

COEDUCATIONAL CLASSES AND PHYSICAL EDUCATION

One of the most widely debated areas of equity in physical education is coeducational classes. In today's society, most teachers would never think of segregating students by different ethnic groups, but some still have a hard time accepting students from different gender groups in the same classes. Segregated classes prevent boys and girls from interacting with one another and learning how to work and play together. Segregation by gender limits opportunities for boys and girls to reconsider their stereotypical assumptions in the physical domain.

Placing boys and girls in the same physical education class is only the first step toward providing students with the opportunity to examine their preconceived ideas about the opposite gender. The figure below shows six steps to equity. Not every teacher needs to pass through all six steps; however, you should be able to identify the step you currently occupy. Step Six is complete equity, including opportunities for both genders to demonstrate skills, answer questions, receive feedback, and feel respect from the teacher and other students. It also includes an environment in which the teacher uses inclusive language (referring to the class as "students" instead of "you guys") and omits stereotypical phrases (e.g., "You throw like a girl").

As you progress through Steps Two through Five, continually reflect on your own teaching behaviors. When boys and girls appear to not be working well together, examine the learning environment and determine what might be causing the problem. Often I hear physical educators state that the boys won't let the girls touch the ball. Sometimes, the physical educator states that a girl must touch the ball before the team can score. When I question the teacher as to whether or not all the boys in her class refuse to share, she typically responds, "No, it is a few aggressive boys." This tells me that the situation has little to do with coeducational physical education, since these same boys are also preventing the other boys from touching the ball. The remedy is either to make a rule that everyone must touch the ball, or better yet, reduce the size of the teams, so that everyone on the team must be involved for the team to be successful. Requiring that a girl must touch the ball before scoring sends the message that girls need special treatment, which only serves to reinforce the stereotype that the girls are not as competent as the boys. (Mohnsen 1997)

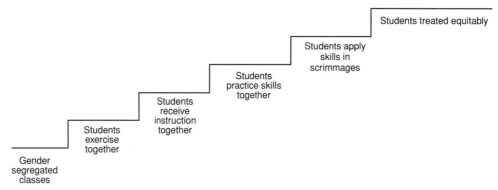

Reprinted, by permission, from B. Mohnsen, 1997, *Teaching Middle School Physical Education: A Blueprint for Developing an Exemplary Program*. (Champaign, IL: Human Kinetics), 51.

224

Teaching the Limited English– or Non-English–Speaking Student in Physical Education

A student who doesn't speak English as his first language can succeed in and enjoy physical education. The following may help such a student:

- Assign an English-speaking buddy to help the student in physical education class. If possible, choose someone who speaks the same language as the non-English–speaking student (Mohnsen 1997).
- Physically move a student through a skill to help her comprehend what you want.
- Use gestures and other visual aids, such as toy people and small balls (Mohnsen 1997).
- Use facial expressions and voice inflections to emphasize your points.
- Remember to speak slowly and enunciate clearly, as you would in the regular classroom (Mohnsen 1997).
- Emphasize the target skill's key word or phrase, as you work with the student, and have the student's buddy do so as well.
- Encourage the student to repeat the words or phrases, as she executes the skill, so she will learn the vocabulary that goes with the actions.
- Learn some of the important words and phrases from the child's native language.

Reprinted from Human Kinetics, 1999, *Physical Education Methods for Classroom Teachers*. (Champaign, IL: Human Kinetics).

nity you provide for girls because of religious beliefs, you might discuss other options with the student and her parents. You might involve a school counselor or administrator in such a discussion as well, depending on the circumstances. If religious beliefs mandate that girls not wear shorts, for example, you can discuss appropriate alternatives with the family and determine some other appropriate dress for participating in physical activity (e.g., culottes—looks like a skirt, but functions like shorts; Mohnsen 1997). Keep in mind that not everyone in a class has to dress alike to be able to benefit from physical activity. As another example, Hispanic girls in one class would not perform any type of straddle stretch, so their teacher offered *all* students a choice from a group of stretch pictures (Lowy 1995). Building in choices helps build on cultural diversity, rather than trying to eliminate it.

Ability Inclusion

Some students are either extremely talented or extremely challenged (but not classified as having a disability); they deserve inclusion, too.

The Physically Elite Child

Although Sara, who can run a mile in under six minutes, or Jimmy, who can do 150 curl-ups, may not need much of your attention, don't neglect these students. You may find the physically elite make good peer tutors. This will help keep them interested in your program, and it may also help them build social skills. However, do not have them tutor so much that their own needs go unmet or that other students sense favoritism. In addition, challenge the physically gifted students in your classes to explore advanced participation in physical activity. A student who might otherwise be bored, and, as a result, disrupt class, is instead challenged and an asset to the class. For example, you might have a physically elite high school student read a book on becoming a personal trainer and then serve as an assistant during class helping other students. You might also make arrangements for this student to interview a personal trainer at the local health club and write a report. Show interest in such a student's extracurricular sport activities, and have her share her experiences with the rest of the class. Encourage independence and fitness gains in

Teaching Tip: Reaching Students Afraid to Try

Ben came up to me after the first class and quietly, but in a serious tone, said, "Mr. Hichwa, that was a good talk, but, you know, I don't do gym." Ben informed me that he was cut from his fourth-grade travel soccer team, his physical education experience in the elementary school was far from positive, and he did not intend to expose himself to further failure or ridicule in the sixth grade. . . . I thanked Ben for being so forthright and suggested that he come to our next class as an observer, which he agreed to do. At the end of that class, I asked him if he thought he could feel comfortable taking part in future class activities. Because I took the time to listen to Ben, showed respect for his concerns, and gave him time to feel comfortable in his new environment, Ben agreed to give it a try! Throughout the year, Ben tried his best, participated fully, and eventually learned to enjoy the many challenges.

At the beginning of sixth grade, Clare was very tall for her age, fairly heavy, and extremely clumsy. She would go through the motions, but even encouragement from her peers was construed as a personal affront and caused her great anguish. But by making developmentally appropriate changes, the activities became less threatening. Clare started to experience a little success, and her self-concept began to rise. She excelled at the problem-solving initiatives and slowly gained respect from the other students. Her running times improved as she participated more enthusiastically; she didn't feel inadequate when competing with herself and enjoyed monitoring her progress. By eighth grade, Clare felt confident enough to demonstrate the layup shot in basketball!

John Hichwa
Educational Consultant
Redding, Connecticut
1993 NASPE Middle School Physical Education Teacher of the Year

From J. Hichwa, 1998, *Right Fielders Are People, Too*. (Champaign, IL: Human Kinetics.)

secondary students, by encouraging them to use health-related fitness training principles to continually challenge themselves.

The Physically "Awkward" Child

Wall (1982) defines the physically "awkward" child as one "without known neuromuscular problems who [fails] to perform . . . motor skills with proficiency." Don't assume a physically awkward child will outgrow the problem on his own; many do not (Schincariol 1994). Such children tend to get discouraged and, consequently, drop out of physical activity never to return, compounding their problems.

First, screen such a student for motor skill delays by administering a test of motor proficiency (Schincariol 1994). For example, the Test of Gross Motor Development (Ulrich 1985) may give you useful information. Then consult with an adapted physical education specialist and the child's parents to individualize the child's physical education program (Schincariol 1994).

The physically awkward child needs remedial help in the form of extra practice time,

instruction, and encouragement (Schincariol 1994). This student may need one-on-one help, the same as a student with special needs; if so, arrange for a trained volunteer, teacher's aide, or peer tutor.

Create learning situations in which the child who is physically awkward can learn, succeed, and have fun, making it more likely the child will learn the value and benefits of physical activity. Offering choices and variety are especially critical to enticing the physically awkward child to persist in physical activity. For example, in conducting a fitness circuit with a jump rope station, you can also offer the choice of doing step aerobics (step up and step down) to those physically awkward children who are unable to jump rope. This allows those children to participate in an activity when their lack of motor skills might otherwise prevent them from getting a good workout.

The Low-Fit or Obese Child

There are many causes of poor fitness and obesity: lack of physical activity, poor diet,

Physically elite students can build social skills by serving as peer tutors.

cultural beliefs, family situation, and too much time watching TV and playing video games, to name a few. Your job as a physical educator is to motivate all students to strive for greater levels of fitness (no matter their weight). Do not, however, assume these conditions arise from laziness. More likely, the younger obese or low-fit child tries harder in your classes, even though the results are poor. The older obese or low-fit student may avoid physical activity, by failing to dress for class or by simply refusing to participate, due to embarrassment and fear of failure.

First, take or have taken percent body fat measurements to determine the severity of the problem (see chapter 9). Then ensure that the child's problems are not caused by disease, health disorders, or hereditary problems (McSwegin 1994). This is best done through the family doctor at your request. Keep in mind that a little diplomacy can go a long way, so always maintain the student's privacy and respect the family's wishes. Consider holding a parent-teacher-student conference, in which you express your concern and desire to help. If there are medical conditions involved, work with the family doctor and parents to establish parameters for the student's participation in class. Secondary students may benefit from several forms of sharing their personal negative physical activity and body composition experiences and personal concerns. A private conference with you or a journal-writing opportunity that allows the student to air his or her feelings may lead to improved attitudes toward appropriate physical activity and nutritional practices.

Once medical concerns have been ruled out, work with the student and family to set appropriate goals and design an individualized fitness plan, emphasizing fun and variety. An obese student also needs extra nutritional guidance. Stress the benefits of even mild exercise, as obese students are often discouraged by being expected to do too much too soon. Let the student set an individual pace within each activity and in regard to the principle of progression. Encourage the entire family to become more active to increase the student's total physical activity time and sense of support. Reinforce achievements by having the student chart progress and by offering other rewards, such as the right to choose the game the class will play or the music the class will listen to.

It is important to deal sensitively with overweight and overfat children when exercising, to ensure that activity sessions are positive experiences for everyone. Some guidelines include the following. (The following list is reprinted, by permission, from J. Harris and J. Elbourn, 1997, *Teaching Health-Related Exercise at Key Stages 1 and 2*. (Champaign, IL: Human Kinetics), 25-26):

- Treat pupils as individuals, not comparing and contrasting them.

- Encourage a range of physical activities, including nonweight-bearing exercises, such as swimming, exercise in water, and cycling.

- Encourage low-impact activities, such as walking, and provide low-impact alternatives (such as marching) to high-impact exercises (such as jogging).

- Schedule rest periods to allow recovery from activity.

- Ensure correct exercise technique to minimize the risk of injury.
- Permit a choice of exercise clothing that reduces embarrassment.
- Ensure the wearing of supportive footwear during weight-bearing activities, and use soft surfaces, rather than hard surfaces, (such as concrete) where possible.
- Provide differentiated tasks to cater to a wide range of abilities, including low-level, easier tasks.
- Be aware of potential problems, such as breathing difficulties, movement restriction, edema (fluid retention resulting in swelling), chafing, excessive sweating, and discomfort during exercise.
- Encourage routine activity around the home and school.
- Where possible, provide opportunities for overweight and obese children to be active in a private, rather than a public, context.
- Enable obese children to follow an individually designed exercise program, based on their particular needs and capabilities.
- Encourage guidance and support from school, family, and friends.
- Always provide positive feedback and constant encouragement.

Other Health Concerns

Other health concerns may also affect a student's ability or willingness to fully participate in the classroom. Asthma is one relatively common example. People who have asthma are liable to narrowing of the airways, which makes breathing difficult. This narrowing can be sparked off by a number of factors (such as irritants, allergens, weather changes, viral infections, emotions, and exercise), which differ among individuals and may vary over time.

Exercise-induced asthma may occur during or after exercise. The usual symptoms are wheezing, coughing, tightness of the chest, and breathlessness. However, as regular physical activity has specific benefits for children with asthma (such as decreased frequency and severity of attacks and reduction in medication), over and above the benefits it has for children in general, it is important that they are encouraged to be active and are integrated as fully as possible into physical education lessons and sporting activities. Children with asthma should be able to participate in activities alongside their peers, with minimal adaptation. A child is most likely to suffer exercise-induced asthma when performing continuous aerobic exercise at a relatively moderate intensity for more than six minutes in cold, dry air (for example, cross-country running).

Although it is important to treat each child individually, here are some general recommendations that should be followed during exercise. (Reprinted, by permission, from J. Harris and J. Elbourn, 1997, *Teaching Health-Related Exercise at Key Stages 1 and 2.* (Champaign, IL: Human Kinetics), 26-27.):

- Encourage the use of an inhaler 5 to 10 minutes before exercise.
- Encourage children to have a spare inhaler readily available for use.
- A child arriving for activity with airway constriction should be excused from participation for that session.
- Allow a gradual warm-up of at least 10 minutes.
- Permit and encourage intermittent bursts of activity interspersed with reduced intensity exercise.
- Permit lower intensity (easier) activity.
- Encourage swimming—the environmental temperature and humidity of an indoor pool are well tolerated by people with asthma.
- In cold, dry weather conditions, encourage the wearing of a scarf or exercise face mask over the mouth and nose in the open air.
- Encourage breathing through the nose during light exercise—this warms and humidifies the air.
- Do not permit children with asthma to exercise when they have a cold or viral infection.

A Word About Inhalers

Although you should encourage children with asthma to participate in physical education as fully as possible, you must be aware of possible limitations. Children should have free and easy access to their inhalers. It is not wise for schools to keep asthma medication in a central store. Teachers who are better informed are more able to help children with asthma lead a normal life.

Adapted, by permission, from J. Harris and J. Elbourn, 1997, *Teaching Health-Related Exercises at Key States 1 and 2.* (Champaign, IL: Human Kinetics), 27.

- Where possible, advise children with severe asthma to avoid exercise during the coldest parts of the day (usually early morning and evening) and in times of high pollution.
- If symptoms occur, ask the child to stop exercising, and encourage them to use an inhaler and to rest until recovery is complete.
- In the case of an asthma attack, send for medical help, contact the child's parents, give medicine promptly and correctly, remain calm, encourage slow breathing, and ensure that the child is comfortable.

Nothing prevents the vast majority of children with mild to moderate asthma from participating in a range of physical activities with minimal difficulty, providing that they take appropriate precautions before and during exercise.

Summary

Inclusion in health-related physical fitness education means making it possible for all students to succeed in *and enjoy* physical activity. Thus, inclusion helps students meet the ultimate goal of becoming adults who value and pursue physical activity as a way of life. At the same time, inclusion teaches other valuable life lessons: social skills, cultural respect, and the feeling that you do not have to accept limitations unfairly assigned by those with limited visions of what people can be. To be truly inclusive in your program (as opposed to simply going through the motions), make a commitment to the planning and effort it takes. But you don't have to do so alone: Collaborate with both school and nonschool resource personnel to make the task of inclusion become easier. Collaboration will also ensure you have the input you need to tailor your program to *your* students' needs.

Part IV

Assessment in Health-Related Physical Fitness Education

Chapter 16

Principles of Assessment

If you hired a health fitness instructor or personal trainer, you would not expect to receive a letter grade as a result of working with this expert. You would expect the expert to assess your fitness level and then prescribe or advise a course of action so you could work efficiently and safely toward a higher fitness level. The same needs to be true for today's physical education teacher: Students should expect to have their health-related fitness levels assessed, and then, to be advised as to the best course of action, based on those assessments. After all, a grade does not tell a student what she needs to know to become more fit. Some assessment tools lend themselves well only to certain situations.

In an ideal world you would not have to assign a grade. You would have plenty of prep time to write detailed reports of each student's current fitness status, each grading period. Then you would sit down for an hour or two with each parent and student and communicate this information in full, set goals, and help with plans to meet those goals—in a private, quiet, and comfortable office. Yet, although this is not possible, you can provide detailed feedback and adequate input into goal setting and physical activity planning, based on appropriate assessment data.

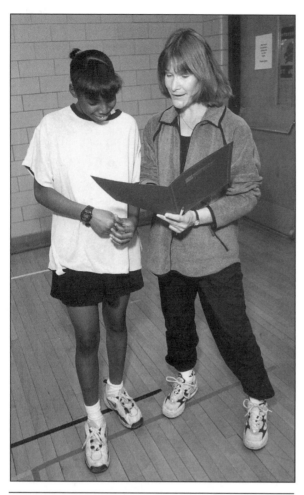

Assessment can be motivating for students when they are able to track progress toward their individual goals.

It's important to understand that grading and assessment are not one and the same: They have very different purposes. Assessment tells you and your students how they are improving in specific health-related components or what they need to work on. Grading attempts to communicate, mainly to parents, all that the individual has done in your physical education program in a single number or letter (Graham 1992). In this chapter, we first explore the issues and tools of assessment, then outline appropriate ways to use this information, if you must assign physical education grades.

Assessment

There are many approaches to evaluation (grading) and assessment. *Traditional assess-ment* is generally considered to be when the results of written tests are the main data used to assess student learning. In physical education, this has often taken the form of rules tests (e.g., for specific games and sports), skill test results, and teacher observation, all used for determining course grades. Today, the term *alternative assessment* is often used interchangeably with *authentic assessment*, although they are not quite the same. "Alternative" means tools other than traditional standardized testing, such as portfolios, journals, and role-playing. Alternative assessment becomes "authentic" when the assessment takes place in a real-world type setting, such as analyzing a child's running stride during natural play on the playground, or having a student set up a personal fitness plan that will actually be used and altered over time. Melograno (1998) defines assessment as authentic "if the student demonstrates the desired behavior in real-life situations rather than in artificial or contrived settings" (p. 10). Applied specifically in physical education, developmentally appropriate authentic assessment means that "teacher decisions are based primarily on ongoing individual assessment of children as they participate in physical education class activities (formative evaluation) and not on the basis of a single test score (summative evaluation)" (Graham 1992, p. 7). A student should make progress in the physical, affective, and cognitive domains, developing health-related fitness itself, a positive attitude, and fitness knowledge. To avoid being "artificial or contrived," authentic assessment in health-related physical fitness education teaches and motivates each student to apply fitness knowledge in the real world. In this section, we outline how. Specifically, we discuss the national standards in relation to assessment, stress the importance of assessment, and describe effective assessment tools.

The National Standards and Assessment

As mentioned in chapter 11, the Physical Best program uses the national guidelines for physical education, health education, and dance education, and their corresponding benchmarks to help determine what curricula to teach (see tables 11.1–11.3; see also *Adapted Physical Education National Standards*, 1995, National Consortium for Physical Education and Recreation for Individuals with Disabilities). In turn, these standards and benchmarks are the guidelines by which a health-related physical fitness education program should assess student achievements. In other words, students should be assessed based on whether or not they have reached the desired program standards as they relate to effort, improvement, and understanding. When student assessments are used to evaluate the effectiveness of a program, the circle of instruction is completed: curriculum design (as a result of program assessment), pretest, diagnosis, prescription, instruction, assessment, prescription, instruction, assessment, and so on.

Importance of Assessment

Given the time and energy commitment assessment takes, you may be wondering, "Why bother?" But assessment provides

- opportunities to focus on each individual,
- specific feedback to guide each student's personal goal setting,
- feedback on the effectiveness of your teaching,
- feedback on the effectiveness of the overall program,
- important feedback about student instructional needs,
- information to guide future planning, and
- credibility in the minds of administrators and parents.

Most importantly, however, carefully constructed and administered assessment allows you to teach and motivate students more effectively.

Both formal and informal assessments are important to a quality health-related physical fitness education program. Formal assessment lets you know more precisely how individual

Informal assessment can take place as trained professionals assist children who are learning how to adjust their safety harnesses before a wall-climbing activity.

students are progressing and gives you data for assessing your overall program. Informal assessment conducted by you is less time consuming, yet helpful. Informal self-assessment conducted by students allows them to practice strategies they can use on their own outside your program—it is an important instructional strategy.

Many of the same assessment tools can be used either informally or formally. For example, an informal assessment of journal entries may simply involve the instructor ensuring the student completed the work assigned, while a formal assessment may involve applying a rubric to assess the thoughtfulness and thoroughness of the entries.

Formal Versus Informal Assessment

One way to manage the time and energy that authentic assessment takes is to recognize the difference between formal and informal approaches. In general, a formal assessment

- is conducted by the instructor or trained adult assistant,
- takes place under strictly monitored conditions, and
- is officially recorded by the instructor in some way.

In general, informal assessment may

- be conducted by the student or a peer,
- be less closely monitored by a trained professional,
- be recorded by the student, instructor, or not recorded at all,
- involve simpler methods, such as an instructor quickly surveying the class to get a general idea of student success rates, and
- help the student to practice strategies to use on his or her own outside the physical education setting.

Teaching Through Assessment

Assessment does not need to be time consuming when it is planned as part of your instructional strategy. Indeed, assessment is critical for defining for students essential information about performance. Emphasize self- and peer assessment, personal responsibility, and goal setting to make assessment a learning tool in itself. In these ways, we teach students *how* to learn, not just why. This, in turn, empowers students to reach the Physical Best goal of becoming adults who know how to be physically active for life in safe, effective, and enjoyable ways. (We might add that this goal is shared by *FITNESSGRAM* and the CDC's *Healthy People 2010* plan.) Your job is to facilitate this process while each student is in your program. We discuss self- and peer assessment later in this chapter in the section titled Recommended Assessment Tools.

Goals should be set based on current personal health-related fitness status, feelings of self-efficacy, knowledge of FITT principles, training principles, access to various types of programs and activities, and purpose for setting goals. See the discussion in chapter 2.

Motivating Through Assessment

Of course, knowing how to be physically active for life isn't enough: Students must want to pursue such a lifestyle. Giving students the responsibility for tracking their own progress is highly motivating (Hichwa 1998). Avoid comparisons among students. Instead, focus on helping students set goals for personal improvement, so they are more likely to feel successful each time they participate in physical activity. Even a very young child can set a simple goal, such as playing physically active games after school three times a week instead of watching television. To guide self-assessment and goal setting, set benchmarks by which students can monitor their own progress (see also chapter 2). This process makes students more accountable for their own learning and progress. This is in keeping with our philosophy of helping students move from depending on our guidance to independently pursuing health-related fitness as a way of life.

Specifically, what is motivating is carefully monitoring self-recorded progress toward goals set for the student with the teacher. Sufficient time must be given to allow for progress. Be satisfied with small steps toward improvement or the goal. It is the small steps that can actually be seen in the student's own writing that are the most motivating. These become fuel for developing a sense of competence.

Recommended Assessment Tools

To assess authentically, you must apply a variety of tools to gather accurate information about a student's progress, because a student might find one form of assessment easier to perform in and interpret than the others, due to his or her individual strengths. By balancing the types of tools you use, you give each student a chance to excel in one way or another as well as to develop weaker avenues of learning and learning intelligences. In addition, the tools you select should help students move toward self-assessment, because they can apply them throughout life. Naturally, however, you must adjust each tool to fit the age and ability of each student.

Finally, when selecting an assessment tool and designing an assessment assignment be sure the results will help you answer the question, "Is the student moving toward the ultimate goal of health-related physical fitness education, that of becoming an adult who values, enjoys, and participates in physical activity?"

Many different assessment tools work well in health-related physical fitness education. The following sections describe several.

Rubrics

A rubric is a scoring mechanism. Rubrics are the means by which teachers, individual students, and peers may evaluate the information gathered by most of the assessment tools we describe in this chapter. A rubric can also double as a task sheet to keep students focused during class, or an observation checklist to guide feedback given by teachers and peers. Thus, being able to create effective rubrics is a vital teaching skill.

An effective rubric

- is shared with students before assessing them to help guide their practice and application attempts,
- accurately reflects the components you have taught,
- includes only the components you have told students they'll be assessed on,
- lists standards to assess by,
- helps you assess with greater equity among students,
- states these components and standards clearly, and
- teaches students how to learn.

You can assess a rubric's effectiveness only through its application. In other words, a rubric that looks and sounds good only assists authentic assessment, if it fits the teaching-learning situation. Take special care, then, when selecting rubrics you did not write yourself, to ensure they fit the specific material you are teaching. However, rubrics from reliable sources can and should guide you in your teaching and assessing—if the components featured meet your students' needs.

Teacher Observations

Every lesson, as you circulate among students applying the concepts and practicing the skills you have introduced, you should be continuously observing and assessing both each class's overall performance and each individual's performance. This informal process is an important part of "thinking on your feet," that is, adjusting lessons as they progress, based on the needs you see arise, rather than rigidly and blindly sticking to your lesson plan. For example, you observe that many students are having trouble finding a

Stay Focused

If another curricular area is involved, be sure you're assessing health-related physical fitness education, not the other area. For example, provide a calculator for figuring heartbeats per minute when only a fraction of a minute, is counted. That way, you're assessing application of fitness knowledge, not multiplication or division skills. If you still feel poor understanding in another subject area is interfering with what you're trying to teach, work with the appropriate colleague to create a cross-curricular approach to overcome this barrier. This can be a great opportunity to develop a more interdisciplinary approach to your curriculum.

Teaching Tip

Partners can check each other's heart rates by counting pulses and recording both scores, tracking and verifying the data simultaneously. I have found this to be the most reliable way to assess each student's ability to accurately find and count heart rate.

Marian Franck
Physical Best Steering Committee NASPE Representative
McCaskey High School, Lancaster, Pennsylvania

site at which they may count their heart rates, so you regain their attention and review the two main sites.

If you have the equipment available to you, videotaping student performance is one observation technique that can help you assess students as well. Consider requiring each student to bring in a blank videotape at the beginning of the school year. Then you can periodically videotape each student performing a fitness skill for closer scrutiny and analysis. Parents or older students can help with videotaping.

You can assess, as you replay the video, using a rubric (see previous section), freeing you to concentrate on management during class. You can also have students self- or peer assess via videotape, perhaps at one station on a circuit. Video can even help both you and your students see how the class is doing affectively. Finally, if you collect video clips over time, it will help you communicate better with both students and parents regarding each individual's progress (Clark and Sanders 1997).

A rubric turns an informal observation into a more formal one. Figure 16.1 shows an example of a rubric for assessing knowledge needed to calculate and use heart rate information, appropriate for middle and high school students. To gather the data for this rubric, you might interview students at one station on an aerobic endurance activities circuit.

You may wish to add or delete target components based on which ones you've focused on in class.

Journal and Log Entries

Journal and log entries provide a way to integrate writing into the health-related physical fitness education curriculum. Students can record either their feelings in journals and/or log their activities for you to review. Although logs can contain reflections on performance, strictly speaking, they are mainly for recording performance and participation data. For example, students can jot down the dates and times of each aerobic endurance activity they engage in outside of physical education. They can also record heart rates before, during,

Assessing Knowledge of Calculating and Using Heart Rate

Student's name_____ Date_____ Score_____
Class_____

Target component	Score 1 point	Score 2 points
Can demonstrate site(s) at which to count the pulse	Knows one site	Knows two sites
Understands how heart rate information indicates intensity	Some understanding	Clearly understands
Can accurately count the pulse for a fraction of a minute, then accurately calculate heartbeats per minute with calculator	Sometimes	Most of the time
Can describe ways and reasons to increase or decrease heart rate	Some understanding	Clearly understands

Figure 16.1 Example of a rubric to assess knowledge of calculating and using heart rate.

Sampling: A Time Saver

Program assessment differs from individual student assessment. You don't need to assess every child every time to assess your program. You can select and assess a sampling of students to give you a general feel for how effective your instruction is.

and after each activity, or analyze whether their total aerobic endurance time each week has been sufficient to maintain or improve aerobic endurance. A journal entry may include such data as well as a written record of how a student felt emotionally and physically before, during, and after each activity. Logging and journaling gives students opportunities to review their progress, which often motivates them to continue being physically active.

You can give each student a small booklet and have students write on the right-hand pages, leaving the left-hand pages blank for your comments. See chapter 19 for more about how to set up well-organized physical activity logs and journals. *Moving Into the Future: National Standards for Physical Education* (NASPE 1995) also offers good examples and guidelines.

Reflection is a type of journal entry that involves thinking about the learning process itself to help improve performance and attitude (Melograno 1998). Reflect on likes, and dislikes, and positive and negative feelings about participation. For example, you could have students list three specific ways they think they can improve their muscular strength.

For all journal entries, however, remember to focus mainly on understanding of the assignment, not spelling and grammar. While you should reinforce learning in other curricular areas, don't spend too much time on these issues and/or encourage other teachers to assess them as part of a cross-curricular, team-teaching approach. If neatness and spelling counts with you, let students know ahead of time; otherwise, settle for legibility and being able to understand what they mean. Have students complete journal assignments on a computer, if appropriate and available.

Finally, if you ask for opinions or for students to share their feelings, keep in mind

there are no right or wrong answers, only degrees of thoroughness and thoughtfulness. NASPE (1995) offers sample criteria and scoring guidelines for journal entries made during an adventure education experience (e.g., ropes course, wall climbing, and the like):

Criteria for assessment:

1. Analyzes and expresses feelings about physical activity.

2. Identifies evidence of success, challenge, and enjoyment present in the activity.

3. Explains challenge that adventure activities provide.

4. Describes the positive effects friends and companions bring to this experience.

Scoring:

- Exemplary: Expresses feelings of personal participation and in sharing it with friends.

- Acceptable: Identifies feelings of personal participation.

- Needs improvement: Has difficulty expressing feelings about participation.

- Unacceptable: Does not make journal entries.

Reprinted, by permission, from NASPE 1995.

Student Projects

Student projects are multitask assignments that encourage individuals, partners, or small groups to apply basic fitness knowledge in real-life settings. Under teacher guidance, a student, or group of students, explores an area of interest, sets goals, plans how to achieve those goals, and then strives for those goals (Melograno 1998). For example, a student investigates how muscular strength and endurance may enhance performance in a favorite sport, then formulates, tests, and reports on (verbally or in a journal) theories as to exactly what helps performance. Projects tend to be cross-curricular in nature, bringing to bear skills developed in several subject areas. Use a rubric to assess each part of such a project (see appendix G), having teachers in other subject areas assess their areas, if possible.

NASPE (1995) offers the following guidelines for developing and using projects effectively (The following list is reprinted from *Moving Into the Future: National Standards for Physical Education* (1995) with permission from the National Association for Sport and Physical Education (NASPE), 1900 Association Drive, Reston, VA 20191-1599.):

- Use a variety of teaching styles.
- Start with small projects in the early grades to prepare them for more complex projects later.
- Explain criteria for assessment and scoring procedures at the beginning of the project.
- Have others also score the project, for example, community experts or colleagues in other disciplines.
- Pilot test any major project before using the results as a basis for promotion or graduation.
- Use this opportunity to individualize your program to meet each student's needs.
- Design a scoring rubric for each part of the project.

In addition, be sure to design group projects so that cooperation with peers is essential for success. This interdependence builds social as well as health-related fitness skills. For example, a group works together to design a training circuit to enhance health-related fitness components. Then they oversee the circuit, while another group performs the activities.

Evaluate group projects both on overall group product and on individual performance.

In other words, make sure you make both each group and each individual accountable. In this way, you will know who are the "slackers," those who are just along for the ride, and who are the "workers," those who put a lot of effort into the project. You might, for example, use a rubric to assess the group's efforts, then have each individual turn in a journal entry or take a quiz to determine individual learning.

The *Physical Best Activity Guide—Elementary Level* and *Physical Best Activity Guide—Secondary Level* provide many suggestions for both individual and group projects in health-related physical fitness education.

Role Plays

Role-playing is an informal way to assess students. Use it mainly to assess the affective domain, but keep in mind it may also reveal clues as to degree of cognitive understanding. To create an effective role play, have students assume roles in a simulated social situation or psychological dilemma related to health-related fitness. For example, have small groups act out how they might convince a friend not to smoke, or how they might encourage an obese friend to join a physical activity.

When assessing a role-playing performance, you should listen for students to incorporate specific information in the dialogue and actions they develop. For example, in the case of convincing a friend not to smoke, you should hear several specific points, such as the increased risks of heart attack and cancer.

Easier Said Than Done

In group projects, assessment of both the group's and each individual's performances to ensure everyone has done their fair share is *very* difficult, a big assessment issue in itself. For one thing, it is difficult to design the rubrics for these. Take care to make students aware of the criteria by which you will be judging them at the beginning of each project. Simply sharing the rubrics you will use is very helpful. Then consider allowing groups and individuals to assess themselves and each other, alongside your professional assessments. For example, if three group members each privately rate the fourth group member poorly, this may support your conclusions regarding this student as well. But be careful! These can be touchy issues. Developing a supportive and open teaching environment is the key to getting the best work out of everyone. Discussing any large discrepancies with those involved can be a valuable teaching technique. Using an individual accountability tool, such as a journal entry or quiz, can also help. See chapter 20 for more on assessment in the affective domain.

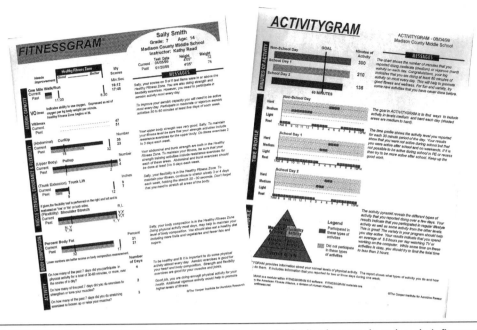

Figure 16.2   *FITNESSGRAM* and *ACTIVITYGRAM* provide students individualized reports based on their fitness test scores. Reprinted, by permission, from The Cooper Institute for Aerobic Research, in press, *FITNESSGRAM Test Administrator's Manual, 2nd Ed.* (Champaign, IL: Human Kinetics).

An event task, however, is a more open-ended role-playing situation through which you encourage students to problem solve. For example, you could challenge students to design and demonstrate a flexibility training circuit for helping a student in a wheelchair increase flexibility. The possible correct solutions are perhaps endless, as long as they follow the overload, progression, specificity, and FITT principles. Not surprisingly, event tasks are often the basis of effective group and individual projects.

To effectively manage role-playing activities, allow groups time to develop and practice their ideas. Then have them take turns performing in front of class, at a station, or in small groups, while you circulate from one to the next.

Health-Related Fitness Tests

Fitness tests, such as *FITNESSGRAM* (developed by the Cooper Institute for Aerobics Research and endorsed by AAHPERD), provide standardized methods for assessing each area of health-related fitness (figure 16.2). As part of an authentic assessment approach, use such test results to help students plan how to maintain or improve each component. Teach students to perform fitness tests inde-

pendently and informally. These self-testing opportunities are vital to preparing them for designing their own health-related fitness programs throughout their lives. Then, perhaps test students more formally each semester or quarter. Have the purpose of such testing firmly in mind, however. Know if you are using test results for individual goal setting or overall program evaluation. Teach realistic goal setting as described earlier in this chapter and in chapter 2 to teach students how to safely apply the principles of overload and progression. We explore fitness testing in more detail in chapter 17.

Written Tests

Written tests are a traditional form of assessment in physical education and most other subject areas. They are, however, often maligned in physical education theory, probably because they have been overemphasized and overvalued in the past. But written tests still have their place as a valid assessment tool. Whereas less formal assessments, such as role plays and discussions, can reveal important general information as to who understands the concepts you're teaching and who doesn't, written tests can provide more specific and accurate data on what each individual knows and doesn't know. Just beware the potential problems: Written tests don't always assess what has been taught or learned; instead, a teacher may write a test based on what is important to him or her, regardless of what was actually taught. In addition, teachers tend to focus on only one form of written test, instead of using a variety of formats to draw important information from students.

Objective tests, such as multiple choice or true-false, take little time to administer and are easier to score. Subjective tests, such as short-answer or essay tests, provide deeper insights into student understanding and are occasionally worth the teacher follow-up time they require. Figure 16.3 shows three examples of written tests appropriate for health-related physical fitness education. Choose the format that best fits the content you're teaching and the ages and abilities of the students you're testing.

Manage the workload by only giving written tests to one or a few classes at a time and by keeping the tests brief—no more than 10 quick questions (e.g., multiple choice, true-false, short answer) or one to three essay questions. Save class time further by asking the classroom teacher to administer quick written tests. This approach probably works best at the elementary level or at other levels that have self-contained classrooms.

Discussions

Interview students at one station on a circuit, briefly pause mid-activity throughout a lesson, or lead a whole-class discussion to provide closure to a lesson. For a good discussion, set a clear objective, plan the questions that will guide students through the topic, keep students focused on the desired content of the discussion, and summarize the discussion at its end to provide effective closure.

To increase participation and therefore effectiveness, you might try the following (adapted from Woods 1997):

- Make sure you wait at least three seconds before calling on anyone, so all have time and motivation to ponder the question first.

- Ask one individual or group to provide an answer, but have the rest of the students in class raise their hands if they agree with the answer.

- Have everyone respond verbally at the same time at a signal. You can also do this nonverbally by having students signal thumbs-up/thumbs-down for true/false and yes/no.

- Direct partners to share their answers with each other, then raise their hands when they believe you have stated the correct answer (verbal multiple choice).

- Keep questioning quick and to the point; don't take too much total time or unnecessarily disrupt the momentum of the class activities.

Discussions are quick, paperwork free, and especially helpful in assessing those students

A brief discussion with a student at a circuit station can provide a quick assessment.

a

Name: _____

Grade: _____4_____

1. When I run for a long time my heart
   (a) beats slower
   (b) stays the same
   (c) beats faster
   (d) almost stops

2. Which of the following is an example of muscular strength?
   (a) playing soccer
   (b) lifting a 50-pound bag of dog food
   (c) doing the sit-and-reach test
   (d) jumping rope

3. Being physically active is
   (a) fun
   (b) good for my heart
   (c) a way to stay well
   (d) all of the above

b

Name: _____

Grade: _____7_____

1. Target heart rate means
   (a) the rate you always want your heart to beat
   (b) the maximum heart rate you can achieve
   (c) the ideal heart rate at which to work out to improve aerobic endurance
   (d) the lowest rate your heart can go

2. Which of the following is an example of muscular strength?
   (a) running a mile
   (b) bench-pressing 150 pounds one time
   (c) doing 35 push-ups
   (d) riding an exercise bike for 30 minutes

3. To gain basic health benefits from physical activity you must
   (a) work out every day for at least 30 minutes at 75% of your maximum heart rate
   (b) sweat out at least one pint of water during your workout each day
   (c) be moderately active for 30 minutes on most days of the week
   (d) feel slight pain in your legs and arms after each workout

c

Name: _____

Grade: _____10_____

1. Determine the target heart rate for a person who is 17 years old (please show your work):

2. Define muscular strength and provide an example:

3. List five benefits of regular participation in physical activity:

Figure 16.3 Examples of written tests appropriate for assessing the health-related fitness knowledge of students in 4th grade (*a*), 7th grade (*b*), and 10th grade (*c*).

who find written communication difficult (Woods 1997). However, they are not appropriate forums in which to assess individuals.

Polls

Polls can give you some of the same information as discussions, but more quickly. You can pose the same questions and have students "vote" in response. Older students can secretly mark a ballot, whereas younger students might enjoy participating in a "poker chip survey" (Graham 1992), in which they place one of two colors of poker chips to indicate "yes" or "no," "true" or "false," "disagree" or "agree," and so on. Students can cast their votes on the way out of class. Use the results of a poll as a group assessment to help you plan reteaching lessons and to revise and improve lessons for future use.

Applying Assessment Tools

Some assessment tools lend themselves well only to certain situations. Other assessment tools work well in a variety of situations. In this section, we discuss which assessment tools work well for self- and peer assessment and teacher assessment through portfolios. In chapters 17–20, we discuss which tools work best for assessing in each domain— cognitive, physical, and affective.

Self-Assessment

Teaching students how to self-assess is an important key to reaching our ultimate goal of producing adults who know how to design appropriate physical activity programs for themselves. It also helps students focus on performance "process," rather than "product," because students understand the critical elements (process components) better, which, in turn, informs performance standards and achievement. You can have students use rubrics, journals, or logs to monitor their progress and assess their performances in fitness testing, role-playing, and group and individual projects. Journals and logs also help you make students accountable for staying on task during class. Journals provide

opportunities to reflect on the learning process through assignments such as the following:

- "Help your friend. . . ." Have students describe in writing how to do a particular health-related fitness activity safely.
- Record feelings. Occasionally or regularly have students record how they feel physically and emotionally after physical education class and other physical activity.
- Record performance. Have students record the number of times they performed a health-related activity, such as each stretch, by making check marks. Young children might enjoy recording a smiley or frowny face next to each check mark to indicate how they felt about each performance (Schiemer 1996). Or make appropriate selections from a pair or series of pictures that show right and wrong ways to perform.
- Analyzing performance. Have students record how well they feel they did on different fitness activities, and what exactly they will work on to improve their performances.

Peer Assessment

Peer assessment is an important part of developing physical, cognitive, and social skills. Analyzing others' performances helps a student focus on the key parts of a skill, reinforcing his or her own learning. Most students, however, need repeated instruction to learn to assess peers effectively. Make sure they have rubrics or other clearly listed criteria available, so they can evaluate and make judgments accurately.

To organize peer assessment, have students work together in pairs or small groups to analyze each other's performances. Then have students use the same rubrics as used for self-assessment. Teach students specific strategies for giving helpful feedback, such as those described in chapter 12. Role-playing acceptable peer assessment behaviors can be helpful.

Finally, when daily peer and self-assessment occurs, students learn more, retain more of what they learn, perform more accurately, and are more accountable. Thus using multiple peer and self-assessments provides very important information about student understanding, retention, and accuracy of data collection and recording.

Teacher Assessment of Students

Although most of your ongoing assessment should be informal, as in day-to-day observations and peer and self-assessment, you should periodically perform more formal assessments. For example, you should be the one to fill out a rubric, and you should be the one to select certain self- and peer assessments and class assignments for closer scrutiny.

One popular and effective way to create a more complete and therefore, more authentic picture of each student's progress, is to create a portfolio system (figure 16.4). A portfolio gives you a ready reference for assessment, grading, and parent-teacher conferences. Although sometimes described as an assessment tool in itself, we view the well-designed portfolio as a "tool kit" of sorts—a collection of tools that help you do a thorough job of assessing each individual. Because portfolios do an excellent job of showcasing student progress, they are a powerful way to build feelings of self-efficacy in students, those feelings that make students believe they have the ability to learn and the competence to participate.

What should you put into each portfolio? Select a wide variety of assignments and assessments to form a more complete picture of each student's progress and achievements.

Portfolio Management

Assessing student portfolios is very time consuming. Be careful what you choose to spend your time on. Then think through a plan for dealing with portfolios that you can handle. Follow these tips to help turn portfolios into the teaching, learning, and assessing tool they are meant to be, without giving up your family life:

- First, determine the purpose for your use of the portfolio.
- Obtain, or have students or volunteers make, sturdy portfolios. Use a traditional three-hole folder, a folded piece of 12- by 18-inch construction paper with pockets added, a flat box, a hanging file, or another appropriate container.
- Store portfolios by class in milk crates, portable hanging file boxes, or larger bins. At the elementary level, try to get the classroom teacher to store the container and bring it to each physical education class.
- Train students to file their papers for themselves or for younger students (but maintain confidentiality). Color coding by class or grade level can help. Establishing class management procedures for filing papers helps, too.
- Establish protocols for passing out and collecting portfolios.
- Periodically, select and/or have students select representative pieces from their assessment activities to retain in their portfolios. This leaves fewer bits and pieces for you to sort through. Designate how many pieces to select, taking the time to discuss what creates a good cross section of items. Send the rest home, after stamping them with a message, such as "COMPLETED ON TIME," to indicate you do care, but that you're not using it as part of your assessment of a student. This will eliminate much paperwork in a professional manner. *Note*: If you designate pieces to select after the work is completed, students will be motivated to try their best on each assignment.
- Staple or glue certain ongoing assessments, such as a fitness testing record sheet, into the front or back cover of each portfolio.
- Decide whether you wish to staple in several sheets of paper to form journals inside each portfolio, use a separate notebook for journals, or add individual sheets to portfolios with journal-type entries as they are written.

Figure 16.4 A portfolio system can provide an authentic assessment of student progress.

Include both informal and formal assessments: periodic fitness testing results; rubrics that reflect affective, cognitive, and physical development; journal entries; and projects. The older the students, the more you should strive to teach them to select their own portfolio pieces, based on criteria you set. This is part of making each student an independent learner.

Another advantage of portfolios is that they can go with students from grade to grade and school to school, making monitoring of long-term progress and persistent problems possible. Portfolios are also a tool for monitoring a program's effectiveness in terms of delivering a sequentially designed curriculum.

Using Assessment Results Appropriately

For all the time and energy assessment takes, it's important to use the information you collect to the greatest advantage. Whenever you're not sure how to use assessment data, simply ask yourself if your use of it furthers a student's chances of reaching our ultimate goal—that of becoming a physically active adult. Ranking students according to fitness test results will not; however, using assessment information to help students set realis-

tic goals and to shape future program and instruction plans, can. Here we examine how to effectively share results with students and parents and use data to improve your planning for their continued learning.

Sharing Information With Students and Parents

Be sure to inform everyone—both students and parents—ahead of time what you're looking for in terms of development and participation and effort levels. This approach can prevent many misunderstandings. Communicate through newsletters, parent-teacher conferences, and detailed report cards. If you focus, as we believe you should, on self-assessment, students will know their results already, but set up teacher-student conferences, perhaps as part of an activity circuit, so you can help each individual set goals based on your feedback and the student's personal objectives. Finally, ensure student and family privacy when interpreting and sharing assessment results. Remember, the idea is, over the course of a K–12 program, to guide each student up the Stairway to Lifetime Fitness (Corbin and Lindsey 1993), empowering each to take individual responsibility for health-related fitness.

Planning

Assessment for its own sake is a waste of time. Instead, it must work in a continuous cycle. In this way, assessment provides feedback to help you plan a program and individual units and lessons that better meet the needs of your particular students. Next, you teach from your revised plans, then you reassess, and the cycle continues indefinitely.

Grading

As mentioned in the opening to this chapter, assessing and grading have very different purposes. Assessment tells you and your students how they are improving or what they need to work on. Grading attempts to communicate, mainly to parents, all that the individual has done in your physical education program in a single number or letter (Graham 1992). It needs to represent a compilation of many assessments and measurements of improvement—not a limited or single test of student status. In this section, we show you how to create an acceptable relationship between assessing and grading.

Develop parameters for testing and grading in order to grade students fairly, including the weight you will give to each component of the grade. Then communicate these criteria to students and parents—*before* collecting data. Safrit (1995) suggests refraining from using fitness test score improvement as the basis for grading, unless you have provided sufficient class time for improving fitness. In addition, use evidence of cognitive development, as long as you have taught the concepts you're measuring. Include data regarding fitness skills, physical activity effort, and affective skills, as well. Finally, collect explicit documentation to maintain accountability. A portfolio system can do much of the record keeping for you.

Unfortunately, however, a grade in physical education doesn't really tell students and parents how an individual is doing. For example, a student who does not understand health-related fitness concepts may receive a "Satisfactory" simply for behaving in physical education class and trying hard (Graham 1992). Instead, give separate grades for affective, physical, and cognitive performances. Create a form to send home with the rest of

Grades and Fitness Scores

Remember, neither *FITNESSGRAM* nor Physical Best believes that fitness test scores should count toward grades. Only ability to self-test and improvement of scores are fair and authentic areas in which to assess students in relation to fitness testing. In addition, keep in mind that students who start off with a high level of fitness, either due to healthy lifestyle choices or genetics, will show a lower percentage of improvement, relative to baseline fitness testing, than will students who begin a course at lower levels of fitness. Take care, then, to not penalize high-fit students, if you choose to give grading credit for improvements in fitness levels.

the report card or at the end of each unit, noting areas of improvement and offering tips as to how the student can overcome problem areas, as appropriate. Even if you must still enter a total grade on the regular report card, by offering students and parents specific information, you will help students learn through grading, making it more valuable. See figure 16.5 for a sample grading form.

Objective and thorough grading should do the following:

- Help the students understand where they can improve
- Help you recognize if students are meeting program objectives and content standards

Weighty Matters

What weight should you give each area you plan to rate in the final grade? This will vary according to district mandates, personal preferences, and program goals. We recommend that, in a health-related physical fitness education program, you strive for a balance of program aspects—cognitive, affective, and physical assessment data—because each of these areas affects how students will be empowered to make lifestyle decisions, regarding physical activity and health-related fitness.

Fitness education sample grading criteria form

____ Knowledge of fitness concepts (25%) (see chapter 18)
____ Fitness testing (ability to self-test and improvement level) (20%) (see chapter 17)
____ Physical activity effort (in and outside of class) (25%) (see chapter 19)
____ Fitness skill application (e.g., ability to take pulse, pace while running) (20%) (see chapter 8)
____ Attitude toward physical activity (10%) (see chapter 20)

Physical Education Progress Report: Grades 3–4

Student: _____ Date: _____

Teacher: _____

_____ 1st qtr. (Nov.) _____ 2nd qtr. (Feb.) _____ 3rd qtr. (April) _____ 4th qtr. (June)

	Working to achieve	Needs improvement	Achieved
Intellectual			
1. Knows rules and procedures governing movement activities and games	❏	❏	❏
2. Recognizes the effects of space, time, force, and flow on the quality of movement	❏	❏	❏
3. Applies basic mechanical principles that affect and control human movement	❏	❏	❏

Comments: _____

	Working to achieve	Needs improvement	Achieved
Social			
1. Respects rights, opinions, and abilities of others	❏	❏	❏
2. Shares, takes turns, and provides mutual assistance	❏	❏	❏
3. Participates cooperatively in student-led activities	❏	❏	❏

Comments: _____

	Working to achieve	Needs improvement	Achieved
Emotional			
1. Assumes responsibility for giving and following directions	❏	❏	❏
2. Makes decisions on an individual basis			
3. Responds freely and confidently through expressive bodily movement	❏	❏	❏
	❏	❏	❏

Comments: _____

	Working to achieve	Needs improvement	Achieved
Values			
1. Carries out tasks to completion	❏	❏	❏
2. Displays preferences for various forms of movement	❏	❏	❏
3. Engages in movement activities voluntarily	❏	❏	❏

Comments: _____

	Working to achieve	Needs improvement	Achieved
Physical			
1. Executes all locomotor movements in response to rhythmic accompaniments	❏	❏	❏
2. Controls body while balancing, rolling, climbing, and hanging	❏	❏	❏
3. Shows body control in manipulating playground ball, while stationary and moving	❏	❏	❏

Comments: _____

Figure 16.5 Sample grading form. This form has been tailored to a specific school district's curriculum.

Reprinted, by permission, from V. Melograno, 1998, *Professional and Student Portfolios for Physical Education*. (Champaign, IL: Human Kinetics), 109.

- Show you where you should change your program (provided grades are plotted on a graph to summarize trends)
- Promote your health-related physical fitness education program to the school and community
- Justify the ongoing need for health-related physical fitness education in the curriculum

Therefore, you should grade students based on, for example, age-appropriate abilities to self-test, interpret test results, knowledge of fitness information, and how well they plan personal programs (Pangrazi and Corbin 1994). This approach will help students become adults who understand the process of achieving and maintaining healthful levels of fitness and who are physically active for life. Grades based solely on test results, however, can discourage students from continuing to be physically active after they leave your program.

Summary

To be truly authentic, assessment in health-related physical fitness education must allow students to demonstrate, in real-life settings, that they are moving toward our goal of becoming physically active adults. Thus, your program should motivate students to apply fitness knowledge in the real world, as they make progress in the physical, affective, and cognitive domains. In chapters 17 through 20, we show you how to apply the tools discussed in this chapter in specific ways to assess physical, affective, and cognitive progress of health-related fitness concepts and skills.

Chapter 17

Assessing Health-Related Physical Fitness

Today, most fitness testing conducted in physical education focuses on the components of health-related fitness. It uses scores for goal setting, checking progress. Records are individualized and include physical activity participation data, not merely one-time scores. Teachers look for improvement in every student, and the focus is on how a student's personal choices can impact each health-related physical fitness component.

Fitness testing has had a sometimes controversial history, however. In the past, more emphasis was placed on skill- or sport-related fitness, such as speed, as measured by an individual's 100-yard dash time. Tests compared students to other students, leading many children, who were actually healthy individuals, to perceive themselves as unfit. Conversely, some students who were practicing unhealthy behaviors were still able to achieve good scores, giving them a false picture of their present and future health and fitness. For example, these students may have matured physically earlier than most students of similar age, or may have inherited good upper-body strength, thus scoring higher on some tests, even though they were not physically active (something that would catch up to them later in life). Today, there is greater

Many students are turned off to physical activity when awards are based on outperforming others rather than personal improvement.

awareness that comparing students does more harm than good. Therefore do not

- use fitness test results as the only criteria for assigning grades,
- use fitness test results as the sole indicator of program effectiveness,
- post test results, or
- base awards on outperforming others, rather than on personal improvement.

In addition, sometimes test results were inconsistent: A student may pass in one test and fail when taking another similar test in a different battery. This problem had to do with assessment design, not teacher practices, creating problems even for teachers who used fitness testing appropriately.

Administered correctly, *FITNESSGRAM* overcomes the problems fitness testing has experienced in the past. *FITNESSGRAM* sets performance standards that reflect the basic health-related fitness levels required for good health (called "healthy fitness zones"), instead of comparing children's performances (figure 17.1). Thus, the likelihood that each child feels successful in fitness testing is greatly increased, thereby increasing the likelihood he or she will view physical activity and health-related fitness in a positive light.

Yet even when health-related fitness testing is conducted properly and with sensitivity, some still argue that health-related fitness

testing is too artificial and contrived to be part of authentic assessment. Physical Best asserts, however, that developmentally appropriate health-related fitness testing, conducted in a sound physical education program, helps teach students *how* to be fit for life. Moreover, it provides a "snapshot" of each student's current fitness level, allowing for both teacher and student to plan for improvement.

You Stay Active!

You Stay Active! is a recognition program developed by AAHPERD and the Cooper Institute for Aerobics Research. The goal of the program is to recognize all children and youth who are physically active and who achieve the Healthy Fitness Zone of the *FITNESSGRAM* physical fitness test. *You Stay Alive!* is being continually updated—for more information you can contact AAHPERD, The Cooper Institute for Aerobics Research, or the American Fitness Alliance. See appendix C for contact information.

Health-Related Fitness Testing and Authentic Assessment

To make fitness testing a viable component of authentic assessment, it must do the following:

1. Demonstrate the desired behavior—teaching students to self-test gives them opportunities to demonstrate the behaviors they'll need to create their own effective physical activity programs throughout life.

2. Link directly to the curriculum—self-testing as a self-teaching activity helps make health-related fitness concepts "essential content" of the curriculum.

3. Occur on an ongoing basis—self-testing makes it easy to test on an ongoing basis, because it saves teacher time. More important, it individualizes the instruction and sequence of learning.

4. Make students both capable and likely to apply the tests and set goals for achieving physical gains in real life—self-testing gives students the practical experience they need to feel confident and capable in their abilities to apply the tests and seek improvement in real life.

Some children will need more supervision and help than other children. Teach all students proper procedures and periodically conduct more formal tests, no matter what

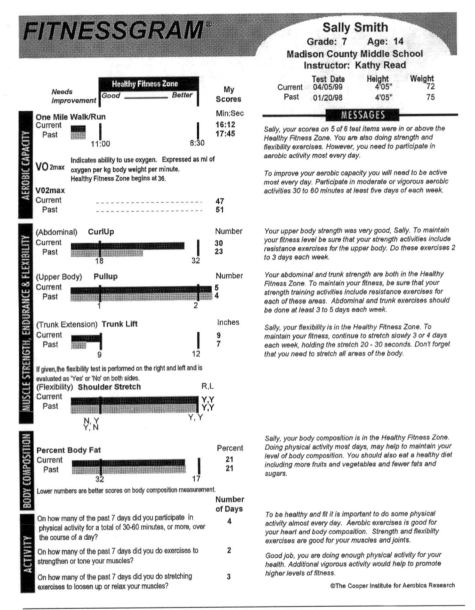

Figure 17.1   The *FITNESSGRAM* report focuses on helping students set self-improvement goals.

Adapted, by permission, from The Cooper Institute for Aerobic Research, in press, *FITNESSGRAM Test Administrator's Manual, 2nd Ed.* (Champaign, IL: Human Kinetics).

your students' levels of independence. Figure 17.2 shows a continuum from just beginning to learn how to self-test to formal, but independent self-testing, depending on goals. The more experienced the student, the more independent he should be of teacher supervision, because the ultimate goal is to produce adults who can conduct their own tests in the context of self-designed physical activity programs. Some students may, however, stay at one stage on the continuum longer than

	Format	Goal
1	Teacher-directed, self-testing practice	To familiarize students with testing procedures
2	Formal, teacher-administered testing	To provide accurate baseline data
	Goal setting	To focus training efforts
	Physical activity	To reach goals
3	Informal self-testing, checked by peer	To compare to baseline data, to provide more testing practice, and to ensure accuracy
	Reset goals (if necessary)	To focus future efforts
	Physical activity	To reach goals
4	Informal self-testing	To self-monitor progress, to provide more testing practice
	Reset goals (if necessary)	To focus future efforts
	Physical activity	To reach goals
5	Formal self-testing, checked by teacher	To ensure accurate current data
	Reset goals (if necessary)	To focus future efforts
	Physical activity	To reach goals
6	Formal self-testing, not checked	To monitor progress independently

Figure 17.2 An example of a continuum for moving students from teacher-directed testing to self-testing.

others, depending on their needs and abilities. For example, most elementary students will require a high degree of direct teacher supervision, but middle schoolers will likely be capable of cycling through the first three steps (teacher-directed, self-testing practice; formal, teacher-administered testing; and informal, self-testing, checked by peer) repeatedly, but may not progress to informal self-testing (without being checked), until they are older. High school students should be able to progress to formal, self-testing (not checked by peer or teacher). Note that goal setting and physical activity are important steps after the initial self-testing practice (checked by teacher) and will perpetuate a continuous cycle of testing, goal setting, and participating in physical activity as discussed in chapter 16. Figure 17.3 shows how *FITNESSGRAM* fits into the components of a quality health-related physical fitness education program.

Administering *FITNESSGRAM*

Fitness testing doesn't have to be an administrative nightmare. By following some simple guidelines, your *FITNESSGRAM* experience should be a positive one.

Preparing for Testing

Simply being ready to administer fitness testing makes the entire process flow more smoothly. The following suggestions will help streamline the process of administering *FITNESSGRAM*. (The following list is adapted, by permission, from The Cooper Institute for Aerobic Research, in press, *FITNESSGRAM Test Administrator's Manual, 2nd Ed.* (Champaign, IL: Human Kinetics).):

1. Prepare students for the test—Allow two to six weeks for students to practice test items and increase their fitness levels. Administering the tests at the very beginning of the school year may lead to muscle soreness and discouragement. It may also cause misleading follow-up test results, as students improve more rapidly, once they get used to the testing procedures. (See also the following section, Involving Students.)

2. Read all test instructions carefully—These are located in the FITNESSGRAM *Test Administrator's Manual* (Second Edition).

3. Collect the necessary testing equipment—Obtain the testing equipment you need, and ensure it is working properly. Sources of equipment are listed in the

Prepare for testing

— Precede with regular enjoyable exercise
— Explain reasons for testing
— Precede with knowledge of how to take tests
— Precede with knowledge of exercise warm-up
— Explain recognition opportunities

Testing

— Follow basic exercise principles
— Test properly
— Consider student feelings
— Consider student confidentiality
— Teach while you test
— Consider self-testing opportunities

After testing

— Report results
— Interpret results
— Recommend program of exercise
— Carry out program

Implement recognition programs

— Explain recognition philosophy
— Use recognition to foster competence and confidence
— Use recognition to promote regular exercise
— Use recognition to stimulate intrinsic motivation
— Use recognition to foster parent interest
— Implement recognition for everyone

Quality physical education program

— Learn about fitness and exercise
— Learn to self-test
— Learn to interpret test results
— Learn to plan personal program
— Do regular vigorous exercise
— Learn to enjoy exercise

Figure 17.3 Testing is part of the overall educational process leading to a physically active, healthy lifestyle.

This material is reprinted with permission of R. Pangrazi and C. Corbin, 1994, *Teaching Strategies for Improving Youth Fitness*, page 5, a publication of the American Alliance for Health, Physical Education, Recreation and Dance, 1900 Association Drive, Reston, VA 20191.

FITNESSGRAM *Test Administrator's Manual* (Second Edition).

4. Prepare record-keeping forms—Reproduce necessary forms (see FITNESSGRAM *Test Administrator's Manual* [Second Edition]). Record student names as appropriate, depending on the form you use.

5. Organize testing stations—Create a kind of circuit, such as that shown in figure 17.4. Be sure your setup allows both you and your students to flow easily from one station to the next. In addition, ensure you can see the entire activity area, making adequate supervision easier. Make sure forms, pencils, and clipboards are available at each station to allow students to record their test results.

6. Organize students—Decide in advance how to group students and which group will begin at which station.

7. Maximize instruction—Plan testing with other activities to continue the learning process and keep all students active.

In addition, if you are new to fitness testing or unsure of a procedure, practice administering the test to a small group of students or colleagues prior to testing on a larger scale.

Involving Students

We all learn best by doing, so, if our goal is to produce students who can self-direct their own physically active lifestyles, we must involve them as fully as possible in each part of our programs—including fitness testing. As previously discussed, at the heart of this approach, is teaching students to self-test. You should also give students feedback to help them establish appropriate goals, such as to improve the number of laps they are able to complete on the PACER test, or to improve their sit-and-reach score. Beyond this, have students record their own test results. Even second graders can record numbers, if you take the time to show them the appropriate place on the form. The new *FITNESSGRAM* software is simple enough for almost all students to be able to enter their own scores. For any of

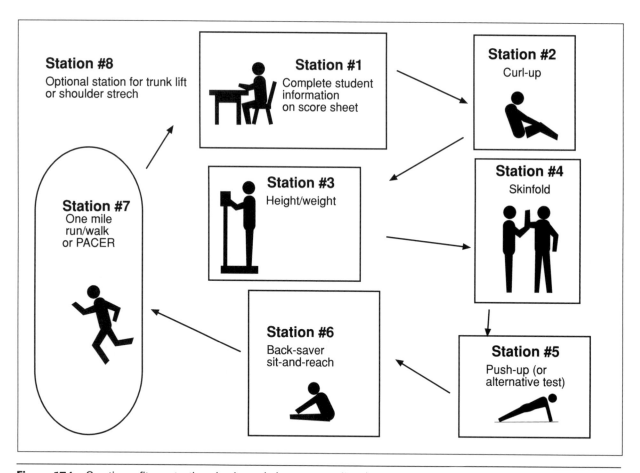

Figure 17.4 Creating a fitness testing circuit can help you streamline the testing process.

Effective Test Item Practice

To encourage optimal test performance, students need to practice each item ahead of time, repeatedly. The following are simple suggestions for making this practice worthwhile:

- Discuss and demonstrate the correct techniques involved in each test item. Deliver this information in multiple forms: posters, listed critical steps in word or picture form, checklists of test steps for self- and peer checking.

- Have students practice the test items with a friend. This partner can provide feedback on technique and emotional support. Then have them practice and practice some more.

- Make testing stations available during class so students can self-test regularly. Use posters to guide students.

- Assign fitness homework that involves parents. Shape Up Across Oregon (pages 26–27) is an example of a program that gets parents and students to work together at home.

- Send weekly workout reports home.

Finally, encourage students to make their best efforts when they practice the tests.

Norm-Referenced Versus Criterion-Referenced Testing

Norm-referenced tests—no matter the subject area—are tests for which a student's score depends on a comparison to other students' performances. In fitness testing, norm-referenced tests use a large sampling of student performances to determine who is fit and who is not, relative to each other. So, for example, the old versions of the President's Challenge test battery only awarded the "President's Physical Fitness Award" to students who score at the 85th percentile on all the test items, meaning, to earn this award, a student has to perform better than 85 out of 100 sample students for whom data was collected; criterion-referenced standards are now available for this test battery, however. Another example is the AAU Physical Fitness Program. This program gives its top award to those who score in the "Outstanding" (as compared to others) range in all five test items (*TEPE* 1994).

In contrast, *FITNESSGRAM* is a *criterion-referenced test*, in that student scores are compared to standards of health-related fitness that indicate levels of fitness necessary for health, regardless of others' scores. The goal is to score in the *Healthy Fitness Zones* (HFZs).

Criterion-based self-testing: In some situations teachers may elect to have students stop the test when they have achieved a score equal to the upper limit of the Healthy Fitness Zone. Stopping the test performance in this manner can reduce required testing time. It may also reduce the possibility of embarrassment and avoid creating a threatening environment, caused by assessments for students who are less capable. If this approach is used, parents should be informed about the process, so they understand that the performance reported on *FITNESSGRAM* does not necessarily represent a maximal effort. Also, if performance during class time does not allow a maximal effort, it is good to provide those more highly motivated students the opportunity to do a maximal test at some other time. An after-school fitness challenge may prove to be very popular with students who are high-level performers.

FITNESSGRAM acknowledges performances above the HFZ but does not recommend this level of performance as an appropriate goal level for all students [note, too, that scoring above the HFZ in body composition is undesirable at all times]. However, students who desire to achieve a high level of athletic performance may need to consider setting goals beyond the HFZ [e.g., a gymnast who needs exceptional flexibility for a variety of reasons, or a basketball player who can use additional flexibility to improve shooting accuracy]. Students, especially younger students, may need assistance in setting realistic goals.

These scores allow students to achieve a level of fitness associated with good health. More students can be successful and score in the HFZ than in norm-referenced tests. This method of scoring takes the competition out of fitness testing and puts the focus back on achieving health-related fitness, rather than on outdoing peers. This means that far more students can experience feelings of success through the testing experience.

Adapted, by permission, from The Cooper Institute for Aerobic Research, in press, *FITNESSGRAM Test Administrator's Manual, 2nd Ed.* (Champaign, IL: Human Kinetics).

these administrative tasks, you can train older students and parents to assist you, as long as you ensure the privacy of tested students.

Test Protocols

As mentioned, prepare the test setting in advance, so you're ready to supervise, troubleshoot, and discuss results with students, during the actual testing. Adequate preparation also makes it easier to record results efficiently. (See Preparing for Testing earlier in this chapter.) Beyond preparing thoroughly, the following suggestions help make fitness

testing a positive experience for both teacher and students:

- Explain the testing procedures and purposes to students over several preceding lessons. Have them practice, practice, practice. Review this information on test days.

- Always announce test days in advance. "Pop-quiz" fitness testing can lead to negative attitudes toward both fitness testing and physical activity.

- Conduct the test under good environmental conditions. Postpone fitness testing if the testing environment is too hot or too

Teaching Tip: Spreading Out Fitness Testing

Instead of administering an entire fitness test battery all at once, you can incorporate fitness testing with other units and activities throughout the school year. Specifically, you can test various health-related fitness components at various times, as the assessments match the concepts the students are studying. Students will be more motivated to self-test, as they see the connections between concepts, class activities, and testing. This saves time and "kills several birds with one stone," because you are teaching concepts, relating assessment to each concept, and having students practice self-assessment all at once. This can be more beneficial than conducting a formal testing time.

Laura Borsdorf
Professor, Exercise and Sport Science Department
Ursinus College, Collegeville, Pennsylvania

cold. Encourage students to dress appropriately. Provide water before, during, and after strenuous items, such as the PACER or one-mile run.

• Set the tone for student-friendly testing by always focusing on personal improvement and by carefully guarding student privacy. Do not allow fitness testing to become a competitive sport. Never compare one student's performance to another's. Refrain from judging student effort. For example, telling a student, "You're not even trying," discourages rather than motivates.

• Teach, through testing, by teaching the concepts behind each test and discussing results with students.

• Train and use parent, community, and student volunteers to make test day proceed more smoothly. Be sure to brief them as to your testing philosophy.

Tailoring Health-Related Fitness Testing

FITNESSGRAM is designed to meet the needs of students within a wide range of abilities. As

Health Fitness Standard Establishment

Research findings were used as the basis for establishing the *FITNESSGRAM* health fitness standards. Blair et al. (1989) reported that a significant decrease in risk of all-cause mortality results from getting out of the lower 20 percent of the population in regard to aerobic fitness level. They also reported that risk level continues to decrease as fitness levels increase, but not as dramatically as simply getting out of the bottom 20 percent. Aerobic capacity standards for the HFZ have been established so that the lower end of the Healthy Fitness Zone corresponds closely to a fitness level equal to getting out of the lower 20 percent of the population. The upper end of the Healthy Fitness Zone corresponds to a fitness level that would include up to 80 percent of the population.

Percentage fat is calculated from equations reported by Slaughter et al. (1988). Detailed information on the development of these equations and other issues related to the measurement and interpretation of body composition information is available in *Advances in Body Composition Assessment* (Lohman 1992). Williams et al. (1992) reported that children with body fat levels above 25 percent for boys and 30 to 35 percent for girls are more likely to exhibit elevated cholesterol levels and hypertension. The beginning of the HFZ corresponds to these levels of body fatness.

Little or no data exist to indicate levels of musculoskeletal fitness associated with good health. Standards in this area of fitness were established to correspond in level as closely as possible to those in aerobic capacity and body composition.

Reprinted, by permission, from The Cooper Institute for Aerobic Research, in press, FITNESSGRAM *Test Administrator's Manual 2nd Ed.* (Champaign, IL: Human Kinetics).

Tips for Conducting Skinfold Testing

Many teachers feel uncomfortable measuring percent body fat for a variety of reasons, including the following:

- A student may feel embarrassed by his or her test results.
- A teacher may be reluctant to touch students in any manner.
- The test is less tangible than the other test items are, so setting and reaching goals may seem more difficult to students.
- It takes training and practice to measure accurately.

You can take several steps to address these concerns. First, get the training and practice you need to take accurate measurements. AAHPERD provides workshops and in-services on Physical Best, including *FITNESSGRAM* testing techniques (contact AAHPERD for details). You may also elect to invite a qualified fitness instructor, university physical education instructor, school nurse, or certified athletic trainer to conduct this testing for you.

Second, protect students' feelings by insisting students be considerate of others' feelings and by providing a separate room or screens for private testing. Consider teaching students to

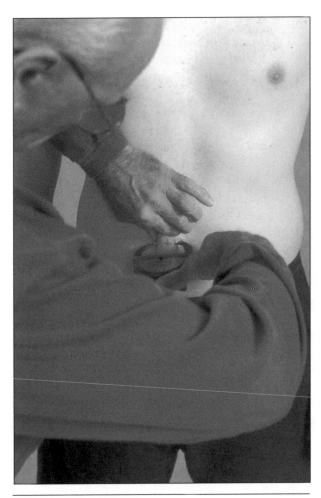

Protect students' feelings by conducting skinfold tests in a separate room.

use inexpensive calipers to measure their friends' skinfolds—as long as a student does not feel this will invade his or her privacy. This way, students will be too busy measuring to make fun of each other (Pangrazi and Corbin 1994). But be sensitive: If you have overweight children in a class, you may not want to have students measure each other and, thus possibly, expose the overweight children to ridicule. On the other hand, it's also important to teach your class that people come in all different sizes, and that all people should feel welcome and comfortable in physical activity settings. Regardless of positive habits, people are made differently.

Third, focus on making students aware of the personal choices we all make that affect our body composition. This helps students set goals based on the *process* of a physically active and healthful lifestyle, rather than the *product*. In addition, teach students that both too much and too little body fat can be harmful. If age appropriate, discuss eating disorders (see also chapters 9 and 10). Finally, if you are especially concerned that you may be accused of touching a student improperly, arrange to have a knowledgeable second adult attend the testing, have friends measure each other, or opt for calculating body mass index instead (see chapter 9).

a general rule, teach and use alternative test items, if they fit your program and students' needs better. For example, in using the one-mile run, if your students represent a wide range of aerobic endurance, you will have many low-fit students running long after the fit students are done, which could result in the lower fit kids feeling very self-conscious. In such a case, you might choose the PACER test, instead, in which higher fit students finish last. Thus, the lower fit students are far less likely to be "exposed." You can also stagger the start in the one-mile run, so it is more difficult for others to discern who is running slower. Or have students of similar ability run in small groups together.

Elementary or Inexperienced Students

These students need to practice individual test items more and need more supervision, during both formal and informal testing. Pair younger or inexperienced students with older or more experienced students or adult volunteers for both the test item practice sessions and actual test days. Be sure to thoroughly train your helpers, however. Consider introducing, teaching, practicing, and then testing each test item in a given time period, perhaps integrating it into a three-week skills unit, before introducing another test item during the next skills unit. For example, focus on flexibility (e.g., back-saver sit-and-reach test item), while teaching an educational gymnastics unit. This approach helps younger and inexperienced students get used to one test item at a time, while teaching them the health-related fitness component in the context of a real-life activity. A test circuit may consist of alternating warm-up and test stations, all related to a single health-related fitness component and its corresponding test item.

Middle and High School Students

Be sure to offer older students increasing independence within the context of adequate supervision. Overdirecting students sends the unwelcome and counterproductive message that you consider the students to be incapable of functioning fully in the test situation. Carefully gauge the maturity and understanding levels of each student and strive to provide the right level of independence and self-direction. Viewing yourself as more of a fitness consultant than teacher can help you assume a more low-key role in the testing environment. You can also train older students to help younger or less-experienced students learn to be more self-directed. This may motivate the tutor to learn the material to be taught more thoroughly, in order to do a good job teaching another student.

Reluctant or Overanxious Students

These students may have had poor fitness testing experiences in the past. Create the most positive fitness testing environment you can to help these students and to prevent such problems from developing in other students. As described earlier, one of the best actions you can take is to have students practice the test items frequently, over an extended period of time, before conducting more formal testing. You can also offer a choice of test items that test the same component, such as aerobic endurance—the PACER, the one-mile run, and the walk test (for secondary students). Work hard to ensure student privacy regarding test scores, and students will learn to trust you. Treat student feelings in a sensitive manner to reassure them that personal achievement is the focus of your program. Finally, allow extremely anxious students to exempt themselves from formal testing, no matter their reasons. They will still gain much from self-test practice, but nothing from being forced to perform in more formal tests. In fact, forcing the issue can reinforce negative feelings toward physical activity—the opposite of the ultimate goal.

Students With Special Challenges

In general, where appropriate and possible, you should use the same definitions, components, test items, and standards of health-related fitness for individuals with disabilities as you do for those without disabilities (Winnick 1995). You can, however, modify *FITNESSGRAM* to meet the needs of many students with disabilities. You may need, for example, to provide assistance to varying degrees to help the student with a disability perform a test. Or, if the tests do not measure the abilities an individual needs to lead an active and independent life, you may need to apply alternative tests. For example, a person who does not have use of the legs may benefit more from testing and developing flexibility in the upper body, rather than of the back and hamstring muscles (Winnick 1995).

As you design an individualized fitness program for a person with disabilities, keep in mind that a major reason for fitness testing should be to measure an individual's ability to function in everyday activities. Thus, it's important to look at each individual, assess needs and limitations, and design alterna-tives to bypass limitations. An individual's interests should be taken into account as well. For example, if an individual in a wheelchair would like to be able to play wheelchair basketball more proficiently and with greater stamina, the fitness program should work to enhance the person's abilities in this area. Fitness testing should then discern whether or not the individual is making progress in areas relevant to enjoying this interest. Whenever possible, the individual should be part of this design process: "A personalized program should be planned *with*, rather than *for*, individuals with disabilities" (Winnick 1995).

Using Results Appropriately

We can attribute much of the "bad press" related to fitness testing, both in the past and the present, to improper use of test results.

As you design an individualized fitness program for a person with disabilities, keep in mind that a major reason for fitness testing should be to measure an individual's ability to function in everyday activities. An individual's interests should be taken into account as well; if a student in a wheelchair would like to improve his or her ability to play wheelchair basketball, then the fitness program should work to enhance the student's abilities in that area.

Health-Related Fitness Tests for Persons With Disabilities

FITNESSGRAM tests can be modified for students with disabilities (see *Physical Best and Individuals with Disabilities: A Handbook for Inclusion in Fitness Programs*). As a complement to the *FITNESSGRAM*, the Brockport Physical Fitness Test also tests the health-related fitness of individuals with disabilities (Winnick and Short 1999). The Brockport tests are specifically designed to accurately assess the physical fitness of individuals with a wide range of physical and mental disabilities.

All the following Brockport Physical Fitness Test resources are available separately or as part of a kit through the American Fitness Alliance (see appendix C for contact information):

- *The Brockport Physical Fitness Test Manual*
- *The Brockport Physical Fitness Training Guide*
- *The Brockport Physical Fitness Test Administration Video*
- *The Fitness Challenge Software*

Sharing Results With Students and Parents

From the first lesson in which you introduce a test item through formally testing that item, you should discuss and explain the reasons for the tests and the meanings behind the results. With students, you can do this as part of your set induction at the beginning of a lesson. Contact parents with a letter that explains your testing philosophy and approach and how you plan to use the results. It is especially important to reassure both students and parents that you will do your utmost to guard student privacy. Share the actual forms you will use to record and interpret the test results, so all involved can clearly see what you plan to focus on (see relevant forms provided in the FITNESSGRAM *Test Administration Manual* [Second Edition] and software). These actions set the stage for clear and productive communication when test results become available.

When sharing test results, use blank *FITNESSGRAM* forms to review the purpose of the test items and the meaning of the test results. Distribute individual report forms in a private manner, such as in a sealed envelope or during a student-teacher or parent-teacher conference. You may find it helpful to set up a station on a physical activity circuit at which you privately discuss test results, while the rest of the student's group participates in an activity.

To be the most effective, share information and offer guidance as to how each student can improve performance, along with test results and interpretations. Help the student set realistic goals and subgoals at this time, as well.

Planning

Testing just to test is a waste of both teacher and student time. To be part of authentic assessment, fitness testing must provide feedback to shape your health-related physical fitness education program into the best it can be. So use test results to help both you and your students plan for future learning and fitness gains. For example, if you find that students are making little or no progress in muscular strength and endurance, design and use more activities that enhance these areas. Involve older students in this problem-

Learning Self-Responsibility

The addition of a student interactive component is a new feature of *FITNESSGRAM*, Revision 6.0. Students can now enter their own scores into the student version of the software. The interactive software allows students to learn more about fitness and the importance of physical activity. By entering their own scores, students will also learn that fitness is personal and that they can take responsibility for their own fitness and physical activity.

ACTIVITYGRAM

A new feature of *FITNESSGRAM*, Revision 6.0, is the inclusion of physical activity assessments. These assessments were added because of the need to reinforce to students the importance of developing lifetime habits of regular physical activity. While fitness is important, it cannot be maintained, unless students remain physically active as adults.

The *ACTIVITYGRAM* assessment is a recall of the student's previous day's physical activity, based on a validated physical activity instrument known as the Previous Day Physical Activity Recall (PDPAR) (Weston et al. 1997). In the assessment, the student reports his or her activity levels for each 30-minute block of time during the day. The format is designed to accommodate both school and nonschool days.

The assessment, provided through the available software, provides detailed information about the student's activity habits and prescriptive feedback about how active he or she should be. It is very similar to the *FITNESSGRAM* assessment.

Because of the cognitive demands of recalling physical activity, it may be difficult for young children to get accurate results. Thus, it is recommended that the *ACTIVITYGRAM* program be used with students in fifth grade and higher.

Why Reward Effort Instead of Results?

The goal of a quality physical education program is to develop a lifelong pattern of physical activity among our total population. This focus is different from other subjects, such as math or driver education, where there is a need to be able to do primary tasks prior to moving forward. The difference is the desired outcome. Presumably, once you learn to add, subtract, multiply, and divide or learn to drive a car, you'll be able to do it correctly for the rest of your life. However, when it comes to health-related fitness, scores today do not necessarily indicate long-term results. The fifth grader born with the "right" genes might score well on the one-mile run without much effort, whereas a classmate might make a great effort, but still record a poor time. However, in the long run, if the student with the good time becomes a "couch potato," and the student with the poor time continues to put forth outstanding, or even moderate, effort, it is likely that the latter student will live a healthier life.

Ultimately, we want a nation of physically active, healthy citizens, not a nation of ex-athletes, who follow a couple of years of excellent fitness levels with 50 years of TV-watching that results in declining health, high medical bills, and poor productivity. Reward effort and participation because that is what will, in the long run, result in lifelong health and fitness.

It is fine to encourage results, as well as participation, but this needs to be individualized. The *FITNESSGRAM* criteria helps us obtain appropriate results for a broad range of individuals, set individual goals for improvement, and provide encouragement for reaching higher levels. For example, did the student with the best one-mile run time in class really put forth the best effort he or she could? You might challenge that student to do even better; maybe he or she will end up running cross-country and really enjoy it. Encourage excellence! However, don't let that discourage students who don't have the genetic potential to be star athletes, but who will benefit just as much from physical activity. Remember, challenge each student individually to be his or her individual Physical Best and reward that effort.

solving process. Encourage students to set specific related process-oriented goals, such as "I will do push-ups fours times a week, and each week, I will try to increase the number of push-ups I do, until I reach my healthy fitness zone. I will then continue to do push-ups four times a week to maintain upper-body strength in the healthy fitness zone. If I'm able, I will attempt to continue to increase the number I can do." This helps students learn to tailor their personal fitness programs to their own specific needs. By following up on results, you continue the planning-teaching-assessing-planning cycle discussed in chapter 16.

Features of the *FITNESSGRAM* Report

FITNESSGRAM has numerous special features that will help make communicating effectively with students and parents easier (see also figure 17.1):

1. Generates highly personalized output.
2. Indicates current and past test performance.
3. Makes individualized recommendations based on assessment results.
4. Includes recommendations and feedback.
5. Evaluates performance based on criterion-referenced health standards. Classifies scores in the Needs Improvement area, the Healthy Fitness Zone, or above the Healthy Fitness Zone.
6. Includes a bar graph of current and past assessment results.
7. Provides an estimated $\dot{V}O_2$max adjusted according to kilograms of body weight per minute, which will allow comparison between performances on alternative test items.
8. Reports changes in height and weight.

From the FITNESSGRAM *Test Administrator's Manual* (Second Edition).

Grading

Despite the difficulty of assigning grades, it is a reality that most teachers have to deal with. However, we cannot emphasize enough that fitness test results should *not* be used as a basis for grades. Grades should be based on age-appropriate abilities to self-test, interpret test results, gain knowledge of fitness information, and plan personal programs (Pangrazi and Corbin 1994). Such emphases help students become adults who are physically active for life in self-designed, enjoyable fitness programs. In contrast, grades based solely on test results are likely to discourage students from continuing to be physically active after they leave your program. Finally, if you choose to give credit for showing improvement in fitness test scores, remember that improvements will come in smaller increments for students who have already achieved a high level of fitness than for those who have not, and your grading system should not penalize high-fit students for this reason. See also chapter 16.

Summary

Misuse of results, inappropriate test selection, and insensitive testing protocols have given fitness testing a controversial past. Appropriately applied, however, *FITNESSGRAM* is an excellent health-related fitness test battery, which provides an up-to-date and sensitive health-related fitness testing program that is easy to implement. Use the information in this chapter to plan, conduct, and follow up on fitness testing that teaches students what they need to know to participate for life in effective, personally designed fitness programs. *FITNESSGRAM* also offers software to help make record-keeping easier. The new student version of the software allows you to put increasing responsibility on each student to keep his or her own records to move each student toward self-responsibility for personal health-related fitness. Then, interpret and apply test results to your planning process to help you create the highest quality physical education program possible.

Chapter 18

Assessing Health-Related Fitness Knowledge

Helping your students understand health-related fitness knowledge is a crucial component of a quality physical fitness education program for many reasons:

• Knowledge of physical fitness and personal exercise behavior are related. Sallis et al. (1986) report that subjects' adoption and maintenance of physical activity was directly related to their health and exercise knowledge.

• Understanding the science behind health-related physical fitness exercises prepares students to sort fact from fiction, when reading advertisements for quick weight-loss plans or new "miracle" exercise equipment.

• Knowing how to exercise, such as appropriate stretching, correct strength-training techniques, and proper hydration, when running in heat, prepares students to safely benefit from physical activity.

• Knowledgeable students are better prepared to make informed decisions in starting and maintaining physical activity programs.

In order to find out what your students have learned about fitness and what they still need to learn, you need to periodically test their knowledge. You can assess students' fitness knowledge through a variety of assessment tools, from traditional written tests to interviews to projects. Even asking for student opinions can reveal knowledge level. Managing knowledge testing, however, can be cumbersome, so in this chapter, we share several practical assessment tools and tips you can use, without taking much time away from physical activities.

Strategies for Assessing Fitness Knowledge

Graham (1992) warns that cognitive assessment needs to be manageable and to reflect what you have taught. Keep these parameters in mind, as you review the following assessment tools applied to the cognitive domain.

Discussions

As when assessing in other areas, simply asking pointed questions can give you a quick reading on whether or not students are learning the fitness concepts you're targeting. Younger students also enjoy responding physically to a discussion question by simply showing you the answer with their bodies. For example, in response to the request "Name one physical activity that can build aerobic endurance," students could mimic the action of their favorites (e.g., run in place, demonstrate a swimming stroke with their arms, and so on). High school students often like to debate issues. For example, ask students to debate the merits of a new piece of exercise equipment advertised on an infomercial, or the latest celebrity diet advertised in a tabloid. Urge students to back up their opinions with what they've learned about how their bodies work.

Polls

As mentioned in chapter 16, polls can give you some of the same information as dis-

cussions, but in a quicker format. The following are examples applied to fitness knowledge assessment. Take a poker chip survey or vote (see chapter 16) to have students tell on the way out of class whether or not they think you have performed a fitness skill correctly:

- Teacher demonstrates how to take the pulse at the neck. Did she place her fingers in the correct area?
- Teacher performs a stretch. Did he do so safely?
- Teacher lifts a weight. Did she follow the correct procedure?
- Teacher mimes or calls out a physical activity. Would performing this activity intensely and long enough enhance aerobic endurance?

Tailor your polls and methods to each group's age and cognitive ability range.

Role Plays

As mini-simulations, role-play situations can reveal student knowledge, while reinforcing the importance of that knowledge. For example, students might

- explain to a friend how to increase aerobic endurance,
- convince a friend to give up smoking,
- teach a younger student how to count heart rate,
- explain to a new student what *intensity* means in regard to flexibility, or
- pretend to be on an infomercial, but, instead of trying to sell customers on a fad diet, try to convince the audience (the rest of the class) on the merits of a physically active lifestyle and balanced nutrition, as the most effective method of weight control.

Written Tests

As mentioned in chapter 16, written tests still have their place as a valid assessment tool. Simply be sure you do not overemphasize or

FitSmart

FitSmart was developed to provide a standardized physical fitness knowledge test appropriate for high school students. Developed by Weimo Zhu, Margaret J. Safrit, and Allan Cohen, FitSmart has carefully established test qualities (reliability and validity) and is designed to help teachers determine their students' learning of physical fitness concepts. FitSmart assesses the following content:

- Concept of health-related fitness—definition, relationship with physical activity and health
- Scientific principles of exercise—physiological and psychological
- Components of health-related fitness—aerobic endurance (cardiorespiratory function), muscular strength and endurance, flexibility, and body composition
- Effects of exercise on chronic disease risk factors
- Exercise prescription—frequency, intensity, time (duration), type (mode), self-evaluation, and exercise adherence
- Other factors—exercise and nutrition, warm-up and cool-down, injury and illness, consumer issues, and equipment

FitSmart was developed to provide a standardized physical fitness knowledge test appropriate for high school students.

The test needs to be scored using a computer software program to convert raw scores to standard scores, and to provide feedback to students about their test results. FitSmart is available now for high school students, and, at a later date, a similar test will be released for middle school and, possibly, for upper elementary students.

overvalue them. Design written tests of knowledge to pinpoint what you've taught, so you can collect assessment data on what each individual knows and doesn't know. Carefully choose the format (objective—e.g., multiple choice, true-false; subjective—e.g., short answer, essay) that best fits the content you're teaching and the ages and abilities of the students you're testing. Refer also to the time management tips in chapter 16.

Journal and Log Entries

Physical educators generally use logs to have students keep track of physical activity data

and record their physiological and psychological reactions to physical activity. But you can also have students record their personal responses to discussion questions in their journals, allowing you to monitor individual understanding. These questions should be related to the other data, and affective responses recorded in the journal. For example, a high school class that has logged physical activity data and made notes about how they're feeling about physical activity, might also explain the biochemical reasons why participating in physical activity can enhance a person's sense of well-being (if you have taught them this).

Reports

Most upper elementary through high school students are capable of learning to research a topic. This skill and practice can enhance a student's learning across the entire school curriculum. The ability to research is a life skill that meets most schools' overall mission to prepare students to learn how to learn. Certainly, research has its place in health-related physical fitness education. Through research, students take what they already know about health-related fitness and teach themselves more. Then you assess the quality and value of each student's research in relation to how it might help him or her pursue an active lifestyle.

Mohnsen (1997) asserts "Research is a viable option related to every standard that has a cognitive component. As a physical educator, however, you must be sure that students possess the necessary skills to conduct the research." Work with teachers in other subject areas (e.g., language arts, math, science) to develop research skills and to coordinate students' writing health-related fitness reports, using the Internet, library books, and CD-ROMs as research tools. Consider having students work in partners or small groups to collect data, but to individually report on it. Try topics such as the following:

- Pick an athlete, movie star, singer, or some other celebrity and research what that person does (or doesn't do) to stay physically active and fit. Pretend you are this person's personal trainer, and write an analysis of this person's personal fitness plan, based on what you've learned about health-related fitness. What does this person do well and what does this person do less well regarding fitness? Then make suggestions as to what this person could do to improve his or her plan. If you believe his or her plan is already excellent, show why you think this. Either way, be sure to address each component of health-related fitness.

- Pick a specific health condition (e.g., cancer, diabetes, asthma, heart disease), and

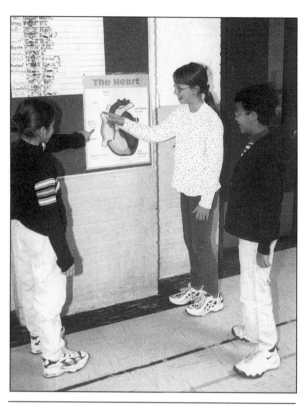

Having students give oral reports is appropriate, but you may want to limit the reports to a few each day to avoid interfering with physical activity time.

research what benefits physical activity can have in helping a person with this condition improve his or her health.

- Find diet ideas and products advertised and analyze them for safety, effectiveness, and value to health.

Another option for elementary or less-experienced students is to provide "raw" research information in lecture settings and have students briefly summarize it orally or in writing (see chapter 14).

While having students create reports is appropriate at times, beware of spending too much physical education time on having students research, write, or share them. As mentioned, work with teachers in other appropriate disciplines to save physical education class time. Use such assignments as homework. Post reports in the gymnasium or display at health fairs, parent events, or in the library. If you wish to have students report orally, only have a few do so each day, until all have had a turn.

Assessing Written and Oral Reports

Using a rubric makes assessing written and oral reports and projects both simpler and more uniform. It also provides information about expectations, thus enhancing the student's potential for success. Here's an example:

Research topic: Research the health benefits of lifetime physical activity, and write a three- to five-page typed, double-spaced report summarizing your findings. Rubric:

Excellent = You have found at least five health benefits of physical activity, which you have referenced appropriately. You have provided an introductory paragraph, at least one well-organized paragraph explaining each health benefit in detail, and a summary paragraph. Your paper is at least three, but no more than five, typed, double-spaced pages. You have no spelling errors. You have no grammatical errors.

Outstanding = You have found at least four health benefits of physical activity, which you have referenced appropriately. You have provided an introductory paragraph, at least one paragraph explaining each health benefit in detail, and a summary paragraph. Your paper is at least three, but no more than five, typed, double-spaced pages. You have two or fewer spelling errors. You have two or fewer grammatical errors.

Acceptable = You have found at least three health benefits of physical activity, which you have referenced appropriately. You have provided an introductory paragraph that introduces your paper, at least one paragraph explaining each health benefit in detail, and a summary paragraph. Your paper is at least three, but no more than five, typed, double-spaced pages. You have four or fewer spelling errors. You have three or fewer grammatical errors.

Needs work = You have found at least two health benefits of physical activity, which you have referenced appropriately. You have provided an introductory paragraph that introduces your paper, an explanation of each health benefit in detail, and a summary paragraph. Your paper is at least three, but no more than five, typed, double-spaced pages. You have six or fewer spelling errors. You have four or fewer grammatical errors.

Projects

Projects allow students to use avenues of communication, other than the written word, to create products from their research and what you've taught them. The following is a list of sample group or individual project ideas you might use or adapt to assess fitness knowledge:

- Design a strength-training circuit.
- Create an audiotape explaining how body composition stems from the other components of health-related fitness.
- Make a "newscast" video (or untaped skit) to dispel the latest health-related fitness myths.
- Act out a "commercial" to sell physical activity to a "couch potato."
- Have students write questions and answers that the class could use in a TV game show format on a rainy day or other designated time.

If students work in small groups, design a method for assessing individual learning to use in tandem with the group activity, such as a short written test or journal entry as a follow-up assignment.

Using Results Appropriately

Remember, Physical Best recommends that you use a balance of assessment tools to assess in the cognitive domain. Avoid overemphasizing written tests and undervaluing role playing and projects. A well-designed portfolio gives students the chance to "show their knowledge stuff" through many different avenues. Then share results with students, parents, and administrators, as well as tailor your plans accordingly.

Sharing Results With Students and Parents

Share cognitive assessment feedback with students and parents, within the context of your entire assessment program. In other words, reinforce that you are using a balance of assessment tools across all domains to assess each student, by presenting knowledge assessment alongside affective and physical assessments. This will help both students and parents see how knowledge enhances development in other areas and vice versa.

Work to use cognitive assessment as a teaching tool—not just a check for current understanding. You can do this by discussing each item on a returned written test, having students share their research or projects with classmates (perhaps at one station in a circuit), asking students how they think you can help them learn more, and helping students design cognitive self-assessments and learning activities that they feel will be helpful to them and their peers. You might also borrow a TV game show format, such as *Jeopardy*, to liven up review sessions.

Planning

The temptation to overdo lecture lessons, in response to poor cognitive assessment results, may be great, but resist this urge. Certainly, lecture settings have their place in the health-related physical fitness education program; however, keep students as physically active as possible. In short, help them learn while they *do*. For example, if students are having trouble learning how to pace themselves while running the mile, design an active game that teaches this concept—or have groups of students do so.

Daniel Midura and Donald Glover (1999) suggest teaching pacing by setting up a 50-meter track and demonstrating the pace to make one lap in exactly 15 seconds (figure 18.1). Have students practice in groups, build-

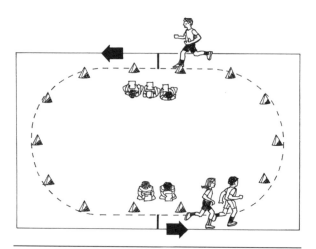

Figure 18.1 Help students learn by doing—for example, teach pacing by using an active game.

Adapted, by permission, from D. Midura, 1999, *The Cooperation-Competition Link*. (Champaign, IL: Human Kinetics), 89.

ing from one lap to four laps. This can be extended to different levels of fitness by changing the lap time, which should range from 12 to 18 seconds to be a realistic preparation for health-related fitness testing.

Grading

Avoid giving too much weight to cognitive assessment in final grades, particularly results of written tests. However, recognize the need for students to learn a body of knowledge to enhance physical development. But, by including it in the grade, today's health-related physical fitness education program values knowledge as an important aspect of reaching our ultimate goal of graduating adults who value and can independently pursue physical activity. Thus, assessment of knowledge of fitness skills and concepts needs to be part of a student's physical education grade. As always, avoid misunderstandings by fully informing parents and students as to what weight you will give to this area, and what types of assessments you will use. Remember, strive for balance and clear communication.

Summary

Fitness knowledge is a vital component in a well-designed physical education program, making it well worth the time it takes to assess. The following lists ways to make the process more meaningful and efficient:

- Use less-formal (less paperwork) methods, such as role playing and discussions to screen for basic understanding

- Use more formal methods, such as written tests, only occasionally.

- Make sure you assess what you have taught, not what you planned to teach and didn't quite cover.

- Use a variety of assessment tools.

- Use knowledge assessment results as only part of a grade, and communicate your exact intentions to parents and students.

- Alter your plans once you know what your students know.

- Assess your students' ability to *apply* their knowledge.

Chapter 19

Assessing Participation in Health-Related Physical Activity

When students leave a quality physical fitness education program, they should be prepared to apply their health-related fitness knowledge and skills. In this chapter, we focus primarily on how to answer the question, Can each student actually *apply* the knowledge in meaningful ways? This is an essential process in producing students who are capable of engaging safely and profitably in physical activity, after they leave your program. Indeed, students who have mastered fitness skills have moved closer to independence on Corbin and Lindsey's Stairway to Lifetime Fitness (figure 3.1). We also discuss strategies to assess physical activity effort and frequency and explore effective ways to use the assessment information you collect (figure 19.1).

Strategies for Assessing Fitness Skills

As discussed in chapters 11, 13, and 14, students need to develop many skills to become self-sufficient in health-related fitness activities. Of course, exactly what you target for assessment directly depends on your curriculum (i.e., what you've taught) and on what is age appropriate. For example, it is appropriate

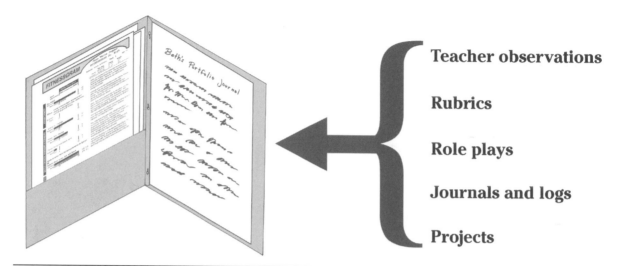

Figure 19.1   Use a portfolio system to organize the assessment information you collect.

to expect kindergartners to be able to place a hand over the heart to "check" heart rate and to understand that a faster heartbeat means the heart is working harder, but not to count the pulse or calculate target heart rate zone.

Teacher Observations

A quick, informal way to see if students know how to apply fitness information is simply to observe them performing fitness skills as you circulate around the activity area. To take a closer look, post yourself at a station on a circuit and target a specific skill to check for. Videotaping a skill, such as a student's running stride, can better allow both you and students to determine if a student uses pacing correctly. Determine the critical elements you want to see prior to an observation to help you focus during the observation. A short checklist or rubric works well.

Rubrics

Add a rubric to an observation, and it becomes more formal. Students can also use rubrics to assess themselves, and peers, teaching them to analyze themselves so they can continue to do so after your program. Keep in mind, too, that rubrics provide structure and focus, helping keep students on task. Figure 19.2 shows a rubric to assess pacing while running.

Role Plays

As extensions of class discussions, role playing is an effective way to assess whether or not students can apply fitness knowledge. Set up role-play situations that call for students to demonstrate fitness knowledge in a real-life context. The following are examples of role-play challenges that help a teacher determine fitness skill competence.

- Practice how you would teach a younger student how to run correctly as pace changes. Be sure to demonstrate that you know the components of a good running stride to look for.
- Demonstrate two ways to take your pulse.
- Teach your small group three safe stretches, and explain what makes them safe.
- Pretend your partner has sprained his ankle. Demonstrate how you might help him treat his injury safely following the RICES guidelines (rest, ice, compression, elevation, support).
- Have one student take the role of a famous local athlete. Have other students interview this person to find out what he or she has done to improve his or her athletic achievement (adapted from NASPE 1995).

Be sure to provide any necessary equipment for students to practice using, such as a clock with a second hand for counting heart rate or

Jogging Criteria

Doer 1 _____ Date _____
Doer 2 _____ Class _____

Level III

Observer: Give the doer some pointers about their jogging form. Use the tips below to help you. Try to be friendly.

Doer: Jog at a moderate pace. When the teacher signals, slow down—then change roles.

	DOER 1		DOER 2	
	Yes	No	Yes	No
1. Runs tall, leans slightly forward.				
2. Swings legs from hip, knees bent.				
3. Lands on heels with weight rolling along the outside portion of foot to toes.				
4. Points toes straight ahead, lands heel directly under knee.				
5. Swings arms straight forward and backward, hands relaxed.				
6. Breathes from stomach in an even rhythm.				

Figure 19.2 A rubric for assessing running stride.

Reprinted, by permission, from *Fitness Education for Children.* (Champaign, IL: Human Kinetics), 32.

an "ice pack" (e.g., beanbag) for a sprained ankle.

Role playing simulates real-life situations, giving students valuable practice even as you also assess their competence. Remember, assessment that teaches is a more efficient and effective way to use precious class time (see also chapter 16).

Journals and Logs

Students can learn to log frequency, intensity, time, and type information in their journals. As discussed in chapter 16, being able to review this information over time is highly motivating. Activity charts and graphs help students see evidence of how far they've progressed. This process can help students stay motivated as adults, as well. In addition, the practical experience helps create greater awareness of health-related training principles' real-life applications.

Teach students how to set up well-organized logs, such as the one shown in chapter 14 (figure 14.2). When assessing, look for good organization, ongoing and up-to-date data, and thoughtful personal notes—both negative and positive. Older students may enjoy logging FITT information on a computer disk. You may also opt to duplicate a form for students to fill out, instead of using a computer or notebook-type journal.

Projects

Well-designed group and individual projects provide the time and space for students to thoroughly demonstrate how to apply fitness knowledge. The following are some examples of effective project assignments:

- Design and make a poster that outlines an interesting aerobic endurance workout.
- Keep a log of the physical activity done outside of physical education class.
- Design a calendar for the month. Consider the FITT principle as you fill in each day's strategies (e.g., doing strength exercises on alternate days), and address each component of health-related fitness.
- Make a resource file (using 3 × 5 cards) of physical activities to do with family, by yourself, at school, in the neighborhood, and with a friend. Then demonstrate that you have used the file over a three-week period by recording your activities in your journal.

Physical Best Activity Guide—Elementary Level and *Physical Best Activity Guide—Secondary Level* offer many additional project ideas.

Strategies for Assessing Physical Activity Effort

These strategies are especially helpful in assessing each student's effort level. Interviews, perhaps at one station on a circuit, can also reveal valuable information.

A Middle School Assessment Example

Effective assessment requires an assessment plan. Here's one example of how to plan assessments for middle school students (see also appendix G):

1. *Establish Desired Course Outcome:* A physically educated person assesses, achieves, and maintains physical fitness.

2. *Define Domain Analysis* (what will be assessed):
   - Creation of and participation in a personal plan of activities and exercises to achieve and maintain a level of physical fitness determined by the needs and goals of the student
   - Application of principles of training and conditioning (progression, overload, frequency, intensity, duration (time), and type (specificity)
   - Management of personal life style and responsibilities for inclusion of participation in regular physical activity

3. *Select Dimension Components* (which dimensions are most important): This assessment is intended to determine mastery of both the processes (principles of training and management of adult life roles) and the product (participation and goals). Assess and score each student on an individual basis with the results used for the purpose of prescribing further sequential instruction, including remediation and enrichment. Focus on achieving cumulative skills and knowledge, resulting from multiple units of study on fitness education, goal setting, and motivation. Achievement will occur through participation in and out of the gymnasium. All students in the system will be assessed as a requirement for promotion to the high school level work.

4. *Identify Implementation Characteristics* (what other issues need to be considered): The student will design a personal fitness profile to be used to plan a realistic personal program of regular physical activity. The profile will use the results of previous health-related fitness tests, recognized standards for fitness levels for good health, and personally set goals. Allow instructional time to master the skills of fitness testing, review the requirements of the assessment, and assist students in researching information needed for both the profile and the plan. In addition, conference time outside of class may be needed to provide feedback relative to accuracy and completeness in designing, implementing, and reporting progress toward achievement of the assessment. The focus of this assessment on life skills for adult roles requires that students be responsible for solving the same problems for engaging in regular physical activity that adults do. Therefore, the teacher becomes an advisor who guides the search for information.

5. *Establish Specifications* (what the student will do): Each student will complete a Personal Fitness Profile (test results, current status of health fitness levels, and personally established realistic goals), a Personal Fitness Plan, implement the Personal Fitness Plan (including appropriate warm-up, workout, and cool-down activities and principles of training and conditioning), and report on the results of participation in the plan. Sample forms are in appendix B. Achievement will be determined based on the following criteria:
   - Accurately assess and interpret personal fitness status
   - Set appropriate and realistic goals to improve or maintain fitness status
   - Apply principles of training and conditioning in designing personal plan
   - Document accurately and neatly, implementation of the designed plan
   - Achieve personal fitness goal
   - Reflect on enjoyment, benefits, and/or risks of participation in physical activity

6. *Administration:* This assessment, including scoring, should be presented to the students at the beginning of the school year. You may spend several class periods reviewing the skills required for assessing fitness status, interpreting personal data, and determining research needs and procedures. Time lines for the completion of each component should be established to ensure completion by deadline dates. Students may work in pairs when fitness status, goals, interests and accessibility for implementing personal plans are similar.

Adapted, by permission, from PSAHPERD, 1994, *Designing Assessments: Applications for Physical Education.*

Journals and Logs

Logging physical activity information in a log or journal, as described earlier in this chapter, provides you with evidence of actual total time spent in physical activity. Depending on your students, you may wish to have parents or guardians verify student participation by signing their child's log or journal periodically. Teach students to use the perceived exertion scale as shown in figure 19.3 so they can record these data in their logs as well.

Heart Rate Monitors

According to Kirkpatrick and Birnbaum (1997), heart rate monitors make it possible to fairly assess each student's level of effort. Heart rate monitor data provides accurate individualized feedback as well, making it a kind of self-assessment test a student can use to plan health-related fitness activities. For example, a student may find it is no longer possible to elevate the heart into the target heart rate zone by walking fast. The student can determine the need to choose to perform a more vigorous aerobic endurance activity, such as jogging or playing one-on-one basketball, to increase aerobic endurance. This process enhances physical activity independence.

Using Results Appropriately

Many questions arise when deciding how to use fitness skill and physical activity assessment data. Should you set a minimum out-of-school physical activity participation level for a grade (e.g., three hours per week is an "A")? What if the child's family or day care situation makes engaging in physical activity outside of school difficult? Should you fault the student who cannot yet run properly, but who is trying hard to learn? What about the child whom you know participates in many extracurricular activities, but does not keep a journal up to date? Use the following information to deal with these common dilemmas in ways that encourage, rather than discourage,

physical activity participation and, therefore, improve health-related fitness.

Sharing Information With Students and Parents

Keeping parents informed in these areas helps you gain their support. As suggested in chapter 16, communicate through conferences, detailed report cards, and newsletters. Be sure to inform everyone—both students and parents—ahead of time what you're looking for in terms of development and participation level. Consider emphasizing improvement in fitness skills and physical activity effort by giving bonus points for doing more or better. Make clear your view on the child who does not possess outstanding motor skills but who tries hard. Make accommodations for students whose family situations make it difficult for them to participate in physical activity outside of school. These tactics both help individualize your approach and prevent many misunderstandings, especially when assessing the fairly subjective idea of effort.

Follow up further by making yourself available for parent and student consultation. Help

6	No exertion at all
7	
8	Extremely light
9	Very light
10	
11	Light
12	
13	Somewhat hard
14	
15	Hard (heavy)
16	
17	Very hard
18	
19	Extremely hard
20	Maximal exertion

Borg RPE scale
© Gunnar Borg, 1970, 1985, 1994, 1998

Figure 19.3   If you teach your students to use the Borg Rating of Perceived Exertion scale, they can record this data in their activity logs.

TIMING IS EVERYTHING

Perhaps the most significant change Marian Franck (McCaskey High School, Lancaster, Pennsylvania) has made to her assessment program is *when* she gives assessment forms to students. The first year she used the forms, she passed them out at the end of the fitness unit and expected students to follow the fitness plan on the forms outside of class, while the class moved on to another unit. At that time, her fitness unit consisted of four lessons on each component of health-related fitness (three lessons a week for nine weeks)—just enough for exposure, not real learning. The unit's final exam was completing the written plan using this form. She was disappointed when only about a quarter of the class could complete it to a meaningful level—that is, prepare an appropriate plan based on their decisions about the health-related component on which they chose to focus.

The second year, Marian spent three lessons summarizing the health-related components, did an initial fitness test to give students benchmark information about their status in all components, and then asked the students to select one on which they would focus for the rest of the nine weeks. She believes that this is when she really began to teach in a meaningful way, and behavior changes and fitness test scores reflected this. While it did mean managing five different components being worked on in the class at the same time, providing resource materials for all components at the same time, and monitoring the written and physical activity work of five different groups of students, much better and more communication with each individual resulted. This led to far more "need-to-know" questions and the teaching opportunities these bring. At the same time, there was very little repetition, because only those students who did not know something had to be taught.

The results were stunning! Students brought informational resources from home, athletes passed on learning to teammates, and self-testing skills skyrocketed. Students needed much less teacher guidance because they were so enthusiastic about what they were working on—because they chose their focus and goals. For example, students adhered to test protocols with less teacher prompting. Most importantly, discipline problems were minimized, because students felt empowered and engaged. At the end of the unit, she asked students to rewrite their plans, focusing on the same or a different component to continue using the plan outside of class during the next quarter. This time, using the form and activity as a final exam was authentic. To keep tabs on implementation of plans, she required weekly reports to indicate regular physical activity participation, which were counted as homework over the next nine weeks, while the class moved on to another unit.

Marian learned that teaching students to be responsible for their own learning is a whole set of skills to cover in themselves. Once the students learn these skills, the process goes more quickly and smoothly. Moreover, individualizing instruction to include personal choice and realistic personal goals provides the incentive to try learning new things, even if a student has already decided he or she is not interested.

Heart Rate Monitors and Authentic Assessment

Heart rate monitors provide the concrete, objective data for measuring effort, creating for the first time true accountability in physical education. Heart rate monitors are useful in providing information about why students don't run or shouldn't run. Heart rate monitors take the guesswork and teacher subjectivity about student participation out of the picture. Specifically, you can download heart rate data to a computer, then print it out. Place the printouts in students' portfolios for accurate, ongoing documentation. Give students and parents copies, teaching them how to interpret the information, so that families can address fitness in specific ways. Heart rate monitors also help students enjoy physical activity more—not because they view them as technological toys, but because they feel empowered to function and achieve at their own ability levels.

One class set of monitors can be reused throughout the school day—and beyond. It is also wise to make a personal elastic chest strap available for purchase to students. This eliminates the need to constantly clean the straps between uses. Have students put on the straps (stored by the teacher) while changing clothes for class. To maximize school purchases and still have full use of heart rate monitors, the coaches and physical education teachers in your school can share the heart rate monitors, one department using them during the day, the other after school.

Heart Rate Monitors, Motivation, and Grades

Kirkpatrick and Birnbaum (1997) have this to say about heart rate monitors, motivation, and grades:

> Measuring heart rates with a heart rate monitor encourages each student to exercise at a sufficiently strenuous level. The self-esteem of students at lower fitness levels than their peers, especially those who typically avoid exercise, increases dramatically as they take part in physical activity and achieve grades proportional to their documented efforts. In other words, using a heart rate monitor allows you to base grades on level of effort and degree of improvement, rather than on absolute achievement—very encouraging to less fit students and motivating to students at all fitness levels. Remember, however, that strenuous activity is not always necessary for improved aerobic endurance. Instead, look for a student to increase intensity over time when he or she feels ready.

Using heart rate monitors can help students individualize their fitness programs.

each individual set goals based on your feedback and the student's personal objectives (see chapter 16). Brainstorm with the family who finds it difficult to fit in physical activity because of work, day care, and neighborhood situations.

Planning

As with other areas we have examined, all worthwhile assessment feeds back into the planning process. If you find a majority of students do not possess a fitness skill, you must plan how you will backtrack and reteach it (remediation). If a majority of students do possess a certain skill, work to give them a variety of real-world application opportunities (enrichment). But don't forget the few students who have not mastered that skill. Design ways to help them catch up, such as working with a peer tutor or meeting you for special instruction, while the rest of the class works independently. Consider using pull-out times as well as before and after school time slots and intramural opportunities. Finally, remember to ask yourself, What could I do elsewhere in the curriculum or in earlier grades to ensure all students come to this course better prepared?

Grading

Once again, it is important to be up front with students and parents regarding what weight you will give fitness skills and physical activity effort in the final grade. Be sure to reward effort—both in attempting fitness skills and

participating in physical activity. Remember, the gifted athlete who does not try to do his or her personal best is not getting nearly as many benefits from physical activity as the less gifted child who participates fully. And possessing fitness skill knowledge does not do any good for an individual who does not know how to apply it to the greatest benefit. Still, it can be difficult to be the judge and jury deciding how much effort a child puts forth. Be sure to use a variety of assessment tools as described in this chapter and other chapters in part IV to support the grades you assign.

Summary

Can each of your students actually *apply* fitness knowledge in meaningful ways? Use the tips and tools described in this chapter to determine the answer to this question for each individual in your program. Keep in mind that knowledge, without the ability to apply it, will not lead to adults who are physically active for life. Each student who passes through your program, then, must become equipped, and therefore, empowered to seek fitness independently. For the second grader, this may mean, for example, knowing that "huffing and puffing" is a signal that the exercise is beneficial to the heart. For the seventh grader, this may mean being able to keep accurate accounts of physical activities to quantify the personal benefit of his participation. For the high school senior, this may mean regular participation in physical activity in a self-designed fitness program, as evidenced by log entries.

Chapter 20

Assessing in the Affective Domain

With the ultimate goal of having your students become adults who value and enjoy physical activity as an important lifestyle choice, being tuned into each student's attitude and motivation level is vital. But how should you go about deciding if an individual's attitude is "good" or motivation is "high"? Then what do you do with this information? Certainly, if you want students to be honest, you should not penalize anyone for revealing a dislike of an activity or of physical activity in general.

Attitude, Motivation, and Authentic Assessment

As defined in chapter 16, assessment is authentic "if the student demonstrates the desired behavior in real-life situations rather than in artificial or contrived settings" (Melograno 1998). This includes the affective domain, especially regarding developing a positive attitude toward physical activity. Authentic assessment in health-related physical fitness education teaches and motivates each student to apply fitness knowledge in the real world. Of course, the primary way to initially motivate students is to conduct a fun program

A major goal of health-related fitness education is for students to self-initiate participation in physical activity outside of your program.

in a supportive, caring, well-managed environment. Then, to assess attitude and motivation, you must find ways to monitor, not only a student's in-class attitude and motivation level, but also, self-initiated participation in physical activity outside your program.

The hard part can be determining whether or not students are participating to get a good grade or simply because they want to. Emphasizing intrinsic over extrinsic motivation can help in this regard. After all, we want students to participate for the joy they find in physical activity, not for stickers or points. Remember, no one is likely to offer extrinsic rewards to a student at the age of 43! Focus, then, on rewarding students who respond to affective assessment assignments in a timely, thorough, and thoughtful manner.

Strategies for Assessing Attitude and Motivation

You can assess attitude and motivation in a variety of formal and informal ways. Be sure,

however, you make it safe for students to respond honestly. Here, we look at several specific strategies for monitoring and assessing attitude and motivation.

Discussions

Simply encouraging students to share how they feel about an activity at the end of a lesson can help you assess attitude and motivation. Ask questions such as the following:

- How do you feel about running the mile?
- How do you feel about stretching at home while watching TV?
- How do you feel about continuing to design ball games that help increase aerobic endurance?
- How do you feel about today's activity?

Although class discussions can put you on the spot more than more private responses can, encourage students to respond honestly by letting them know you accept their opinions. For example, if a student proclaims, "That was the stupidest activity ever!" refrain from taking offense. Instead, ask probing questions that may uncover more helpful informa-

All Feelings Are OK

Part of you may balk at letting students say whatever they think about class activities and physical activity in general. But, as you review student responses to affective assessment assignments, keep in mind that all feelings are OK. Not until the bad feelings come out can the good feelings follow (Faber and Mazlish 1980; 1995). Accept students' attitudes—positive or negative—and you'll find they become empowered to move on to better attitudes. So, avoid getting upset over honest responses. Focus, instead, on how the information is presented (e.g., timely [completed on time], thorough, thoughtful—not disruptive, superficial, or disrespectful), and how it can help you improve your overall program, so that it better meets the needs of each student and better reaches toward the ultimate goal.

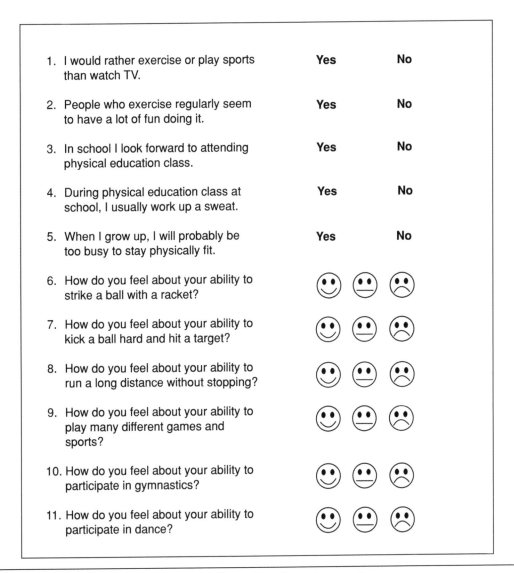

1. I would rather exercise or play sports than watch TV.   **Yes   No**

2. People who exercise regularly seem to have a lot of fun doing it.   **Yes   No**

3. In school I look forward to attending physical education class.   **Yes   No**

4. During physical education class at school, I usually work up a sweat.   **Yes   No**

5. When I grow up, I will probably be too busy to stay physically fit.   **Yes   No**

6. How do you feel about your ability to strike a ball with a racket?

7. How do you feel about your ability to kick a ball hard and hit a target?

8. How do you feel about your ability to run a long distance without stopping?

9. How do you feel about your ability to play many different games and sports?

10. How do you feel about your ability to participate in gymnastics?

11. How do you feel about your ability to participate in dance?

Figure 20.1   Discussion can begin from written questions you assign as homework.

Reprinted, by permission, from G. Graham, 1992, *Teaching Children Physical Education*. (Champaign, IL: Human Kinetics), 159.

tion, such as, "You sound frustrated, Joe. Can you tell us one part of the activity you found especially frustrating?" Then put the responsibility back on students by asking questions such as, "Class, how can we make this activity more helpful to people who were as frustrated as Joe?" Through this process, you teach students to be physical activity problem solvers—a powerful life skill to possess.

Discussion can also begin from written questionnaires you assign as homework, such as the one appropriate for upper elementary students, shown in figure 20.1. Follow up by reviewing student answers and discussing results with students in a future lesson. Consider making such questionnaires anonymous,

to increase the likelihood that students will be completely honest.

Polls

Quick polls after class help when you don't have enough time for a full discussion, but still give you a general feel for what students think of an activity. In addition, some types of poll taking also allow for anonymity. For younger students, Graham (1992) suggests conducting a "Smiley-Face Exit Poll." Students can deposit a smiley, neutral, or frowny face in a coffee can as they leave the lesson in answer to a question you have posed. Upper elementary and middle school students may respond with a thumbs-up or thumbs-down to indicate what they are thinking. High school students may prefer to mark a simple ballot or write "yes" or "no" on a slip of paper to turn in anonymously. If responses are mostly negative, ask follow-up questions during the next lesson to help you plan how to better meet student needs and interests.

Role Plays

Role playing is a dynamic way to monitor attitude and motivation. Have groups of students act out how they feel about an activity or how they might change another's opinion about physical activity. First, have groups brainstorm possible actions and statements among themselves. Next, have each group act out their ideas for the rest of the class. Then, discuss, as a class, which statements and actions are most likely to be helpful in a real-life situation. Ask students for suggestions of other issues they'd like to explore in this way.

Journals and Logs

Journals and logs provide a method for individual students to respond to your program

privately. As a homework assignment, journaling offers the time to reflect and respond thoughtfully. Affective entries can simply be individual responses to discussion questions or they can be more involved, such as logging feelings toward physical activity over several exercise sessions. Hichwa (1998) found it helpful to have his middle school students list the top 10 reasons why students enjoy physical education. He then found it personally and professionally helpful to list the 10 most important aspects of physical education (see figure 20.2).

Rubrics

Usually we think of rubrics as guides for assessing physical performances, but rubrics have been used successfully in other subject areas to assess affective performance, as well. You can design rubrics that target, for example, such social behaviors as cooperating in a group (see figure 20.3) or attitudes and levels of motivation (see figure 20.4). These examples are self-assessments, because this approach helps make students aware of important behaviors and attitudes. They also function as surveys of student attitudes and

Students' Top 10 List	Teachers' Top 10 List
10. We get to grade ourselves.	10. Have enough equipment for each student.
9. We are taught to make goals for ourselves and to try our hardest to achieve them.	9. Chart each child's progress and motivate him/her to do his/her personal best.
8. We have plenty of supplies.	8. Play the game.
7. The activities are challenging.	7. Make lessons interesting, progressive, and challenging.
6. Physical education relieves stress from our day.	6. Keep the development of self-responsibility as a top priority.
5. We are always doing different things, so it's interesting, and you never get bored.	5. Develop individual and cooperative skills.
4. Teachers are supportive, understanding, and are easy to get along with.	4. Provide equipment that is developmentally appropriate.
3. We get a good workout.	3. Present a variety of offerings so that each child can experience success.
2. We are always active.	2. Keep students physically active as much as possible.
1. Teachers make physical education fun!	1. Treat each child fairly and with respect.

Figure 20.2 John Hichwa had his students create a list of the top 10 reasons they enjoy physical education (on the left) and then he created his own list of what he felt were the 10 most important aspects of effectively teaching physical education (on the right).
Reprinted, by permission, from J. Hichwa, 1998, *Right Fielders Are People, Too.* (Champaign, IL: Human Kinetics).

I worked well with my group	Seldom	Sometimes	Always
I listened when others shared their ideas.			
I offered thoughtful comments to help others in my group improve.			
I followed the teacher's directions and used everyone's time wisely.			
I cheerfully tried others' suggestions.			
Share what you found the most difficult in working with this group: List at least two possible solutions to this problem:			

Figure 20.3   Sample rubric that targets social behaviors.

What I think of this activity	Seldom	Sometimes	Always
I think the activities in this class can help me become more fit.			
I try class activities during my free time.			
I recommend class activities to friends.			
I like class activities.			
Write any other comments you would like to make:			

Figure 20.4   Sample rubric that targets motivation levels.

social behaviors, helping students reflect on their own affective development.

Portfolios

As described in chapter 16, a portfolio gives you a comprehensive way to look at an individual student. A well-designed portfolio—one that includes a balance of physical, cognitive, and affective assignments—can provide invaluable insights into a student's overall attitude and motivation level. For example, a portfolio that reflects the minimum of work in all areas may indicate the student is not very interested in physical activity. In contrast, a portfolio that reflects an enthusiasm for physical activity through up-to-date, detailed logs and thoughtful journal answers may indicate a student who values physical activity. Be careful, however, to confirm your hunches, as students with learning disabilities may have difficulty expressing their feelings in writing. And any student eager to please may mislead you. Of course, making such judgments can be a touchy issue. These extremes call for further investigation, perhaps in the form of private teacher-student conferences. You should also be sure to view the portfolio as a whole. Remember, it is a forum for viewing several different types of assessments collected over time to give you a more complete picture of a student's participation and attitudes.

Using Results Appropriately

As mentioned earlier, it is vital to accurate assessment that you ensure it is safe for your students to share their feelings about physical activity. It is also imperative that you emphasize intrinsic over extrinsic motivators. What, then, do you do with the affective information you collect? Handle with care all affective assessment data you gather so that students will be honest with you, helping you make your program the best it can be.

Sharing Information With Students and Parents

As with the physical and cognitive domains of physical education, parents need to know how their child is doing in the affective domain. Parent-teacher conferences are an excellent way to share this information. This personal touch makes it easier to convey information in a positive and genuinely caring manner. If you cannot meet systematically with every parent, try to at least meet with the parents of students who seem especially reluctant to participate in physical activity. Invite the student, as well. At the conference, brainstorm ways to help the student enjoy physical activity more. Express any specific health concerns you may have, and explain your physical education program philosophy. Remember to be diplomatic and to ask for honest feedback on your program. Find out what lifestyle activities you can help the family build on, such as a love of fishing, and suggesting they expand this love of the outdoors and nature to include hiking and canoeing. At the end of the conference, thank parents for their time, and invite them to contact you whenever they have concerns, comments, or questions.

If you cannot hold conferences, send a detailed attitude and motivation report. Provide space for parent feedback, and leave the door open for further communication.

Finally, involve parents in fun family events to help families learn to enjoy physical activity together.

Planning

Your primary reason for using your valuable time to assess affective issues should be to learn how to tailor your program to meet individual needs. Adapt activities that turn

kids off; they'll be glad to suggest how. The process of working together, not only improves your program, it also helps model problem-solving skills. Remember, if students do not enjoy the physical activity in your program, they are much less likely to pursue it as a lifestyle choice. Naturally, this defeats your attempts to produce adults who love physical activity and seek it as a way of life. Be sure to include a variety of movement forms, not only health-related fitness and sport activities; for example, dance, outdoor pursuits, and adventure programming can spark interest in physical activity in otherwise reluctant students.

Grading

Remember, assessing and grading are not quite the same. But, at a certain point, you may need to assign a grade. Try, as suggested in chapter 16, to offer a separate affective grade, even if this means creating your own health-related physical fitness education report card.

If students learn to enjoy physical activity in your program, they are more likely to also be physically active on their own after school and on weekends.

Anytown Middle School
Physical Education Department
1000 North Scenic Drive
Anytown, IL 00000

September 1, 2000

Dear Parents/Guardians:

We are looking forward to an exciting year at Anytown Middle School. Our objective as physical education teachers is to provide all our students with the knowledge, skills, attitudes, and behaviors needed to live physically active, healthy lives. We believe in an individualized approach to physical education, and we will do our best to help your son or daughter become his or her physical best.

We will provide progress reports throughout the year, and we welcome your questions at anytime. However, at the end of the semester and at the end of the year, we will give a single letter grade, as dictated by school policy. The purpose of this letter is to explain how this grade will be determined for your son or daughter. The physical education grade will be determined as follows:

25% of the grade will be based on knowledge of health-related fitness and a variety of physical activities and sports, as determined through written tests and quizzes.

25% of the grade will be based on the completion of a physical education portfolio, which will include work sheets, homework assignments, research projects, and journal writing.

25% of the grade will be based on appropriate participation in class activities, discussions, and fitness testing, with an emphasis on self-responsibility.

25% of the grade will be based on improvement, including improvement of motor skills specific to sports and activities, and improvement of health-related fitness.

Again, if you have any questions, please feel free to contact me or any member of the physical education staff. Please sign this letter, and have your son or daughter return it, so I will know that you have had a chance to read it.

Sincerely,

Jane Doe
Physical Education Department Chair

Parent signature   Date

_____   _____

Figure 20.5 It is important to clearly communicate to parents exactly how you will determine letter grades in your physical education class.

Make the thoughtfulness and care a student puts into completing affective assessment assignments your main focus—not a student's actual attitude toward physical activity. This encourages students to be honest. There are exceptions, however, for example, the student who persistently poisons the class with unhelpful negative comments and refuses to join you in troubleshooting disliked areas, or the student who never stops trying, despite poor physical abilities. Both of these students especially need to know their approach affects their grade. As always, the key is to be open and up front about what weight you plan to give a perceived attitude and motivation level in the final physical education grade, as well as exactly what you'll be looking at (e.g., level of out-of-class participation, expressiveness in written assignments, faithfulness and timeliness in completing affective assignments, and so on).

If your school policy is that you must give one letter grade for physical education, you might give students a handout to bring home and have parents sign (so you know parents read it) that outlines exactly what will be taken into account in assigning that one letter grade (see figure 20.5).

Summary

Assessing attitude and motivation, and then using that information wisely, are the keys to developing a health-related physical fitness education program that teaches students physical activity is enjoyable and worthwhile. Strive to get to know each student's likes, dislikes, and fears, then help him or her discover enjoyable physical activities to increase the likelihood of independently pursuing physical activity. Include parents in this process by keeping them informed and asking them for suggestions. Finally, grade students on how thoughtful, timely, and thorough their responses are to affective assessment assignments—not how much they say they liked an activity or not.

Part V

Physical Best
Study Guide

Chapter 21

Preparing for the Physical Best Health-Fitness Specialist Certification Exam

This chapter is designed to help you review the information in chapters 1–20, giving you an opportunity to reflect on the material and prepare for the Physical Best Health-Fitness Specialist Certification Exam. Use the questions and exercises to help you focus on some of the key concepts this book discusses. However, as you look for answers and ideas, it is suggested that you carefully review *all* the material.

The recommended manner in which you should approach these questions and exercises is to

1. answer them, based on your memory of the material; then,

2. confirm or change your answers, based on the information in the text; and, finally,

3. check your answers against those listed starting on page 307.

Chapter 22 provides a practice Physical Best Health-Fitness Specialist Certification Exam for further review.

Answers on pages 307–308.

Study Guide for Part I

Terminology Review

1. In your own words, explain the differences among the terms *exercise*, *physical activity*, and *health-related physical fitness* (chapter 1).

2. In your own words, define *health-related physical fitness education* (chapter 3).

Fact Review

1. As a quality health-related physical fitness education program, the ultimate goal of the Physical Best program is (chapter 1):

_____

_____

2. Name at least five physical and mental benefits of regularly participating in physical activity (chapter 1):

_____

_____

_____

_____

_____

3. Name three personal and three environmental factors that may influence physical activity behavior (chapter 2).

Personal: _____

_____

_____

Environmental:_____

_____

_____

4. List the 10 basic strategies for successful goal setting with students (chapter 2):

_____   _____

_____   _____

_____   _____

_____   _____

_____   _____

Study Guide for Part I

5. List the six main characteristics of a quality health-related physical fitness education program (e.g., Physical Best; chapter 3):

_____   _____

_____   _____

_____   _____

6. In regard to integrating skill development, students (and, ultimately, adults) need to be skillful enough to obtain fitness benefits without needless

_____ or _____ (chapter 3).

7. List at least five hazards potentially present in the physical education environment (chapter 4):

_____

_____

_____

_____

_____

8. List four main effective ways you can advocate for your health-related physical fitness education program (chapter 4):

_____

_____

_____

_____

Application Practice and Research

1. Review the NASPE/COPEC statements regarding developmentally appropriate practices for elementary, middle school, and high school students in chapter 1. Choose *one* component (e.g., active participation, physical fitness activities, warm-up). Visit a different school and observe another teacher's approach to this component. What do you observe that is developmentally appropriate? Inappropriate? How would you change an inappropriate practice to an appropriate one? (Choose a practice you observed; or, if none were observed, list one you recall from your own personal experience as a physical education student.) How might this change impact student learning and attitudes? *Note:* Be sure to speak to the recommendations for the specific age group being taught.

2. After reading the sidebar titled Dressed for Success in chapter 2, tell what you liked/disliked about your high school gym uniform or dress code. Design a uniform or create a dress code that today's typical 17 year old would enjoy (or at least not mind) wearing. Keep in mind sanitation, good taste, and safety requirements. Write a description and make a sketch of your ideas. Vote among your classmates/colleagues as to whose design or code would be most appealing to students, teachers, and administrators alike. Discuss how an appealing uniform or code can positively impact attitudes toward physical activity.

3. Reread the sidebar titled Why Change? in chapter 3. In this sidebar, two physical education teachers explain why they feel it is necessary to continually update their programs through the years. What would you tell your principal if he or she asked why you would change your physical education program?

4. You have developed innovative ways to extend your students' physical activity time at school (e.g., after-school fitness club, intramural games over lunch periods). Now your school administration is threatening to cut funding for physical education classes, so that you will meet with your students fewer times per week (elementary level) or fewer semesters per middle or high school career. You're told, "Students play enough over lunch and after school. We need more time for academics." Draw on all the information in part 1 to refute this argument. Hold a debate with your classmates with one side taking the side of the administration (playing "devil's advocates") and the other side taking the position that health-related physical fitness education is as vital to promoting student success in life as academics.

5. Create a health-related fitness assignment that uses computers in some way. State what age level this assignment is intended for. Tell why the use of technology in this assignment is important to student learning. Think about the statement, "Remember, high-tech can help you teach, but it is no substitute for a solid program. So don't turn technology into expensive toys. Make sure your reasons for using each item are sound and that your applications of the technology are relevant, both to your students and your program goals" (chapter 4). List nontechnological alternatives that may potentially achieve the same learning.

Reflection Questions

1. After reading the section titled How Physical Best Is Different in chapter 1, which of the following statements would most likely be made by a teacher who follows the Physical Best philosophy:

"I teach children and young adults the hows and whys of a physically active, healthy lifestyle."

"I teach football, basketball, volleyball, and softball."

"I teach students sports skills."

Explain why.

2. After reading the section titled Motivating Students to Be Active for Life in chapter 2, explain the statement "Young children naturally want to move. What happens, then, to this natural inclination to be physically active as children grow into early adolescence?" Name at least three specific ways a quality health-related physical fitness education program can build on the natural inclination to enjoy movement, thereby combating the trend toward sedentary living among adolescents and adults.

3. After reading the section titled Age-Appropriate Practical Applications in chapter 3, compare and contrast appropriate approaches to elementary and secondary students. How are the approaches to helping students progress up Corbin and Lindsey's (1993) Stairway to Lifetime Fitness similar? How are they different? Offer reasons for the similarities and differences.

4. After reading the section titled Collaboration in chapter 4, discuss the well-known African proverb, "It takes a whole village to raise a child" in relation to the Physical Best and health-related physical fitness education goal of producing adults who seek physical activity as a way of life.

Study Guide for Part II

Answers on page 309.

Terminology Review

Match each term with the definition that most closely describes it:

a. aerobic fitness
b. body composition
c. calorie
d. diet
e. flexibility
f. frequency
g. homeostasis
h. hypermobility
i. intensity
j. kilocalorie
k. laxity
l. muscular endurance
m. muscular strength
n. nutrient density
o. overload
p. percent body fat
q. progression
r. solutes
s. time
t. type

1. how often a person performs the targeted health-related activity _____
2. a measure of the heart's ability to pump oxygen-rich blood to the rest of the body _____
3. providing a greater stress or load on the body than it is normally accustomed to _____
4. the duration of a physical activity _____
5. the ability of a muscle or muscle group to exert force over a period of time against a less-than-maximum resistance _____
6. dissolved chemicals _____
7. the way in which an individual should increase overload _____
8. the ratio of lean body mass to body fat _____
9. the amount of a given nutrient per calorie _____
10. the degree of abnormal motion of a given joint _____
11. how hard an individual exercises _____
12. double-jointedness; a form of excess range of motion _____
13. the amount of energy it takes to raise the temperature of one gram of water 1°C _____
14. the ability of a muscle or group of muscles to exert a maximal force against a resistance _____
15. the specific physical activity chosen to improve a component of health-related fitness _____
16. a method of expressing body composition _____
17. 1,000 calories, or one kcal; often mistakenly called a "calorie" _____
18. the ability of a joint and the muscles and tendons surrounding it to move freely and comfortably through its intended full range of motion _____
19. the proper level of hydration _____
20. the total intake of food consumed in a five-to-seven-day period _____

Study Guide for Part II

Fact Review

Fill in the blanks with the words that best complete the sentences:

1. Basic training principles are the _____ of physical activity (chapter 5).

2. The _____ principle describes how one safely applies the principles of overload and progression (chapter 5).

3. Monitor children to ensure intensity does not reduce the _____, increasing the chances of _____ (chapter 5).

4. Properly _____ before and _____ after a workout is vital to preventing injuries and then returning the body to a more rested state, respectively (chapter 5).

5. What actually causes an imbalance of health-related component fitness levels in a particular individual depends on _____ (chapter 5).

6. Aerobic fitness is measured by gauging _____, known as _____ (chapter 6).

7. Aerobic fitness activity can be accumulated throughout the day in segments of no less than _____ minutes each (chapter 6).

8. The four main training methods to maintain or increase aerobic fitness are: _____, _____, _____, and _____ (chapter 6).

9. Add motor skills to _____ activities and incorporate aerobic fitness training into _____ learning (chapter 6).

10. Because children respond differently to exercise than adults, build in frequent rest periods, and regardless of age, provide _____ before, during, and after physical activity (chapter 6).

11. To develop _____, the overload principle dictates increasing the resistance against the muscles involved to a level greater than that used before (chapter 7).

12. To develop _____, increase the number of repetitions, increase the length (time) of the repetition, or decrease the rest interval between activities (chapter 7).

13. In developing muscular strength and endurance, we can gauge _____ by calculating the percentage of one-repetition maximum (RM) (chapter 7).

14. Four appropriate ways to develop muscular strength and endurance in health-related physical fitness education are _____, _____, _____, and _____, depending on the age and ability of the students (chapter 7).

Study Guide for Part II

15. Lifting maximal weights should be delayed until all the long bones have finished growing at about _____ years of age (chapter 7).

16. Flexibility—and the stretches that foster it—can be classified as _____, _____, _____, and _____ (chapter 8).

17. Stretching encourages the body to release _____ that lubricate the _____ (chapter 8).

18. Never make flexibility training _____; instead, emphasize correct _____ and _____ (chapter 8).

19. The three main keys to safe stretching in the physical education setting are: _____, _____, _____ (chapter 8).

20. If you believe a student has severe problems with flexibility, refer the student to _____ (chapter 8).

21. Muscular strength and endurance affect body composition because muscle cells use more _____ at rest than _____ cells (chapter 9). (Keep in mind that this effect takes place over a long period of time, and it is more difficult for women to obtain because it is more difficult for women to build large muscle mass.)

22. Aerobic fitness affects body composition because aerobic activities burn calories and raise _____ (chapter 9).

23. Because weight charts (e.g., body mass index [BMI]) do not take percent body fat into consideration, a person might be overweight without being _____ (chapter 9).

24. _____ is the most accurate way of measuring body composition generally available to the physical educator (chapter 9).

25. The BMI for a female who is 5'4" tall and weighs 125 lbs. is _____. This _____ considered obese (chapter 9).

26. Although all foods have _____ value, clearly some foods are more _____ than others (chapter 10).

27. _____ or _____ pressures may influence adolescents' nutritional choices (chapter 10).

28. Poor childhood habits in both _____ and _____ often lead to health problems in adulthood (chapter 10).

29. _____, _____, and _____ can cause dehydration (chapter 10).

30. The body breaks down starches and sucrose into simple sugars for _____ (chapter 10).

Application Practice and Research

1. After studying chapter 6, consider a 16-year-old student who wishes to move from a base health-related fitness level of aerobic fitness to an intermediate health-related fitness level. Use table 6.1 to counsel this student.

2. Calculate the appropriate target heart rate zone (THRZ) for the student in question 1.

3. After studying the section titled Safety Guidelines for Muscular Strength and Endurance Activities in chapter 7, including the sidebar titled NSCA Youth Resistance Training Guidelines, list a set of safety rules that would be appropriate for students to follow during muscular strength and endurance activities (including weight training). State these rules as succinctly as possible. (You might also compare these guidelines to the policy statement by the American Academy of Pediatrics on strength training, weight and power lifting, and body building by children and adolescents—this policy statement can be found on the Internet at **http://www.aap.org/policy/03327.html**.)

4. After studying the information in the section titled Flexibility Training Methods in chapter 8, hold a debate with classmates: One side advocates static stretching only in high school physical education, and the other side advocates teaching ballistic stretching as well as static stretching.

5. Discuss how you might handle measuring percent body fat, the type of test, privacy issues, and so on at the elementary, middle school, or high school level. Give reasons for your decisions (chapter 8).

6. Prepare a response for a parent who expresses the concern that his or her child may suffer from an eating disorder (chapters 9 and 10).

7. After studying part II, design a family fitness night appropriate for a middle school setting. What is/are your goal(s)? What topic(s) and activities will you include? How will you organize the activities for safety and enjoyment? How will you generate interest in the event? (See also chapter 4, Public Relations and Program Advocacy.)

Study Guide for Part III

Answers on pages 310–312.

Terminology Review

Define the following terms in your own words:

Ch. 11:

      1. health-related physical fitness education curriculum

      2. exit outcomes

      3. delivering up

Ch. 12:

      4. intratask variation

      5. teaching by invitation

Ch. 13:

      6. developmentally appropriate

      7. task presentation

      8. class management

Ch. 14:

      9. personal lifetime health-related fitness course

Ch. 15:

     10. inclusion

     11. least restrictive environment

     12. mainstreaming

     13. task analysis

Fact Review

Write "T" for true or "F" for false for each statement. Change the wording of false statements to make them true.

1. Before planning your curriculum, you should identify the lesson outcomes you want students leaving your program to have achieved (chapter 11). _____

2. When designing curriculum, work backward from exit-level outcomes, so that, ultimately, each unit and lesson enhances each student's chance of achieving those outcomes (chapter 11). _____

3. When selecting and designing units, you should take into account the facilities, equipment, and community opportunities available, as well as student ages and interests (chapter 11). _____

4. Your program should not worry about what people actually do in real life to stay fit (chapter 11). _____

5. Music can welcome students, signal station changes, and be a fun background (chapter 12). _____

Study Guide for Part III

6. To create an effective learning environment, you should avoid comparing students to each other, making idle threats, being sarcastic, humiliating students, using physical activity as a punishment, and overreacting (chapter 12). _____

7. Teaching by invitation is "simply a way of allowing children to adjust the task so they can be successful—and challenged" (Graham 1992; chapter 12). _____

8. Understanding how objects orient in space is the strong suit of individuals with high linguistic intelligence (chapter 12). _____

9. Age, choice, attitude, and goals are not important when deciding if a competitive or cooperative activity is appropriate (chapter 13). _____

10. When selecting physical activities for learning, be sure they are developmentally appropriate, purposeful, sequential, connected to real life, and enjoyable (chapter 13). _____

11. Choosing how to communicate ideas appropriate to the content being presented is vital to effective teaching (chapter 13). _____

12. To monitor "type" (the second "T") in the FITT principle, students need to learn to keep an accurate log or journal that includes information about exactly what a student is engaging in to reach set goals (chapter 13). _____

13. The current trend in secondary education is to not require students to take and pass a personal lifetime health-related fitness course (chapter 14). _____

14. Providing opportunities to discuss, debate, and write about fitness concepts is one way to foster logical-mathematical intelligence in health-related physical fitness education (chapter 14). _____

15. The occasional thoughtful written response from a teacher makes no difference in a student's physical activity behavior (chapter 14). _____

16. Your program must offer reasonable opportunities for physical activity to students of both genders (chapter 15). _____

17. Collaborating with peer tutors, parents, other volunteers, and colleagues is one approach to inclusion (chapter 15). _____

18. Cultural diversity is not a major area in which to address issues of inclusion (chapter 15). _____

19. Physically elite and physically awkward children deserve the full benefit of inclusion in health-related physical fitness education (chapter 15). _____

20. With obese students, you should stress the benefits of even mild exercise, as these students are often discouraged by being expected to do too much too soon (chapter 15). _____

Application Practice and Research

1. Reread the sidebars titled Pride in Physical Education: Take Ownership of New Curriculum, Career Paths and Physical Education, and Lifetime Physical Education in chapter 11. Discuss how and why physical educators of today have to design curricula that meet the needs of their target populations.

2. After studying chapter 12, select two styles of teaching (e.g., command, reciprocal, guided discovery), and describe how you might use these styles to teach the concept of pacing when running the mile. State the age group and experience level of the students you are targeting. Compare how the two styles do and do not enhance these students' chances of learning this concept.

3. After studying chapter 12, choose a health-related fitness topic, and design a lesson that addresses the topic through at least three of Gardner's intelligences. List the age and experience of the students you are targeting.

4. After studying the section titled Communicate Clearly and other tips in chapter 13, make a checklist of effective communication. Observe a colleague or mentor teaching a lesson, and report on how often this teacher used these techniques.

5. After reviewing the section titled Professionalism and the sidebar titled Should Physical Educators Be Fit? in chapter 13, hold a debate with your colleagues. Have one side argue that sharp clothing and fit bodies are important to effective teaching in health-related physical fitness education and the other side argue that these issues are not very important—after all, it is the curriculum and effective teaching of that curriculum that matter the most.

6. After reviewing the information about various approaches to lifetime personal health-related fitness courses in chapter 14, design a lesson to teach high school students about consumer issues related to health-related fitness (e.g., false advertising, purchasing equipment). Be sure to apply the principles discussed in the section titled Teaching Principles for Classroom-Based Lessons, which appears later in the chapter, to your lesson design. (See example assignments in the section titled Becoming a Good Fitness Consumer, as well.)

7. After studying the section titled Leading Effective Discussions in chapter 14, take turns with a small group of colleagues leading a discussion on a health-related fitness topic. Give each leader a point each time they remember to employ one of the teaching tips listed in the text. Compete to see who scores the highest, or make this a cooperative activity by keeping a collective score (adding up everyone's points).

8. After reading the sidebar titled Responding to Journal Entries in chapter 14, write a response to a student who complains, "I hate this class!" in his or her journal.

9. After studying part III, address three of the following barriers to participating in lifetime physical activities, offering physical activity homework ideas for helping students overcome these barriers: fear of the unfamiliar, expense, fear or dislike of competition, lack of skill, lack of knowledge, and lack of time. Note for which age group (primary, upper elementary, middle school, or high school) each idea is appropriate.

10. After studying chapter 15, design a physical activity pyramid appropriate for a specific student with special needs. What physical activities might be appropriate for this individual? What FITT guidelines might be appropriate for this individual? Whom might you consult with to answer these questions accurately? Sketch your pyramid, offering art notes, if you cannot draw pictures well. If possible, take pictures of the student performing the activities to decorate a poster of your pyramid.

Study Guide for Part IV

Answers on pages 313–314.

Terminology Review

For each definition, write "T" for true or "F" for false. Change the wording of false definitions to make them correct.

Ch. 16:

1. *Traditional assessment* occurs when the results of written tests are the main data used to assess student learning.

2. *Alternative assessment* occurs when tools, other than traditional standardized testing, are used to assess student learning.

3. Alternative assessment becomes *authentic*, when the assessment takes place in a contrived setting.

Ch. 17:

4. *Norm-referenced tests* score a student on how he or she compares to health-related fitness standards that indicate true health, regardless of others' scores.

5. *Criterion-referenced tests* score a student on how he or she compares to other students' fitness performances.

6. The *Healthy Fitness Zone* indicates the range of *FITNESSGRAM* test scores necessary for maintaining good health.

Fact Review

1. Authentic assessment in health-related physical fitness education teaches and motivates each student to apply fitness knowledge in the _____ (chapter 16).

2. _____ assessment, conducted by students, allows them to practice strategies they can use on their own outside your program (chapter 16).

3. List the six characteristics of an effective rubric (chapter 16):

_____   _____

_____   _____

_____   _____

4. To make health-related fitness testing (e.g., *FITNESSGRAM*) go smoothly, you should _____, _____, and _____ (chapter 17).

5. You can _____ *FITNESSGRAM* to meet the needs of students with special needs or use a test specifically designed for such students (chapter 17).

6. You should _____ and _____ the reasons for health-related fitness tests and the meanings behind the results to students and parents (chapter 17).

Study Guide for Part IV

7. Knowing _____ to exercise (e.g., correct strength-training techniques) prepares students to _____ benefit from physical activity (chapter 18).

8. In assessing knowledge, _____ allow students to use avenues of communication, other than the written word, to create products from their research (chapter 18).

9. It is important to be sure you are assessing what you have _____, not what you _____ to teach and did not cover (chapter 18).

10. As extensions of class discussions, role playing is an effective way to assess whether or not students can _____ fitness knowledge (chapter 19).

11. Heart rate monitors are one way to fairly assess a student's level of _____ in aerobic endurance activities (chapter 19).

12. If a majority of students do not possess a fitness skill you have taught, you must _____ how you will backtrack and _____ it (chapter 19).

13. You should focus on how _____, _____, and _____ responses to affective assessment assignments are (chapter 20).

14. It is important that students feel safe giving _____ answers to affective assessment assignments (chapter 20).

15. When assessing in the affective domain, a well-designed portfolio can provide invaluable insights into a student's overall _____ and _____ level (chapter 20).

Application Practice and Research

1. Create a sample rubric to assess a colleague's push-up or curl-up technique. Then have the colleague assess your push-up or curl-up technique, using the rubric you created. Discuss how the rubric helps you assess (chapter 16).

2. After studying part IV, keep a physical activity journal on your own physical activity for at least a week. Be sure to comment on your feelings regarding each physical activity session. What did you enjoy about keeping the journal? What did you find difficult? How might you use this information when requiring students to keep physical activity journals? Trade journals with a colleague, and use the criteria for assessment listed on page 239. Rate each other's work (Exemplary to Unacceptable) and state how you arrived at this conclusion.

3. After studying part IV, role-play a conference with a student who is having trouble passing your health-related physical fitness education class and his or her parents. Define what the problems are (e.g., not completing assignments, not working well with others, not taking content seriously, and the like). Practice being firm, but diplomatic, while guiding the student toward better behavior or work. See the information regarding sharing results with students and parents in chapters 16–20 for ideas. In addition, keep in mind a conference is a teaching opportunity, not a "punishment." Therefore, follow the teaching principles outlined in part III (e.g., be positive, remember you're dealing with an individual).

4. After studying chapter 20, design a five-question written test to assess student attitudes about flexibility training appropriate for primary students (K-3). Rewrite the test to be appropriate for high school students. Explain why you made the changes you did. State which domain you are assessing.

5. Internet research: Use the Internet to find listservs, websites, and discussion groups grappling with assessment issues in elementary and/or secondary education. Check out the issues in both physical education and other disciplines. How are the issues similar? Different?

6. After studying part IV, explain how self-assessment experience and competency helps a student reach the ultimate goal of becoming an adult who participates in health-related physical activity as a way of life.

7. After studying chapter 16, explain the difference between assessment and grading.

8. After studying part IV (especially chapter 17), hold a debate with colleagues. One side takes the stand that fitness testing results should not count toward grades. The other side plays the role of administrators who want evidence that the physical education department is productive enough. See also program advocacy suggestions in the section titled Public Relations and Program Advocacy in chapter 4.

9. After studying the section titled Reluctant or Overanxious Students in chapter 17, role-play how you might help a reluctant or overanxious student learn to enjoy health-related fitness testing. Speak to issues of program philosophy, your own attitudes, and student choice.

10. After studying the section titled Projects in chapter 18, choose an idea from the list of project suggestions. How would you assess the work of the group? How would you assess the knowledge each individual gained through doing the project?

11. Chapter 18 suggests borrowing a TV game show format, such as *Jeopardy*, to liven up review sessions. Choose a health-related fitness topic, and design a game show to review the facts students should learn related to this topic. Play the game with colleagues, then revise it based on their feedback.

12. Chapter 19 discusses assessment of participation in physical activity. Write your own personal goal for participating in physical activity for the next week and then keep track of your activity for that week. At the end of the week, compare your goal with your actual results. If you didn't achieve your goal, what factors were to blame? How do you plan to overcome these factors in the future?

Answers: Part I

Terminology Review

1. Answer should paraphrase the definitions offered in chapter 1, for example: "In a nutshell, *physical activity* is something you *do. Physical fitness* is something you *acquire*—a characteristic or an attribute one can achieve by being physically active. *Exercise* is structured and tends to have *fitness* as its goal" (Michael Pratt, as quoted from draft of USDHHS 1999).

2. Sample answer: A health-related physical fitness education program teaches students how and why to engage in lifelong, individualized, health-related physical activity *and* inspires them to do so.

Fact Review

1. Sample answers: to help young people develop the skills, knowledge, attitudes, and behaviors that lead to physically active, healthy lifestyles

2. Sample answers: physical benefits—enhances all components of health-related fitness (muscular strength, endurance, and flexibility; aerobic endurance; body composition), enhances appearance, can prevent many diseases and illnesses (e.g., diabetes, premature death); mental benefits—reduces stress, increases sense of well-being, and can reduce symptoms of depression.

3. Sample answers: personal—biological factors, such as obesity, gender, and age, and psychological factors, such as knowledge, cues to be active, and feelings of self-efficacy; environmental—social factors, such as family and peer influences, and physical factors, such as season of the year and safety of neighborhood.

4. involve students, start small and progress, focus on personal improvements, set specific and measurable goals, set challenging and realistic goals, write goals down, provide strategies, support and give feedback about progress toward goals, create goal stations, provide opportunities for periodic evaluation

5. individualized, fair, health oriented, educational, enjoyable, realistic

6. injury, frustration

7. unstable bleachers, slippery floors, poor heating or ventilation, unlit water fountains, debris or unused equipment lying around a field or gymnasium, ungroomed fields, holes on fields, cracked blacktop surfaces, dangerously loose gym floorboards, high flood areas and deep water on playing fields, sports fields too close to playgrounds, unsafe traffic conditions

8. offer an excellent program, seek professional development, let your school and students' parents know about your program, let the community at-large know about your program

Application Practice and Research

1. Answers will vary, but be sure to speak to the age-appropriate recommendations for the age group observed.

2. Designs and codes will vary, but should consider the constraints of sanitation, safety, good taste, and current fashion.

3. Answers will vary, but might include the need to update various stretches and exercises based on new research, the need to keep current with changing student interests, the need to take advantage of new technology, and the need to provide students with the most up-to-date information on what research tells us about physical activity and health.

4. Content of the debate will vary but should focus on the value of physical activity and preparing students for a lifetime of health and wellness.

5. Answers will vary, but be sure to list the nontechnological alternatives to the high-tech approaches.

Reflection Questions

1. The first statement would be more typical of a Physical Best health-related physical fitness educator. The first statement reveals that quality health-related physical education seeks to give students the tools they need to be physically active for life. The second statement reveals a philosophy of teaching games or skills without connecting them to lifetime health-related fitness pursuits.

2. Most young children are inclined to participate in physical activity, at least on their own terms. But, in the past, some poorly designed physical education and recreational experiences and socialization factors have turned children off to physical activity, contributing to the trend toward sedentary living seen in many adolescents and adults. Programs that foster, for example, intrinsic motivation through offering choices; fostering skill competency; providing the necessary information; and focusing on student interest, fun, and excitement are more likely to motivate students to be physically active now and in the future than those that are boring, designed based on irrelevant or unrealistic goals, or otherwise inappropriate (e.g., espousing the "no pain, no gain" theory; overly competitive).

3. Opportunities for development of psychomotor skills and ample exposure to a variety of activities that teach of love of physical activity are the hallmarks of a quality health-related physical fitness education program for young children. Sensitivity to issues of self-esteem and physical appearance and emphases on self-evaluation and personal program planning are especially important to secondary students. Secondary guidelines build on elementary ones, overlapping especially in regard to allowing personal choices and issues of self-efficacy (feelings of competence in physical activity, e.g., skill development at the elementary level to self-evaluation and program design at the secondary level).

4. Answers should paraphrase: Helping students make healthy life choices is the job of the entire school and the community, not just the health-related physical fitness education program. A school should educate the whole child in a coordinated effort, through developing a comprehensive school health and wellness program, and otherwise, tapping into parent and community resources. An atmosphere of cooperation and collaboration among those most interested in students' well-being creates a nurturing and supportive school atmosphere, thereby facilitating learning.

Answers: Part II

Terminology Review

1. f; 2. a; 3. o; 4. s; 5. l; 6. r; 7. q; 8. b; 9. n; 10. k; 11. i; 12. h; 13. c; 14. m; 15. t; 16. p; 17. j; 18. e; 19. g; 20. d

Fact Review

1. hows; 2. FITT; 3. quality of performance, injury; 4. warming up, cooling down; 5. that individual's needs; 6. maximum oxygen uptake, $\dot{V}O_2max$; 7. 10; 8. continuous, circuit, interval, and Fartlek training; 9. aerobic endurance, motor skill; 10. water; 11. muscular strength; 12. muscular endurance; 13. intensity; 14. body weight training (calisthenics), partner-resisted training, resistance band training, weight training; 15. 17; 16. ballistic, static, dynamic, PNF; 17. fluids, joints; 18. competitive, technique, personal bests; 19. using controlled movements (static stretches), warming up first, and individualizing; 20. a trained health care professional; 21. calories, fat; 22. resting metabolism rates; 23. obese; 24. skinfold caliper testing; 25. 21, is not; 26. nutritional, valuable; 27. social, peer; 28. physical activity, nutrition; 29. sweating, vomiting, urinating; 30. absorption

Application Practice and Research

1. Advise the student to apply the principles of overload and progression safely by gradually increasing only one component of health-related fitness at a time. For example, if the student increases intensity, he or she should not increase frequency, until the body adjusts to the increase in intensity.

2. 60–75% of Max HR for a 16 year old is calculated as follows:

$220 - 16 = 204$ (Max HR)

$.60 \times 204 = 122.4$ (122 rounded to the nearest whole number)

$.75 \times 204 = 153$

Thus, THRZ for this student is 122–153.

3. Sample answer: warm up first; learn and use correct technique; compete against yourself, not others; always have a spotter; do not attempt maximum weights; return equipment to its proper place.

4. Use the arguments for and against each type of stretch discussed in chapter 8.

5. Sample answer: At the high school level, I would invite a health care professional or certified fitness instructor (so I can still teach the rest of the class) to calculate percent body fat for interested students. I would make this an optional activity, so that students don't feel embarrassed or pressured to participate. I would set up a screened area to ensure privacy. I would have all students find their BMI on the chart to record privately in their physical education journals, cautioning them that this does not indicate percent body fat, but can help identify potential body composition problems.

6. Sample answer: I would not try to "diagnose" a student. Instead, I would refer the parent to a health care professional, trained in identifying and treating eating disorders.

7. Answers will vary.

Answers: Part III

Terminology Review
Sample answers:

1. provides an integrated framework within which students learn the necessary health-related physical fitness concepts, so they can apply them in real life in a developmentally appropriate K–12 progression

2. the ultimate desired achievements of students who graduate from a K–12 curriculum (e.g., the national standards)

3. teaching

4. selecting a way to make a task easier for a lower skilled student or more difficult for a higher skilled student

5. a way of allowing children to adjust the task so they can be successful and challenged

6. activities that are appropriate based on a student's developmental level, age, ability level, interests, previous experience and knowledge

7. the method(s) through which a learning experience is presented for maximal learning

8. maintaining appropriate control of students and the teaching environment to ensure that all students are safe and can learn

9. a course that teaches the basic training principles of health-related fitness, fitness safety, nutrition, fitness consumer awareness, benefits of physical activity, and that lifelong physical activity is individual and can be enjoyable; typically taught in high school and required in many states

10. all students (regardless of needs, abilities, or cultural or religious beliefs) are included in an appropriate manner so that each student can reach his or her maximum potential

11. the practice of including persons with disabilities to the greatest extent possible in the situations their peers without disabilities automatically have access to

12. the practice of placing students with special needs with students without special needs for classes, such as music, art, and physical education, and in the regular classroom for limited times

13. the process of breaking down a task into its component parts

Fact Review

Suggestions for changing false statements to true are sample answers. Synonyms for the new wording suggested are acceptable.

1. F, change "lesson" to "exit"; 2. T; 3. T; 4. F, change "not worry about" to "reflect"; 5. T; 6. T; 7. T ; 8. F, change "linguistic" to "spatial"; 9. F, delete "not"; 10. T; 11. T; 12. T; 13. F, delete "not"; 14. F, change "logical-mathematical" to "linguistic"; 15. F, change "makes no difference in" to "can greatly impact"; 16. T; 17. T; 18. F, delete "not"; 19. T; 20. T

Application Practice and Research

1. Sample answer: Today's physical education curriculum must appeal to the student population, prepare students for the real world, and be responsive to individuals' needs. Programs must also be able to compete with other subject areas and priorities to survive budget cuts.

2. Sample answer: **Command style**—simply tell students that they should run at a medium pace, not too fast and not too slow—try to be steady. **Discovery**—students are asked to try running as fast as they can for the mile—they will be unable to do this and will have to stop and walk, until they recover, and they can run again. Ask students what they think would work better in terms of getting a good time in running the mile. The command style might be more appropriate because it makes sure the information is available before a problem arises. The guided discovery style could be dangerous in this case because students may injure themselves before they learn what they need to know to be safe. However, if students are properly warmed up, the discovery style could work in this example, as long as you carefully monitor your students and stop anyone who appears to be pushing too hard.

3. Sample answer: **Topic**—increasing flexibility with a class of second graders. **Set induction,** *naturalistic intelligence*—discuss more- and less-flexible animals (e.g., monkeys and snakes are flexible, armadillos aren't very, and so on) and how flexibility may help certain animals survive. Then compare this to the human need for flexibility. **Core lesson activity**, *logical-mathematical intelligence*—focus on the first "T" in FITT, time, by counting the number of seconds for an effective stretch (e.g., 1000-1, 1000-2, and so on, to gauge seconds). **Closure**, *interpersonal intelligence*—have partners check each other to ensure they are counting reasonably accurately.

4. Sample answer: List the following aspects of clear communication, and leave a space under each to check off when pertinent examples occur—set induction, logical sequencing of information, examples, nonexamples, using student names, drawing on students' personal experiences, repetition, double-checking student understanding.

5. Answers will vary.

6. See sample assignments in the section titled Becoming a Good Fitness Consumer in chapter 14, for ideas.

7. Keep score on the following aspects of effective discussion leading: asking an open-ended question, giving students time to think before calling on anyone, establishing/insisting that everyone has a right to be heard and respected, requiring a new speaker to summarize previous speaker's comments (on same question), accepting a student's opinions without immediately evaluating them, acting as a facilitator by asking pointed questions, listing key points, ending a line of discussion with a brief summary before students get bored.

8. Use the sample responses in the sidebar as models. Be sure to refrain from becoming defensive.

9. Use the suggestions in the section titled Selecting Appropriate Lifetime Activities in chapter 11, to help you get started. Sample answers: **Topic**—fear of the unfamiliar (e.g., physical activity facilities in the local area); **homework idea for high school students**—visit a local health club or YMCA to learn about membership, facility, and activity options, costs, and sign-up procedures. **Topic**—expense; **homework idea for middle school students**—visit a local sporting goods shop to price check equipment and compare the expenses of various activities. Then visit a shop that sells used equipment and compare to the first shop. **Topic**—lack of skill; **homework idea for elementary students (K–6)**—practice running stride with a checklist of components with which a parent may perform a simple task analysis.

10. Answers will vary.

Answers: Part IV

Terminology Review

1. T; 2. T; 3. F, change "contrived" to "real-world"; 4. F, change "health-related fitness standards that indicate true health, regardless of others' scores" to "other students' fitness performances"; 5. F, change "other students' fitness performances" to "health-related fitness standards that indicate true health, regardless of others' scores"; 6. T

Fact Review

1. real world

2. informal

3. accurately reflects the components you have taught, includes only the components you have told students they'll be assessed on, lists standards to assess by, helps you assess with greater equity among students, states these components and standards clearly, and teaches students how to learn

4. Sample answer: prepare for the testing, involve students in self-testing before administering formal testing, and follow test protocols explained in the testing manual; see other hints in the section titled Preparing for Testing in chapter 17

5. modify

6. discuss, explain

7. how, safely

8. projects

9. taught, planned

10. apply

11. effort

12. plan, reteach

13. timely, thorough, thoughtful

14. honest

15. attitude, motivation

Application Practice and Research

1. Be sure to include key components of the skill on the rubric. A rubric helps you systematically focus on the same components of the skill for each student.

2. Sample answer: I enjoyed seeing all I had done and really felt a sense of accomplishment. I found it difficult to take the time to include much detail in my comments. I rated my colleague as "Exemplary" because his comments met all four criteria listed.

3. Answers will vary.

4. Sample answer (to be read aloud to nonreaders): (1) I like to do the stretches. [smiley face, frowny face] (2) I feel good after stretching. [smiley face, frowny face] (3) I sometimes do stretches outside of school. [smiley face, frowny face] (4) I would like to teach a stretch to a friend or family member. [smiley face, frowny face] (5) I hope we learn more stretches. [smiley face, frowny face]; for high school students, I would write "Yes" and "No" for them to circle, instead of faces, and reword the questions as follows: (1) I like to stretch out. (2) I feel relaxed and calm after stretching. (3) I sometimes work on flexiblity on my own time. (4) I can see how good flexibility has helped me in health-related fitness and other activities. (5) I think I would benefit from learning and doing new stretches. I changed the format and wording to be more appropriate to the older age group. Assessing attitudes is part of assessing the affective domain.

5. Answers will vary.

6. Self-assessment experience and competency prepares a student to monitor his or her own progress, independent of organized programs and formal, professional guidance. This helps empower the student to take responsibility for his or her health-related fitness.

7. Answer should paraphrase: Assessment tells you and your students how they are improving or what they need to work on. Grading attempts to communicate, mainly to parents, all that the individual has done in your physical education program in a single number or letter (Graham 1992).

8. Debate content will vary.

9. Role-playing comments should take the following into consideration: create the most positive fitness testing environment you can, have students practice test items frequently ahead of time, offer a choice of tests within each component, guard student privacy, be sensitive to feelings, and allow students to exempt themselves from formal testing. You might, for example, say to *all* students, "You will not be graded on your performances. Instead, I am interested in finding out where you are physically right now, so I can plan activities that will help you improve. I am most interested in your learning to test yourself, so you can do so outside of class."

10. Sample answer: **project**—commercial to sell physical activity; **group assessment**—a rubric that lists components of the project, including showing they know the benefits of physical activity and speaking to how well they worked together; **individual assessment**—a journal entry at the end of class, without referring to notes, listing at least three benefits of physical activity.

11. Results will vary.

12. Answers will vary.

Chapter 22

Physical Best Health-Fitness Specialist Certification Practice Exam

Chapter 1

1. Which of the following is one reason today's children are more likely than in the past to display one or more risk factors for eventually developing heart disease?

   a. a decline in daily participation in physical education

   b. reductions in state requirements for physical education

   c. the teaching of physical education by unqualified classroom teachers

   d. all of the above

2. Which statement best describes why the Physical Best program was developed?

   a. Physical education provides the best opportunity to prepare all young people to live physically active lives and to inspire them to do so.

   b. A number of veteran physical educators wanted to share what they had learned about improving physical education curriculums to meet the needs of all students.

   c. Increasing students' scores on fitness tests is the most important goal of physical education.

   d. both a and b

3. Which of the following is most likely to help ensure a quality physical activity program?

   a. preventing parents from interfering in program activities

   b. establishing policies that promote enjoyable, lifelong physical activity among young people

   c. establishing as competitive a learning environment as possible

   d. implementing curricula that is not individualized to fit participants' needs

Chapter 2

4. Which of the following *best* outlines the personal factors that may influence physical activity behavior?

   a. gender, age, obesity, knowledge, self-efficacy

   b. family exercise habits, peer exercise habits, safety of neighborhood

   c. gender, age, obesity, season of the year

   d. none of the above

5. Which of the following statements *best* describes extrinsic motivation?

   a. involves inborn motivation

b. involves factors inside the individual

c. involves factors beyond a teacher's control

d. involves factors outside the individual

6. Which of the following is *least* likely to be a reason a young person does not participate regularly in physical activity?

a. a perception of a lack of time

b. feelings of competence in physical activity

c. belonging to a family that enjoys sedentary leisure activities

d. having friends who prefer playing video games

7. Which of the following is *most* likely to motivate students to be more physically active?

a. focusing on activities that are for older or younger students

b. setting the intensity level students must work at for them

c. building in opportunities for all to succeed, increasing students' confidence

d. emphasizing the long-term benefits of physical activity

8. Which of the following is *not* an appropriate step for helping students set goals?

a. giving feedback about progress toward goals

b. setting goals for students without involving them in the process

c. writing down goals

d. setting challenging yet realistic goals

Chapter 3

9. What does it mean to say a health-related physical fitness education program is "realistic"?

a. focuses on accessible lifetime activities applicable to real-life settings

b. focuses on the fact that some students just can't learn

c. focuses on the fact that some students will never be fit

d. focuses on having fun, even if the fitness value of an activity is poor

10. Corbin and Lindsey's (1993) Stairway to Lifetime Fitness

a. shows how to help a student follow teacher directives better

b. outlines developmentally appropriate guidelines for various age groups

c. outlines the process through which a student becomes independently physically active

d. provides assessment strategies

11. In a quality health-related physical fitness education program, what does "individualized" mean in "lifelong, individualized, health-related physical activity"?

a. engaging in activities that maintain or improve any of the components of health-related fitness

b. possessing the knowledge, skills, and self-motivation to regularly engage in physical activities

c. having choices of activities and the knowledge to modify each activity to meet one's needs, without losing its health-related fitness effectiveness

d. performing activities to meet one standard, regardless of ability, needs, or interests

12. Which statement *best* describes an approach to motor skill learning appropriate for high school students in health-related physical fitness education?

a. teaching and drilling them in all the skills they have not yet acquired

b. offering opportunities to learn the skills they need to enjoy participating in the physical activities they find interesting

c. helping an individual find other ways to stay involved, when he or she simply cannot master a skill despite repeated instruction

d. both a and b

e. both b and c

Chapter 4

13. An advantage of block scheduling at the high school level is:

a. not having to see students every day

b. having time to take trips to explore community resources during class time

c. not having time to explore health-related fitness topics in greater depth

d. more time spent on administrative chores

14. Which of the following is an equipment fundraiser *most* in tune with the goals of a quality health-related physical fitness education program?
    a. selling magazine subscriptions
    b. having a book sale
    c. conducting a jog-a-thon
    d. both a and b

15. Caring properly for equipment involves, for example,
    a. tossing it into the equipment room wherever it will fit
    b. discarding owner's manuals to prevent clutter
    c. letting students use the equipment without briefing them as to appropriate procedures
    d. regularly inspecting it

Chapter 5

16. Which of the following statements is correct?
    a. *Progression* is the way in which an individual should deal with specificity.
    b. *Overload* provides a greater stress, or load, than the body is used to.
    c. *Frequency* in the FITT principle is how long an individual exercises.
    d. *Time* in the FITT principle is how often an individual exercises.

17. An appropriate warm up
    a. allows the heart to gradually increase the rate at which it pumps blood to the rest of the body
    b. is anything that gives you time to take attendance
    c. targets the muscles the participant will not use during the workout, so that all areas of the body are exercised
    d. is not essential

18. Base health-related fitness refers to the
    a. maximum level of fitness required by an individual
    b. minimum level of fitness required for health benefits to occur
    c. level of fitness required to succeed in formal interscholastic sport competition
    d. level of fitness required for optimally enjoying recreational sports, activities, and good health

Chapter 6

19. Which of the following fitness tests measures aerobic fitness?
    a. the back-saver sit-and-reach
    b. the mile run
    c. the curl-up test
    d. the pull-up test

20. Which of the following physical activities is most likely to develop aerobic fitness?
    a. sit-ups
    b. bowling
    c. biking
    d. weight lifting

21. What do you need to know to help a student design safe and enjoyable aerobic fittness training sessions?
    a. whether or not the student has serious health conditions, such as asthma
    b. the student's current aerobic endurance fitness level
    c. the aerobic endurance activities the student prefers
    d. all of the above
    e. none of the above

Chapter 7

22. Which fitness test measures one aspect of muscular strength and endurance?
    a. the PACER
    b. the step test
    c. skinfold caliper tests
    d. the curl-up test

23. How might intensity be measured in muscular strength and endurance?
    a. heart rate
    b. amount of resistance and speed of movement, or percent of 1 RM
    c. frequency of workouts
    d. number of push-ups

24. Which of the following is an advantage of training muscular strength and endurance with body weight exercises?
    a. does not require equipment
    b. does not require instruction
    c. cannot quantify repetitions
    d. both a and b

Chapter 8

25. In regard to flexibility, what is "time" in the FITT principle?

 a. how often an individual stretches

 b. the specific muscles an individual stretches

 c. the same as overload

 d. how long an individual holds a stretch multiplied by the number of times performed

26. Which type of stretching is considered most appropriate for the physical education setting?

 a. ballistic

 b. static

 c. dynamic

 d. PNF

27. Which of the following is a key to safe stretching?

 a. bouncing

 b. stretching first thing in a warm-up

 c. using slow, controlled movements

 d. having everyone hold a stretch for the same length of time

(*Note:* Ballistic stretching is not recommended for use in physical education classes.)

Chapter 9

28. Which of the following is a good teaching guideline for teaching students about body composition?

 a. Insist that students participate in skinfold caliper testing.

 b. Be sure to diagnose an eating disorder before referring a student to a health care provider.

 c. Respect each student's privacy.

 d. Outline the absolute indicators of good and poor health related to body composition.

29. How does muscular strength and endurance affect body composition?

 a. Muscle cells use more calories at rest than fat cells do.

 b. Muscular strength and endurance activities burn more calories than other types of physical activities.

 c. Muscular strength and endurance activities raise heart rates enough.

 d. Fat will turn into muscle if it is exercised enough.

30. Which is the *most* accurate method of measuring percent body fat generally available to physical educators?

 a. body mass index charts

 b. underwater weighing

 c. skinfold caliper measurements

 d. height-weight charts

Chapter 10

31. Thirst signals the body's need for water, but

 a. it is unhealthy to drink during exercise

 b. this signal is slow to express the need

 c. sodium and potassium concentrations in the blood will decrease as the body becomes dehydrated

 d. an individual should only drink when he or she feels thirsty

32. Which of the following is true in regard to learning about nutrition?

 a. Students need help separating myth from reality.

 b. "No fat" means you can eat more of the particular food and not worry about weight gain.

 c. There is substantial proof that supplementing the diet with vitamins and minerals beyond the Recommended Daily Allowance (RDA) greatly enhances nutrition.

 d. Cultural and social values and beliefs are not likely to influence an individual's diet.

Chapter 11

33. A curriculum progression should do which of the following?

 a. teach the same material year after year in the same way

 b. ignore student ages and abilities

 c. help students apply and extend their knowledge as they mature

 d. never repeat or reinforce skills

34. Of what are the National Physical Education Standards an example?

 a. lesson outcomes

b. a model curriculum

c. unit outcomes

d. exit outcomes

35. Which of the following is an example of tailoring a health-related physical fitness education curriculum to meet the target population's needs?

a. using fitness test results as the sole basis of grades

b. designing a high school course that helps students meet college entrance requirements

c. waiving certain students' mandated physical education credits

d. downplaying issues of self-esteem and social skill development

Chapter 12

36. Which of the following lists three aspects of an effective teaching-learning environment?

a. enjoyable and active learning environment, a positive class atmosphere, sarcasm used only when necessary

b. enjoyable and active learning environment, a positive class atmosphere, efficient running of class

c. a positive class atmosphere, minimal supervision, efficient running of class

d. active supervision, developmental appropriateness, offering negative feedback frequently

37. Which of the following is an example of the reciprocal style of teaching?

a. allowing students to choose a range of performance levels

b. teacher offering a task sheet to guide individual students as they practice curl-ups independently

c. teacher giving instructions to teach students how to calculate a target heart rate zone

d. partners giving each other feedback as they practice swimming technique

38. Which of the following targets intrapersonal intelligence?

a. calculating a target heart rate zone

b. exchanging performance feedback with a partner

c. personal goal setting

d. enjoying nature while hiking

Chapter 13

39. Among these choices, which is the most developmentally appropriate way to develop aerobic endurance in kindergartners?

a. riding stationary bikes

b. swimming laps

c. playing tag

d. in-line skating

40. Which statement best reflects an appropriate philosophy regarding "fun" in a quality health-related physical fitness education program?

a. Fun is a by-product of effective teaching.

b. Fun is the ultimate goal.

c. Fun is not important.

d. Fun is an important extrinsic motivator.

41. An effective demonstration

a. is accurate

b. uses student demonstrators whenever possible

c. ends with a check for understanding

d. all of the above

42. Which of the following helps a teacher give effective cues?

a. giving lengthy lectures before allowing students to practice

b. designating a reminder word or phrase to help students focus on the target idea

c. offering several ideas at once to ensure students have the information they need

d. not identifying the most important features of a task

Chapter 14

43. Which of the following is *not* recommended core course content for a high school lifetime personal fitness course?

a. understanding the personal nature of fitness

b. knowledge of the benefits of physical activity

c. competitive fitness testing

d. consumer education

44. What is one way a health-related physical fitness educator can offer variety in a lecture setting?

    a. always being sure to lecture at length on different topics

    b. designing activities and assignments to address various types of intelligences

    c. forgetting about technology; the choices are simply expensive toys

    d. sticking with the most natural teaching style

45. Which of the following is *most* likely to help an instructor manage behavior in the lecture setting?

    a. not worrying about keeping class activities varied and developmentally appropriate

    b. not wasting time adapting physical activity setting procedures to the particular classroom setting

    c. allowing students to show disrespect for others' opinions

    d. establishing protocols, such as requiring students to raise their hands to speak

Chapter 15

46. Which of the following *best* illustrates an appropriate application of the term *least restrictive environment*?

    a. allowing a student with special needs to join his nondisabled peers only for special classes, e.g., music, art, and physical education, without taking his needs and abilities into account

    b. including a student with disabilities in every activity her nondisabled peers have access to, regardless of the individual's needs

    c. including a student with cerebral palsy to the greatest extent possible to meet his identified needs

    d. automatically offering a student with special needs the best in separate, but just as good, physical activity programs

47. Which of the following is an appropriate way to be culturally inclusive in health-related physical fitness education?

    a. using physical activities from other cultures, such as active games or sports, to develop aerobic endurance

    b. paying little attention to the interests of students from cultures different from your own or the majority of your student population

    c. insisting on certain uniforms or dress codes to minimize differences even if they go against the cultural or religious beliefs of certain students' particular cultures

    d. banning students from sharing their personal physical activity experiences with the class

Chapter 16

48. A norm-referenced fitness test battery

    a. is the most sophisticated way to assess a student's physical fitness

    b. compares a student to health-related fitness standards that indicate true health, regardless of others' scores

    c. compares a student to other students' fitness performances

    d. is the recommended method of assessing a student's fitness in health-related physical fitness education

49. Asking students to think about the learning process (e.g., How could you improve your flexibility?) and record their thoughts is an example of which assessment tool?

    a. a journal entry

    b. a rubric

    c. a role play

    d. a teacher observation

50. Having students act out how they might convince a friend to quit smoking is an example of which assessment tool?

    a. a journal entry

    b. a rubric

    c. a role play

    d. a teacher observation

Chapter 17

51. Which of the following is *not* an appropriate way to share fitness test results with students?

    a. holding a brief, but private, conference to interpret results

    b. posting test results in the locker room

c. guiding the class through a blank report form

d. sending home the test results sealed in an envelope with a letter of explanation

52. To be part of authentic assessment, fitness testing must

a. not be used for setting personal fitness goals

b. not be used to plan for future learning and fitness gains

c. be conducted in isolation from the rest of the health-related physical fitness education program

d. link directly to the curriculum

53. What should you reward in health-related fitness testing (e.g., *FITNESSGRAM*)?

a. only those students who use correct technique

b. only those students scoring in the Healthy Fitness Zone

c. physical prowess, because this will motivate students to try harder and become more fit

d. effort and participation, because these are more likely to result in health-related fitness

Chapter 18

54. Which of the following might be an appropriate way to assess fitness knowledge at the high school level?

a. conducting a smiley-face exit poll seeking opinions

b. holding a class debate on a fitness topic

c. giving a "pop" abdominal strength fitness test

d. having students record their feelings about a workout in a journal

55. Which of the following is *not* an appropriate way to use cognitive assessment as a teaching tool?

a. discussing each item on a returned written test

b. disregarding results when planning future lessons and units

c. having students share their research or projects with their classmates

d. asking students how they think you can help them learn more

56. Which of the following is an appropriate way to use the results of knowledge assessment in calculating health-related physical fitness education grades?

a. giving no weight to this area

b. using results as the main basis of grades

c. not telling students and parents what weight will be given to results

d. making results a balanced part of grades

Chapter 19

57. Which of the following will *not* help you assess if a student can apply fitness knowledge?

a. a journal or log entry

b. a fitness knowledge test

c. a role-playing scenario

d. a teacher observation

58. Which of the following will *not* help you assess student effort in physical activity?

a. reviewing a student's current criterion-referenced health-related fitness test scores

b. interviewing a student

c. reviewing a student's physical activity log

d. reviewing a student's heart rate monitor data

Chapter 20

59. Which of the following is an example of a question that may reveal student attitudes about physical activity?

a. How do you feel about dancing to build aerobic endurance?

b. How do you calculate a target heart rate zone?

c. How many curl-ups did you perform today?

d. What are some ways to assess your flexibility?

60. What is an important aspect of encouraging students to share their feelings about physical activity?

    a. not overreacting to negative comments

    b. making it safe for students to be honest

    c. taking student feelings into account when designing future lessons and units

    d. all of the above

61. Which of the following statements might belong on an affective assessment rubric?

    a. I know how to take my pulse at two sites.

    b. I enjoy learning how to swim better.

    c. In the front crawl, I bend my elbows during the recovery phase.

    d. I can enter heart rate monitor data into the computer.

Chapter 22 Answers

1. d	22. d	43. c
2. d	23. b	44. b
3. b	24. a	45. d
4. a	25. d	46. c
5. d	26. b	47. a
6. b	27. c	48. c
7. c	28. c	49. a
8. b	29. a	50. c
9. a	30. c	51. b
10. c	31. b	52. d
11. c	32. a	53. d
12. e	33. c	54. b
13. b	34. d	55. b
14. c	35. b	56. d
15. d	36. b	57. b
16. b	37. d	58. a
17. a	38. c	59. a
18. b	39. c	60. d
19. b	40. a	61. b
20. c	41. d	
21. d	42. b	

Appendix A

CDC's *Guidelines for School and Community Programs to Promote Lifelong Physical Activity Among Young People*

1. **POLICY**

   Establish policies that promote enjoyable, lifelong physical activity among young people.

   - Require comprehensive, daily physical education for students in kindergarten through grade 12.

   - Require comprehensive health education for students in kindergarten through grade 12.

   - Require that adequate resources, including budget and facilities, be committed for physical activity instruction and programs.

   - Require the hiring of physical education specialists to teach physical education in kindergarten through grade 12, elementary school teachers trained to teach health education, health education specialists to teach health education in middle and senior high schools, and qualified people to direct school and community physical activity programs and to coach young people in sports and recreation programs.

   - Require that physical education instruction and programs meet the needs and interests of all students.

2. **ENVIRONMENT**

   Provide physical and social environments that encourage and enable safe and enjoyable physical activity.

   - Provide access to safe spaces and facilities for physical activity in the school and the community.

   - Establish and enforce measures to prevent physical activity–related injuries and illnesses.

   - Provide time within the school day for unstructured physical activity.

   - Discourage the use or withholding of physical activity as punishment.

   - Provide health promotion programs for school faculty and staff.

3. **PHYSICAL EDUCATION**

   Implement physical education curricula and instruction that emphasize enjoyable participation in physical activity and that help students develop the

knowledge, attitudes, motor skills, behavioral skills, and confidence needed to adopt and maintain physically active lifestyles.

- Provide planned and sequential physical education curricula from kindergarten through grade 12 that promote enjoyable, lifelong physical activity.
- Use physical education curricula consistent with the national standards for physical education.
- Use active learning strategies and emphasize enjoyable participation in physical education class.
- Develop students' knowledge of and positive attitudes toward physical activity.
- Develop students' mastery of and confidence in motor and behavioral skills for participating in physical activity.
- Provide a substantial percentage of each student's recommended weekly amount of physical activity in physical education classes.
- Promote participation in enjoyable physical activity in the school, community, and home.

4. HEALTH EDUCATION

Implement health education curricula and instruction that help students develop the knowledge, attitudes, behavioral skills, and confidence needed to adopt and maintain physically active lifestyles.

- Provide planned and sequential health education curricula from kindergarten through grade 12 that promote lifelong participation in physical activity.
- Use health education curricula consistent with the national standards for health education.
- Promote collaboration among physical education, health education, and classroom teachers, as well as teachers in related disciplines who plan and implement physical activity instruction.
- Use active learning strategies to emphasize enjoyable participation in physi-

cal activity in the school, community, and home.

- Develop students' knowledge of and positive attitudes toward healthy behaviors, particularly physical activity.
- Develop students' mastery of and confidence in the behavioral skills needed to adopt and maintain a healthy lifestyle that includes regular physical activity.

5. EXTRACURRICULAR ACTIVITIES

Provide extracurricular physical activity programs that meet the needs and interests of all students.

- Provide a diversity of developmentally appropriate competitive and noncompetitive physical activity programs for all students.
- Link students to community physical activity programs, and use community resources to support extracurricular physical activity programs.

6. PARENTAL INVOLVEMENT

Include parents and guardians in physical activity instruction and in extracurricular and community physical activity programs, and encourage them to support their children's participation in enjoyable physical activities.

- Encourage parents to advocate for quality physical activity instruction and programs for their children.
- Encourage parents to support their children's participation in appropriate, enjoyable physical activities.
- Encourage parents to be physically active role models and to plan and participate in family activities that include physical activity.

7. PERSONNEL TRAINING

Provide training for education, coaching, recreation, health care, and other school and community personnel that imparts the knowledge and skills needed to effectively promote enjoyable, lifelong physical activity among young people.

- Train teachers to deliver physical education that provides a substantial percentage of each student's recommended weekly amount of physical activity.
- Train teachers to use active learning strategies needed to develop students' knowledge about, attitudes toward, skills in, and confidence in engaging in physical activity.
- Train school and community personnel how to create psychosocial environments that enable young people to enjoy physical activity instruction and programs.
- Train school and community personnel how to involve partners and the community in physical activity instruction and programs.
- Train volunteers who coach sports and recreation programs for young people.

8. HEALTH SERVICES

Assess physical activity patterns among young people, counsel them about physical activity, refer them to appropriate programs, and advocate for physical activity instruction and programs for them.

- Regularly assess the physical activity patterns of young people, reinforce physical activity among active young people, counsel inactive young people about physical activity, and refer young people to appropriate physical activity programs.

- Advocate for school and community physical activity instruction and programs that meet the needs of young people.

9. COMMUNITY PROGRAMS

Provide a range of developmentally appropriate community sports and recreation programs that are attractive to all young people.

- Provide a diversity of developmentally appropriate community sports and recreation programs for all young people.
- Provide access to community sports and recreation programs for young people.

10. EVALUATION

Regularly evaluate school and community physical activity instruction, programs, and facilities.

- Evaluate the implementation and quality of physical activity policies, curricula, instruction, programs, and personnel training.
- Measure students' attainment of physical activity knowledge, achievement of motor and behavioral skills, and adoption of healthy behaviors.

CDC's *Guidelines for School and Community Programs to Promote Lifelong Physical Activity Among Young People* can be reproduced and adapted without permission. Copies of the guidelines can be downloaded from the Internet at **http://www.cdc.gov**. On the CDC home page, click on *MMWR*, select *Recommendations and Reports,* and then select March 7, 1997. Print copies are available from CDC, Division of Adolescent and School Health, ATTN: Resource Room, 4770 Buford Highway, Mailstop K-32, Atlanta, GA 30341-3742; phone: 888-CDC-4NRG.

Appendix B

Worksheets and Blackline Masters

Fitness Goals Contract

To improve my personal fitness level, I, with the help of my teacher, have set the following fitness goals. I will participate in the activities outlined in this plan to achieve improved physical fitness. Based on my current level of fitness, I believe that these goals are reasonable.

Fitness component test item (Circle appropriate item.)	Score Date: _____	My goal	Activities to improve physical fitness	Follow-up score Date: _____
Aerobic fitness *One-mile walk/run* *PACER*				
Body composition *Percent body fat* *Body mass index*				
Muscular strength and endurance and flexibility *Curl-up*				
Trunk lift				
Push-ups *Modified pull-ups* *Pull-ups* *Flexed-arm hang*				
Back-saver sit-and-reach *Shoulder stretch*				

Student: _____   Date: _____   Teacher: _____

Reprinted, by permission, from AAHPERD, 1999, *Physical Best Activity Guide—Secondary Level.* (Champaign, IL: Human Kinetics), 222.

Activity Goals Contract

Week of _____ My plans are to do:

	Activity I plan to do	Time of day	Friend(s) who will be active with me
Monday			
Tuesday			
Wednesday			
Thursday			
Friday			
Saturday			
Sunday			

Student: _____ Date: _____ Teacher: _____

Reprinted, by permission, from AAHPERD, 1999, *Physical Best Activity Guide—Secondary Level*. (Champaign, IL: Human Kinetics), 219.

Estimated Energy Expenditures for Common Activities

Activity	Cal/min/lb	Cal/min/140 lb	Cal/10 min/lb
Badminton	0.214	29.9	2.14
Baseball (except pitching)	0.132	18.5	1.32
Basketball	0.304	42.6	3.04
Billiards	0.095	13.3	0.95
Bowling	0.207	29.0	2.07
Canoeing (leisurely pace)	0.099	13.9	0.99
Card playing	0.055	7.7	0.55
Carpet sweeping	0.101	14.2	1.01
Circuit training	0.408	57.1	4.08
Cooking	0.101	14.2	1.01
Cycling, 5.5 mph (11:00/mile)	0.141	19.7	1.41
Cycling, 9.4 mph (6:25/mile)	0.220	30.9	2.20
Dancing, aerobic (moderate)	0.225	31.5	2.25
Dancing, modern	0.159	22.2	1.59
Eating	0.051	7.1	0.51
Field hockey	0.304	42.6	3.04
Fishing	0.141	19.7	1.41
Food shopping	0.132	18.5	1.32
Football	0.291	40.7	2.91
Frisbee	0.220	30.9	2.20
Gardening	0.198	27.8	1.98
Golf	0.187	26.2	1.87
Grass mowing	0.247	34.6	2.47
Ice hockey	0.346	48.4	3.46
Jogging, 5.3 mph (11:30/mile)	0.298	41.7	2.98
Jogging, 6.7 mph (9:00/mile)	0.425	59.6	4.25
Jogging, 7.5 mph (8:00/mile)	0.461	64.5	4.61
Judo	0.432	60.5	4.32
Jumping rope, 70/min	0.357	50.0	3.57
Jumping rope, 125/min	0.390	54.6	3.90
Jumping rope, 145/min	0.436	61.1	4.36
Karate	0.445	62.3	4.45
Lacrosse	0.328	46.0	3.28
Lying at ease	0.048	6.8	0.48
Mopping	0.132	18.5	1.32
Sitting quietly	0.046	6.5	0.46
Standing quietly	0.057	8.0	0.57
Tennis	0.240	33.6	2.40
Walking, normal pace	0.176	24.7	1.76
Writing (sitting)	0.064	8.9	0.64

Reprinted, by permission, from AAHPERD, 1999, *Physical Best Activity Guide—Secondary Level*. (Champaign, IL: Human Kinetics), 228.

Aerobic Activity Frequency Log

Name: _____ Date begun: _____

	Sun	Mon	Tue	Wed	Thu	Fri	Sat	Total
Week 1 (beginning _____)								
Week 2 (beginning _____)								
Week 3 (beginning _____)								
Week 4 (beginning _____)								
Week 5 (beginning _____)								
Week 6 (beginning _____)								
Week 7 (beginning _____)								

Using this worksheet: Monitor your heart rate during physical activity. You earn one point for each 10-minute session that your heart rate stays in the aerobic fitness training zone. At the end of each day, write the number of points you earned that day in the box.

Reprinted, by permission, from AAHPERD, 1999, *Physical Best Activity Guide—Secondary Level.* (Champaign, IL: Human Kinetics), 220.

Borg Ratings of Perceived Exertion Scale

6	No exertion at all
7	Extremely light
8	
9	Very light
10	
11	Light
12	
13	Somewhat hard
14	
15	Hard (heavy)
16	
17	Very hard
18	
19	Extremely hard
20	Maximal exertion

Fitness Workout Plan

Name: _____   Date: _____

Week beginning:

Component	Activity	Mon	Tue	Wed	Thu	Fri	Weekend
	Warm-up						
Aerobic fitness							
Muscular strength and endurance							
Flexibility							
Body composition							
	Cool-down						

Reprinted, by permission, from AAHPERD, 1999, *Physical Best Activity Guide—Secondary Level*. (Champaign, IL: Human Kinetics), 223.

Muscular Strength and Endurance Training Log

Name: _____   Date: _____

Monday	Week 1	Week 2	Week 3	Week 4	Week 5	Week 6
	2 × 5	2 × 5	2 × 5	2 × 5	2 × 5	
	2 × 5	2 × 5	2 × 5	2 × 5	2 × 5	
	2 × 10	2 × 10	2 × 10	2 × 10	2 × 10	
	2 × 5	2 × 5	2 × 5	2 × 5	2 × 5	
	2 × 10	2 × 10	2 × 10	2 × 10	2 × 10	
	2 × 5	2 × 5	2 × 5	2 × 5	2 × 5	
	2 × 10	2 × 10	2 × 10	2 × 10	2 × 10	
	2 × 10	2 × 10	2 × 10	2 × 10	2 × 10	

Thursday	Week 1	Week 2	Week 3	Week 4	Week 5	Week 6
	2 × 5	2 × 5	2 × 5	2 × 5	2 × 5	
	2 × 10	2 × 10	2 × 10	2 × 10	2 × 10	
	2 × 5	2 × 5	2 × 5	2 × 5	2 × 5	
	2 × 5	2 × 5	2 × 5	2 × 5	2 × 5	
	2 × 5	2 × 5	2 × 5	2 × 5	2 × 5	
	2 × 10	2 × 10	2 × 10	2 × 10	2 × 10	
	2 × 10	2 × 10	2 × 10	2 × 10	2 × 10	
	2 × 10	2 × 10	2 × 10	2 × 10	2 × 10	

Comments

Date | | | | | | INT

Reprinted, by permission, from AAHPERD, 1999, *Physical Best Activity Guide—Secondary Level*. (Champaign, IL: Human Kinetics), 225.

Appendix C

Working With National Programs

Aerobic and Fitness Association of America
15250 Ventura Boulevard, Suite 200
Sherman Oaks, CA 91403
818-905-0040

American Academy of Pediatrics
141 Northwest Point Boulevard
Elk Grove Village, IL 60007-1098
847-228-5005
http://www.aap.org

American Alliance for Health, Physical Education, Recreation and Dance
1900 Association Drive
Reston, VA 20191
703-476-3400

American Cancer Society
1599 Clifton Road, NE
Atlanta, GA 30329
404-320-3333
800-ACS-2345 (800-227-2345)

American College of Sports Medicine
P.O. Box 1440
Indianapolis, IN 46206-1440
317-637-9200

American Council on Exercise
5820 Oberlin Drive, Suite 102
San Diego, CA 92121
619-535-8227

American Diabetes Association
1660 Duke Street
Alexandria, VA 22314
703-549-1500

American Dietetic Association
216 West Jackson Boulevard, Suite 800
Chicago, IL 60606
312-899-0040

American Fitness Alliance Youth Fitness Resource Center
P.O. Box 5076
1607 N. Market Street
Champaign, IL 61825-5076
Toll-free: 800-747-4457
http://www.americanfitness.net

American Heart Association
7272 Greenville Avenue
Dallas, TX 75231
214-373-6300

American Lung Association
1740 Broadway
New York, NY 10019
212-315-8700

American Medical Association
515 North State Street
Chicago, IL 60610
312-464-5000
http://www.ama-assn.org

American Red Cross
Attn: Public Inquiry Office
11th Floor
1621 North Kent Street
Arlington, VA 22209
703-248-4222
http://www.redcross.org

American Running and Fitness Association
4405 East-West Highway, Suite 405
Bethesda, MD 20814
301-913-9517

Bicycle Federation of America
1506 21st Street, NW, Suite 200
Washington, DC 20036
202-463-6622

Centers for Disease Control and Prevention
1600 Clifton Road, NE
Atlanta, GA 30333
http://www.cdc.gov

IDEA-International Association of Fitness Professionals
6190 Cornerstone Court East, Suite 204
San Diego, CA 92121
619-535-8979

International Health, Racquet & Sportsclub Association
263 Summer Street
Boston, MA 02210
617-951-0055

League of American Bicyclists
749 North 26th Street
Philadelphia, PA 19130
215-232-7543

National Association for Girls and Women in Sport (NAGWS)
1900 Association Drive
Reston, VA 20191-1599
Office: 703-476-3450
Fax: 703-476-9527
http://www.aahperd.org/nagws/

National Association for Sport and Physical Education (NASPE)
1900 Association Drive
Reston, VA 20191
1-800-213-7193 ext. 410
E-mail: **naspe@aahperd.org**
http://www.aahperd.org/naspe/

National Association of Governors' Councils on Physical Fitness and Sports
201 S. Capitol Avenue, Suite 560
Indianapolis, IN 46225

National Coalition for Promoting Physical Activity
P.O. Box 1440
Indianapolis, IN 46206-1440
317-637-9200

National Recreation and Park Association
P.O. Box 6287
Arlington, VA 22206
800-626-6772

National Safety Council
1121 Spring Lake Drive
Itasca, IL 60143
Fax: 630-775-2310
Office: 630-285-1121
E-mail: **webmaster@nsc.org**
http://www.nsc.org

National Youth Sports Safety Foundation
3335 Longwood Avenue, Suite 202
Boston, MA 02115
617-277-1171

President's Council on Physical Fitness and Sports (PCPFS)

200 Independence Avenue, SW
Hubert H. Humphrey Building, Room 738H
Washington, DC 20202-0004
202-690-9000
E-mail: **cspain@osophs.dhhs.gov**

Shape Up America

6707 Democracy Boulevard, Suite 306
Bethesda, MD 20817
301-493-5368

Sporting Goods Manufacturers Association

200 Castlewood Drive
North Palm Beach, FL 33408-5696
561-842-4100

Young Men's Christian Association (YMCA)

101 North Wacker Drive
Chicago, IL 60606
312-977-0031

Young Women's Christian Association (YWCA)

726 Broadway
New York, NY 10003
212-614-2700

Appendix D

Biochemistry of Meeting the Six Fundamental Nutritional Needs

The body is a complex chemical factory that takes raw material from the diet and the air and creates an astounding array of products—including the human body itself. The body needs different nutrients to meet each of its six fundamental needs.

TYPES OF NUTRIENTS

The body needs nutrients from each of the following types for proper functioning and growth. Each type has unique roles in meeting the six fundamental needs and cannot be completely eliminated from a healthful diet.

Water and Electrolytes

Water is essential to life. No other substance is as widely involved in so many diverse functions. Water

- makes up slightly more than half of the normal body weight;
- transports nutrients throughout the circulatory system for delivery to cells and tissues;
- removes waste products, by transporting them from cells and tissues, through the

circulatory system to the kidneys, and then, out of the body in the urine;
- contributes greatly to the buffering system, which maintains the acid-alkaline balance in the body;
- is an important coolant as a temperature-regulation mechanism; and
- is involved as a reactant or solvent in almost every chemical reaction that occurs in the body.

Water may be bottled or delivered by tap. You can also consume water in milk and juices, which contain additional nutrients. Fruits, vegetables, and other foods, as well, contain water and nutrients. Water, however, is the most important nutrient. The body loses two to three quarts of water per day through normal activity—and even more with greater physical activity. Therefore, one must consume at least two to three quarts of various beverages and water daily to maintain adequate levels in the body. Humans can only survive four to five days without water.

Some beverages can actually lead to greater water loss. Caffeine (found in many soft drinks, tea, and coffee) and alcohol are both diuretics—that is, they cause the body to lose more water, usually through increased kidney function. Active people need to replenish their water, not lose even more.

Energy Sources and Building Blocks

Food provides the fuel for maintaining the energy-requiring processes that sustain life. We must constantly replenish energy reserves through nutrients that provide "burnable fuel": carbohydrates, fats, and proteins. Energy is measured in calories. Every calorie, no matter what the source, is equal.

The First and Second Laws of Thermodynamics show us the relationship between energy and nutrition. The First Law tells us that energy can neither be created nor destroyed. It can, however, be converted from one form to another. In nutritional terms, if energy is taken in as food and not used, it is stored as fat. The Second Law states that all systems in the universe have a tendency to become disorganized and chaotic. Preventing this chaos requires continuous energy expenditure. In nutritional terms, there are millions of cells in our body breaking down every second. Nutritional fuels provide the energy to repair, replace, and operate these cells.

Metabolism is a series of chemical reactions, in which the body converts food to useful energy and heat, which it then uses to operate, build, and repair body tissues. Two processes work at the same time. One process, called *anabolism*, joins smaller molecules together to form larger molecules; it occurs, for example, in the growth and repair of cells and tissues. The other process, called *catabolism*, splits larger molecules into smaller molecules; it occurs, for example, when the body splits complex carbohydrates into simple sugars.

Each individual has his or her own rate at which to convert the potential energy available in foodstuffs into stores of body energy. Through physical activity and proper nutrition, a person can improve this rate of conversion: the *resting metabolic rate* (RMR)—or the amount of energy the body requires at rest to carry out such basic physiological functions as breathing, blood flow, and basal nerve and muscle activity. These functions alone consume 60 to 75 percent of the body's daily energy budget.

RMR varies with genetics, age, sex, physical activity level, and body type. Body type is determined by bone and muscle structure. A muscular person will have a higher RMR than a less muscular person of the same weight, because muscle tissue requires more energy to maintain itself than does fat tissue.

Another consequence of the First Law of Thermodynamics is the need to take in building materials. Just as we can only change the form of energy, not create or destroy it, we can only change the form of matter, not create or destroy it. The matter forming the body must come from somewhere; that somewhere is the diet. The body uses nutrients in different ways as raw material for life's energy and structures, just as we might use wood to heat houses or build them.

Carbohydrates

Carbohydrates, both sugars and starches, are the body's principle source of energy. One gram of carbohydrate yields four calories (kilocalories). The body converts all sugars to glucose, the form of sugar that the cells use for energy. Glucose is the building block for other sugars (lactose, maltose, and galactose), amino acids, and nucleic acids.

The body stores any glucose it does not immediately use, since (under the First Law) it can't simply destroy the energy. It converts some of the glucose to glycogen and stores it in the liver and muscle; it converts the rest of the glucose to fat.

Although all cells require some glucose, the brain and nervous system rely almost completely on glucose for energy. The brain and nervous system use two-thirds of the glucose the body requires—about 500 calories a day. Although one can survive longer without carbohydrates than without water, feelings of hunger, sluggishness, and irritability set in, when the glucose levels in the blood drop.

When carbohydrate intake is too low, the glucose and glycogen stores in the liver will be depleted within 24 hours. Although the body can use fat for two-thirds of its energy requirements, it cannot use fat directly for energy in the brain and nervous system. Furthermore, in the absence of sugar, the body breaks down fat into toxic ketone bodies, leading to *ketosis*. The body must look for other stores of glucose to help fuel the brain and nervous system; it breaks down protein sources in the body to make amino acids, which are converted, in turn, to sugars to prevent ketosis.

An adult needs between 120 and 160 grams of simple and complex carbohydrates each day to provide sufficient glucose. There are two types of carbohydrates. The simple sugars—glucose, fructose, sucrose, galactose, and lactose—are found primarily in fruits, vegetables, soft drinks, cakes, candies, and milk. The bloodstream rapidly transports these simple carbohydrates to body tissues. Starches are complex carbohydrates containing linked glucose molecules, and they occur in grains, grain products, and potatoes.

Dietary fibers are complex, indigestible carbohydrates that come from plants. *Insoluble* fiber absorbs water and helps provide the diet with needed bulk for the proper elimination of waste. *Soluble* fiber combines with waste substances to assist in their removal from the body.

Almost all foods, both natural and processed, contain carbohydrates. Grains, fruits, vegetables, and sweets, such as candies and baked goods, all contain both simple and complex carbohydrates to fuel the body. Whole grains and fruit or vegetable seeds and skins contain insoluble dietary fiber, whereas oat bran, apples, barley, beans, carrots, and other vegetables contain soluble fiber.

Proteins

The body uses protein both for fuel and as raw material for synthesizing tissues and hormones. *Proteins* are giant molecules consisting of chains of various of the 20 amino acids, strung together like beads. Protein synthesis requires the simultaneous presence of all 20 amino acids. The body can synthesize 10 of these amino acids, so they are termed *nonessential*. The other 10 amino acids, called the *essential* amino acids, must come from the diet because the body is unable to make them. The breakdown and synthesis of protein is a normal function of the human body. As already mentioned, sugars are the primary fuel for the body. Proteins can be used for fuel, if necessary, because the body can break them down to simple sugars and waste products with a complex series of chemical reactions. Proteins have the same caloric density as carbohydrates—that is, one gram of protein equals four calories.

Dietary protein is broken down into amino acids, which are then absorbed into the bloodstream. Each cell synthesizes the proteins it needs, including enzymes to facilitate and direct chemical reactions and key structural elements of the cell. The body also uses proteins as building blocks for antibodies (which protect the body from invading organisms), blood clots, hormones (such as insulin), and neurotransmitters. Finally, amino acids are precursors in the construction of the nucleic acids DNA and RNA.

The nutritional value of proteins depends on their complement of essential amino acids and their ease of digestion and absorption. Not all sources of proteins in the food supply are equal. A complete protein meal contains all the essential amino acids in the correct amounts required by the human body. Animal sources, such as poultry, meat, fish, eggs, and milk, provide complete proteins. Vegetable sources of protein, such as legumes and grains, are incomplete, because (with the exception of soy protein) they don't provide all the essential amino acids. Vegetarians can obtain complete proteins (and still not eat animal products) by consuming legumes and grains together to create a complete protein.

Fats

Fats play important roles, not only as fuel sources for the body, but also by adding pleasure, satiety (feeling of satisfaction), and taste to foods. The term *fat* refers to all lipids: triglycerides (fats and oils), phospholipids (lecithin), and sterols (cholesterol). Fats are the most dense caloric energy source—one gram of fat equals nine calories.

Triglycerides, the most common form of fat, are composed of three long-chain, fatty acid hydrocarbon molecules joined to a glycerol. Like carbohydrates, fatty acids are composed of carbon, hydrogen, and oxygen. However, fatty acids have many more atoms of carbon and hydrogen in proportion to their oxygen, and so, they supply more energy per gram. Few fatty acids that occur in foods or the body are free. Instead, they are usually found incorporated into trigylcerides. In the body, 99 percent of the stored body lipids are triglycerides.

There are two major types of fatty acids: saturated and unsaturated. Saturated fatty acids, found in shortening and animal fats, are usually solid at room temperature and contain the maximum number of hydrogen atoms per carbon atom; thus, they have no double bonds. Unsaturated fatty acids contain one or more double bonds; they tend to remain liquid at room temperature and to come from plants. Oils, such as olive and canola, are rich in monounsaturated fatty acids, which have only one double bond. Polyunsaturated fatty acids, which are found in vegetable and some fish oils, contain more than one double bond. Margarine is a chemically saturated vegetable oil.

Stored body fat (triglycerides) provides a source of energy, thermal insulation, and protection from mechanical shock. Fatty acids serve as starting materials for important hormonal regulators. The phospholipids and sterols contribute to the cells' structures. Cholesterol serves as the raw material for steroid hormones, vitamin D, and bile. The lack of fat in the diet may lead to hair loss, abnormal skin conditions, failure to resist infection, and poor absorption of fat-soluble vitamins.

Fats can be found in a wide variety of foods, in varying forms and amounts. Triglycerides in the diet deliver fat-soluble vitamins; bring flavor, aroma, and tenderness to foods; slow digestion; and contribute to a sense of satiety. Fats are found in foods of both plant and animal origin. They also are in processed sources, including breads, cakes, candy, dairy products, and cooking fats, such as oils, shortening, and butter. In food, 95 percent of the lipids (triglycerides) are fats and oils, and the remaining 5 percent are other lipids, such as phospholipids and sterols.

Only when fats are consumed in high quantities do they become a threat to an individual's health and well-being. Fats, eaten with awareness and appreciation, can bring pleasure to a meal. If eaten unconsciously and unnecessarily, however, they offer no such benefits. While eating special low-fat foods can, in theory, be beneficial for weight management, make sure your students recognize that most people tend to eat *more* of these reduced fat foods, and may therefore, fail to reduce their caloric intake.

Other Nutrients

Carbohydrates, proteins, and fats are the body's sources for energy for most of its structure. But these nutrients by themselves aren't enough. The body also needs vitamins and minerals to build chemical structures and to make and use energy.

Vitamins

Vitamins are small organic molecules. After it was discovered that a deficiency of vitamins causes disease, they were determined to be essential substances. Only very small amounts of each vitamin are typically required in the diet. Vitamins differ from carbohydrates, fats, and proteins in many ways: They cannot be synthesized by our bodies and must be obtained, instead, from the diet. Furthermore, they can be *oxidized*, or broken down, and rendered unable to perform their duties. Consequently, vitamins must be treated with respect in cooking and storing food.

We know enough about the structure and function of each vitamin to be able to synthesize all of them. Synthetic vitamins are identical in their activity to those of natural origin. The body converts all vitamins to either *coenzymes*, which assist enzymes with cell metabolism and energy production, or regulatory hormone-like molecules.

The nine water-soluble vitamins (see table D.1) dissolve in water and cannot be stored in the body. Therefore, water-soluble vitamins need to be consumed more often than fat-soluble ones.

Table D.1   Water-Soluble Vitamins

Vitamin	Functions	Sources
Thiamine (B_1)	Assists in energy metabolism; has a site on nerve-cell membrane to aid in muscle and tissue response.	Whole-grain foods
Niacin	Energy-transfer reactions and the metabolism of glucose, fat, and alcohol; oxidation-reduction reactions.	Milk, eggs, meat, poultry, fish, whole-grain and enriched breads and cereals
Riboflavin (B_2)	Coenzymes in energy metabolism; supports vision and skin health.	Milk, yogurt, cottage cheese, meat, green leafy vegetables, whole-grain bread and cereals
Biotin	Part of coenzyme used in energy metabolism, fat synthesis, amino-acid metabolism, and glycogen synthesis.	Widespread in foods
Pantothenic acid	Energy metabolism.	Widespread in foods
Pyridoxal (B_6)	Helps make red blood cells; energy metabolism, amino-acid metabolism.	Green leafy vegetables, meats, fish, poultry, legumes, fruits, whole grains
Folate	New cell formation; nucleic-acid metabolism.	Green leafy vegetables, legumes, seeds, liver
B_{12}	New cell synthesis; maintains nerve cells; helps break down some fatty acids and amino acids.	Animal products (meat, fish, poultry, dairy, eggs)
Vitamin C	Collagen synthesis; antioxidant; amino-acid metabolism; absorption of iron.	Citrus fruits, cabbage-type vegetables, dark green vegetables, cantaloupe, strawberries, peppers, tomatoes, potatoes

Reprinted, by permission, from AAHPERD, 1998, *Physical Best Activity Guide—Elementary Level*. (Champaign, IL: Human Kinetics), 75.

The four fat-soluble vitamins (see table D.2) dissolve in fat and can be stored in the body. They are found in oils, greens, milk, and eggs. Given the proper precursors, the body can manufacture vitamins A and D. For example, the body can convert beta carotene, which is found in melons, squash, and carrots, to vitamin A. Sunlight on the skin helps transform cholesterol to vitamin D.

Minerals

Minerals are inorganic elements that dissolve in water to become charged particles. Minerals cannot be changed, so they keep their chemical identity. Nevertheless, they may be incorporated into proteins and other body structures. Minerals are involved in many aspects of the body's functioning. For example, they are important in both electrolyte balance and acid-base balance. Nerve and muscle func-

Table D.2 Fat-Soluble Vitamins

Vitamin	Functions	Sources
Vitamin A	Vision, maintenance of the cornea, epithelial cells, mucous membranes; growth of skin, bone, and teeth.	Fortified milk, cheese, eggs, spinach, broccoli, orange fruits and vegetables
Vitamin D	Bone metabolism.	Sunlight, fortified milk, egg yolk, liver, fatty fish
Vitamin E	Antioxidant, stabilization of cell membranes.	Plant oils, green leafy vegetables, wheat germ, egg yolks
Vitamin K	Blood clotting; bone metabolism.	Liver, green leafy vegetables, milk

Reprinted, by permission, from AAHPERD, 1998, *Physical Best Activity Guide—Elementary Level*. (Champaign, IL: Human Kinetics), 76.

Table D.3 Major Macrominerals

Macromineral	Functions	Sources
Calcium	Bone building; regulation of muscle activity; vision.	Milk products
Magnesium	Bone building; glucose utilization.	Nuts, avocados
Phosphorus	Bone building; cellular structure; cellular energy transfer.	Meat, fish, milk products
Sodium	Electrolyte balance; nerve and muscle function.	Salt
Potassium	Electrolyte balance; nerve and muscle function.	Bananas
Chloride	Electrolyte balance; nerve and muscle function.	Salt
Sulfur	Joint lubrication (in body-synthesized amino acids); allergic inflammation.	Meat, fish, milk products

Reprinted, by permission, from AAHPERD, 1998, *Physical Best Activity Guide—Elementary Level*. (Champaign, IL: Human Kinetics), 76.

tioning depends critically on minerals, and many enzymes require minerals as a cofactor (necessary helper) in order to function. The structures of many cells and tissues, particularly bone, also rely on minerals.

The body requires the major minerals (*macrominerals*) in the largest amounts (see table D.3). Minerals, except for calcium, are readily absorbed into the blood, freely transported, and rapidly excreted by the kidneys.

As a result, the only mineral that the body stores is calcium; the others are quickly used or lost in waste products. Thus, mineral-rich foods must be eaten regularly to replenish the body's supply.

Minerals are plentiful in the food supply, except for calcium and magnesium. Not enough people eat dairy products, which can supply 80 percent of the available calcium in a typical diet. Inadequate dietary calcium is the most common serious mineral deficiency. While we must realize sodium's importance, too much sodium can lead to high blood pressure.

Trace elements are also vital to one's health. They are the minerals (see table D.4) that must be consumed in small amounts, hence they are called *microminerals*. There are 10 essential trace elements, the best known of which are iron, copper, zinc, iodine, and selenium. Trace elements, used as enzyme cofactors, are a crucial part of systems for oxygen transport, respiration, and the regulation of metabolism.

FOODS, FOOD GROUPS, AND NUTRITIONAL VALUE

Just as the body needs nutrients of each type previously discussed, it needs to obtain those

Table D.4   Trace Elements

Trace element	Functions	Sources
Iron	Hemoglobin protein; oxygen transport; respiration.	Red meats, fish, poultry, shellfish, eggs, legumes, dried fruits
Zinc	Insulin; genetic material and proteins; immune reactions; transport of vitamin A; taste perception; wound healing; bone metabolism.	Protein-containing foods; meats, fish, grains, vegetables
Iodine	Thyroid hormone.	Seafood, bread, dairy products
Copper	Respiration; heme synthesis; collagen synthesis; bone metabolism.	Meats, shellfish, nuts
Manganese	Enzyme cofactors; bone and collagen.	Meats, nuts
Selenium	Oxidation reduction, antioxidants, collagen.	Grains, seafood
Fluorine	Tooth and bone development.	Grains
Chromium	Maintains glucose homeostasis.	Meats, unrefined foods, fats, vegetable oils
Molybdenum	Facilitates (with enzymes) many cell processes.	Legumes, cereals, organ meats
Cobalt	Part of vitamin B_{12}; nerve formation and blood formation.	Meat, milk, dairy

Reprinted, by permission, from AAHPERD, 1998, *Physical Best Activity Guide—Elementary Level*. (Champaign, IL: Human Kinetics), 77.

nutrients from a variety of foods. There are no "health foods," in the sense that eating a disproportionate amount of that food will necessarily result in better nutrition or better health. Similarly, there are no "junk foods," in the sense that eating any of that food at all will necessarily result in poor nutrition or poor health.

Tables D.5 and D.6 list the nutritional values of a variety of foods. Table D.5 lists unprepared, basic foods, while Table D.6 includes fast-food menu items likely to be encountered by your students. Keep in mind that the preparation of raw foods can dramatically change their nutritional values. For example, compare the different values for french fries, a plain baked potato, and the total values for that plain baked potato with sour cream.

Table D.5 Nutrient Values of Common Foods

	Measure	E (kcal)	P (g)	C (g)	DF (g)	Fat Total	Fat Sat	Mono	CH (mg)	CA (mg)	I (mg)	S (mg)
Beverages												
Beer												
Regular (12 fl oz)	1 1/2 c	146	1	13	3	0	0	0	0	18	.11	18
Light (12 fl oz)	1 1/2 c	99	1	5	1	0	0	0	0	18	.14	11
Gin, rum, vodka, whiskey (80 proof)	1 1/2 fl oz	97	0	0	0	0	0	0	0	0	.02	<1
Wine												
Red	3 1/2 fl oz	74	<1	2	0	0	0	0	0	8	.44	5
White	3 1/2 fl oz	70	<1	1	0	0	0	0	0	9	.33	5
Carbonated												
Cola beverage (12 fl oz)	1 1/2 c	152	0	38	0	<1	.02	.03	0	11	.11	15
Diet cola w/aspartame (12 fl oz)	1 1/2 c	4	<1	<1	0	0	0	0	0	14	.11	21
Coffee, brewed	1 c	5	<1	1	0	<1	0	0	0	5	.12	5
Gatorade	1 c	60	0	15	0	0	0	0	0	0	.12	96
Tea												
Brewed, regular	1 c	2	0	1	0	<1	0	0	0	0	.05	7
From instant, sweetened	1 c	89	<1	22	0	<1	t	0	0	5	.05	8
Dairy												
Cheese, natural												
Cheddar	1 oz	114	7	<1	0	9	6	2.7	30	204	.19	176
Cottage: small curd, low-fat 2%	1 c	203	31	8	0	4	2.8	1.2	19	155	.36	918
Cream	1 oz	99	2	1	0	10	6.2	2.8	31	23	.34	84
Cream, low fat	1 oz	65	3	2	0	5	3.1	1.4	16	32	.48	84
Feta	1 oz	75	4	1	0	6	4.2	1.3	25	140	.18	316
Mozzarella, part-skim milk, low moisture	1 oz	79	8	1	0	5	3.1	1.4	15	207	.07	149
Swiss	1 oz	106	8	1	0	8	5	2.1	26	272	.05	74
Pasteurized, processed												
American	1 oz	106	6	<1	0	9	5.6	2.5	27	174	.11	405
Half & half (cream & milk)	1 tbs	19	<1	1	0	2	1.1	.5	6	16	.01	6
Cream, sour, cultured	1 tbs	30	<1	1	0	3	1.8	.8	6	16	.01	7
Milk, fluid												
Whole	1 c	150	8	11	0	8	5.1	2.3	33	290	.12	120
2% low-fat	1 c	121	8	12	0	5	2.9	1.3	18	298	.12	122
1% low-fat	1 c	102	8	12	—	3	1.6	.8	10	300	.12	123
Nonfat, vitamin A added	1 c	86	8	12	0	<1	.3	.1	4	301	.1	126
Ice cream, vanilla (about 10% fat)												
Hardened, 1/2 gallon	1 c	267	5	31	<1	15	9	4.2	59	170	.12	106
Soft serve	1 c	372	7	38	<1	22	12.9	6	157	227	.36	106
Chocolate pudding (5 oz can, .55 c)	1 ea	189	4	32	1	6	1	2.4	4	128	.72	183
Vanilla pudding, instant	1/2 c	148	4	26	<1	4	2.3	1.1	14	131	.09	372
Yogurt, frozen, low-fat	1 c	276	6	42	0	10	6	2.8	4	248	.52	152
Eggs												
Whole, w/o shell (raw, large)	1 ea	74	6	1	0	5	1.5	1.9	213	25	.72	63
White (raw, large)	1 ea	17	4	<1	0	0	0	0	0	2	.01	54
Egg Beaters, Fleischmann's	1/4 c	30	6	1	0	0	0	0	0	40	1.08	100

(continued)

	Measure	E (kcal)	P (g)	C (g)	DF (g)	Fat (g) Total	Sat	Mono	CH (mg)	CA (mg)	I (mg)	S (mg)
Fats and Oils												
Butter: stick	1 tbs	100	<1	<1	0	11	7.1	3.4	31	3	.02	117
Margarine: regular, soft (about 80% fat)	1 tbs	100	<1	<1	0	11	1.9	5.1	0	4	0	103
Oils												
Canola	1 tbs	124	0	0	0	14	1	8.2	0	0	0	0
Corn	1 tbs	124	0	0	0	14	1.8	3.4	0	0	0	0
Olive	1 tbs	124	0	0	0	14	1.9	10.3	0	<1	.05	<1
Salad dressings/sandwich spreads												
French, regular	1 tbs	69	<1	3	<1	9	1.5	1.2	9	2	.06	219
French, low calorie	1 tbs	21	<1	3	<1	1	.1	.2	1	2	.06	126
Italian, regular	1 tbs	70	<1	1	<1	9	1	1.6	0	2	.03	118
Italian, low calorie	1 tbs	16	<1	1	<1	1	.2	.3	1	<1	.03	118
Mayonnaise												
Regular (soybean)	1 tbs	100	<1	<1	0	11	1.6	3.1	8	3	.07	80
Regular, low calorie	1 tbs	37	<1	3	0	3	.5	.7	4	<1	0	80
Ranch, regular	1/2 c	436	4	6	0	45	6.7	19.4	47	119	.31	522
Ranch, low calorie	1 tbs	32	0	1	0	3	.5	—	5	11	0	150
Vinegar & oil	1 tbs	72	0	<1	0	8	1.5	2.4	0	0	0	<1
Fruits and Fruit Juices												
Apples: fresh, raw, w/peel, 2 3/4" diam (about 3 per lb w/cores)	1 ea	81	<1	21	3	<1	.1	t	0	10	.25	0
Apple juice, bottled or canned	1 c	116	<1	29	<1	<1	<1	t	0	17	.92	7
Bananas, raw, w/o peel: whole, 8 3/4" long (175g w/peel)	1 ea	104	1	27	2	1	.2	t	0	7	.35	1
Grapefruit: pink/red, half fruit	1 ea	37	1	9	2	<1	t	t	0	13	.15	0
Grapes: Thompson seedless, raw	10 ea	35	<1	9	<1	<1	.1	t	0	6	.13	1
Kiwi fruit, raw, peeled (88g w/peel)	1 ea	46	1	11	1	<1	t	.1	0	20	.31	4
Cantaloupe, 5" diam (2 1/3 lb whole w/refuse), orange flesh	1/2 ea	93	2	22	2	1	.1	.1	0	29	.56	24
Oranges, raw: whole w/o peel & seeds, 2 5/8" diam (180 g w/peel & seeds)	1 ea	62	1	15	3	<1	t	t	0	52	.13	0
Orange juice: fresh, all varieties	1 c	112	2	26	<1	<1	.1	.1	0	27	.5	2
Orange juice frozen concentrate: diluted w/3 parts water by volume	1 c	112	2	27	<1	<1	t	t	0	22	.25	3
Peaches: raw, whole, 2 1/2" diam, peeled, pitted (about 4 per lb whole)	1 ea	37	1	10	2	<1	t	t	0	4	.1	0
Pears: fresh, w/skin, cored: Bosc, 2 1/5" diam (about 3 per lb)	1 ea	83	1	21	3	1	t	.1	0	16	.35	0
Pineapple: fresh chunks, diced	1 c	76	1	19	2	1	t	.1	0	11	.57	2
Raisins, seedless	1 c	435	5	115	5	1	.2	t	0	71	3.02	17
Strawberries: fresh, whole, capped	1 c	45	1	10	2	1	t	.1	0	21	.57	1
Watermelon: raw, w/o rind & seeds, diced	1 c	51	1	11	1	1	.2	.1	0	13	.27	3
Baked Goods: Breads, Cakes, Cookies, Crackers, Pies												
Bagels, plain, enriched, 3 1/2" diam	1 ea	187	7	36	2	1	.1	.1	0	50	2.43	363
Biscuits from refrigerated dough	1 ea	75	1	9	<1	4	.2	1	1	24	.44	158

Food	Amount											
Breads												
French/Vienna, enriched	1 slice	68	2	13	1	1	.2	.3	0	19	.63	152
Mixed grain, enriched	1 slice	62	3	12	2	1	.2	.4	0	23	.87	122
Pita pocket, enriched, 6 1/2" round	1 ea	165	5	33	1	1	.1	.1	0	52	1.58	322
Rye, light (1/3 rye & 2/3 enriched wheat flour)	1 slice	65	2	12	2	1	.2	.3	0	18	.71	165
White, enriched	1 slice	67	2	12	1	1	.2	.4	<1	27	.71	135
Whole-wheat	1 slice	69	3	13	2	1	.3	.5	0	20	.94	147
Cakes, prepared from mixes												
Angel food	1 pce (1/12)	137	3	31	1	<1	.1	t	0	74	.28	397
Devil's food, choc. frosting	1 pce (1/16)	253	3	38	2	11	3.2	6.2	32	30	1.52	230
Pound cake (from recipe w/enriched flour)	1/2" slice	109	3	14	<1	6	3	1.5	0	5	.1	88
Cheesecake	1 pce (1/12)	295	5	23	2	21	10.6	7.1	51	47	.58	190
Cheese puffs/Cheetos	1 oz	155	2	15	<1	10	1.9	5.8	1	16	.67	294
Cookies made w/enriched flour												
Chocolate chip (home recipe, 2 1/4" diam)	4 ea	195	2	23	1	11	3.2	4.2	13	16	.99	144
Fig bars	4 ea	195	2	40	3	4	.7	2.2	0	36	1.63	196
Peanut butter (home recipe, 2 5/8" diam)	4 ea	228	4	28	1	11	2.1	5.2	15	19	1.08	249
Shortbread, commercial, small	4 ea	161	2	21	1	8	2	4.3	6	11	.88	146
Corn chips	1 oz	151	2	16	1	9	1.3	2.7	0	36	.37	179
Crackers												
Graham	2 ea	59	1	11	<1	1	.4	.7	0	3	.52	85
Saltine	4 ea	52	1	9	<1	1	.3	.8	0	14	.65	156
Croissants, 4 1/2 x 4 x 1 3/4"	1 ea	231	5	26	1	12	6.7	3.2	43	21	1.16	424
Doughnuts: cake type, plain, 3 1/4" diam	1 ea	211	3	25	1	11	1.9	4.8	18	22	.98	273
English muffin: plain, enriched	1 ea	134	4	26	2	1	.1	.2	0	99	1.43	264
Muffins, 2 1/2" diam, 1 1/2" high (from commercial mix)												
Blueberry	1 ea	135	2	22	1	4	.7	1.6	21	11	.51	197
Bran, wheat	1 ea	124	3	21	4	4	1.1	2.1	31	14	1.14	210
Cornmeal	1 ea	144	3	22	2	5	1.3	2.4	28	34	.88	358
Pancakes, 4" diam: plain, from mix: egg, milk, oil added	1 ea	52	1	10	<1	1	.1	.2	3	34	.42	170
Pies, 9" diam; crust made w/vegetable shortening, enriched flour												
Apple	1 pce (1/6)	374	3	54	3	17	3.3	9.4	0	17	.71	420
Chocolate cream	1 pce (1/6)	561	10	62	1	32	10	13	105	161	2.04	487
Custard	1 pce (1/6)	319	8	32	2	18	4.2	8.8	50	122	.88	365
Lemon meringue	1 pce (1/6)	375	2	66	2	12	2.2	5.1	63	78	.85	204
Pecan	1 pce (1/6)	552	6	79	5	25	5.2	14.9	44	23	1.45	585
Pumpkin	1 pce (1/6)	433	8	56	6	20	4.2	10.3	41	124	1.63	581
Pretzels: thin twists, 3 1/4 x 2 1/4 x 1/4"	10 ea	229	5	47	2	2	.4	.8	0	22	2.59	1029
Toaster pastries, fortified (Poptarts)	1 ea	212	3	38	1	6	.8	2.2	0	14	1.89	226
Tortilla chips												
Plain	1 oz	140	2	18	2	6	.2	4.4	0	0	0	135
Nacho flavor	1 oz	139	2	18	1	7	1.4	4.3	1	42	.4	198
Tortillas												
Corn, enriched, 6" diam	1 ea	67	2	14	2	1	.1	.2	0	52	.42	48
Flour, 8" diam	1 ea	115	3	20	1	2	.4	1	0	44	1.17	169
Taco shells	1 ea	66	1	9	1	3	.4	1.5	0	22	.35	51

(continued)

(continued)

Measure	E (kcal)	P (g)	C (g)	DF (g)	Fat (g) Total	Fat (g) Sat	Mono	CH (mg)	CA (mg)	I (mg)	S (mg)
Grain Products: Cereal, Flour, Grain, Pasta and Noodles, Popcorn											
Oatmeal or rolled oats											
Plain, from packet	3/4 c	104	4	18	3	2	.3	.6	0	162	6.3	283
Flavored, from packet	3/4 c	167	4	33	2	2	.3	.6	0	172	7	235
Breakfast cereals, ready-to-eat											
All-Bran	1/3 c	70	4	21	10	1	.1	.1	0	23	4.52	315
Cap'n Crunch	1 c	156	2	30	1	3	2.2	.4	0	6	9.81	278
Cheerios	1 c	90	3	16	2	1	.3	.5	0	39	3.66	249
Corn Chex	1 c	110	2	25	<1	1	.1	.2	0	3	1.8	268
Corn Flakes, Kellogg's	1 1/4 c	109	2	24	1	<1	t	t	0	1	1.8	286
Cracklin' Oat Bran	1 c	229	6	41	10	9	2.1	2.3	0	40	3.78	487
Frosted Flakes	1 c	133	2	32	1	<1	t	t	0	1	2.21	283
Grape Nuts	1/2 c	203	7	47	6	<1	t	t	0	5	2.47	396
Kix	1 c	74	2	16	<1	<1	.1	t	0	24	5.44	194
Lucky Charms	1 c	125	3	26	1	1	.2	.4	0	36	5.09	227
Product 19	1 c	125	3	27	1	<1	t	t	0	4	21	378
Raisin Bran, Kellogg's	1 c	152	5	37	5	1	.2	.1	0	17	22.2	271
Rice Krispies, Kellogg's	1 c	114	2	25	<1	<1	t	t	0	5	1.83	213
Special K	1 c	83	4	16	1	<1	t	t	<1	6	3.39	196
Total, wheat, w/added calcium	1 c	116	3	26	4	1	.1	.1	0	282	21	326
Macaroni, cooked, enriched	1 c	197	7	40	2	1	.1	.1	0	10	1.96	1
Egg noodles, cooked, enriched	1 c	213	8	40	2	2	.5	.7	53	19	2.54	11
Popcorn											
Air popped, plain	1 c	31	1	6	1	<1	<1	.1	0	1	.21	<1
Microwaved, low fat, low sodium	1 c	24	1	4	1	1	.1	.2	0	1	.13	28
Popped in vegetable oil, salted	1 c	55	1	6	1	3	.5	.9	0	1	.31	97
Rice, white: regular/long grain, cooked	1 c	267	6	58	1	<1	.2	.2	0	20	2.48	2
Spaghetti, w/o salt, enriched	1 c	197	7	40	2	1	.1	.1	0	10	1.96	1
Meats: Fish and Shellfish											
Catfish, breaded/flour fried	4 oz	325	21	14	1	20	5	9	92	40	1.44	597
Cod, batter fried	4 oz	196	20	8	<1	9	2.2	3.6	64	43	.9	124
Cod, poached, no added fat	4 oz	116	25	0	0	1	.2	.1	61	23	.54	69
Fish sticks, breaded pollock	2 ea	155	9	14	<1	7	1.8	2.9	64	11	.42	331
Halibut, baked or broiled	4 oz	158	30	0	0	3	.5	1.1	47	68	1.21	78
Salmon, baked or broiled	4 oz	244	31	0	0	13	2.2	6	99	8	.62	75
Shrimp											
Cooked, boiled, 2 large (11g)	16 ea	85	18	1	0	1	.2	.2	167	33	2.65	192
Fried, 2 large (15g)	12 ea	218	19	10	<1	11	1.9	3.6	159	60	1.13	309
Swordfish, baked or broiled	4 oz	176	29	0	0	6	1.6	2.2	57	7	1.18	130
Tuna, light, canned, drained, water packed	3 oz	98	22	0	0	1	.2	.1	25	9	1.3	287
Meats: Beef, Lamb, Pork, and Others											
Beef, cooked											
Ground beef, broiled, patty (3 x 5/8") lean, 21% fat	4 oz	316	32	0	0	20	7.9	8.7	114	14	2.78	101
Steak, broiled, choice sirloin, lean only	4 oz	228	34	0	0	9	3.5	3.9	101	12	3.81	75

Food	Serving											
Steak, broiled, relatively fat, choice T-bone												
Lean and fat	4 oz	337	28	0	0	24	9.7	10.1	94	9	3.01	69
Lean only	4 oz	242	32	0	0	12	4.7	4.7	91	8	3.4	74
Pork, cured, cooked												
Bacon, medium slices	3 pce	109	6	<1	0	9	3.3	4.5	16	2	.31	303
Canadian-style bacon	2 pce	87	11	1	0	4	1.3	1.9	27	5	.38	726
Ham, roasted, lean only	4 oz	177	24	0	0	6	2	3	62	8	1	1500
Pork, fresh, cooked												
Chops, loin (cut 3 per lb w/bone)												
Broiled, lean and fat	1 ea	211	24	0	0	12	4.6	5.4	70	17	.76	54
Broiled, lean only	1 ea	151	21	0	0	7	2.6	3.4	57	12	.66	46
Meats: Poultry and Poultry Products												
Chicken, cooked												
Fried, batter dipped												
Breast (5.6 oz w/bones)	1 ea	364	35	13	<1	18	4.9	7.6	119	28	1.75	385
Drumstick (3.4 oz w/bones)	1 ea	192	16	6	<1	11	3	4.6	62	12	.97	193
Thigh	1 ea	238	19	8	<1	14	3.8	5.8	80	15	1.25	247
Roasted												
Breast, w/o skin	1 ea	141	27	0	0	3	.9	1.1	73	13	.89	64
Drumstick	1 ea	95	12	0	0	5	1.4	2	41	5	.57	40
Thigh, w/o skin	1 ea	108	13	0	0	6	1.6	2.2	49	6	.68	46
Turkey												
Roasted, meat only												
Dark meat	4 oz	250	31	0	0	13	4	4	101	37	2.64	86
Light meat	4 oz	223	32	0	0	9	2.7	3.8	86	24	1.53	71
Meats: Sausages and Lunchmeats												
Bologna												
Beef	1 pce	72	3	<1	0	7	2.8	3.2	13	3	.38	226
Healthy Favorites	2 ea	45	7	2	0	1	0	—	15	—	.36	510
Turkey	1 pce	56	4	<1	0	4	1.4	1.4	28	24	.43	246
Frankfurters												
Beef, large link, 8/package	1 ea	180	7	1	0	16	6.9	7.7	35	11	.81	585
Turkey, 10/package	1 ea	101	6	1	0	8	2.7	2.5	39	48	.83	641
Ham lunchmeat, regular	2 pce	103	10	2	0	6	1.9	2.8	32	4	.56	746
Turkey breast, fat free	1 pce	25	4	1	0	0	0	0	10	0	0	310
Turkey pastrami	2 pce	80	10	1	0	4	1	1.2	31	5	.95	595
Mixed Dishes and Fast Foods												
Beef stew w/vegetables, homemade	1 c	218	16	15	2	10	4.9	4.5	64	29	2.94	292
Buffalo wings/spicy chicken wings	2 ea	98	8	<1	<1	7	1.8	2.8	26	5	.4	61
Chicken chow mein, canned	1 c	95	6	18	2	1	0	.1	8	45	1.25	725
Chicken fajitas	1 ea	344	17	43	4	11	2	5	35	71	3	372
Chicken salad w/celery	2 c	268	11	1	<1	25	4	7.2	47	16	.62	201
Chili w/beans, canned	1 c	286	15	30	11	14	6	5.9	43	120	8.75	1331
Coleslaw	1 c	178	2	15	2	13	2	2.9	6	41	.88	324
Egg roll, w/meat	1 ea	114	5	9	1	6	1.6	2.9	38	12	.77	305
Lasagna (w/meat, homemade)	1 pce	382	22	39	3	15	7.7	5	56	258	3.43	745
Macaroni & cheese, homemade	1 c	430	17	40	1	22	8.9	8.8	42	362	1.8	1086
Meat loaf, beef	1 pce	185	14	5	<1	11	4	4.8	72	35	1.61	329

(continued)

(continued)

	Measure	E (kcal)	P (g)	C (g)	DF (g)	Fat Total	Fat Sat	Mono	CH (mg)	CA (mg)	I (mg)	S (mg)
Potato salad w/mayonnaise & eggs	1/2 c	179	3	14	2	10	1.8	3.1	85	24	.81	661
Fried rice (meatless)	1 c	264	5	34	1	11	1.7	2.9	42	30	1.84	286
Spaghetti (enriched) in tomato sauce, with cheese												
Canned	1 c	190	5	38	2	1	0	.4	8	40	2.75	955
Homemade	1 c	260	9	37	2	9	2	5.4	8	80	2.25	955
Sandwiches (on part whole wheat)												
Avocado, cheese, tomato, lettuce	1 ea	454	14	33	5	31	9	12.6	32	277	3.01	525
Bacon, lettuce, tomato	1 ea	398	13	32	3	25	6	9.5	27	73	2.6	753
Cheese, grilled	1 ea	389	18	27	2	24	12.3	7.7	53	405	2.08	1143
Chicken salad	1 ea	366	10	27	2	25	4	7	31	67	2.13	461
Egg salad	1 ea	375	9	27	2	26	4.5	8	146	77	2.36	521
Ham	1 ea	257	17	22	2	11	2.3	4.1	35	56	2.09	1274
Ham & cheese	1 ea	384	22	27	3	21	7.8	6.9	57	236	2.49	1578
Peanut butter & jelly	1 ea	341	11	46	4	14	2.8	6.6	0	73	2.52	305
Reuben, grilled: corned beef, swiss cheese, sauerkraut on rye	1 ea	639	29	40	5	40	13.7	12.8	114	411	3.68	1685
Roast beef	1 ea	311	23	25	2	13	2.8	4.3	34	56	3.33	1254
Tuna salad	1 ea	326	13	30	3	17	3	5	14	67	2.35	557
Turkey	1 ea	267	19	21	2	11	2	3.5	34	53	1.8	1249
Vegetarian burger, no salt added (Worthington)	1/2 c	150	22	7	—	4	—	—	—	—	1.80	170
Nuts, Seeds, and Products												
Almonds: whole, dried, unsalted	1 oz	165	6	6	3	15	1.4	9.6	0	75	1.04	3
Cashew nuts: oil roasted, salted	1 oz	161	5	8	1	14	2.7	8	0	11	1.16	175
Macadamias: oil roasted, salted	1 oz	201	2	4	3	21	3.2	16.9	0	13	.5	73
Peanuts: oil roasted, salted	1 oz	163	7	5	2	14	1.9	6.9	0	25	.52	123
Peanut butter	2 tbs	188	8	7	2	16	3.1	7.6	0	11	.54	153
Sunflower seed kernels: oil roasted	1/4 c	209	7	5	2	19	2	3.7	0	19	2.28	1
English walnuts, chopped	1 oz	180	4	5	1	17	1.6	4	0	27	.69	3
Sweets												
Almond Joy candy bar	1 oz	130	1	16	2	8	4.7	1.5	1	22	.34	38
Milk chocolate												
Plain	1 oz	143	2	17	1	9	5.2	2.8	6	54	.39	23
With almonds	1 oz	147	3	15	2	10	4.8	3.8	5	63	.46	21
Gumdrops	1 oz	108	0	28	0	<1	0	t	0	1	.11	12
Jellybeans	1 oz	104	0	26	0	<1	0	t	0	1	.31	7
Milky Way candy bar	1 ea	251	3	43	1	9	4.7	3.3	12	78	.46	144
Reese's peanut butter cups	2 ea	218	5	21	2	14	10.4	.9	7	35	.49	131
Snickers candy bar (2.2 oz)	1 ea	278	6	37	2	14	7.3	4.1	7	70	.48	164
Chocolate syrup												
Hot fudge type	2 tbs	131	2	22	<1	5	2.2	1.4	5	38	.46	49
Thin type	2 tbs	83	1	22	1	<1	.2	.1	0	5	.81	36
Vegetables and Legumes												
Asparagus, green, cooked, from fresh, cuts and tips	1/2 c	22	2	4	2	<1	.1	t	0	18	.66	10

Food	Amount											
Black beans, cooked	1/2 c	114	8	20	7	<1	.1	t	0	23	1.81	1
Green string beans, cooked from frozen	1/2 c	17	1	4	2	<1	t	t	0	30	.55	9
Broccoli, cooked from frozen, chopped	1 c	51	6	10	5	<1	t	t	0	94	1.12	44
Carrots, raw, whole, 7 1/2 x 1 1/8"	1 ea	31	1	7	2	<1	t	t	0	19	.36	25
Carrots, cooked, from frozen, sliced, drained	1/2 c	26	1	6	3	<1	t	t	0	20	.34	43
Cauliflower, flowerets, cooked from frozen, drained	1/2 c	17	1	3	2	<1	t	t	0	15	.37	16
Celery, pascal type, raw, diced	1 c	19	1	4	2	<1	t	t	0	48	.48	104
Corn, cooked, drained												
From fresh, on cob, 5" long	1 ea	83	3	19	2	1	.2	.3	0	2	.47	13
Kernels, cooked from frozen	1/2 c	66	2	17	2	<1	t	t	0	2	.25	4
Corn, canned												
Cream style	1/2 c	92	2	23	2	1	.1	.2	0	4	.49	364
Whole kernel, vacuum pack	1/2 c	83	3	20	6	1	.1	.2	0	5	.44	286
Cucumber slices w/peel	7 pce	4	<1	1	<1	<1	t	t	0	4	.07	1
Lettuce: iceberg/crisphead, wedge, 1/4 head	1 ea	18	1	3	1	<1	t	t	0	25	.67	12
Mushrooms, raw, sliced	1/2 c	9	1	2	<1	<1	t	t	0	2	.43	1
Onions												
Raw, chopped	1 c	61	2	14	3	<1	t	t	0	32	.35	5
Cooked, drained, chopped	1/2 c	46	1	11	1	<1	t	t	0	23	.25	3
Peas												
Black-eyed, cooked from frozen, drained	1/2 c	112	7	20	7	1	.2	.1	0	20	1.8	4
Green, canned, drained	1/2 c	59	4	11	3	<1	.1	t	0	17	.81	186
Peppers, sweet, green: whole pod (90 g w/refuse), raw	1 ea	20	1	5	1	<1	t	t	0	7	.34	1
Potatoes												
Baked in oven, 4 3/4" x 2 1/3" diam												
With skin	1 ea	220	5	51	5	<1	.1	1	0	20	2.75	16
Flesh only	1 ea	145	3	34	2	<1	t	t	0	8	.55	8
French fried in vegetable oil, strips 2-3 1/2" long	10 ea	155	2	19	2	8	2.5	4	0	8	.68	82
Mashed												
Home recipe w/milk & marg	1/2 c	111	2	18	2	4	1.1	1.9	2	27	.27	310
Prepared from flakes: water, milk, margarine, salt added	1/2 c	124	2	17	1	6	1.6	2.5	4	54	.24	365
Potato chips	14 ea	150	2	15	1	10	3.1	2.8	0	7	.46	166
Refried beans, canned	1/2 c	135	8	23	7	1	.5	.6	0	58	2.24	534
Spinach: raw, chopped	1 c	12	2	2	2	<1	t	t	0	55	1.52	44
Zucchini, cooked	1/2 c	14	1	4	1	<1	t	t	0	12	.31	3
Acorn squash, baked, mashed	1/2 c	68	1	18	5	<1	t	t	0	54	1.14	5
Sweet potatoes: baked in skin, peeled, 5 x 2" diam	1 ea	140	3	28	4	<1	t	t	0	32	2	11
Tomatoes: raw, chopped	1 c	38	2	8	2	1	.1	.1	0	9	.81	16
Tomato juice, canned	1 c	41	2	10	1	<1	t	t	0	22	1.42	881
Tomato paste, canned	1 c	220	10	49	11	2	.3	.4	0	92	7.83	2070
Tomato sauce, canned	1 c	73	3	18	3	<1	.1	.1	0	34	1.89	1482

Reprinted, by permission, from A. Jackson, 1999, *Physical Activity for Health and Fitness*. (Champaign, IL: Human Kinetics), 147-156.

Table D.6 Nutrient Values at Popular Fast-Food Restaurants

Food item	Calories	Total fat (g)	Saturated fat (g)	Cholesterol (mg)	Protein (g)	Sodium (mg)	Carbohydrate (g)
Arby's							
Beef n' Cheddar	487	28	9	50	25	1216	40
Giant Roast Beef	555	28	11	71	35	1561	43
Regular Roast Beef	388	19	7	43	23	1009	33
Junior Roast Beef	**324**	**14**	**5**	**30**	**17**	**779**	**35**
Breaded Chicken Filet	536	28	5	45	28	1016	46
Ham n' Cheese	**359**	**14**	**5**	**53**	**24**	**1283**	**34**
Curly Fries	300	15	3	0	4	853	38
Potato Cakes	**204**	**12**	**2**	**0**	**2**	**397**	**20**
Baked Potato (plain)	**355**	**.3**	**0**	**0**	**7**	**26**	**82**
Deluxe Baked Potato	736	36	16	59	19	499	86
Plain Biscuit	280	15	3	0	6	730	34
Blueberry Muffin	**230**	**9**	**2**	**25**	**2**	**290**	**35**
Garden Salad	**61**	**.5**		**0**	**3**	**40**	**12**
Roast Chicken Salad	**149**	**2**		**29**	**20**	**418**	**12**
Side Salad	**23**	**.3**		**0**	**1**	**15**	**4**
Reduced-Calorie Italian Dressing	**20**	**1**	**0**	**0**	**0**	**1000**	**3**
Reduced-Calorie Buttermilk Ranch Dressing	**50**	**0**	**0**	**0**	**0**	**710**	**12**
Burger King							
Whopper Sandwich (with cheese)	730	46	16	115	33	1350	46
Hamburger	**330**	**15**	**6**	**55**	**20**	**530**	**28**
Cheeseburger	**380**	**19**	**9**	**65**	**23**	**770**	**28**
BK Broiler Chicken Sandwich	530	26	5	105	29	1060	5
Croissan'wich with Sausage, Egg, and Cheese	600	46	16	260	22	1140	25
French Toast Sticks	500	27	7	0	4	490	60
Hash Browns (small)	240	15	6	0	2	440	25
French Fries (medium, salted)	400	21	8	0	3	820	50
Broiled Chicken Salad	**190**	**8**	**4**	**75**	**20**	**500**	**9**
Garden Salad	**100**	**5**	**3**	**15**	**6**	**115**	**8**
Side Salad	**60**	**3**	**2**	**5**	**3**	**55**	**4**
Reduced-Calorie Light Italian Dressing	**15**	**.5**	**0**	**0**	**0**	**50**	**3**
Kentucky Fried Chicken							
Original Recipe							
Wing	140	10	2.5	55	9	414	5
Breast	400	24	6	135	29	1116	16
Drumstick	140	9	2	75	13	422	4
Thigh	250	18	4.5	95	16	747	6
Tender Roast With Skin							
Wing	121	7.7	2.1	74	12.2	331	1
Breast	**251**	**10.8**	**3**	**151**	**37**	**830**	**2**
Thigh	207	12	3.8	120	18.4	504	< 2
Drumstick	97	4.3	1.2	85	14.5	271	< 1
Tender Roast Without Skin							
Breast	**169**	**4.3**	**1.2**	**112**	**31.4**	**797**	**1**
Thigh	106	5.5	1.7	84	12.9	312	< 1
Drumstick	67	2.4	.7	63	11	259	< 1
Chunky Chicken Pot Pie	770	42	13	70	29	2160	69
BBQ Flavored Chicken Sandwich	**256**	**8**	**1**	**57**	**17**	**782**	**28**
Mashed Potatoes and Gravy	**120**	**6**	**1**	**< 1**	**1**	**440**	**17**
Cole Slaw	**180**	**9**	**1.5**	**5**	**2**	**280**	**21**
Potato Salad	230	14	2	15	4	540	23
Corn on the Cob	**150**	**1.5**	**0**	**0**	**5**	**20**	**35**
Green Beans	**45**	**1.5**	**.5**	**5**	**1**	**730**	**7**
BBQ Baked Beans	**190**	**3**	**1**	**5**	**6**	**760**	**33**
Mean Greens	**70**	**3**	**1**	**10**	**4**	**650**	**11**

Nutrient values were obtained from each restaurant's Website.
Bold items denote healthful choices.

Food item	Calories	Total fat (g)	Saturated fat (g)	Cholesterol (mg)	Protein (g)	Sodium (mg)	Carbohydrate (g)
Long John Silver's							
Batter-Dipped Fish (1 piece)	170	11	2.5	30	11	470	12
Batter-Dipped Chicken (1 piece)	120	6	1.5	15	8	400	11
Batter-Dipped Shrimp (1 piece)	35	2.5	.5	10	1	95	2
Flavorbaked Fish	**90**	**2.5**	**1**	**35**	**14**	**320**	**1**
Flavorbaked Chicken	**110**	**3**	**1**	**55**	**19**	**600**	**< 1**
Flavorbaked Fish Sandwich	**320**	**14**	**7**	**55**	**23**	**930**	**28**
Flavorbaked Chicken Sandwich	**290**	**10**	**2**	**60**	**24**	**970**	**27**
Wraps	730	36	7	25	18	1780	83
Fries	250	15	2.5	0	3	500	28
Hushpuppy (1 piece)	60	2.5	0	0	1	25	9
Corn Cobbette (without butter)	**80**	**.5**	**0**	**0**	**3**	**0**	**19**
Rice Pilaf	**140**	**3**	**1**	**0**	**3**	**210**	**26**
Baked Potato	210	0	0	0	4	10	49
Garden Salad	**45**	**0**	**0**	**0**	**3**	**25**	**9**
Grilled Chicken Salad	**140**	**2.5**	**.5**	**45**	**20**	**260**	**10**
Ocean Chef Salad	**130**	**2**	**0**	**60**	**14**	**540**	**15**
Side Salad	**25**	**0**	**0**	**0**	**1**	**15**	**4**
Fat-Free Ranch Dressing	**50**	**0**	**0**	**0**	**2**	**380**	**13**
Fat-Free French Dressing	**50**	**0**	**0**	**0**	**0**	**360**	**14**
McDonald's							
Big Mac	560	31	10	85	26	1070	45
Quarter Pounder With Cheese	530	30	13	95	28	1290	38
Hamburger	**260**	**9**	**3.5**	**30**	**13**	**580**	**34**
Cheeseburger	**320**	**13**	**6**	**40**	**15**	**820**	**35**
Fish Filet Deluxe	560	28	6	60	23	1060	54
Grilled Chicken Deluxe	440	20	3	60	27	1040	38
Egg McMuffin	**290**	**12**	**4.5**	**235**	**17**	**710**	**27**
Bacon, Egg, and Cheese Biscuit	470	28	8	235	18	1250	36
Hash Browns	130	8	1.5	0	1	330	14
Hotcakes (plain)	**310**	**7**	**1.5**	**15**	**9**	**610**	**53**
Cheese Danish	410	22	8	70	7	340	47
French Fries (large)	450	22	4	0	6	290	57
Garden Salad	**35**	**0**	**0**	**0**	**2**	**20**	**7**
Grilled Chicken Salad Deluxe	**120**	**1.5**	**0**	**45**	**21**	**240**	**7**
Fat-Free Herb Vinaigrette	**50**	**0**	**0**	**0**	**0**	**330**	**11**
Low-Fat Apple Bran Muffin	**300**	**3**	**.5**	**0**	**6**	**380**	**61**
Vanilla Reduced-Fat Ice Cream Cone	**150**	**4.5**	**3**	**20**	**4**	**75**	**23**
1% Low-Fat Milk	**100**	**2.5**	**1.5**	**10**	**8**	**115**	**13**
Orange Juice	**80**	**0**	**0**	**0**	**1**	**20**	**20**
Pizza Hut							
Supreme (per slice)							
Thin n' Crispy	250	11	5	20	13	710	24
Pan	300	13	5	25	13	670	32
Chicken Supreme							
Thin n' Crispy	**220**	**7**	**2.5**	**25**	**14**	**550**	**26**
Hand Tossed	**240**	**6**	**3**	**25**	**14**	**660**	**31**
Meat Lover's							
Thin n' Crispy	310	16	7	35	16	900	25
Pan	360	19	6	40	17	870	30
Veggie Lover's							
Thin n' Crispy	**170**	**6**	**2**	**10**	**7**	**460**	**23**
Hand Tossed	**240**	**7**	**3**	**20**	**11**	**650**	**34**

(continued)

Table D.6 *(continued)*

Food item	Calories	Total fat (g)	Saturated fat (g)	Cholesterol (mg)	Protein (g)	Sodium (mg)	Carbohydrate (g)
Cheese							
Thin n' Crispy	**210**	**9**	**4.5**	**20**	**12**	**530**	**21**
Hand Tossed	**280**	**10**	**5**	**25**	**16**	**770**	**32**
Ham							
Thin n' Crispy	**190**	**6**	**3**	**15**	**10**	**560**	**23**
Hand Tossed	**230**	**6**	**3**	**25**	**13**	**710**	**30**
Italian Sausage							
Thin n' Crispy	300	16	6	35	15	740	24
Pan	350	18	6	40	16	740	31
Garlic Bread (1 slice)	150	8	1.5	0	3	240	16
Breadstick	**130**	**4**	**1**	**0**	**3**	**170**	**20**
Subway							
Cold Subs (6 inch)*							
Veggie Delight	**222**	**3**	**0**	**0**	**9**	**582**	**38**
Turkey Breast	**273**	**4**	**1**	**19**	**17**	**1391**	**40**
Ham	**287**	**5**	**1**	**28**	**18**	**1308**	**39**
Subway Club	**297**	**5**	**1**	**26**	**21**	**1341**	**40**
Roast Beef	**288**	**5**	**1**	**20**	**19**	**928**	**39**
Cold Cut Trio	362	13	4	64	19	1401	39
Spicy Italian	467	24	9	57	20	1592	38
Hot Subs (6 inch)*							
Roasted Chicken Breast	**332**	**6**	**1**	**48**	**26**	**967**	**41**
Meatball	404	16	6	33	18	1035	44
Steak and Cheese (+)	383	10	6	70	29	1106	41
Cheese (2 triangles)	**41**	**3**	**2**	**10**	**2**	**201**	**0**
Mayonnaise	37	4	1	3	0	27	0
Light Mayonnaise	18	2	0	2	0	33	0
Mustard	**8**	**0**	**0**	**0**	**1**	**0**	**1**

* Cheese and condiments not included unless indicated with a (+).

Food item	Calories	Total fat (g)	Saturated fat (g)	Cholesterol (mg)	Protein (g)	Sodium (mg)	Carbohydrate (g)
Taco Bell							
Supreme Gordita							
Beef	**300**	**13**	**6**	**35**	**14**	**390**	**31**
Chicken	**290**	**12**	**5**	**55**	**15**	**420**	**30**
Steak	**280**	**11**	**5**	**35**	**18**	**310**	**28**
Fiesta Gordita							
Beef	**290**	**13**	**4**	**25**	**14**	**880**	**31**
Chicken	**280**	**12**	**3**	**45**	**14**	**910**	**29**
Steak	**270**	**10**	**2.5**	**25**	**17**	**800**	**28**
Santa Fe Gordita							
Beef	380	20	4	35	14	440	33
Chicken	360	19	2.5	55	15	470	32
Steak	350	18	2.5	35	18	360	31
Burrito Supreme	440	19	8	35	17	1230	51
Bean Burrito	**380**	**12**	**4**	**10**	**13**	**1100**	**55**
Chili Cheese Burrito	**330**	**13**	**6**	**35**	**14**	**870**	**37**
Grilled Chicken Burrito	**410**	**15**	**4.5**	**55**	**17**	**1380**	**50**
7-Layer Burrito	530	23	7	25	16	1280	66
Taco Supreme	220	14	7	35	10	350	14
Taco	**180**	**10**	**4**	**25**	**9**	**330**	**12**
Soft Taco	**220**	**10**	**4.5**	**25**	**11**	**580**	**21**
Grilled Steak Soft Taco	**230**	**10**	**2.5**	**25**	**15**	**1020**	**20**
Grilled Chicken Soft Taco	**240**	**12**	**3.5**	**45**	**12**	**1110**	**21**
Mexican Pizza	570	35	10	45	21	1040	42
Tostada	**300**	**15**	**5**	**15**	**10**	**650**	**31**
Cheese Quesadilla	350	18	9	50	16	860	32
Country Breakfast Burrito	**270**	**14**	**5**	**195**	**8**	**690**	**26**
Grande Breakfast Burrito	420	22	7	205	13	1050	43
Nachos	320	18	4	30	5	570	34
Pintos n' Cheese	**190**	**9**	**4**	**15**	**9**	**650**	**18**
Cinnamon Twists	**140**	**6**	**0**	**0**	**1**	**190**	**19**

Reprinted, by permission, from A. Jackson, 1999, *Physical Activity for Health and Fitness*. (Champaign, IL: Human Kinetics), 147-156.

Example of High School Performance Criteria

SOUTH CAROLINA HIGH SCHOOL COURSE STUDENT PERFORMANCE CRITERIA

The Performance Criteria

The following student performance criteria were created for the required South Carolina High School physical education course. The required high school physical education course should be conducted so that every student can meet the performance criteria described below:

CRITERION ONE: Demonstrate competency in at least two movement forms.

Description of the criterion

The intent of this criterion is movement competence. The student who has the competence to participate in activities that involve movement skills are more likely to lead an active lifestyle as a youth as well as an adult. Movement competence implies the development of sufficient ability to enjoy participation in physical activities and establishes a foundation to facilitate continued motor skill acquisition. Several factors are related to the potential of a student to attain movement competence. The first is that there must be a sufficient variety of movement activities in the program from which the student can choose to accommodate her or his interest and ability level. People choose to participate in physical activity for a variety of reasons including opportunities for enjoyment and pleasure, challenge, self-expression, health related and physical development concerns, and social interaction. Different activities have varying potential to contribute to each of these aspects. What is important is that a program develop active participants. The second factor is that the student must have sufficient time to develop competence. Although a student may not have the potential to develop high levels of competence in all activities, with sufficient time and quality instruc-

tion each student can develop competence in some activities.

Definitions

Competence Competence implies the ability to independently and safely participate in an activity and maintain a level of continuity in that activity that would make participation enjoyable.

Movement forms Movement forms imply the following categories of activities: aquatics, dance, outdoor pursuits (e.g., backpacking, canoeing), individual activities (e.g., golf, archery), dual activities (e.g., tennis, badminton) and team sports.

Critical Aspects of Performance

1. The student has the ability to participate in the activity safely, enjoyably, and independently.
2. The student has acquired all the basic physical skills, strategies, and rules of the activity to a level of consistency in simple conditions.
3. The student has acquired the basic physical skills of the activity in the context of the activity (game play, independent weight training program, canoe trip, etc.).
4. The student has acquired the knowledge of how to perform the physical skills of the activity and how to perform safely.

Examples of Student Performance Meeting the Criterion

1. The student uses basic offensive and defensive strategies effectively in a three on three basketball game.
2. The student keeps the ball in play for at least four consecutive hits against an opponent of equal ability in a tennis game.

3. The student hits the target in archery at least 50% of the time from a distance of 40 feet.

4. The student choreographs a dance sequence of at least four minutes to music that demonstrates the ability to move efficiently and use movement expressively.

Assessment Examples

1. Portfolio

   The student provides a video tape of their game play in tennis against an opponent of equal ability. (20 minutes)

   ### Assessment Criteria

   A. The student uses all the basic offensive and defensive skills of tennis at least once during the game play.

   B. The game includes several rallies of at least four consecutive hits.

   C. The student demonstrates an understanding of the basic rules of tennis.

2. Teacher Observation (observational record)

   Using a checklist, rating scale, or scoring rubric to observe performance of a choreographed dance, the teacher assesses the extent to which students have demonstrated competence in modern dance.

   ### Assessment Criteria

   A. The student selects and moves to music appropriately.

   B. The student uses the components of body, space, effort and relationships effectively and dynamically to express him/herself appropriately to the theme.

   C. The student demonstrates control of movement.

3. Student Record

   The student submits a verifiable record of participation and achievement performance that meets the performance criteria for a particular activity (e.g., a Red Cross Certificate for a swimming course).

Assessment Criteria

A. The record of achievement is in a content area appropriate to the criterion.

B. The level of performance specified meets the criterion.

CRITERION TWO: Design and develop an appropriate physical fitness program to achieve a desired level of personal fitness.

Description of the Criterion

The intent of this criterion is to ensure that the student has the skills and knowledge to independently assess and develop a personal physical fitness program based on current available knowledge related to physical training and the development of an active lifestyle. Skills to assess fitness should be developed for *real life* environments. The student should be able to interpret the meaning of assessment data and be able to apply principles of training to a variety of alternative ways to develop fitness components.

Critical Aspects of Performance

1. The student has the ability to assess all five components of health related fitness in a real world setting.

2. The student can interpret the meaning of assessment data in terms of identifying the level of health related fitness indicated by the data.

3. The student can design a program that utilizes the principles of training and development to develop a program to maintain and/or improve the level of fitness indicated by the data.

4. The student can *package* a personal and individualized long term program that has the potential to achieve/maintain a desired level of fitness.

Examples of Student Performance Meeting the Criterion

1. The student uses fitness data from class projects on assessment of physical

fitness to: a) establish a personal profile of his/her own fitness level; b) set a personal goal for each component of fitness; and c) design a six week program that utilizes exercise, strength training and participation in tennis to develop/increase current levels of fitness.

2. The student assesses his/her physical fitness independently and at home using techniques of assessment learned in class. The student interprets his/her level of fitness and designs a program of exercise twenty minutes a day, three days a week at home to reach his/her personal fitness goal.

3. The student assesses fitness components in class, interprets the assessments, and designs a personal fitness program to be conducted during nine weeks of a physical education class.

Assessment Examples

1. Written Test

   The student is given a written test with the following questions:

   A. Determine how you would assess the following components of fitness at home: cardiovascular endurance, muscular strength, muscular endurance, body composition, and flexibility.

   B. Given the following results of the above assessment, determine which of the components meet or do not meet a health enhancing level of fitness and establish a six week program to increase the levels of performance on each one of the components.

   ### Assessment Criteria

   A. The student correctly identifies appropriate assessment techniques for each component of fitness.

   B. The student correctly assesses the level of fitness described in the assessment data.

   C. The student appropriately uses the principles of training and development to increase levels of performance for each of the fitness components.

2. Student Project

   The student is given the following project to perform at home.

   A. Assess your level of fitness in each of the five components of fitness.

   B. Chart your level of fitness in terms of the following for each component:

      1. below health enhancing level
      2. at health enhancing level
      3. above health enhancing level
      4. well above health enhancing level

   C. Set goals for either maintenance or improvement based on your data.

   D. Design a nine week program to meet fitness maintenance or improvement goals that utilize the knowledge of principles of training learned in class for each of the components.

   ### Assessment Criteria

   A. The student correctly identifies appropriate assessment techniques for each component of fitness.

   B. The student correctly assesses the level of fitness described in the assessment data.

   C. The student appropriately uses the principles of training and development to increase levels of performance for each of the fitness components.

CRITERION THREE: Participate regularly in health enhancing physical activity outside the physical education class.

Description of the Criterion

The intent of this standard is to help the student make a transition from physical education class to a physically active lifestyle and *real life* opportunities. The high school student should participate regularly in physical activity outside the physical education setting if patterns of participation appropriate for a physically active lifestyle are to be established. Two dimensions of participation are critical. The first is the student should be *exploring* opportunities both in the school and in the community and surrounding areas for participation in a wide variety of physical activities. The second is the student should be developing the ability to make wise choices about how he/she spends time both in terms of the structured activities chosen to participate in as well as choosing more active alternatives in daily living (e.g., taking the stairs rather than the elevator). The student should independently seek opportunities for activity and design activity programs as a lifestyle issue. This criterion can be met through opportunities in the school and community as well as through independently designed programs of physical activity.

Definitions

Regularly   Weekly over a nine week period

School activities   Sport teams, intramural, club activities

Community activities   Church sponsored, parks and recreation programs, YM(W)CA, commercial companies

Health enhancing physical activity   Moderate to vigorous exercise (consecutively and/or totally) for twenty minutes or more a day, three times per week

Components of health related fitness   Cardiovascular endurance, muscular strength, muscular endurance, body composition, and flexibility

Independent programs   Family designed structured programs and independently designed structured programs. (The term *structured* here means designated time and place with planned regularity.)

Critical Aspect of Performance

The student provides evidence of regular participation for a minimum of nine weeks in an activity normally producing moderate levels of physical activity.

Examples of Student Performance Meeting the Criteria

1. The student participates in a youth baseball league in the community.

2. The student sets up a walking club with several other students during the lunch hour.

3. The student sets up a personal fitness program consisting of weight lifting and aerobic exercise on a regular basis.

4. The student participates in folk dance club/hunting club in the community.

5. The student successfully participates as a member of a school athletic team.

Assessment Examples

1. Student Journal

   The student keeps a daily journal of participation in their outside activity recording each day of participation and what they do each day. The student evaluates his/her participation after every three weeks indicating the extent to which he/she is meeting the health enhancing aspect of the criterion; the personal benefits of their participation; and the difficulties they have encountered in participating regularly in the activity. The journals are shared and discussed in the physical education class.

   Assessment Criteria

   A. The student participates in the activity regularly for a period of at least nine weeks.

   B. The student evaluates the level of their participation appropriately.

   C. The student appropriately identifies both the advantages and disadvantages of participation.

2. Student Record

   The student submits a signed form from a responsible adult describing the participation in an independent project.

   Assessment Criteria

   The student meets the criterion for type of activity and regularity of participation.

CRITERION FOUR: Meet the gender and age group health related physical fitness standard as published by the National Association for Sport and Physical Education.

Description of the Criterion

The intent of this criterion is for the student to achieve and maintain a health-enhancing level of physical fitness. While a health-enhancing standard of fitness is considered minimum, the student should be encouraged to develop higher levels of performance necessary for many work activities which are part of an active lifestyle. Expectations for student fitness levels should be established on a personal basis, taking into account variation in entry levels and personal student goals.

Definition

Standard for health-related fitness Currently published by NASPE for each component of health related fitness in the test administration manual for the *FITNESSGRAM*.

Critical Aspect of Performance

The student meets or exceeds the specified standard for his/her age group for each of the health related fitness components as published by NASPE.

Examples of Student Performance Meeting the Criteria

1. A fourteen-year-old male student completes the one mile run/walk in nine minutes and thirty seconds and does equally as well in the other components of fitness.

2. A sixteen-year-old girl reaches 12 inches on the sit-and-reach test and does equally well in the other components of fitness.

Assessment Examples

The student submits acceptable scores on all components of fitness using *FITNESSGRAM* or an equivalent measure.

Appendix E information is reprinted, by permission, from R. Hohn, 1995, *South Carolina High School Course Student Performance Criteria*.

Appendix F

Example Scope and Sequence Progressions

Table F.1   A Guide to Content and Assessment

Standard	Kindergarten	Second Grade
1. Demonstrates competency in many movement forms and proficiency in a few movement forms	• Demonstrate progress toward the mature form of selected manipulative, locomotor and nonlocomotor skills • Demonstrate mature form in walking and running	• Demonstrate mature form in skipping, hopping, galloping and sliding • Demonstrate mature motor patterns in simple combinations (e.g., dribbling while running) • Demonstrate smooth transitions between sequential motor skills (e.g., running into a jump) • Exhibit the ability to adapt and adjust movement skills to uncomplicated, yet changing, environmental conditions and expectations (e.g., partner needs for force production, tossing a ball to a moving partner, rising and sinking while twisting, different rhythms) • Demonstrate control in traveling activities and weight bearing and balance activities on a variety of body parts
2. Applies movement concepts and principles to the learning and development of motor skills	• Identify fundamental movement patterns (skip, strike) • Establish a beginning movement vocabulary (e.g., personal space, high/low levels, fast/slow speeds, light/heavy weights, balance, twist) • Apply appropriate concepts to performance (e.g., change direction while running)	• Identify the critical elements of basic movement patterns • Applies movement concepts to a variety of basic skills • Uses feedback to improve performance
3. Exhibits a physically active lifestyle	• Engage in moderate to vigorous physical activity • Select and participate in activities which require some physical exertion during unscheduled times • Identify likes and dislikes connected with participation in physical activity	• Experience and express pleasure from participation in physical activity • Engage in moderate to vigorous physical activity outside of physical education class • Identify at least one activity associated with each component of health-related physical activity
4. Achieves and maintains a health-enhancing level of physical fitness	• Sustain moderate to vigorous physical activity for short periods of time • Identify the physiological signs of moderate physical activity (e.g., fast rate and heavy breathing)	• Engage in sustained physical activity that causes an increased heart rate and heavy breathing • Recognize the physiological indicators that accompany moderate to vigorous physical activity (e.g., sweating, increased heart rate, heavy breathing) • Identify the components of health-related physical fitness
5. Demonstrates responsible personal and social behavior in physical activity settings	• Apply, with teacher reinforcement, classroom rules and procedures, and safe practices • Share space and equipment with others	• Apply rules, procedures, and safe practices with little or no reinforcement • Follow directions • Work cooperatively with another to complete an assigned task
6. Demonstrates understanding and respect for differences among people in physical activity settings	• Recognize the joy of shared play • Interact positively with students in class regardless of personal differences (e.g., race, gender, disability)	• Play and cooperate with others regardless of personal difference (e.g., gender, ethnicity, disability) • Treat others with respect during play • Resolve conflicts in socially acceptable ways
7. Understands that physical activity provides opportunities for enjoyment, challenge, self-expression, and social interaction	• Engage in physical activities • Associate positive feelings with participation in physical activity • Try new movement activities and skills	• Gain competence to provide increased enjoyment in movement • Try new activities • Express feelings about and during physical activity • Enjoy interaction with friends through physical activity

Standard	Fourth Grade	Sixth Grade
1. Demonstrates competency in many movement forms and proficiency in a few movement forms	• Demonstrate mature form in all locomotor patterns and selected manipulative and nonlocomotor skills • Adapt a skill to the demands of a dynamic, unpredictable environment • Acquire beginning skills of a few specialized movement forms • Combine movement skills in applied settings	• Demonstrate mature form for all basic manipulative, locomotor, and nonlocomotor skills • Demonstrate increasing competence in more advanced specialized skills • Adapt and combine skills to the demands of increasingly complex situations of selected movement forms • Demonstrate beginning strategies for net and invasion games
2. Applies movement concepts and principles to the learning and development of motor skills	• Apply critical elements to improve personal performance in fundamental and selected specialized motor skills • Use critical elements of fundamental and specialized movement skills to provide feedback to others • Recognize and apply concepts that impact the quality of increasingly complex movement performance	• Use information from a variety of sources of internal and external origin to improve performance • Identify and apply principles of practice and conditioning that enhance performance • Recognize general characteristics of movement that can be applied to specific settings (e.g., similarity of the ready position in striking movement forms) • Use basic offensive and defensive strategies in noncomplex settings
3. Exhibits a physically active lifestyle	• Select and participate regularly in physical activities for the purpose of improving skill and health • Identify the benefits derived from regular physical activity • Identify several moderate to vigorous physical activities that provide personal pleasure	• Identify opportunities in the school and community for regular participation in physical activity • Participate daily in some form of health-enhancing physical activity • Analyze personal interests and capabilities in regard to one's exercise behavior • Identify the critical aspects of a healthy lifestyle
4. Achieves and maintains a health-enhancing level of physical fitness	• Identify several activities related to each component of physical fitness • Associate results of fitness testing to personal health status and ability to perform various activities • Meet the health-related fitness standards as defined by *FITNESSGRAM*	• Participate in moderate to vigorous physical activity in a variety of settings • Monitor intensity of exercise • Begin to develop a strategy for the improvement of selected fitness components • Work somewhat independently with minimal supervision in pursuit of personal fitness goals • Meet the health-related fitness standards as defined by *FITNESSGRAM*
5. Demonstrates responsible personal and social behavior in physical activity settings	• Follow, with few reminders, activity-specific rules, procedures, and etiquette • Utilize safety principles in activity situations • Work cooperatively and productively with a partner or small group • Work independently and on-task for short periods of time	• Participate in establishing rules, procedures, and etiquette that are safe and effective for specific activity situations • Work cooperatively and productively in a group to accomplish a set goal in both cooperative and competitive activities • Make conscious decisions about applying rules, procedures, and etiquette • Utilize time effectively to complete assigned tasks
6. Demonstrates understanding and respect for differences among people in physical activity settings	• Explore cultural/ethnic self-awareness through participation in physical activity • Recognize the attributes that individuals with differences can bring to group activities • Experience differences and similarities among people of different backgrounds by participating in activities of national, cultural, and ethnic origins	• Acknowledge differences in the behaviors of people of different gender, culture, ethnicity, and disability and seek to learn more about both similarities and differences • Cooperate with disabled peers and those of different gender, race and ethnicity • Work cooperatively with both more and less skilled peers
7. Understands that physical activity provides opportunities for enjoyment, challenge, self-expression, and social interaction	• Experience enjoyment while participating in physical activity • Enjoy practicing activities to increase skill competence • Interact with friends while participating in group activities • Use physical activity as a means of self-expression	• Recognize physical activity as a positive opportunity for social and group interaction • Demonstrate enjoyment from participation in physical activities • Recognize that success in physical activities leads to recognition from peers • Use physical activity to express feelings • Seek personally challenging experiences in physically active experiences

(continued)

Standard	Eighth Grade	Tenth Grade
1. Demonstrates competency in many movement forms and proficiency in a few movement forms	• Demonstrate competence in modified versions of a variety of movement forms	• Demonstrate competence (basic skills, strategies and rules) in an increasing number of more complex versions of at least three of the following different types of movement forms: aquatics, team sports, individual and dual sports, outdoor pursuits, self-defense, dance, gymnastics
2. Applies movement concepts and principles to the learning and development of motor skills	• Understand and apply more advanced movement and game strategies • Identify the critical elements of more advanced movement skills • Identify the characteristics of highly skilled performance in a few movement forms • Understand and apply more advanced discipline specific knowledge	• Use more specialized knowledge to develop movement competence or proficiency • Identify and apply critical elements to enable the development of movement competence/proficiency • Identify and apply characteristics of highly skilled performance to enable the development of movement competence/proficiency • Understand and independently apply discipline specific information to their own performance
3. Exhibits a physically active lifestyle	• Establish personal physical activity goals • Participate regularly in health-enhancing physical activities to accomplish these goals (in and out of the physical education class) • Explore a variety of new physical activities for personal interest in and out of physical education class • Describe the relationships between a healthy lifestyle and "feeling good"	• Participate regularly in health-enhancing and personally rewarding physical activity outside the physical education class setting • Seek and select physical activities from a variety of movement forms based on personal interest, meaning and fulfillment • Develop and conduct independently a personal physical activity program meeting their needs
4. Achieves and maintains a health-enhancing level of physical fitness	• Participate in a variety of health-related fitness activities in both school and nonschool settings • Assess physiological indicators of exercise during and after physical activity • Understand and apply basic principles of training to improving physical fitness • Begin to develop personal fitness goals independently • Meet the health-related fitness standards as defined by *FITNESSGRAM*	• Participate in a variety of health enhancing physical activities in both school and nonschool settings • Use principles of training for the purpose of modifying levels of fitness • Assess personal health-related fitness status • Begin to design personal health-related fitness programs based on an accurately assessed fitness profile • Meet the health-related fitness standards as defined by *FITNESSGRAM*
5. Demonstrates responsible personal and social behavior in physical activity settings	• Recognize the influence of peer pressure • Solve problems by analyzing causes and potential solutions • Analyze potential consequences when confronted with a behavior choice • Work cooperatively with a group to achieve group goals in competitive as well as cooperative settings	• Apply safe practices, rules, procedures and etiquette in all physical activity settings • Act independently of peer pressure • Resolve conflicts in appropriate ways • Keep the importance of winning and losing in perspective relative to other established goals of participation
6. Demonstrates understanding and respect for differences among people in physical activity settings	• Recognize the role of sport, games and dance in modern culture • Identify behaviors that are supportive and inclusive in physical activity settings • Willingly join others of diverse culture, ethnicity and race during physical activity	• Recognize the value of sport and physical activity in understanding multiculturalism • Invite others with differences (e.g., ethnicity, gender, disabilities) to join in personally enjoyable physical activity
7. Understands that physical activity provides opportunities for enjoyment, challenge, self-expression, and social interaction	• Enjoy participation in physical activity • Recognize the social benefits of participation in physical activity • Try new and challenging activities • Recognize physical activity as a vehicle for self-expression	• Enjoy participating in a variety of physical activities in competitive and recreational settings • Pursue new activities both alone or with others • Enjoy working with others in a sport activity to achieve a common goal • Recognize that physical activity can provide a positive social environment for activities with others

Standard	Twelfth Grade
1. Demonstrates competency in many movement forms and proficiency in a few movement forms	• Demonstrate proficiency in a few movement forms
2. Applies movement concepts and principles to the learning and development of motor skills	• Know and understand pertinent scientifically based information regarding movement performance • Independently apply advanced movement-specific information • Integrate discipline-specific knowledge to enable the independent learning of movement skills
3. Exhibits a physically active lifestyle	• Have the skills, knowledge, interest, and desire to independently maintain an active lifestyle throughout their life • Understand how activity participation patterns are likely to change throughout life and have some strategies to deal with those changes
4. Achieves and maintains a health-enhancing level of physical fitness	• Participate regularly in health-enhancing fitness activities independent of teaching mandates • Demonstrate the skill, knowledge, and desire to monitor and adjust activity levels to meet personal fitness needs • Design a personal fitness program • Meet the health-related fitness standards as defined by *FITNESSGRAM*
5. Demonstrates responsible personal and social behavior in physical activity settings	• Initiate independent and responsible personal behavior in physical activity settings • Accept the responsibility for taking a leadership role and willingly follow as appropriate in order to accomplish group goals • Anticipate potentially dangerous consequences and outcomes of participation in physical activity
6. Demonstrates understanding and respect for differences among people in physical activity settings	• Recognize the influence of participation in physical activity on fostering appreciation of cultural, ethnic, gender and physical diversity • Develop strategies for including persons from diverse backgrounds and characteristics in physical activity they select for leisure pursuits
7. Understands that physical activity provides opportunities for enjoyment, challenge, self-expression, and social interaction	• Enjoy regular participation in physical activity • Recognize that physical activity can provide opportunities for positive social interaction • Enjoy learning new activities • Recognize the positive feelings that result from physical activity participation alone and with others

Reprinted from *Moving Into the Future: National Standards for Physical Education* (1995) with permission from the National Association for Sport and Physical Education (NASPE), 1900 Association Drive, Reston, VA 20191-1599.

Table F.2 Sample Progressive Scope and Sequence for Grades 1-10

Essential learning #1: *The student acquires the knowledge and skills necessary to maintain an active life: movement, physical fitness, and nutrition.*

Components	Grade K learning targets	Grade 1 learning targets
1.1 Develops fundamental physical skills and progresses to complex movement activities as physically able	Demonstrates large muscle coordination in locomotor and nonlocomotor skills	Demonstrates basic locomotor and nonlocomotor movement in combination
	Demonstrates an awareness of personal space	Demonstrates basic rhythm and dance movements
	Demonstrates a feeling for beat and accent through rhythmic activities	Manipulates simple apparatus with basic movement elements
	Responds to visual and verbal signals	
	Performs various activities requiring body management	
1.2 Incorporates rules and safety procedures into physical activities	Demonstrates movement safety of self and others	Demonstrates movement safety of self and others using various movements and pathways
1.3 Understands the concepts of physical fitness and plans and monitors personal fitness plans and goals	Meets age-appropriate fitness criterion	Meets age-appropriate health-related fitness criterion
	Recognizes changes in heart rate during exercise and rest	
1.4 Understands nutrition and food nutrients and how they affect physical performance and the body	Explores the food pyramid and identifies food groups	Identifies relationship of food to growth
	Identifies healthy nutrition choices	Explains the concept of food as fuel

Essential learning #4: *The student effectively analyzes health and safety information to develop health and fitness plans based on life goals.*

Components	Grade K learning targets	Grade 1 learning targets
4.2 Develops a health and fitness plan and a monitoring system	Identifies and establishes short-term class goals	Identifies goal-setting process and makes/monitors appropriate short-term goals
		Assists in establishing class goals for health and fitness

Essential learning #1: *The student acquires the knowledge and skills necessary to maintain an active life: movement, physical fitness, and nutrition.*

Components	Grade 2 learning targets	Grade 3 learning targets
1.1 Develops fundamental physical skills and progresses to complex movement activities as physically able	Demonstrates basic movement and manipulative skills in combination in a variety of activities	Combines locomotor, non-locomotor, and manipulative skills in game situations
	Demonstrates mature movement patterns to teacher-selected rhythm, by using the body as a means of expression	Identifies and demonstrates appropriate movement to accents in music in a variety of ways
	Demonstrates balance skills using various apparatus	
1.2 Incorporates rules and safety procedures into physical activities	Participates safely during activities	Moves safely during activity
		Demonstrates a basic knowledge of rule and specific safety procedures as related to physical activity
1.3 Understands the concepts of physical fitness and plans and monitors personal fitness plans and goals	Meets age-appropriate health-related fitness criterion	ΔMeets age-appropriate health-related fitness criterion
	Explains the relationship of fitness to health	Identifies the components of health-related fitness
		Participates in activities that apply the concepts of duration and intensity, as related to cardiovascular endurance
		Identifies nutritional souces for proteins and carbohydrates
1.4 Understands nutrition and food nutrients and how they affect physical performance and the body	Demonstrates healthy nutritional choices	Identifies factors influencing nutritional choices within the family
	Explains the concept of variety and moderation in food selection	
	Explains the relationship of healthy foods to healthy bodies	

ΔIndicates taught in previous year

(continued)

Essential learning #4: *The student effectively analyzes health and safety information to develop health and fitness plans based on life goals.*

Components	Grade 2 learning targets	Grade 3 learning targets
4.2 Develops a health and fitness plan and a monitoring system		Demonstrates the ability to develop health plans and predicts the benefits of healthy choices

Essential learning #1: *The student acquires the knowledge and skills necessary to maintain an active life: movement, physical fitness, and nutrition.*

Components	Grade 4 learning targets	Grade 5 learning targets
1.1 Develops fundamental physical skills and progresses to complex movement activities as physically able	Combines locomotor, non-locomotor, and manipulative skills in individual, dual, rhythmic, and team activities	Identifies, describes, and demonstrates increasingly complex movement combinations through previously learned progressions
		Integrates multiple movement concepts and patterns in various rhythmic activities
1.2 Incorporates rules and safety procedures into physical activities	Applies rules, safety procedures, and cooperation during active participation in a variety of activities	Demonstrates knowledge of rules and safe participation in a variety of activities
1.3 Understands the concepts of physical fitness and plans and monitors personal fitness plans and goals	ΔMeets age-appropriate health-related fitness criterion	ΔMeets age-appropriate health-related fitness criterion
	Sets and monitors progress toward personal fitness goals	ΔSets and monitors personal fitness goals
	Identifies strength, flexibility, and cardiovascular endurance activities	Analyzes health-related fitness components, as they relate to personal lifestyles
1.4 Understands nutrition and food nutrients and how they affect physical performance and the body	Identifies nutrients provided by a variety of foods, and describes how the body and physical performance are affected	Identifies the influence of advertising and food labeling on nutrition choices

ΔIndicates taught in previous year

Essential learning #4: *The student effectively analyzes health and safety information to develop health and fitness plans based on life goals.*

Components	Grade 4 learning targets	Grade 5 learning targets
4.2 Develops a health and fitness plan and a monitoring system	Establishes and monitors both short- and long-term personal health goals	Monitors progress toward personal health goals and revises, when appropriate

Essential learning #1: *The student acquires the knowledge and skills necessary to maintain an active life: movement, physical fitness, and nutrition.*

Components	Grade 6 learning targets	Grade 7 learning targets
1.1 Develops fundamental physical skills and progresses to complex movement activities as physically able	Performs multiple movement patterns in rhythmic activities Demonstrates age- and developmentally appropriate skills during participation in a variety of individual dual and team activities	Performs age- and developmentally appropriate physical skills and applies them in complex patterns, including leisure and rhythmic activities
1.2 Incorporates rules and safety procedures into physical activities	Participates safely and cooperatively in physical activities	Participates safely, follows rules, and acts cooperatively in a variety of physical activities
1.3 Understands the concepts of physical fitness and plans and monitors personal fitness plans and goals	ΔMeets age-appropriate health-related fitness criterion Performs in personal, health-related fitness assessments, sets fitness goals, and creates/follows personal action plans to achieve fitness goals	ΔMeets age-appropriate health-related fitness criterion Sets personal, health-related fitness goals and explores a variety of activities to maintain appropriate levels of health-related physical fitness
1.4 Understands nutrition and food nutrients and how they affect physical performance and the body	Identifies components of the national dietary guidelines and sets/monitors personal nutrition patterns	Designs nutrition goals based on national dietary guidelines and individual activity needs Understands the results of movement, fitness, and nutrition practices in relation to a healthy lifestyle

ΔIndicates taught in previous year

(continued)

Essential learning #4: *The student effectively analyzes health and safety information to develop health and fitness plans based on life goals.*

Components	Grade 6 learning targets	Grade 7 learning targets
4.2 Develops a health and fitness plan and a monitoring system	Develops and implements a personal health and fitness action plan	Develops a support system and record-keeping system to achieve health and fitness goals

Essential learning #1: *The student acquires the knowledge and skills necessary to maintain an active life: movement, physical fitness, and nutrition.*

Components	Grade 8 learning targets	Grade 9 learning targets
1.1 Develops fundamental physical skills and progresses to complex movement activities as physically able	Applies age- and developmentally appropriate skills related to individual and leisure physical activities Applies knowledge and skill to personal activity patterns outside of school setting	Refines and applies age- and developmentally appropriate skills in individual and leisure physical activities to participate at a recreational level
1.2 Incorporates rules and safety procedures into physical activities	Cooperatively and safely participates in a variety of physical activities Analyzes the risks involved in participating in various physical activities	Applies rules and safety procedures
1.3 Understands the concepts of physical fitness and plans and monitors personal fitness plans and goals	ΔMeets age-appropriate health-related fitness criterion Initiates a personal, health-related fitness plan that includes physical activity, nutrition, and reduction of risk-taking behaviors	ΔMeets age appropriate health-related fitness criterion Refines and monitors individual health-related fitness goals, based on a variety of physical activities, fitness profiles, and nutritional guidelines
1.4 Understands nutrition and food nutrients and how they affect physical performance and the body	Identifies various noncommunicable diseases caused by and/or aggravated by poor nutritional choices and specific effects on the body Identifies how self-esteem, peer pressure, and the media influence nutritional practices	Develops personal nutrition goals based on national dietary guidelines and individual needs

ΔIndicates taught in previous year

Essential learning #4: *The student effectively analyzes health and safety information to develop health and fitness plans based on life goals.*

Components	Grade 8 learning targets	Grade 9 learning targets
4.2 Develops a health and fitness plan and a monitoring system	Modifies and continues to implement a personal fitness plan that includes physical activity, nutrition, and reduction of risk-taking behaviors	Refines personal health and fitness plans to include potential lifetime activities

Essential learning #1: *The student acquires the knowledge and skills necessary to maintain an active life: movement, physical fitness, and nutrition.*

Components	Grade 10 learning targets
1.1 Develops fundamental physical skills and progresses to complex movement activities as physically able	Applies knowledge and skills to personal activity patterns inside and outside of school setting
1.2 Incorporates rules and safety procedures into physical activities	Applies rules and safety procedures, practices sportsmanship, and participates in a variety of physical activities
1.3 Understands the concepts of physical fitness and plans and monitors personal fitness plans and goals	ΔMeets age-appropriate health-related fitness criterion
	Monitors progress on individual health-related fitness goals, based on fitness profiles, individual physical capabilities, and national guidelines in relation to work and leisure goals
1.4 Understands nutrition and food nutrients and how they affect physical performance and the body	Monitors personal nutrition goals based on national dietary guidelines and individual needs
	Compares and contrasts the application of movement, fitness, and nutrition concepts to safe work practices and leisure activities

Essential learning #4: *The student effectively analyzes health and safety information to develop health and fitness plans based on life goals.*

Components	Grade 10 learning targets
4.2 Develops a health and fitness plan and a monitoring system	Implements and monitors a personal health and fitness plan, based on life goals for leisure and employment

ΔIndicates taught in previous year

Contributed by Jeff Carpenter, Coordinator of Health and Fitness Programs at the Olympia School District in Olympia, Washington.

Appendix G

Middle School Assessment Example: P.E.-L.I.F.E. Assessment Project

This appendix is taken from the P.E.-L.I.F.E. assessment project and is meant as an example of middle school physical education assessment. The material is reprinted by permission.

LESSON LEVEL

Step 1: Design Phase

Lesson Outcome Perform the following with good form, until 10 repetitions can be completed: push-up with straight body, hands and toes on the floor. (P.E.-L.I.F.E., Health-Related Fitness—Muscular Strength, p. 22.1.)

Define Domain Analysis (what will be assessed) The primary focus of this assessment is on the process (how) of performing the push-up, as a means of improving or maintaining arm and shoulder strength. The process is critical to defining "good form" and includes lifting, rather than bouncing, swinging, or jerking the body parts through the movement; placement of weight on the body parts involved; and the movement involved. A secondary focus is the product or how many push-ups can be performed in succession.

Select Dimension Components (which dimensions are most important) The intent of this assessment is to determine mastery of the process of performing the push-up. Each student is to be assessed on an individual basis, with the results used for the purposes of prescribing further sequential instruction, including remediation and enrichment and preparation for participation in a fitness assessment of muscular strength and endurance. The focus is achievement of an isolated skill lesson objective, which leads to the achievement of the unit outcome. While achievement may occur through practice over several class periods, the assessment can be administered to an entire class during and within a formal class period. All students in the district will be assessed by the physical education teacher or a trained peer.

Identify Implementation Characteristics (what other issues need to be considered) The class will perform in diads (one partner performs the movement, while the other partner assesses the quality of the movement) for the designated repetitions. The physical education teacher will be free to observe student performance, as well. The time allotted should permit observations and scoring of the entire class during one class period. However, if peer assessment is to be used with only spot (system) assessment by the teacher, multiple assessments over a number of class periods should be used to provide reliability of the results. Score sheets, prepared in advance, provide quick and easy recording of the scores for each student. Codes for recording are established relative to the critical elements. Students are aware of the recording system.

Establish Specifications (what the students will do) Each student will be asked to perform the critical elements of the push-up, as prescribed by the teacher. Each of the following critical elements will be assessed by the teacher/trained peer as the student performs. Each student will perform 10 repetitions of the push-up, demonstrating the following critical elements on each:

A. Maintain a straight body throughout the performance
B. Position hands shoulder-width apart
C. Hold weight on hands and toes
D. Move with slow let-down and lift
E. Bend arms to 90 degrees on the let-down

Scoring Achievement will be scored at three levels:

	Exemplary (+)	Acceptable (√)	Unacceptable (–)
Process	Uses 5 out of 5 critical elements	Uses 5 out of 5 critical elements	Uses fewer than 5 critical elements
Product	Completes 10 repetitions	Completes 5 repetitions	Completes fewer than 5 repetitions

Administration The class may be organized into pairs or groups formed for general class management. Ideas for forming groups for a fitness unit might include fitness level, personal selection of fitness factor of priority concern, and so on. The groups will report to their assigned area for the starting of the class. Distribution of scoring forms and pencils should be similar to other class activities. Pairs for the assessment are determined within each group. Training in these procedures occurs prior to the assessment session. Opportunities to practice the skill should have also occurred. Scoring and reporting forms provide specific information for the teacher, student, parents, and various types of administrators. The purpose for the information dictates the type of report form used.

Scoring Form

Push-Ups

Student: _____

Date: _____ Skill: ____Push-ups____

Place the number of the missing critical element(s) for each trial in each circle. If no elements are missing place a "+" in the circle.

Critical elements:

1—Straight body

2—Hands shoulder-width apart

3—Weight on hands and toes

4—Slow lift and let-down

5—Arms bend 90 degrees on let-down

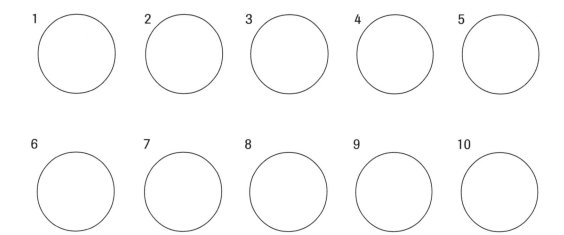

Exemplary _____

Acceptable _____

Unacceptable _____

	Exemplary (+)	Acceptable (√)	Unacceptable (−)
Process	Uses 5 out of 5 critical elements	Uses 5 out of 5 critical elements	Uses fewer than 5 critical elements
Product	Completes 10 repetitions	Completes 5 repetitions	Completes fewer than 5 repetitions

Student/Parent Report Form

Scoring form may be used. (May be used to summarize status of all fitness factors.)

Summary Student/Report Form

Student: _____John_____

A. Fitness score

Muscular strength	Push-up	Sit-up	Other
Endurance	Push-up	Sit-up	
Flexibility	Sit-and-reach	Shoulder	
Cardiorespiratory	PACER	Step test	Mile run
Body composition	Height	Weight	Skinfold

B. Comments for improvement of maintenance of fitness

Administrative Report Form: Teacher, Principal

Report number for those performing at acceptable or better.

	Muscular strength PU SU	Endurance PU SU	Flexibility SR SS	Cardio-respiratory P ST RUN	Body composition WT HT SF
Mary	9				
John	7				
Bill	10				
Helen	10				

Administrative Report Form: Supervisor

Report total number acceptable or better for each section.

Class/ Section	Class size	Muscular strength PU SU	Endurance PU SU	Flexibility SR SS	Cardio-respiratory P ST RUN	Body composition WT HT SF
6-1	30	25				
6-2	28	22				
6-3	32	25				

Step 2: Refinement Phase

Date

Review by peers and others (independent)
 (Will this assess the outcome?)   _____

Rewrite/Revise
 (See examples provided by the committee)   _____

Preliminary testing—pilot testing
 (Small group—three students to a whole class; may not be scored)   _____

Rewrite/Revise
 (if needed)   _____

Field testing
 (Trial operational, all students one level; check consistency of scoring)   _____

Step 3: Implementation Phase

Operational administration   _____

Scoring
 (students, teachers, community experts)   _____

Reporting
 (students, parents, principal, curriculum supervisor, superintendent,
 school board, state department of education)   _____

UNIT LEVEL

Step 1: Design Phase

Unit Outcome Perform planned/personal program of strength fitness for at least four weeks, or until progress is achieved, as determined by preestablished goals. Record daily progress. (P.E.-L.I.F.E. Health Related Fitness—Muscular Strength, p. 47)

Defined Domain Analysis (what will be assessed) Content to be assessed includes planning and participating in muscular strength activities/exercises to achieve a preestablished goal. The content of this assessment includes the process (how) of setting goals and performing a strength-training workout, for the purpose of improving one's status to reach personal goals. Knowledge about training and conditioning principles, skills for assessing status, interpretation of results of assessments of personal status, and skills to perform specific activities that build muscular strength will be needed.

Select Dimension Components (which dimensions are most important) The intent of this assessment is to determine mastery of both the process and the product. Each student is to be assessed and scored on an individual basis, with the results used for the purpose of prescribing further sequential instruction, including skills and knowledge, resulting from multiple lesson outcomes within a unit of study on fitness education and goal setting, which have been experienced over several lessons and which lead to the achievement of the course outcome. Achievement will occur through participation both in and out of the gymnasium. Both process (critical elements of exercises, goal setting, and the components of a workout) and product (goal) are to be scored.

Identify Implementation Characteristics (what other issues need to be considered) Information and direction about this assessment should be given to students at the beginning of a unit of study of muscular strength and endurance and will occur concurrently with other related activities of the unit (i.e., integrated assignments to be completed outside of class or classes of related subjects [health, English, art] in communication, research, and art, which focus on researching and reporting the concepts of conditioning and training). Each student will create a personal fitness profile from muscular strength test results and use the information collected to determine a personal goal. The teacher, trained volunteer (adult/older student who has successfully completed the assessment) will review the profile to determine accuracy of information and appropriateness of the goal. Expanded opportunities may need to be accessed, if class time does not permit training principles of frequency and/or duration (time) to be followed. Students should be given responsibility for establishing workout time outside of class. Therefore, the prescribed event must be transferrable to out-of-class environments for all students. Scoring of end results should be completed by the teacher. Parents may be asked to verify participation outside of class.

Establish Specifications (what the student will do) Each student will perform two cycles of a circuit routine (developed by the teacher and student) designed to increase muscular strength. An individual profile, including a pretest for each muscle group used in the circuit and realistic personal goals will be prepared prior to the workout series. Exercises selected should be appropriate for both in-school and out-of-school environments. The resistance for each exercise should be established, based on the student's pretest status and increased, when the exercise can be performed with good form for 10 repetitions. The student will maintain a log, indicating the date and number of repetitions at each station completed. The following critical elements should be used in scoring:

A. Perform each exercise with proper form and movement throughout the workout

B. Complete the workout as indicated by strength-training principles

C. Maintain personal participation log neatly and accurately

D. Reach established goal

Scoring   Achievement will be scored at three levels:

	Exemplary (+)	Acceptable (✓)	Unacceptable (−)
Performance	Performs all exercises with proper form and movement	Performs all exercises with proper form and movement	Fails to perform all exercises with proper form and movement
Strength training principles	Applies established principles 90%, each time the workout is performed	Applies established principles 80%, each time the workout is performed	Fails to apply principles
Log	Maintains log accurately and neatly	Maintains log accurately	Fails to maintain a log
Goal	Reaches 100% of goal	Reaches 75% of goal	Reaches less than 75% of goal

Administration   The class may be organized into six groups, with each group starting at a different station in the circuit. If exercises are added or deleted, the number of groups may be added or deleted. Each station will have a resource poster, indicating proper form and movement requirements for the exercise and options for adjusting the weight (intensity level) appropriate for each student's profile. Each student will record the results at each station on his or her own individual log. Maintenance of the individual log is the responsibility of the student. Out-of-class participation is to be recorded in the log. An additional summary log of each class experience may be desirable and is to stay with the teacher. The groups will report to their assigned area for the starting of the class. All students will perform the same warm-up, regardless of the station where the circuit is started. All students will perform the same cool-down at the end of the workout. Following the same class management procedures over the duration of the unit will enable the development of habits that allow students to concentrate on the essential learning. Training in this procedure occurs prior to the assessment sessions. Opportunities to practice the skills should have also occurred. Scoring and reporting forms provide specific information for the teacher, student, parents, and various types of administrators. The purpose for the information dictates the type of report form used.

Scoring Forms: Weekly Log

Student:_____ Beginning date:_____

Enter number of repetitions completed for each cycle each date.

Exercise	Pretest	Goal	Intensity Level	Date Cycle 1 2	Date Cycle 1 2	Date Cycle 1 2	Date Cycle 1 2
Wrist rolls							
Push-ups							
Arm curls							
Curl-ups							
Half squats							
Toe rise							
Toe curls							
Other							

Scoring: _____ Exemplary _____ Acceptable _____ Unacceptable

Comments:

Alternate Scoring Forms: Daily Class Record

Print on lined 5" × 8" file card. Record the total number of stations for which two cycles have been completed.

Date	Task	Score	Date	Task	Score
9/15	Strength circuit	14			
9/22	Strength circuit	12			

Reporting Forms: Student and Parents

Use Weekly Log to provide feedback each week. Final scoring may be given on the last week of the circuit.

Administrative Report Form: Teacher, Principal

Report number for those performing at acceptable or better.

	Muscular strength training	Endurance training	Flexibility training	Cardio-respiratory training	Body composition
Nit	12				
John	10				
Juan	16				
Helen	15				

Administrative Report Form: Supervisor

Report total number acceptable or better for each section.

Class/ Section	Class size	Muscular strength training	Endurance training	Flexibility training	Cardio-respiratory training	Body composition
6-1	30	25				
6-2	28	22				
6-3	32	25				

Step 2: Refinement Phase

Date

Review by peers and others
  (independent) (Will this assess the outcome?)
     _____

Rewrite/Revise
  (See examples provided by the committee)
     _____

Preliminary testing—pilot testing
  (Small group—three students to a whole class; may not be scored)
     _____

Rewrite/Revise
  (if needed)
     _____

Field testing
  (Trial operational, all students one level; check consistency of scoring)
     _____

Step 3: Implementation Phase

Operational administration
     _____

Scoring
  (students, teachers, community experts)
     _____

Reporting
  (students, parents, principal, curriculum supervisor, superintendent,
  school board, state department of education)
     _____

Appendix G is reprinted, by permission, from PSAHPERD, 1994, P.E.-L.I.F.E. Project, *Designing Assessments: Applications for Physical Education.*

Appendix H

National Observances Related to Physical Activity

February

American Heart Month
American Heart Association
800-AHA-USA1

1st Thurs.
Girls and Women in Sports Day
Women's Sports Foundation
800-227-3988

March

National Nutrition Month
American Dietetic Association
800-877-1600
312-899-0040

April

National Youth Sports Safety Month
National Youth Sports Safety Foundation
617-449-2499

7th
World Health Day
American Association for World Health
202-466-5883

1st full week
National Public Health Week
American Public Health Association
202-789-5600

May

National Physical Fitness and Sports Month
President's Council on Physical
Fitness and Sports
202-272-3426

National Bike Month
League of American Bicyclists
410-539-3399

National High Blood Pressure Month
National Heart, Lung, and Blood Institute
301-251-1222

1st week
National Physical Education and Sports Week
American Alliance for Health, Physical Education, Recreation and Dance (AAHPERD)
703-476-3412

1st Wed.
All Children Exercise Simultaneously Day
Youth Fitness Coalition, Inc.
201-433-8993

2nd week
American Running and Fitness Week
American Running and Fitness Association
800-776-2732
301-913-9517

3rd Wed.
National Employee Health and Fitness Day
National Association of Governors' Councils
on Physical Fitness and Sports
317-237-5630

4th week
National Water Fitness Week
U.S. Water Fitness Association, Inc.
561-732-9908

July

National Recreation and Parks Month
National Recreation and Park Association
800-626-6772

September

National Cholesterol Education Month
National Heart, Lung, and Blood Institute
301-251-1222

Last Sun.
Family Health and Fitness Day
Health Information Resource Center
800-828-8225

October

Family Health Month
American Academy of Family Physicians
800-274-2237
816-333-9700

1st weekend
American Heart Walking Event
American Heart Association
800-AHA-USA1

1st Mon.
Child Health Day
National Institute of Child Health and Human
Development, National Institutes of Health
301-496-5133

3rd Sun.
World Walking Day
Trim and Fitness International Sport for All
Association (TAFISA) Frankfurt, Germany
011-49-69-67-00-225

November

National Diabetes Month
American Diabetes Association
800-232-3472
703-549-1500

References

Alter, M.J. 1998. *Sport Stretch*. 2d ed. Champaign, IL: Human Kinetics.

———. 1996. *Science of Flexibility* (2d ed.) Champaign, IL: Human Kinetics.

American Academy of Pediatrics Committees on Sports Medicine and School Health (AAPCSMSH). 1987. "Physical Fitness and the Schools." *Pediatrics* 80:449–450.

American Alliance for Health, Physical Education, Recreation and Dance (AAHPERD). 1998. *Physical Best Activity Guide—Elementary Level*. Champaign, IL: Human Kinetics.

———. 1999. *Physical Best Activity Guide—Secondary Level*. Champaign, IL: Human Kinetics.

American College of Sports Medicine (ACSM). 1998. *ACSM Fitness Book*. 2d ed. Champaign, IL: Human Kinetics.

———. 1988. "Physical Fitness in Children and Youth." *Medical Science of Sports and Exercise* 20:422-23.

Arthur, M., and B. Bailey. 1998. *Complete Conditioning for Football*. Champaign, IL: Human Kinetics.

Baechle, T.R. 1994. *Essentials of Strength Training and Conditioning*. Champaign, IL: Human Kinetics.

Baechle, T. and B. Groves. 1996. *Steps to Success: Weight Training Instruction*. 2d ed. Champaign, IL: Human Kinetics.

Banks, J.A. 1988. *Multiethnic Education: Theory and Practice*. Needham Heights, MA: Allyn & Bacon.

Bar-Or, O. 1993. "Importance of Differences Between Children and Adults for Exercise Testing and Exercise Prescription." In *Exercise Testing and Exercise Prescription for Special Cases* (2d ed.), edited by J.S. Skinner, 57–74. Philadelphia: Lea and Febiger.

———. 1994. "Childhood and Adolescent Physical Activity and Fitness and Adult Risk Profile." In *International Proceedings and Consensus Statement*, edited by C. Bouchard, R.J. Shephard, and T. Stephens, 931–42. Champaign, IL: Human Kinetics.

Bell, S. 1995. "Preaching to the Choir." *Teaching Elementary Physical Education* 6 (6):5.

Blair, S.N. 1995. "Youth Fitness: Directions for Future Research." In *Child Health, Nutrition, and Physical Activity*, edited by L.W.Y. Cheung and J.B. Richmond, 147–52. Champaign, IL: Human Kinetics.

Blair, S.N., D.G. Clark, K.J. Cureton, and K.E. Powell. 1989. "Exercise and Fitness in Childhood: Implications for a Lifetime of Health." In *Perspectives in Exercise Science and Sports Medicine:* Vol. 2 of *Youth Exercise and Sports*, edited by C.V. Gisolfi and D.R. Lamb, 401–30. Indianapolis: Benchmark.

Borg, G. 1998. *Borg's Perceived Exertion and Pain Scales*. Champaign, IL: Human Kinetics.

Brehm, B.A. 1998. "Helping Clients Perceive Exertion." *Fitness Management* 14(7):33–34.

Campbell, W., Crim, M., Young, V. & Evans, W. 1994. "Increased energy requirements and changes in body composition with resistance training in older adults." *American Journal of Clinical Nutrition*, 60, 167–175.

Chelminski, Rudolph. 1998. "Your Opponent Must Be Destroyed" *Smithsonian* (Jan.)

Cheung, L.W.Y., and J.B. Richmond, eds. 1995. *Child Health, Nutrition, and Physical Activity*. Champaign, IL: Human Kinetics.

Clark, C., and S.W. Sanders. 1997. "Visually Reporting Skill Performance to Parents." *Teaching Elementary Physical Education* 8 (May):6–7, 19.

Clifford, C., and R.M. Feezell. 1997. *Coaching for Character*. Champaign, IL: Human Kinetics.

Cohen, G. 1993. *Women in Sport*. Newbury Park, CA: Sage.

Cooper, K.H. 1991. *Kid Fitness*. New York: Bantam Books.

Corbin, C.B. 1994. "The Fitness Curriculum—Climbing the Stairway to Lifetime Fitness." In *Health and Fitness Through Physical Education*, edited by R.R. Pate and R.C. Hohn, 59–66. Champaign, IL: Human Kinetics.

———, and R. Lindsey. 1997. *Fitness for Life: Teacher's Annotated Edition* (4th ed.). Glenview, IL: Scott, Foresman.

———, and R.P. Pangrazi. 1998. *Physical Activity for Children: A Statement of Guidelines*. Reston, VA: NASPE.

Council on Physical Education for Children (COPEC). 1998. *Appropriate Practices for High School Physical Education*. Reston, VA: NASPE.

———. 1995. *Appropriate Practices for Middle School Physical Education*. Reston, VA: NASPE.

———. 1992. *Developmentally Appropriate Physical Education Practices for Children*. Reston, VA: NASPE.

Craft, D. 1994. "Strategies for Teaching Inclusively." *Teaching Elementary Physical Education* 5(5):8–9.

Davison, B. 1998. *Creative Physical Activities & Equipment: Building a Quality Program on a Shoestring Budget*. Champaign, IL: Human Kinetics.

de Vries, H.A.. 1986. *Physiology of Exercise* (4th ed.). Dubuque, IA: McGraw-Hill.

———. 1966. "Quantitative Electromyographic Investigation of the Spasm Theory of Muscle Pain." *American Journal of Physical Medicine* 45(3):119–34.

DePauw, K. 1996. "Students With Disabilities in Physical Education." In *Student Learning in Physical Education: Applying Research to Enhance Instruction*, edited by S. Silverman and C. Ennis, 101–24. Champaign, IL: Human Kinetics.

Desmond, S.M., J.H. Price, R.S. Lock, D. Smith, and P.W. Stewart. 1990. "Urban Black and White Adolescents' Physical Fitness Status and Perceptions of Exercise." *Journal of School Health* 60:220–26.

Dishman, R. 1999. "Mental Health." In *Physical Activity and Health*, edited by J. Morrow, Jr., D.W. Hill, and R.K. Dishman, 271–292. Champaign, IL: Human Kinetics.

Dishman, R.K., and J.F. Sallis. 1994. Determinants and Interventions for Physical Activity and Exercise. In *Physical Activity, Fitness, and Health: International Proceedings and Consensus Statement*, edited by C. Bouchard, R.J. Shephard, and T. Stephens, 214–238. Champaign, IL: Human Kinetics.

Dishman, R.K., J.F. Sallis, and D.R. Orenstein. 1985. "The Determinants of Physical Activity and Exercise." *Public Health Report* 100:158–71.

Engstrom, L.-M. 1991. "Exercise Adherence in Sport for All From Youth to Adulthood." In *Sport for All*, edited by P. Oja & R. Telama, 473–83. Amsterdam: Elsevier.

Ennis, C.D. 1996. "Designing Curriculum for Quality Physical Education Programs." Pp. 13–37 in *Physical Education Sourcebook*, edited by B.F. Hennessy. Champaign, IL: Human Kinetics.

Epstein, L.H., A. Valoski, R.R. Wing, K.A. Perkins, M. Fernstrom, B. Marks, and J. McCurley. 1989. "Perception of Eating and Exercise in Children as a Function of Child and Parent Weight Status." *Appetite* 12:105–18.

Faber, A. 1995. *How to Talk So Kids Can Learn—at Home and in School.* New York: Rowan Associates.

Faber, A., and E. Mazlish. 1980. *How to Talk So Kids Will Listen & Listen So Kids Will Talk.* New York: Avon.

Florida Department of Education. 1984. *Personal Fitness Curriculum Framework/Student Performance Standards.* Tallahassee, FL: Department of Education.

Franks, B.D., and E.T. Howley. 1998. *Fitness Leader's Handbook* (2d ed.). Champaign, IL: Human Kinetics.

Fuchs, R., K.E. Powell, N.K. Semmer, J.H. Dwyer, P. Lippert, and H. Hoffmeister. 1988. "Patterns of Physical Activity Among German Adolescents: The Berlin-Bremen Study." *Preventative Medicine* 17:746–63.

Gardner, H. 1993. *Multiple Intelligences: The Theory in Practice.* New York: Basic Books.

———. 1983. *Frames of Mind: The Theory of Multiple Intelligences.* New York: Basic Books.

Giangreco, M.F., and J.W. Putnam. 1991. "Supporting the Education of Students With Severe Disabilities in Regular Education Environments." In *Critical Issues in the Lives of People With Severe Disabilities*, edited by L.H. Meyer, C.A. Peck, and L. Brown, 245–70. Baltimore: Paul H. Brookes.

Glover, D.R., and D.W. Midura. 1992. *Team Building Through Physical Challenges.* Champaign, IL: Human Kinetics.

Graham, G. 1992. *Teaching Children Physical Education: Becoming a Master Teacher.* Champaign, IL: Human Kinetics.

Greene, L., and R. Pate. 1997. *Training for Young Distance Runners.* Champaign, IL: Human Kinetics.

Griffin, J.C. 1998. *Client-Centered Exercise Prescription.* Champaign, IL: Human Kinetics.

Grineski, S. 1996. "Improving Practices in Elementary Physical Education: Obstacle Courses and Learning Stations." *Teaching Elementary Physical Education* 7 (September):14–15.

Hannaford, C. 1995. *Smart Moves: Why Learning Is Not All in Your Head.* Arlington, VA: Great Ocean Publishers.

Harris, J., and J. Elbourn. 1997. *Teaching Health-Related Exercise at Key Stages 1 and 2.* Champaign, IL: Human Kinetics.

Heyward, V.H. 1998. *Advanced Fitness Assessment & Exercise Prescription* (3d ed.). Champaign, IL: Human Kinetics.

Hichwa, J. 1998. *Right Fielders Are People Too: An Inclusive Approach to Teaching Middle School Physical Education.* Champaign, IL: Human Kinetics.

Hill, J.O., and J.C. Peters. 1998. "Environmental Contributions to the Obesity Epidemic." *Science* 280 (May 29):1371–74.

Hinson, C. 1998. "Should PE Teachers Be Fit?" *Teaching Elementary Physical Education* 9(3):23.

———. 1995. *Fitness for Children.* Champaign, IL: Human Kinetics.

Hopple, C. 1995. *Teaching for Outcomes in Elementary Physical Education: A Guide for Curriculum and Assessment.* Champaign, IL: Human Kinetics.

Houston-Wilson, K. 1995. "Alternate Assessment Procedures." In *Physical Best and Individuals With Disabilities: A Handbook for Inclusion in Fitness Programs*, edited by J.A. Seaman, 91–109. Reston, VA: AAHPERD.

Human Kinetics. 1998. *Active Youth: Ideas for Implementing CDC Physical Activity Promotion Guidelines.* Champaign, IL: Human Kinetics.

Hutchinson, G.E. 1995. "Gender-Fair Teaching in Physical Education." *Journal of Physical Education, Recreation and Dance* 60(2):23–24.

International Life Sciences Institute (ILSI). 1997a. "Physical Activity Message for Parents From New Survey: No More Excuses." Press release, July 1.

———. 1997b. "Improving Children's Health Through Physical Activity: A New Opportunity." Pamphlet. Washington, DC: ILSI.

Jackson, A.W., et al. 1999. *Physical Activity for Health and Fitness.* Champaign, IL: Human Kinetics.

Jobe, M. 1998. "Disabilities Awareness Field Days." *Teaching Elementary Physical Education* 9 (August):10-11.

Johnson, D.J., and E.G. Harageones. 1994. "A Health Fitness Course in Secondary Physical Education." In *Health and Fitness Through Physical Education*, edited by R.R. Pate and R.C. Hohn, 165–75. Champaign, IL: Human Kinetics.

Kann, L., S.A. Kinchen, B.I. Williams, J.G. Ross, R. Lowry, C.V. Hill, et al. 1998. "Youth Risk Behavior Surveillance—United States, 1997." In CDC Surveillance Summaries, August 14, 1998. *Morbidity and Mortality Weekly Report* 47 (SS-3): 1–89.

Kirkpatrick, B., and B.H. Birnbaum. 1997. *Lessons From the Heart: Individualizing Physical Education With Heart Rate Monitors.* Champaign, IL: Human Kinetics.

Kraemer, W.J., and S.J. Fleck. 1993. *Strength Training for Young Athletes.* Champaign, IL: Human Kinetics.

Kraft, R.E. 1989. "Children at Play: Behavior of Children at Recess." *JOPERD* 60:21–24.

Kuntzleman, C.T., and G.G. Reiff. 1992. "The Decline in American Children's Fitness Levels." *Research Quarterly for Exercise and Sport* 63:107–11.

Lavay, B.W., R. French, and H.L. Henderson. 1997. *Positive Behavior Management Strategies for Physical Educators.* Champaign, IL: Human Kinetics.

Lipowitz, S. 1997. "Have a Heart—A Healthy One." *Teaching Elementary Physical Education* 8(2):16–17.

Lohman, T.G. 1992. *Advances in Body Composition.* Champaign, IL: Human Kinetics.

Lowy, S. 1995. "A multicultural perspective on planning." *Teaching Elementary Physical Education* 6 (3):14–15.

Martens, R. 1997. *Successful Coaching* (Updated 2nd ed.) Champaign, IL: Human Kinetics.

McCall, R. 1998. "Ride for Life." *Teaching Elementary Physical Education* 9(3):12 and 27.

McKenzie, T.L., and J.F. Sallis. 1996. "Physical Activity, Fitness, and Health-Related Physical Education." In *Student Learning in Physical Education: Applying Research to Enhance Instruction,* edited by S.J. Silverman and C.D. Ennis, 223–46. Champaign, IL: Human Kinetics.

Melograno, V.J. 1998. *Professional and Student Portfolios for Physical Education.* Champaign, IL: Human Kinetics.

Middle and Secondary School Physical Education Council (MASSPEC). 1995. *Appropriate Practices for Middle School Physical Education.* Reston, VA: NASPE.

———. 1998. *Appropriate Practices for High School Physical Education.* Reston, VA: NASPE.

Midura, D.W., and D.R. Glover. 1999. *The Competition-Cooperation Link: Games for Developing Respectful Competitors.* Champaign, IL: Human Kinetics.

Mohnsen, B.J. 1997. *Teaching Middle School Physical Education: A Blueprint for Developing an Exemplary Program.* Champaign, IL: Human Kinetics.

Morris, G.S.D., and J. Stiehl. 1998. *Changing Kids' Games* (2d ed.). Champaign, IL: Human Kinetics.

Mosston, M., and S. Ashworth. 1994. *Teaching Physical Education.* New York: Macmillan Publishing Co.

Murphy, D.R. 1991. "A Critical Look at Static Stretching: Are We Doing Our Patients Harm?" *Chiropractic Sports Medicine* 5(3):67–70.

National Association for Sport and Physical Education (NASPE). 1999. "Healthy People 2010." *NASPE News* No. 52 (Winter): 1.

———. 1995. *Moving Into the Future: National Standards for Physical Education.* St. Louis: Mosby.

———. 1993. *Shape of the Nation 1993: A Survey of State Physical Education Requirements.* Reston, VA: NASPE.

National Consortium for Physical Education and Recreation for Individuals With Disabilities. 1995. *Adapted Physical Education National Standards.* Champaign, IL: Human Kinetics.

National Strength and Conditioning Association (NSCA). 1985. "Position Paper on Prepubescent Strength Training." *NSCA Journal* 7 (4):1–9.

———. 1996. "Position Paper and Literature Review of Youth Resistance Training." Colorado Springs, CO: NSCA.

Nilges, L. 1996. "Ingredients for a Gender Equitable Physical Education Program." *Teaching Elementary Physical Education* (October) 7(5):28–30.

Ormrod, J.E. 1995. *Educational Psychology Principles and Applications.* Columbus, OH: Merrill.

Pangrazi, R.P. 1994. "Teaching Fitness in Physical Education." In *Health and Fitness Through Physical Education,* edited by R.R. Pate and R.C. Hohn, 75–80. Champaign, IL: Human Kinetics.

———, and C.B. Corbin. 1994. *Teaching Strategies for Improving Youth Fitness.* 2d ed. Reston, VA: AAHPERD.

Pate, R.R. 1995. "Promoting Activity and Fitness." In *Child Health, Nutrition, and Physical Activity,* edited by L.W.Y. Cheung and J.B. Richmond, 139–45. Champaign, IL: Human Kinetics.

Pate, R.R., M.L. Small, J.G. Ross, et al. 1995. "School Physical Education." *Journal of School Health* 165(8): 312–318.

Pate, R.R., and R.C. Hohn. 1994. *Health and Fitness Through Physical Education.* Champaign, IL: Human Kinetics.

Raffini, J.P. 1993. *Winners Without Losers: Structures and Strategies for Increasing Student Motivation to Learn.* Needham Heights, MA: Allyn & Bacon.

Ratliffe, T., and L.M. Ratliffe. 1994. *Teaching Children Fitness: Becoming a Master Teacher.* Champaign, IL: Human Kinetics.

Reedy, M.E. 1996. "Cecil County Schools Leading the Way." *Teaching Secondary Physical Education* 1(2): 22–25.

Rink, J.E. 1998. *Teaching Physical Education for Learning* (3d ed.). Boston: McGraw-Hill.

———. 1994. "Fitting Fitness Into the School Curriculum." In *Health and Fitness Through Physical Education,* edited by R.R. Pate and R.C. Hohn, 67–73. Champaign, IL: Human Kinetics.

———. 1993. *Teaching Physical Education for Learning.* St. Louis: Mosby.

Russell, T.T. 1992. "The K-5 Health and Wellness Magnet School." *Teaching Elementary Physical Education* (Nov.): pp. 14–15.

Sadker, M., and D. Sadker. 1995. *Failing at Fairness: How Our Schools Cheat Girls.* New York: Simon & Schuster.

Safrit, M.J. 1995. *Complete Guide to Youth Fitness Testing.* Champaign, IL: Human Kinetics.

Sallis, J.F. 1995. "A Behavioral Perspective on Children's Physical Activity." In *Child Health, Nutrition, and Physical Activity,* edited by L.W.Y. Cheung and J.B. Richmond, 125–38. Champaign, IL: Human Kinetics.

———. 1994. "Determinants of Physical Activity Behavior in Children." In *Health and Fitness Through Physical Education,* edited by R.R. Pate and R.C. Hohn, 31–43. Champaign, IL: Human Kinetics.

Sallis, J.F., M.J. Buono, J.J. Roby, F.G. Micale, and J.A. Nelson. 1993. "Seven-Day Recall and Other Physical Activity Self-Reports in Children and Adolescents." *Med. Sci. Sports Exerc.* 25:99–108.

Sallis, J.F., Haskell, S.P. Fortman, K.M. Vranizan, C.B. Taylor, and D.S. Solomon. 1986. Predictors of adoption and maintenance of physical activity in a community sample. *Preventive Medicine* 15:331–346.

Saltman, P., J. Gurin, and I. Mothner. 1993. *The University of California at San Diego Nutrition Book.* Boston: Little, Brown.

Saunders, L. 1997. "Strength Training Tips for Children." *Teaching Elementary Physical Education* 4 (8):26–27.

Saunders, S. 1998. "Skill Development, Technology, Fitness, and Enrichment." *Teaching Elementary Physical Education* 9(1):25–26.

Schiemer, S. 1996. "A Positive Learning Experience: Self-Assessment Sheets Let Students Take an Active Role in Learning." *Teaching Elementary Physical Education* (March) 7(2):4–6.

Schincariol, L. 1994. "Including the Physically Awkward Child." *Teaching Elementary Physical Education* 5 (5):10–11.

Schmidt, R.A., and C. Wrisberg. 1999. *Motor Learning and Performance* (2d ed.). Champaign, IL: Human Kinetics.

Seaman, J.A., ed. 1995. *Physical Best and Individuals with Disabilities: A Handbook for Inclusion in Fitness Programs.* Reston, VA: AAHPERD.

Sharkey, B.J. 1997. *Fitness and Health* (2d ed.). Champaign, IL: Human Kinetics.

Siedentop, D. 1990. *Introduction to Physical Education, Fitness and Sport.* Mountain View, CA: Mayfield.

Simons-Morton, B., N.M. O'Hara, D. Simons-Morton, and G.S. Parcel. 1987. "Children and Fitness: A Public Health Perspective." *Research Quarterly for Exercise and Sport* 58:295–302.

Simons-Morton, B.G. 1994. "Implementing Health-Related Physical Education." In *Health and Fitness Through Physical Education*, edited by R.R. Pate and R.C. Hohn, 137–45. Champaign, IL: Human Kinetics.

Slaughter, M.H., T.G. Lohman, R.A. Boileau, C.A. Horswill, R.J. Stillman, M.D. Van Loan, and D.A. Benben. 1988. "Skinfold Equations for Estimation of Body Fatness in Children and Youth." *Human Biology* 60:709–23.

Steller, J., and D.B. Young. 1994. "Moving to Success: A Comprehensive Approach to Physical Education." In *Health and Fitness Through Physical Education*, edited by R.R. Pate and R.C. Hohn, 177–184. Champaign, IL: Human Kinetics.

Stephens, T., D.R. Jacobs, and C.C. White. 1985. "A Descriptive Epidemiology of Leisure-Time Physical Activity." *Public Health Report* 100:147–58.

Taubes, G. 1998. "As Obesity Rates Rise, Experts Struggle to Explain Why." *Science* 280 (May 29):1367–68.

Teaching Elementary Physical Education. 1994. "A Look at the Fitness Tests." 5(1):6–7.

Teaching Middle School Physical Education. 1995. "Alaskan Teacher Takes Physical Education to Heart." *MSPE* 1(1):17.

Tell, G.S., and O.D. Vellar. 1988. "Physical Fitness, Physical Activity, and Cardiovascular Disease Risk Factors in Adolescents: The Oslo Youth Study." *Preventative Medicine* 17:12–24.

Thigpen, L.K. 1984. "Neuromuscular Variation in Association With Static Stretching." Abstract. In *Abstracts of Research Papers 1984*, edited by W. Kroll, 28. Washington, DC: AAHPERD.

Tipton, J.S., and S.L. Tucker. 1998. "Fundraising Can Be Fun!" *Teaching Elementary Physical Education* 9(3):14.

Turner, B., and S. Turner. 1998. "The Jog-A-Thon: A Fundraiser for Physical Education." *Teaching Elementary Physical Education*, 9(3):5–8.

Ulrich, D. 1985. *Test of Gross Motor Development.* Austin, TX: Pro-Ed Publishers.

USDHHS. 1999. *Promoting Physical Activity.* Champaign, IL: Human Kinetics.

———. 1996. *Physical Activity and Health: A Report of the Surgeon General Executive Summary.* Atlanta: USDHHS, Center for Disease Control (CDC), National Center for Chronic Disease Prevention and Health Promotion.

Vanden Auweele, Yves, et al. 1999. *Psychology for Physical Educators.* Champaign, IL: Human Kinetics.

Verschuur, R., and H.C.G. Kemper. 1985. "Habitual Physical Activity in Dutch Teenagers Measured by Heart Rate." In *Children and Exercise XI*, edited by R.A. Binkhorst, H.C.G. Kemper, and W.H.M. Saris, 194–202. Champaign, IL: Human Kinetics.

Virgilio, S.J. 1997. *Fitness Education for Children: A Team Approach.* Champaign, IL: Human Kinetics.

Wall, A.E. 1982. "Physically Awkward Children: A Motor Development Perspective." In *Theory and Research in Learning Disabilities*, edited by J.P. Das, R.F. Mulcahy, and A.E. Wall, 253–68. New York: Plenum Press.

Walsh, B.T., and M.J. Devlin. 1998. "Eating Disorders: Progress and Problems." *Science* 280 (May 29):1387–90.

Westcott, W. 1996. *Building Strength and Stamina: New Nautilus Training for Total Fitness.* Champaign, IL: Human Kinetics.

Whitehead, J.R. 1994. "Enhancing Fitness and Activity Motivation in Children." In *Health and Fitness Through Physical Education*, edited by R.R. Pate and R.C. Hohn, 81–90. Champaign, IL: Human Kinetics.

Wickelgren, I. 1998. "Obesity: How Big a Problem?" *Science* 280 (May 29):1364–67.

Williams, D.P., S.B. Going, T.G. Lohman, D.W. Harsha, L.S. Webber, and G.S. Bereson. 1992. "Body Fatness and the Risk of Elevated Blood Pressure, Total Cholesterol and Serum Lipoprotein Ratios in Children and Youth." *American Journal of Public Health* 82:358–63.

Williams, J. 1997. Starting Small: The Jonas Clarke Fitness Center. *Teaching Secondary Physical Education* 3(3):11–12.

Winnick, J.P. and Francis X. Short. 1999. *The Brockport Physical Fitness Test Manual.* Champaign, IL: Human Kinetics.

Winnick, J.P. 1995. "Personalizing Measurement and Evaluation for Individuals With Disabilities." In *Physical Best and Individuals With Disabilities: A Handbook for Inclusion in Fitness Programs*, edited by J.A. Seaman, 21–31. Reston, VA: AAHPERD.

Winnick, J.P., ed. 1995. *Adapted Physical Education and Sport* (2d ed.). Champaign, IL: Human Kinetics.

Woods, A.M. 1997. "Assessment of the Cognitive Domain." *Teaching Elementary Physical Education* 8 (3):28–29.

Zwiren, L.D. 1988. Exercise Prescription for Children. In *Resource Manual for Guidelines for Exercise Testing and Prescription*, edited by American College of Sports Medicine, 309–14. Philadelphia: Lea and Febiger.